Steven Spielberg's Children

Steven Spielberg's Children

LINDA RUTH WILLIAMS

Rutgers University Press
New Brunswick, Camden and Newark, New Jersey
London and Oxford

Rutgers University Press is a department of Rutgers, The State University of New Jersey, one of the leading public research universities in the nation. By publishing worldwide, it furthers the University's mission of dedication to excellence in teaching, scholarship, research, and clinical care.

Library of Congress Cataloging-in-Publication Data

Names: Williams, Linda Ruth, author.
Title: Steven Spielberg's children / Linda Ruth Williams.
Description: New Brunswick: Rutgers University Press, 2025. | Includes bibliographical references and index.
Identifiers: LCCN 2024047499 | ISBN 9780813571676 (paperback) | ISBN 9780813571683 (hardcover) | ISBN 9780813575537 (epub) | ISBN 9780813571690 (pdf)
Subjects: LCSH: Spielberg, Steven, 1946—Criticism and interpretation. | Children in motion pictures. | Child actors.
Classification: LCC PN1998.3.S65 W55 2025 | DDC 791.4302/33092—dc23/eng/20241009
LC record available at https://lccn.loc.gov/2024047499

A British Cataloging-in-Publication record for this book is available from the British Library.

∞ The paper used in this publication meets the requirements of the American National Standard for Information Sciences—Permanence of Paper for Printed Library Materials, ANSI Z39.48-1992.

rutgersuniversitypress.org

For Georgia and Gabriel Williams

Contents

Steven Spielberg's Children

Introduction

Steven Spielberg is the consummate director of contemporary cinematic childhood. His films are drenched in youth, as is this book. Children have been his most regular emotional and sentimental focus, particularly in his singular examples of the child's point of view film (*E.T. the Extra-Terrestrial*; *A.I. Artificial Intelligence*), the family adventure film (*Jurassic Park*; *Ready Player One*), and films that painfully situate children's experience in adult contexts (*Empire of the Sun*; *War of the Worlds*). Childhood and adolescence frame and intensify Spielberg's focus on family dysfunction (*Hook*; *Lincoln*; the later *Indiana Jones* films; *The Fabelmans*), historical trauma and social change (*Schindler's List*; *Munich*; *The Color Purple*; *War Horse*), and identity, through meditations on growing up as a boy or a girl, or not growing up at all (the adult as eternal or thwarted child in *Close Encounters of the Third Kind*; *The Terminal*; *Minority Report*).

Scholarly and journalistic critics alike locate children and childhood at the heart of his films and his directorial focus—but they do so mostly in passing. Biography is frequently cited: in 1985 Spielberg told David Breskin, "I use my childhood in all my pictures, and all the time. . . . My childhood was the most fruitful part of my entire life," while Richard Schickel's glossy *Spielberg: A Retrospective* begins with a quote from the director as an epigraph (a stand-alone at the front of the book, before even the title page): "Hardly a single one of my films isn't based on something that happened in my childhood" (2012, 1). The biographical claim on childhood strives to put a full stop on the issue, curtailing any further exploration—as if all childhood references and resonances in these complex texts can be so simply explained. To put it plainly: while everyone knows that Spielberg is interested in children, that he has made films for children, and that his auteur branding is (even as an elder statesman of Hollywood) that of the Peter Pan of contemporary cinema, children and childhood have received scant sustained and serious attention in the analysis of Spielberg.

Steven Spielberg's Children addresses this fascinating complex of concerns. It offers new scholarship into child performers in contemporary Hollywood and analyzes the director's employment of child actors and his methods for eliciting skilled performances from those actors in order to build such resonant representations of boyhood or girlhood (and sometimes of nonhuman childhood). It therefore stages a dialogue between representations of childhood, child labor, and children as primary signifier in and for the career of perhaps the world's most powerful filmmaker. Across the large body of films directed (and sometimes written) by Spielberg, children straddle disparate genres, formats, production budgets, and market sectors; they drive narratives and articulate, represent, or inspire complex subjective formations, from the hapless crying baby of *The Sugarland Express* (quest object for its childlike parents) to the child-ciphers of *Schindler's List* or *Amistad* who turn the screw of affect, to the nimble performance of adventurous girlhood for child audiences developed by Ruby Barnhill in *The BFG,* to the complex oscillation between "adult-ish" mimicry and the child ages and child stages of Christian Bale as Jim/Jamie in *Empire of the Sun*. Even the relatively child-free *Duel* contains one memorable scene of irritating family life from which Dennis Weaver is lucky to escape (*Duel* would have been a very different film if, during the adaptation process, the screenwriter Richard Matheson—who also wrote the original short story—had not been dissuaded from his idea to have "his wife aboard so he would have somebody to talk to" [McBride 2010, 200]). Three of the most detailed case histories in this book concern child actors performing childhood subjectivity in the child's point of view film—not always for child audiences—as formations of the kinds of children (specifically the kinds of *boys*) Spielberg has regularly orchestrated: Elliott in *E.T. the Extra-Terrestrial*, David in *A.I. Artificial Intelligence*, and Jim/Jamie in *Empire of the Sun*. *Steven Spielberg's Children* discusses Spielberg as an employer *of* children and as a marketer *to* children (selling cultural tropes and tickets, as well as toys and merchandise others have been licensed to produce). His films provide an influential space within which the child is fantasized, theorized, and then sold back to children. I also consider what the image of the child signifies to its various implied audiences, drawing on meditations such as Jacqueline Bobo's study of Black women viewers of *The Color Purple* or reception reports of lachrymose reactions to *E.T.* Of course, as well as making films for children, starring children, and about children, Spielberg also makes films for adults and for adults in families. He sometimes represents adults as children and has been accused of both infantilizing his adult audiences and idealizing the child in the adult—issues I will return to in chapters 1 and 8 of this book. Childhood thus signifies in multiple ways. Citing Peter Coveney's *The Image of Childhood*, Robin Wood writes in his essay on the child in cinema, "The figure of the Child . . . reflects the condition of civilization, its health or sickness, as projected in the values and aspirations of its art" (2006, 189). Childhood is central to Spielberg's success across a wide audience demographic, but it has also become a denounced sign of mass-market emotion. The image of the sentimentalized child is often shorthand for the most criticized aspects of the director's work and branding.

This book shows that it is not so simple, posing a set of interconnected questions around childhood. What is a child according to Spielberg? What is it to perform the child in his films? Are his mass-market representations of the child also films for children? What does it mean to venerate children on-screen while simultaneously employing child workers? And what kind of child is the directorial brand of Steven Spielberg—how does youth inflect the filmic persona? All adults have once been children, and one reading of Spielberg's films (and a tenet of popular psychoanalysis) suggests that perhaps they never stop being children. This has informed much biographically oriented discussion of Spielberg as a baby boomer Peter Pan and New Hollywood wunderkind. I will explore this idea in a range of ways in this book, from adults remembering childhood trauma (J. G. Ballard's source book for *Empire of the Sun*; the adult voices of Holocaust survivors accounting for their childhood experiences that informed *Schindler's List* and the many testimonies housed in the Shoah Foundation), to adults performing childhood (either "passing" as children in the sense of twentysomethings such as Leonardo DiCaprio performing a teenager, or childish adults in a regressive state—Robin Williams in *Hook*, the care home residents in *Kick the Can*, Richard Dreyfuss in *Close Encounters of the Third Kind*). *Steven Spielberg's Children* examines contested terms associated with the child, such as innocence and exploitation, but also darker formations, such as monstrosity and knowingness. It situates its youth focus squarely within the era Spielberg has come to define: post-1960s, baby boomer Hollywood, characterized by a veneration of youth culture, narratives, and audiences.

Spielberg's work grew through an era that developed the most savage aesthetic and political castigation of sentimentality in popular critical and academic discourse, which in turn contributed to a long-standing neglect of the director as a serious subject of scholarly inquiry. As chapter 1 will show, the child—as focus and provoker of screen tears par excellence, awash with "debased" emotion yet at the same time acutely tenacious, sometimes tough—is also bound up with the history of critical attitudes toward Spielberg. This is, then, also partly a reception study of how the child has been culturally meaningful in the public life of Spielberg's films. Children and childishness are everywhere in Spielberg, across production, text, and reception, even extending to (the few) films that contain no children at all. This makes him a key symptom of his moment.

Childhood studies is an interdisciplinary area that has mapped out societal attitudes toward the child using historical, sociological, and cultural evidence. It shows that the child is not a stable entity but has swung wildly across definitions framed by diverse discourses such as the noble savage, the abused innocent, original sin, and above all societal construction (see Gittins 2005, 25–38; also Jenks 1996). As Robin Bernstein writes in her powerful and horrifying history of images of children of color in American culture, *Racial Innocence: Performing American Childhood from Slavery to Civil Rights*, "The connection between childhood and innocence is not essential but is instead historically located" (4). In the period she scrutinizes, innocence is "raced white" (8), suggesting indeed "that only white children *were* children" (2011, 16). As she richly shows, despite this the child is never "one thing"—though often represented as white and male and Western. Historically, of course, the child has been variously represented as monstrous, or a creature of instinct with unique powers of insight, or, latterly, as someone who "deserves" the privileged space of childhood. The child in antiquity was seen as an imperfect adult, incomplete if full of potential. It was only with the Romantic deification of the (usually white) child as an '"authentic" innocent in the late eighteenth and early nineteenth centuries that a cultural interest in childhood as a singular phase and state began in earnest in the West, burgeoning through the Victorian period in tandem with an intensification of representations of the child in literature, painting, and later film, and the development of social movements promoting children's legal rights, particularly around child labor and poverty. Contemporary Western models of the child are consequently both culturally and historically limited, but also, as the pathbreaking childhood theorist Philippe Ariès established in *Centuries of Childhood* (1962), culturally relative. For Ariès, models of childhood are historically mutable. For instance, the Middle Ages contained no fixed child image, he argues, and it certainly was not coded as innocent. After a short infancy, once the medieval child reached a fairly self-sufficient age (between five and seven), they became a mini-adult. Historians have continued to counter Ariès's position with evidence of the early exaltation of the child (particularly through images of the Christ child), a debate that inaugurated models of childhood as a culturally and historically determined construct rather than a universal and transhistorical absolute. Studies of American childhood followed this cue: William Kessen's 1979 paper on American childhood and child psychology concluded that "the American child, like any other, was a cultural invention" (quoted by Heywood 2001, 4). The question posed by the sixteenth-century cleric Thomas Becon—"What is a child, or to be a child?"—is followed by the suggestion that childness is always already a state of fallenness: "A child in scripture is a wicked man, or he that is ignorant and not exercised in godliness and God's word, be he old, or be he young."[1]

Crucially, many of the multifarious notions of childhood propounded in these extensive debates—images of the child across the history of childhood—are also present in Spielberg's work, somewhere, in some form. Spielberg—as a white male American pillar of Hollywood—mostly spotlights white characters, though not always. The 1985 adaptation of Alice Walker's *The Color Purple* is an interesting case in this story, to which I will return. The historical slavery story *Amistad* also features some children, mostly mute but certainly coded "innocent" in Spielbergian visual language. The persecuted children of *Schindler's List* will also form a case study in chapter 7. Rarely does he represent the originally sinning, truly monstrous child—the child of Hobbes, perhaps—who is ubiquitous in horror cinema but largely absent from Spielberg. Even his darkest children have a reason for being so, more rooted in the contingency of family than the theological absolute of fallenness. An exception is the puppet mistress of historical trauma in *Amistad*, eleven-year-old Queen Isabella of Spain, played by a fourteen-year-old Anna Paquin, a slave owner who demands compensation for the loss of her property—the slaves aboard the *Amistad*. By contrast, the initially alien robot child of *A.I.* (whose quest, like Pinocchio's, is to become a "real boy"), and the human bully boys who torture him are each more sinned against than sinning, and this is a more characteristic Spielbergian approach. This book acknowledges (indeed, is built on) the notion that the child is a central element in auteur branding (from the self-image Spielberg presents, through the young audiences who buy his products, through the children he employs and the representations they bear out), which risks suggesting that, in the world of Spielberg, there is an entity akin to the Romantic idea of "a timeless figure of essential childhood" (Plotz 2001, 5). "Romantic discussions of childhood," writes Plotz, "tend to focus on single figures called 'the child,' 'the boy,' 'infancy,' 'childhood'" (23). However, analysis of Spielberg's films shows that there is no single view of the child across this varied body of work, and his children are arguably less "Spielbergian" when they originate in novels, or are female, or are non-American. Indeed, they are as diverse as his adults: curious, manipulative, victimized, resourceful, able to experience areas of life unavailable to adults, and vulnerable to having their experience limited by the power of adults.

They are of course gendered: Spielberg represents boys and boyhood more extensively and intimately than girls and girlhood (I will investigate formulations of boyhood in chapters 3, 4, and 7, and girlhood in chapters 5 and 6). Indeed, boys precede any film or story. The boy child is quite literally branded onto the logos of Spielberg's two production companies: the Amblin logo features the silhouette of a boy on a bicycle with E.T. in its basket, while the DreamWorks logo stars a boy child at leisure, fishing from a crescent moon. Warren Buckland places these children in cultural histories as a lonely adventuring suburban boy and a Tom Sawyer–esque country boy evoking an "idyllic, idealistic, sentimental, Norman Rockwell–type" landscape (2006, 25). But within what might seem to be a boy monoculture, there is difference: there are lonely children (*E.T.*), abused children (*The Color Purple*), endangered children (*Jurassic Park* and *The Lost World: Jurassic Park*), imprisoned and refugee children (*Empire of the Sun*), children on the cusp of adulthood (*Catch Me If You Can*; *War of the Worlds*), dead children (*Jaws*; *Schindler's List*). They are far more likely to find themselves in dangerous or difficult scenarios than in comfortable, safe idylls. This is not just a function of exciting storytelling but an ongoing interest in exploring the child in the context of different genres and is perhaps the starkest evidence of Spielberg's complexity. Like representations of women for other filmmakers, children show Spielberg at his darkest as well as his sweetest.

Childness and Childishness

Children are also not necessarily young. Everyone—until *A.I.*'s factory-built robot children become a reality—is a child, whatever their age, in that they are the genetic offspring of two (and, from 2016, sometimes three) parents.[2] In English etymologically "child" is rooted in descriptions not of youth but of procreation and family: "child" first appeared in 1175 from the Old English word *cild*, which is cognate with various Scandinavian terms for "brood," "litter," and "offspring," as well as Gothic and Sanskrit words for "womb" and "pregnancy." At root, then, a child is not necessarily a minor or young human: a child is everyone who has been begotten. Of course this book does not analyze children in Spielberg through discussion of *all* human/mammalian figures just because we are all child offspring. The etymology signifies because Spielberg's films themselves are already underpinned by it, in their insistence that children and families need to be read together. Toward the end of this book I will look also at failing parents and grown-ups as child offspring—characters like Indiana Jones, his father and his son in the later installments of the franchise, or Avner (Eric Bana) in *Munich*, or Peter Banning (Robin Williams) in *Hook*, who are defined by the (in)ability to be fully the parent of a child or the child of a parent, and are sometimes marked by a perverse childishness. While Spielberg scholarship is only now seriously scrutinizing the child, it has more readily focused on the parent of the child than the child of the parent (Pomerance 2017; Williams 2017).

The child and the childish adult are of course not the same thing and are legally distinct. "Minor" and "juvenile" accurately refer to many Spielbergian children who are actually underage and correspond to these terms in the accepted sense. But the numerous adults who behave as juveniles are often outsider figures who have few of the responsibilities or—sometimes—the rights associated with reaching the age of majority (e.g., Victor Navorski [Tom Hanks] in *The Terminal*). Though these images have appeared in Spielberg's films at the perfect postwar moment for boomer significance, they have long cultural roots. Childishness is itself an ancient concept. Despite those histories of childhood that date its provenance as only from the Romantic period of the early nineteenth century, an Old English word for "childish"—*cildisc*—dates from before the year 1000. Children are of course often childish—the term itself means "the nature and character of a child." But in common parlance it is a far more pejorative term, used to denigrate puerile or immature adults, those who should know better or should have grown better. Roy Neary in *Close Encounters of the Third Kind* is childish, as is Lou Jean Poplin in *The Sugarland Express*. When they are male, these regressing or childish adults are often taken as directorial alter egos, even though the wider point of view of the films themselves might reserve judgment or positively disapprove of them. Children (young humans) can also be the opposite of childish: the adult-aspiring or "mature" child is said to be behaving like a grown-up. Critics who, for instance, have praised Haley Joel Osment for seeming older than his years or Christian Bale for a preternaturally mature performance have echoed this. Since this is a book that focuses on childhood, I use the word "adult" to mean simply not-child, despite the fact that the word has come to imply excessively "adult" works of a sexual nature. In the context of this book, "adult" signifies the culture of the grown-up—though inevitably this is a contested concept given debates around the family film and its fluid audience, and the highly tenuous adulthood of some of Spielberg's man-child characters. Avoiding the childishness of the term "grown-up" and avoiding the sexualization of the word "adult" is an interesting part of writing about children and the child in Spielberg. "Adultish" may be the best (if not the most elegant) signifier for children who perform adult modes of behavior.[3]

There are then children proper—Spielberg provides images of many such young humans, up to about thirteen years of age, who function to convey a range of positions, sensibilities, symbols, and emotions: Lex and Tim in *Jurassic Park*, Rachel in *War of the Worlds*, Barry in *Close Encounters*, numerous bit-part children in *Jaws* and almost every other film Spielberg has made, even *Schindler's List*'s girl in the red coat. These are child actors playing children. There are also adolescent figures, through whom transitional or threshold states between childhood and adulthood are explored: Jamie/Jim in *Empire of the Sun* (a 13-year-old playing a 13-year-old); Albert in *War Horse* (20-year-old Jeremy Irvine playing a 15-year-old); Robbie in *War of the Worlds* (22-year-old Justin Chatwin playing a teenager); Frank in *Catch Me If You Can* (a 27-year-old-Leonardo DiCaprio playing a 15-year-old—"just a kid" according to Tom Hanks's Hanratty). The adult actor "passing" as a minor is an interesting formation of screen childhood and is distinct from the failing adult for whom the failure is childishness. Since the mid-1980s, Spielberg has become increasingly interested in the child-turning-adult—he has argued that *Empire of the Sun* moved him forward into discussion of loss of innocence rather than innocence itself (which his earlier films are said to simplistically celebrate). Of course, it makes employment sense to hire a twentysomething who looks young rather than someone who may be the age of the character but who, as a minor, is subject to the strictures of shorter working days and on-set guardians. Making an adult pass as a child also enables the character to age credibly, toward or past the actor's own age (DiCaprio, Irvine). Child performers dread the moment—usually around 14 or 15—when employment dries up because, unless they look young enough to be able to perform a 10-year-old, casting agents prefer to choose young-looking adults for legal and contractual reasons. So there is something special about Christian Bale performing a 13-year-old child-becoming-adult at the age of 13: it is not a role a youthful adult could take on.

The Cultural Child

This book is indebted to a long history of scholarship into the historical child, philosophies of childhood, and children's culture. Discussion of children's film work, performance, and filmmaking practice focused on childhood is in its infancy, yet critical engagement with children's literature is as old as children's literature itself. Literary scholarship frequently reads the form's key historical phases (from the first golden age of writing for children in the nineteenth century, through to the second golden age after World War II, through to the more recent period of "contemporary classics") in terms of a literary challenge to, or confirmation of, wider Romantic, nineteenth- and twentieth-century cultural ideas and ideals about what the child is, which are indelibly marked by race and sex. But following Ariès, many familiar models of the child were challenged or rewritten around the time baby boomer Spielberg came of age; certainly his films draw on earlier models and myths of the child (established by religious doctrine, Romantic idealization, and Victorian sentiment), but his career is most clearly coterminous with a late twentieth-century explosion in cultural, historical, and social scientific revision of how the child is understood and—most recently—with the child in film.[4] It is this last surge of interest that is most useful here. Just as academic accounts of childhood frequently use literary forms as historical evidence (Wordsworth, Blake, Dickens, and Beecher Stowe are regularly cited when developing a picture of the child in the nineteenth century and beyond, just as Hobbes and Rousseau are used for earlier accounts), so filmic images form attitudes toward the child in the late twentieth and early twenty-first centuries. In this century a wellspring of scholarly work has developed on child-focused cinema, but it usually positions itself through textual analysis as an adjunct of adaptation and children's literary studies or else reads film as illustrating episodes in the social history of childhood. This book draws on a range of studies focused on representations of children and cinema, including Kathy Merlock Jackson's *Images of Children in American Film: A Sociocultural Analysis* (1986), Emma Wilson's *Cinema's Missing Children* (2003), Vicky Lebeau's *Childhood and Cinema* (2008), Debbie Olson's *Black Children in Hollywood Cinema: Cast in Shadow* (2017), and edited collections including Debbie Olson and Andrew Scahill's *Lost and Othered Children in Contemporary Cinema* (2012). These texts, mostly discussing representations and theory, are underpinned by film-historical work (Bazalgette and Buckingham 1995; Staples 1997; Wojcik-Andrews 2000; N. Brown 2017), which informs this book's understanding of cinema for children, child audiences, and the rise of the family adventure film. Most Spielberg scholarship touches on his work as a nexus for these issues, but rarely in a sustained way. Two exceptions are Emilio Audissino's study *L'infanzia nel cinema di Steven Spielberg* (2010), an early exploration of representations of childhood in Spielberg, whose readership is as yet limited to Italian readers. The collection *Children in the Films of Steven Spielberg* (2016), edited by Adrian Schober and

Debbie Olson, covers a range of questions and texts, including some neglected films (two readings of *Hook*, an analysis of *The Adventures of Tintin*, and Spielberg-produced television) and discussions of lost children and trauma. A further wave of work focused on child actors and creative labor was spearheaded by the *Screen* article "Child Performance Dossier Introduction" (Lawrence and Smith 2012), which emerged from what may have been the first symposium in the area at the University of Sunderland in 2011.[5] One year earlier, Karen Lury's *The Child in Film: Tears, Fears and Fairy Tales* (2010) combined a focus on representations with discussion of performance and performers.

This all provides fertile ground for an extended analysis not just of representations of childhood within Spielberg's films but also of his role as an employer of children. A skilled director of children, he has fostered strong working relationships with his young actors and is known for his ability to nurture and provoke powerful performances. His career coincides with the exponential growth of child-focused cinema globally and—with the explosion of child-marketed genres—the employment of children for screen purposes on a historically unprecedented scale. I frame film analysis through questions of the politics and pragmatics of employing children as actors and pay close attention to what these young performers bring to the work. In addition to its contribution to Spielberg studies and wider understanding of contemporary genre and popular cinema, this book therefore also contributes to this emerging scholarship on child performers. Caroline Steedman's brilliant *Strange Dislocations: Childhood and the Idea of Human Interiority 1780–1930* engages with shifting ideas and ideals of childhood, but it also focuses its materialist gaze on real historical children while keeping "an analytic separation between real children . . . and the ideational and figurative force of their existence" (1995, 5). It is equally important to recognize that "the child" in Spielberg's work is a culturally constructed image specific to post-1960 America but also is borne out by actual children—actors—performing in a job of work.

Just as the child is everywhere in Spielberg, so Spielberg's children speak to these long-standing debates. How do we define childhood—through its end point? (eighteen or twenty-one? puberty? the shifting age of consent? the shifting age of criminal responsibility?); through its racial, gendered, and class distinction? (what is it to grow up Black and female in the 1930s [*The Color Purple*], or as a boy in the suburban United States in the 1980s [*E.T.*], or as the son of ex-colonial Britain in China in the 1940s? [*Empire of the Sun*]). What of children who have childhood taken away from them—slaves (*Amistad*), laborers, or prisoners (*Schindler's List*), or perhaps even the child actors who perform them? What do artificial children (in *A.I.*) tell us about real ones? Childhood is both the "best years of our lives" and a time of immense suffering, inflected with nostalgia and horror, misunderstanding and pain. This book shows that many historical discourses about the child continue to battle it out in Spielberg's child meanings, but the result is contradictory and complex. It also draws from a particular thread in American studies that identifies the historical child alongside women and slaves as a focus for pity and emotion. But as with counterhistories that have celebrated first-person slave narratives and women's culture as a way of mitigating the sentimentalized othering of dominant culture, so the self-authored voice of the child speaks occasionally through adult-produced childhood histories. And so the child is identified in this book sometimes against the grain of adult filmic discourse.

The focus of this book is therefore threefold: childhood in film, child actors in film, and films for children, all read through Spielberg's directorial work. Childhood may be analyzed with child actors, but the result may not necessarily be a children's film. Indeed, the very term is highly contested in the burgeoning literature around the subject. Cary Bazalgette and Terry Staples demarcate this on national grounds: "the family film (essentially American)" is distinct from "what we shall call the 'children's film' (essentially, but no longer exclusively, European)" (1995, 94–95). Despite its title (*Children's Films: History, Ideology, Pedagogy, Theory*), Ian Wojcik-Andrews's 2000 book focuses primarily on representations of children and films about childhood in a range of variously genred films, including those not likely to be watched by children, while Noel Brown's extensive body of work primarily on the family film identifies the difficulties of categorizing films based on their protagonists or audiences. Brown's study *The Children's Film: Genre, Nation and Narrative* examines films with and for children in the context of nationality, marketing and distribution, censorship, and merchandising, reading the child viewer and protagonist in and of Hollywood cinema in the context of new multimedia conglomeration and production modes (2017, 35–60). Hollywood, he asserts, mostly "makes 'family films' rather than 'children's films'" (35), and I will explore what this might mean for Spielberg's child audiences—who these films are for, as well as who they star, and who authored them.

Genre and Melodrama

Tears are not an accidental special effect. Spielberg's generic master stroke has been to wed melodrama to other genres through the use of children. Children "mess up" genre with emotion and reaction, and through the manifestation of their bodies "acting out." This is reminiscent of the historical use of women in classical Hollywood, bringing a particular affective and somatic appeal for women audiences, as evidenced in the substantial history of scholarship form the 1980s onward (see Gledhill 1987; Bratton, Cook, and Gledhill 1994). But children in Spielberg function in a distinct way and for a wider audience demographic. They inflect films that might be thought of as non-melodramas with the feelings and responses of melodrama, just as women have done across this history of cinema. This happens in a variety of ways, as the focus of domestic pressure or repression (evoking Thomas Elsaesser's foundational 1986 framing of women across the genre) and as physical beings (representations of children, but also performed by children) embodying "the performative rhetoric of melodrama. . . . The body as site of meaning" (Bratton, Cook, and Gledhill 1994, 2). Melodrama intervenes in Spielberg's favored popular genres (science fiction; the family adventure film; the war film) because, quite simply, children and childhood enable a privileging of feeling over more cerebral signification. Spielberg himself said in 1981 that he sees "movies through youngsters' eyes. . . . I don't make intellectual movies" (Schickel 1981, 56); post-*Schindler's List*, this may be revised: childhood is explored across this wide range of genres, but all are altered by the presence of the child. Vivian Sobchack has argued that in horror and science fiction the child creates an affinity between these genres and "the newly revitalized family melodrama" (1991, 2–30). I want to put it more starkly, by deploying a noun as a verb. Linguistically awkward though this might seem, permit me to do so in order to build some scaffolding for this book. The child in Spielberg functions to "melodrama" these other genres. This mobilizes the idea of melodrama as process, as mode, rather than (or as well as) noun and genre category—the literal melding of music with story. Children add something else. Children at risk, in pain or out-and-out visibly emoting, turn the screw of affect (to borrow from Henry James's famous formulation). Of course, it might be argued that melodrama is everywhere in Spielberg. He did declare in 1988, "I don't think I've ever *not* made a melodrama" (Friedman and Notbohm 2000,65). Perhaps there are some marginal cases (the early *Indiana Jones* films? *1941*?), but the point stands. Nor has he made a film entirely without children or child figures. As a multigenred filmmaker, he has said that the director he admires most is Victor Fleming because Fleming was a hired hand director making eclectic project choices and working across genres within the studio system (Ebert and Siskel 1991, 40). This is a version of Spielberg's career arc: though no longer exactly a hired hand, he has ranged across genres and forms. But to this genre eclecticism he adds the child.

The child in Spielberg thus functions as a generic mobilizer: like women, children bring melodrama straight into the heart of other genres. It is the child in Spielberg who enables him to make the melo-hybrid genres with which he works "Spielbergian." The child enables Spielberg to reinflect other genres with the pull of melodrama—the child (to which he always has to turn, even when he thinks he is making a movie with no children, as he said of *Schindler's List* at its inception) enables him to reinflect genres. It is the child (rather than the woman) who "melodramas" other genres, which then in turn become vehicles for the most agonized of family romances.

The "Master Images"

Let us put the question of the child in Spielberg the other way around by asking, what does "Spielbergian" mean? Auteurist neologisms (Hitchcockian, Wellesian) can be a useful shorthand, but they are highly essentialist and often focused around traditional auteurist ideas about visual style, and are welded to a "great man" model of cultural history. "Spielbergian" may refer to the primarily historical or industrial—his family adventure action films as consummate examples of New Hollywood, huge-scale works produced in a particular context, for instance. It may refer to the segueing of sentiment and score, or repeated cinematographic or stylistic techniques (as Warren Buckland's 2006 book forensically pins down), or to repeated themes and obsessions—World War II, the "greatest generation," and the Holocaust; absent fathers; airplanes, even. But he is also a director of exquisite imagistic "moments," which are for me more interesting than his roller-coaster signature virtuoso sequences, and frequently focus the child. These are visual metonyms in which complex significance is condensed into simple resonant images: the trembling water in *Jurassic Park*, the toddler obliviously singing to himself while a beachful of people panic, or the dog's stick floating on the waves in *Jaws*. Or *Schindler's List*'s girl in the red coat. Or the "affecting" moment from *Empire of the Sun* when Jim is haloed by light, which may be both the departure of a woman's soul and the explosion at Nagasaki. Nigel Morris (2007) reads what we might call the "light story" across Spielberg's work as cinematically self-reflexive. Throughout this book key moments of the Spielbergian sublime serve to establish the child through characteristic lighting set-ups, as spectacular light resonators, as radiant bodies with a particular curiosity about light, in order to specify the question of what it would be to consider the child as an auteurial motif. Spielberg himself has pinpointed this as his "signature image." On March 22, 1990, he told Gene Siskel that the vision of toddler Barry Guiler silhouetted by the aliens' bright lights is the signature "master image" of his career: "I think it's the little boy in *Close Encounters* opening the door and standing in that beautiful yet awful light, just like fire coming through the doorway. And he's very small, and it's a very large door" (Ebert and Siskel 1991, 72) (figure 1). Children are repeatedly called upon to apprehend/comprehend forms and sources of illumination. They are lit as if they themselves radiate the light; they are backlit and silhouetted against an "awful" cosmic or divine light; they give it scale and brightness.

Two of the arguments that run through *Steven Spielberg's Children* are therefore that (1) the child is central to what we understand as "the Spielbergian" (which becomes more complex as a surprisingly diverse image of the child emerges), and (2) children inflect the genres in which Spielberg most commonly works with emotions more "appropriate to" other genres. Chapter 1 examines Spielberg's auteur identity as a grown-up Peter Pan, permutations of sentimentality read as resonating and marketable emotion, and as a current sweeping against the tide of the American New Wave. Spielberg's authorial persona is set against the ubiquitous notion that children in his films are infused with a "Spielbergian" ethic/aesthetic that coexists with a powerful popular notion that "the Spielbergian" has itself been built through ideas of the child, including the child self. Because Spielberg as director is the organizing principle of this book, for reasons of clarity I have deliberately avoided discussion of the numerous films on which he has a producer credit but no director credit (however much he seems to have had a leading

FIGURE 1 Spielberg's "master image": Barry Guiler (Cary Guffey) opens the door in *Close Encounters of the Third Kind.*

influence on some projects—*Poltergeist* would clearly be an excellent focus here). The auteur story told in this book is also built through the child. He claims to be a team player ("camera position and editing is what it's all about. . . . Beyond that, I'm open to collaboration" [B. Cook 1977, 28]) and resists the auteur label ("I'll tell you how—really, the only way—I see myself becoming an auteur. I am an auteur when I pick up my 8mm camera and shoot my girl watching television" [29]).[6] Yet not only has the focus on the child (as protagonist, theme, and performer) throughout this directorial corpus been one of the most consistent places where childhood is represented on mainstream screens, but the child is central to how Spielberg's directorial persona has developed in the marketing of his films.

This fascinating circularity is complicated by the question of which came first. But, as chapter 2 explores, other forces are at play: despite his undoubted power in controlling the images he delivers (relative to other directors), his child performers, his source material, and the genres he works with all bring their own resonances, qualifications, and resistance into the filmmaking mix. Chapters 3 through 8 focus on films, performances, and the child as a mobilizer of genre: science fiction and boyhood in chapter 3; science fiction and synthetic childhood in chapter 4; girlhood in horror, the family adventure film, the children's film, and historical melodrama in chapters 5 and 6; the child in war in chapter 7; the adult child in chapter 8 across a range of genres. Ardent fans and serious scholars of Steven Spielberg will have flocked to see the intensely autobiographical *The Fabelmans* (2022), a bookend film that threads through this discussion but to which I will return at the close of this book in an afterword, since it is (at time of writing) Spielberg's latest and last film. It is of course a fictional autobiography, perhaps the other genre that he has "never not made."

These chapters, in distinct ways, identify darkness at the heart of Spielberg's work and extend the reach of foundational studies such as Nigel Morris's *The*

Cinema of Steven Spielberg: Empire of Light (2007) and James Kendrick's *Darkness in the Bliss-Out: A Reconsideration of the Films of Steven Spielberg* (2014). I am also indebted to the growing corpus of scholarship cited throughout this study that situates Spielberg against a larger canvas of postclassical American cinema, including Lester Friedman's pathbreaking *Citizen Spielberg* (2006); Andrew Gordon's *Empire of Dreams: The Science Fiction and Fantasy Films of Steven Spielberg* (2008); and the collection *Steven Spielberg and Philosophy: We're Gonna Need a Bigger Book* (2008), edited by Dean Kowalski. However, given the importance of Spielberg to the history of cinema, these are just the beginnings of what promises to be a substantial critical industry.

Since there is some investigation of the autobiographical as part of Spielberg's persona in this book, please indulge this brief autobiographical anecdote, which also serves to anchor the chain of tears that are dotted through the analysis. With all the savagery of teenage scorn, my son emerged from a screening of *Inside Out* with the dismissive comment "It was like punching children in the face until they cried." This very same child watched *E.T.* at age five and wept copious tears for Elliott, E.T., and probably himself. *Steven Spielberg's Children* starts with a simple question that riffs on this familiar scenario: How can it be that the most family-friendly of filmmakers is also prone to making children cry, on set, on-screen, and in the audience (one often resulting from the other)? Making children cry is surely one of the things responsible adults are precisely *not* supposed to do, not least in this most public of arenas. But given that the figure of the child *within* the film also helps to generate Spielberg's audiences *for* the film, the child in the audience is a particular target of Spielberg's affecting viscerality, delivering the physical attractions of cinema to his young viewers as much as any carnival show supremo. As well as employing children, his films also tell children how to be children; "Spielberg's children" in the widest sense are then both consumers and consumed, often through extreme emotional scenarios. They are targeted as audience members and provoked into particular consumerist, identificatory, and emotional responses. Does this suggest a rather darker vision of Spielberg than the cuddly mainstream figure we have swallowed—and then regurgitated—whole, provoked into rejection by the dominant anti-sentimentalist critical discourse that has prevailed in U.S. cinematic culture since the 1960s? Why, then, has Spielberg's association with childhood and children become tangled up with implications of screen sentimentality, and why has sentiment fared so badly in critical discourse (if not among mass audiences) since the 1970s? Tears have mostly served the critical case against Spielberg as a serious filmmaker. However, they are splashed through this book as key physical evidence in an alternative case I make for a different, darker Spielberg. Children turn every genre they touch into a melodrama. Tears are the body fluid of melodrama, and in Spielberg's films children's tears feed the engine of melodrama most affectively.

1

"You Are the Child"

Steven Spielberg and Peter Pan

In the week that *E.T. the Extra-Terrestrial* was released in the United States in 1982, Steven Spielberg purchased the sole surviving Rosebud sled, made for the filming of *Citizen Kane*. Lucky visitors to his Pacific Palisades home later saw it on display, collected for real just as it had been first collected by the fictional Charles Foster Kane. It then hung at Amblin, a sign of childhood play in an institution named for a film of youth.[1] What the sled means to Kane is complex, opaque, and, of course, one of the most debated interpretative questions in film history. Its power circulates around the dream of a lost (fantasy of) childhood—lost freedom, lost family, lost ordinariness, lost innocence. Equally, we do not know what this object means to Spielberg personally. It is an evocative placeholder for *Citizen Kane* itself, infused with the youthful genius of its director, Orson Welles. While it took some time for Spielberg to garner serious attention, Welles was lauded from the start. Still, the two directors are comparable in terms of preternatural achievement: if Welles was the boy wonder of classical Hollywood, Spielberg is the Peter Pan of contemporary cinema. Peter W. Kaplan's *Washington Post* report on the Rosebud purchase begins, "One boy genius bought another boy genius's toy sled Wednesday" (Kaplan 1982).[2] Like the (initially) overachieving Welles, Spielberg landed a directing contract with a studio at an extraordinarily early age (though just how young is a matter of dispute, as we shall see) and negotiated an eternally youthful image well into old age. As the copious press materials around Spielberg evidence, the "boy wonder" image was by turns nurtured and resisted. His conscious and repeated return to the story of Peter Pan itself forms one of the narratives on children and childhood in his work, and around his work.

Welles's famous line from *F for Fake*—"I started at the top and have been working my way down ever since"—is often taken as a career statement, post-*Kane*; by contrast, Spielberg's has been post–classical Hollywood's most resounding success story. He is, as Lester Friedman denotes, Hollywood's "Citizen Spielberg." So what do we know about him? That he has made some of the most successful movies of all time? That his public image is of a barely grown-up movie geek—the cinephile who parlayed his fandom and a childhood "messing about with cameras" into blockbuster filmmaking? That he has a special affinity to childhood and the child? That a counterdiscourse of "growing up" also runs through his films and public image? Spielberg's ownership of Rosebud connects these known qualities. Of course the sled is the holy grail—or perhaps the not-so-lost ark—of movie memorabilia.[3] Along with Dorothy's ruby slippers, the eponymous statuette from *The Maltese Falcon*, or the Little Tramp's bowler hat and cane, it is a prime relic of American cinema history.[4] Whatever the movie-mad director's personal reasons, I do not think he bought it just because he could, or because, as he professed, it is "a symbolic medallion of quality in movies" (Kaplan 1982).[5] I think he bought it because on many levels Rosebud *is* cinematic childhood.

One of the arguments of this book is that Spielberg's films have provided some of contemporary cinema's most popular articulations of what it is to be a child—most regularly, of the child as an idealized figure of conscience and consummate humanity. This is only the first of several paradoxes around the child that this book encounters, since children are also regularly identified as prehuman or subhuman by cultures habituated to deem fully human that which is legally adult and consenting. Sometimes, surprisingly, his films have also critiqued common Hollywood views of childhood, an against-the-grain view that is only marginally acknowledged. Childhood is also a mode of performance, a marketing device, and an element of auteurial/authorial identity. It is intrinsic to Spielberg's public directorial persona and to promoting his success across diverse audience demographics—sometimes generically centering *on* children makes him popular *with* children (and their adults). In almost single-handedly inventing the family adventure film, he has roundly ignored W. C. Fields's famous dictum, "Never work with children or animals." In this he was encouraged by François Truffaut, who, Spielberg has said in interview, "helped inspire me to make *E.T.* simply by saying to me, on the *Close Encounters* set, 'I like you with *keeds*, you are wonderful with *keeds*, you must do a movie with *keeds* . . .' And I said, 'Well, I've always wanted to do a film about kids, but I've got to finish this [*1941*]. . . . And Truffaut told me I was making a big mistake. He kept saying, 'You are the child'" (Sragow 2000, 113).[6]

Of course Spielberg has since done many movies "with *keeds*": because he is regular employer of children, his work is indelibly marked by their performances. Chapter 2 of this book focuses on child actors, informed by and informing the scholarly area of child stardom and performance. But Truffaut's final statement tellingly slides from one child formation to another: featuring the child as a central narrative focus and being a skilled director of children have become conflated in the persona of Spielberg himself as a grown-up kid. This resonant cultural layering of children in film, films for children (or not), and the director's identity as both a son/child and a father—cinematically and through the biographical elements worked in the public dissemination of his branding—underpins the approach to Spielberg developed in this book. The work of this chapter is to unpick the historical development of Spielberg as child—fostering, resisting, but nevertheless unshakably associated with a popular cultural Peter Pan.

Central to Spielberg's filmic mythology is an anxious focus on the way adults use children, partly to indulge fantasies about themselves as children—innocence conceived as an adult's fantasy of childhood that saves the adult (or what Peter Biskind has called Spielberg's "sentimental view of our better self as the inner child" [1998, 363]). This is the basic principle of childhood put to work as the gauge by which authentic or debased adulthood is judged—it is the motivating fantasy of *Hook* (Robin Williams's Peter must relearn how to be a child) and also of *Close Encounters of the Third Kind* (Richard Dreyfuss's Roy is chosen by the childlike—and child-performed—aliens because he is more child than father in his family). Rosebud, and Kane's lifelong preservation of it, suggests just this personal, retrospective view of the child, one that goes up in flames in the final frame.[7] It may be that this most cinematic view of a childhood idyll that the early-life scene in *Kane* presents is also significant because it shows the child to be meaningful only if he is meaningful to the adult (not least his own adult self). Childhood as directed by Welles is one element in a range of memories, dreams, and symptoms that define the knowing or unknowing of the adult man. What happened to the boy Kane is key to the complexities of the adult Kane, a key that is snatched away from the audience (and the investigator, Thompson, who is trying to crack the code of Kane the man) as the film ends. It is a prime example of the child functioning as a metonym for and of the man. This may suggest Wordsworth's idea of the child as father of the man, but in narratives where the grown-up is the primary point of view the child becomes just another clue deployed to solve the complex puzzle of adulthood.

This is not (always) true of Spielberg, as this book shows. A number of films, particularly child-point-of-view films, explore and extend the subjectivity of the child, albeit as written, produced, and in all other ways made by an adult filmmaking team as directed by Spielberg. Within the considerable constraints and freedoms of maximum-budgeted mass-market filmmaking, Spielberg's films often present the child as a stand-alone entity, not simply a being who signifies primarily as a reference point for the adult (though you may well counter this with the argument that since I am an adult, I am in no position to judge). The very idea that a product that is adult-authored cannot be child-identified springs partly from Jacqueline Rose's important analysis of children's literature inflected through the case of *Peter Pan*. "Peter Pan offers us the child—for ever," she famously writes. "It gives us the child, but it does not speak *to* the child" (1993, 1). The image of Pan is an enforced infantilization courtesy of adult fantasy: he is "a little boy who does not grow up, not because he doesn't want to, but because someone else prefers that he shouldn't. Suppose, therefore, that what is at stake in *Peter Pan* is the adult's desire for the child" (3). There is, then, something predatory about how the child is posited as object within children's fiction ("Children's fiction sets up the child as an outsider to its own process, and then aims, unashamedly, to take the child *in*" [2]). This may also speak to movies for children, starring children, about children, though the process of production, and the opportunity for reframing the child, might itself reframe the question. As yet, we lack a significant child-authored sector of film production, at least commercially and professionally, though widespread access in developed countries to mobile phones, as well as (to a lesser degree) digital cameras, editing software, and web-based modes of self-distribution, now underpins a proliferation of amateur, online, and indie work by under-eighteens. Children may be closer to developing a child-originating film production industry that self-imagines the child than they are to taking over the publishing industry and helming their own (possible rather than impossible, to deploy Rose's terms) children's literature. *The Fabelmans*, Spielberg's autobiographical account of his child self as a developing filmmaker, "gives us the child" by the adult that the child became.

One of the primary ways in which the image of the child actor circulates is paradoxically through the postchildhood dramas of what happens to them when they grow up (when they "fail" to be a child, and forge an uneasy public path to unembraced adulthood), and I will examine the "former child actor" in chapter 2. Spielberg as a filmmaker for children himself started as a child filmmaker, and only perhaps reluctantly graduated to adult filmmaker status. In 1977 he said, "I was born with a camera glued to my eye" (Austin 1977, 29). Accounts of his childhood are peppered with examples of the young Spielberg as a local cultural magnet and an inventive director—as a storyteller who would terrify other children in order to film their terror (*Newsweek* 1977, 98; Janos 1980, 238). At age eleven he codirected a play about Peter Pan for his elementary school (which he replicated in an early scene in *Hook*) (Bahiana 1992, 14). More significant for his cinematic future, he also directed a silent Western for his Eagle Scout photography merit badge, which he cites as formative: "I was making something happen that I could relive over and over again, something that would only be a memory without a camera in my hand" (Janos 1980, 238). Before the cheap, portable technology available to young filmmakers today, Spielberg first used his father's 8mm Brownie movie camera, inventing narratives based on the genre films he loved and starring his school friends as actors, or dramatizing films to accompany records of film soundtracks that he collected. Joseph McBride (2010) notes the ubiquity of 8mm or 16mm camera ownership in middle-class families among Spielberg's Phoenix neighborhood, and Steven regularly collaborated in particular with three other children who were also budding amateur filmmakers.[8] A local children's TV program, *The Wallace and Ladmo Show*, showcased these young filmmakers' work in its "Home Movie Winners" spot.[9] He was also child (with a TV set and, later, through cinematic screenings) who hosted and curated other children's viewing. He became an exhibitor at age twelve, showing 16mm versions of theatrically released films on a borrowed GE 16mm projector in the family room at his house,[10] as well as using his own films as program fillers. The profits were split between charity donations and the purchase of film stock for subsequent work. These were, he has said, "my first audience-youngsters": "The audience was usually composed of children under 12. I sold tickets for a dime (later raising it to a quarter) and they'd come over to my house. We'd use the family room and they'd sit on card-table chairs" (Poster 2000, 60).

Spielberg was then a child producer of children's culture. "Some kids get involved in a Little League team or in music . . . or watching TV. I was always drowning in little home movies. That's all I did when I was growing up," he said in interview in 1978 (Tuchman 1978, 50). So his first films are not his TV work at Universal, or *Duel* or *The Sugarland Express*; they are *The Last Gunfight* (made in fifth grade), *Fighter Squad* (made in seventh grade), and the prizewinning *Escape to Nowhere*, which is reimagined in *The Fabelmans* (started when he was thirteen and finished when he was sixteen), all featuring his young friends (figure 2). A number of profiles of Spielberg around the release of *Close Encounters of the Third Kind* in 1977 lay out this childhood film work because one of the key films he made then, *Firelight*, is often read as a prototype for the 1977 science fiction classic. The Spielberg-produced *Super8*—the story of children making a film—was, according to director J. J. Abrams, inspired by Spielberg's work as a child filmmaker.[11] One of his grade school teachers sees his early filmmaking as being on a continuum with his adult work: "I wasn't a bit surprised by his filmmaking. He *was a filmmaker*. Always, from the early days" (quoted by McBride 2010, 93). Spielberg argues that his filmmaking career started in childhood: "I've been really serious about [filmmaking] as a career since I was twelve years old. . . . I don't excuse those early years as a hobby. . . . I really did start then" (McBride 2010, 66).[12] These were films starring and crewed by "youngsters my own age who went to the same school and had nothing to do on Saturdays—just like me" (Poster 2000, 58).[13] Of course, we do not know Spielberg for his juvenilia but for his adult-helmed films. At present almost all films about children and starring children—certainly theatrically released films—are made by adults. But does this mean that they only present the child in an

FIGURE 2 "I was born with a camera glued to my eye": Spielberg reimagines his filmmaking childhood self in *The Fabelmans*.

adult-signifying manner? Given that his films are so successfully sold to children, what is at stake when Spielberg directs children for children?

These questions are not lost on child audiences. Eleven years after his purchase of Rosebud, Spielberg made time in a busy schedule wrapping the *Schindler's List* shoot in Poland by day and editing *Jurassic Park* by night to attend a ceremony organized by children at Łęg, near Kraków, at which they bestowed upon him the Order of the Smile ("the highest recognition that the Polish children had at their disposal" [Palowski 1999, 142]). Preceded by a live theatrical entertainment in which E.T. defies a frightening dragon from Polish mythology, the child-directed ritual suggests the sweetest confection critics accuse Spielberg of himself concocting: "Spielberg is sworn in: that he will always be full of joy and will strive to bring joy and happiness to all the children in the world" (146). He then is tested on whether he can drink a glass of lemon juice and smile afterward (he passes) and is interviewed by children about making films for children, featuring children (he cannot recall a film of his which does not feature children), and the specifics of whether he likes Polish children: "'Of course,' is Steven's immediate reply. 'In *Schindler's List*, which is not a film for children, there are only Polish children and they are excellent actors. Besides, I came here with my own children, who made a lot of friends in Poland'" (146–147). Here, then, is a tentative distinction of what constitutes a film for children (or not), articulated for an audience of child viewers, which folds in the child performer while also gesturing toward the director's own public image as a father—which the seriousness of *Schindler's List* was helping to reinforce.[14] This complex of public/private articulations is only one of many ways in which Spielberg contextualizes his work through the child, and in turn uses the child as context for his directorial style and image.

The Man-Child

What, then, of the adult producer/creator of child-focused cultural objects, who is himself publicly identified and sometimes marketed as an adult child? Spielberg has repeatedly returned to Peter Pan, in his film *Hook* (1991), in the evocative moment in *E.T.* when Mary (Dee Wallace) reads Gertie (Drew Barrymore) J. M. Barrie's novelized version of the story, and in the many references to this story sprinkled across *A.I.* Many critics mention childhood in the context of the contemporary family, psychoanalysis, or psychobiography, yet the Pan-Spielberg connection is more contradictory than casual references across the burgeoning biographical corpus suggest. Indeed, "Peter Pan" has become a popular designation for something quite other than its original meaning. From the character's first appearance in an adult novel in 1902 (*The Little White Bird*), followed by the 1904 stage play *Peter Pan, or The Boy Who Wouldn't Grow Up*, right up to twenty-first-century spin-offs and productions (*Peter Pan in Scarlet* by Geraldine McCaughrean, the official 2006 sequel to *Peter and Wendy*, for example, or *Pan*, a live-action origins story directed by Joe Wright), Peter Pan has continued to be a provocative image of the child and product for the child, able to adapt to the nuances and demands of disparate historical cultural moments. As Allison Kavey argues, it is a cultural history that spans almost every art form, and plays equally powerfully to adults and children. The collection *Second Star to the Right: Peter Pan in the Popular Imagination* (coedited by Kavey and Lester Friedman) is one recent scholarly work that uncouples *Peter Pan* from its primary association with children's culture. "I know of no other story," writes Kavey, "that consistently inspires such personal and intense reactions in adults" (2009, 3). The essays in Kavey and Friedman's book read Pan as a queer icon (Munns 2009, 219–242), an outsider (Tuite 2009, 112), and an image as much of child hating as of child loving (Holmes 2009, 137). The novel *Peter and Wendy* appeared in 1911, with its famous first sentence underlining the inevitability of most young humans' fate alongside the specific case of Peter, who escapes it: "All children, except one, grow up."

However, the term has more recently switched to its opposite: since at least the 1960s it has come to mean not a child but an adult, and not one who cannot grow up but one who refuses to, or is in denial about the fact that he has. It would be odd to call an actual child a Peter Pan. In theatrical performance—stage musicals and pantomime—it is usually an adult woman who plays Peter, and has been since the first performances by Nina Boucicault in London in 1904 and Maude Adams in New York in 1905, though the most famous "principal boy" Peter is Mary Martin on Broadway in 1954, which was followed by a series of popular telecasts and rebroadcasts throughout the 1950s and 1960s (key decades, of course, for Spielberg's own TV viewing). When a boy child is given the role, he is often an adolescent, on the cusp of puberty, all the better to be heterosexually linked to Wendy (e.g., P. J. Hogan's *Peter Pan* [2003], with a teenage Jeremy Sumpter as Peter). The term "Peter Pan" thus has the most popular cultural significance as a label for the adult who has failed to grow up but who is seen to have grown up anyway, the adult man who persists in identifying himself with youth despite having aged. In the title of Dan Kiley's 1983 pop psychology best-seller, those suffering from "the Peter Pan syndrome" are "men who have never grown up."[15] This vanity of youth and tortured masculinity suggests a kind of temporal rift, which designates mind/inner self as young but tragically or playfully out of sync with an aging body, a mismatch between body and performed identity, an uneasy insertion of childlikeness into a grown body. What one critic has called Spielberg's need to keep "the adult world at arm's length" is, then, simply one, singular, instance of the generational sensibility of the "teens of the 60s [who] may have settled down but they haven't really turned into adults" [Kilday 1982]). "Peter Pan" has then become a synonym for "eternally youthful." This baby boomer Peter Pan is precisely *not* a child. All children, including this one, grow up.

Consider, then, a critical consensus that has consistently represented an increasingly aging adult as "a cinematic Peter Pan," as Myra Forsberg called Spielberg in 1988 when he was already in his forties (2000, 127). A few years earlier a *Rolling Stone* profile titled "Will Hollywood's Mr. Perfect Ever Grow Up?" had overdone the age obsession. "Steven Spielberg still looks like a kid," Lynn Hirschberg begins, before exploring his long-standing desire to direct a film version of Peter Pan: "'I won't grow up' has been the battle cry of Spielberg's films, and the director himself only seems half his age. . . . The allegorical nature of this story, the parallels between Peter Pan and his own life, are not lost on him. . . . He seems about fifteen" (1984, 38). By 1998, Peter Biskind was diagnosing the fiftysomething director's "Peter Pan complex" through work that can "return the boomers to the sandbox" (1998, 363). Ironically, there are scant uses of the term "Peter Pan" in reception material focused on Spielberg in the 1970s, when he was still actually quite young, but the extreme youth of the "kid director" was a common theme from the mid-1970s onward: a *Newsweek* profile around the release of *Close Encounters* begins, "Isn't it nice that they're letting kids make movies these days" (1977, 98). The term comes more clearly into focus from the 1980s onward, used increasingly as the man himself gets older and older, the dominant auteurial moniker (along with "wunderkind" and "young lion") as he progresses through middle age and into what should be elder statesmanship ("Boy Wonder" was a headline in the *L.A. Weekly* in 1986 when Spielberg was nearly forty [Carson]). In 1982, Gregg Kilday was writing in the *Los Angeles Herald-Examiner* that Spielberg "is the eternal teen-ager who's found that his own teen-age obsessions (with fantasy and technology) are shared by millions of others. Addicted to junk food and video games, Spielberg at 34 manages to live pretty much as if he were still a teen-ager."

Citing his age (or more precisely his youth) is commonplace (as it was for Orson Welles), which is particularly ironic since Spielberg seems to have fudged his history in order to appear even younger than he was. The story that he was eighteen in 1966 when he absconded from the Universal tour bus and pretended to be "some kid related to some mogul" (Hirschberg 1984, 35), and found work while hiding under the radar, emerges in different forms in various biographical accounts. It has become one of the foundational stories of Spielberg history, but it is not true, even if it conflates a series of events that have been shuffled over the years. Joseph McBride opens his demystification of the myth with a quote from a 1972 *TV Guide* profile of Spielberg: "Poke a Hollywood legend with the needle of fact and it usually blows up in your face" (McBride 2010, 109). Spielberg was born on December 18, 1946, but this was initially widely misreported; age checks cited in press in the 1970s and 1980s are usually two years out, in favor of making Spielberg appear an even younger (and therefore higher) high achiever—a child, in fact. "At 33," wrote Robert Moss (erroneously) in 1981, "Spielberg must be the most convincing incarnation of the boy genius to hit Hollywood since Irving Thalberg" (12). A *New York Times* profile titled "Spielberg at 40: The Man and the Child" was published in 1988, when he was in fact already nearly forty-two. Press surveys of his preternaturally early start are anchored to the Universal moment: He "made the pilot of 'Night Gallery' at Universal when he was 21" (Loynd 1977); he told the *Hollywood Reporter* in 1971 that he was twenty-one when he "sneaked past the guard at Universal, found an empty bungalow, and set up office . . . it took Universal two years to discover I was on the lot" (McBride 2010, 109). Spielberg did indeed have a legitimate pass to work at Universal during his summer holidays in 1964 and 1965 when he was just seventeen and eighteen, getting invaluable experience of the end of the studio system, observing production, and networking.[16] But he then went back to high school and eventually on to Long Beach State University, having failed to get into the prestigious film program at the University of Southern California ("I was a kind of orphan abandoned in Long Beach" [McBride 2010, 138]). He shot *Amblin'*, the short calling-card film that helped him to secure his seven-year contract at Universal, when he was twenty-one, and while the *Hollywood Reporter* gives his correct age as twenty-one in its announcement of December 12, 1968 ("Spielberg, 21, is believed the youngest filmmaker ever pacted by a major studio"), this is just under the wire—he turned twenty-two six days later (despite this, by 1984 he was telling the journalist Lynn Hirschberg, "I was still several months shy of my twenty-first birthday").

His first job was directing Joan Crawford in a 1969 episode of *Night Gallery*. Spielberg promotes the "boy director" angle of this break ("I quit college so fast I didn't even clean out my locker. I went from Cal State at Long Beach to Stage 15 at Universal—where Joan Crawford met me at the door" [quoted by McBride 2010, 169]), and Crawford hilariously endorses it. "When I suggested we go to lunch," Spielberg declared in 1981, the veteran actress replied, "I'm not going to be seen in public with you. People will think you're my child" (Reilly 1981, 76). Bette Davis had reportedly dropped out of the role because Spielberg was too young, only to be replaced by her lifelong rival, who insisted on denoting serious authority on her director by calling him "Mr. Spielberg," for the benefit of a crew that balked at his youth.[17] Crawford's biographer also notes that she was used to a commanding steer from her directors; she "never lost that need for the firm, parental voice of authority, even when the director was young enough to be her grandson" (Thomas 1978, 241). So at the beginning Spielberg's struggle was to promote himself as *more* adult than he seemed: "'I expected hostility when I started on this,' said the long-haired very youthful appearing tyro, on the final day of shooting. But no one seemed to think it was unusual. Nobody called me, 'Hey Kid'" (Hull 1969, 8). This workplace "adultization" was short-lived, and press continued the extreme-youth angle: "Child prodigy Steven Spielberg," wrote *Esquire* in February 1975, "directed Joan Crawford on TV when he was only twenty-one." In June 1975, *Playboy* further cited the director as "still six weeks shy of his 21st birthday" when he shot *Night Gallery*, and concluded the profile with "Orson who?" While twenty-one (or less) may not be much younger than twenty-two, in some U.S. states the age of majority remains twenty-one, so losing that year signifies an even smaller step from childhood.[18]

To the roll call of people who present themselves as younger than they are—child actors (and their agents) seeking to extend their tenure within a lower "playing age,"[19] and those women who view aging as the enemy of power—we must then add film directors seeking to secure the "youngest ever" badge of honor. Extreme youth is deployed as a rhetorical strategy to give extreme success further relief. Particularly in the wake of the massive success of *Jaws* and *Close Encounters*, the younger Spielberg is portrayed, the more freakishly extraordinary are his achievements. The monstrous success of *Jaws* provided a particularly ripe opportunity. "He doesn't look like a Hollywood Colossus," wrote Ruth Taylor in 1975, "but, at an age when many of his contemporaries scuffle for pittances, Steve is a multi-millionaire." By 1980 it was reported that "he is only thirty-two years old but has already earned a measure of immortality by becoming the only director in movie history to have two films—*Jaws* and *Close Encounters of the Third Kind*—on the all-time top-ten list of box-office champions." A year later Sue Reilly reported, "'My dream,' director Steven Spielberg proclaimed only five years ago, 'is that people will stop calling me a prodigy'" (1981, 74).

The adult man as child is perhaps a questionable entity, but when this becomes a framework for marketing and criticizing a mass-cinematic career, Peter Pan-ism materializes as a significant cultural phenomenon rather than an individual issue. Pauline Kael is often cited as the origin of the "infantilization" charge, but she is not alone. J. Hoberman, who cast *Empire of the Sun*–vintage Spielberg as "shamelessly kiddicentric," is one among many for whom the child and the childish have underpinned critical suspicion. Spielberg may be the most commercially successful filmmaker of all time, but from the early 1980s until around 1993 (his annus mirabilis when between the marketplace poles of *Schindler's List* and *Jurassic Park* he garnered much of the critical and peer acclaim previously denied), he was increasingly reviled on childish terms. It became particularly common for writers to entwine financial success with aesthetic failure in making a case for Spielberg as conservative filmmaker par excellence. In 1986, Andrew Britton's influential "Blissing Out: The Politics of Reaganite Entertainment" used Pauline Kael's eulogistic response to *E.T.* ("It's a dream of a movie—a bliss-out" [1987, 347]) as the key to unlock what he saw as most ideologically retrograde about 1980s Hollywood cinema. That same year Robin Wood published *Hollywood from Vietnam to Reagan*, an important collection of essays that also fixed Spielberg together with George Lucas in its sights.[20] Reflecting on this New Hollywood history later in the 1990s, Peter Biskind placed Spielberg in "the pantheon of profit"; along with Lucas, he had "finally succeeded in turning the counterculture upside down" (1998, 364). Political objection is then crystalized through an age- and stage-inflected language. In distinct ways each of these writers (and they are not alone) articulate filmmaking perceived as politically retrograde through a discourse of childishness. Though he is addressing *Star Wars* primarily here (making sideways references to Lucas's *Indiana Jones* collaborator), the language Biskind uses is more characteristic of a strain that even today continues to dog writing about Spielberg: "Lucas and Spielberg returned the 70s audience, grown sophisticated on a diet of European and New Hollywood films, to the simplicities of the pre-1960s Golden Age of movies. . . . They marched backward through the looking glass, producing pictures that were the mirror opposite of the New Hollywood films of their peers. They were . . . infantilizing the audience, reconstituting the spectator as child, then overwhelming him and her with sound and spectacle, obliterating irony, aesthetic self-consciousness, and critical reflection" (343–344).

This formulation, linking film-political conservatism and regression to infancy, riffs on a pattern that became increasingly familiar through the 1980s. The argument posits that conservative films render their viewers childlike, at the same time enveloping them in a fog of unquestioning bliss; indeed, films that promote infantilization (and filmmakers perceived as valuing this quality) are deemed by definition conservative. Mass-market film replaces religion as the opium of the people, with childishness as the ultimate state of political impotence. Against this, countercultural or challenging films supposedly act on viewers in the reverse way, provoking them to grow up into politicized adults. Aesthetic and political "maturity" is preferred over blissful, pleasurable wonder (which are effectively the only choices given). Childishness, then, is not just an element represented *within* Spielberg's films; it is an action of cinematic affect, a tool enforcing aesthetic regression. So Spielberg's films are not simply *about* children. The weight of critical response would have us believe that they force us all to *become* children. Across his career, "infantilization" has consistently been the most pejorative term wielded against the director.

Wood's savage account of fantasy and ideology in the Reagan era made a bold attempt to gather all this together while distinguishing the teller from the tale: "I am not positing some diabolical Hollywood-capitalist-Reaganite conspiracy to impose mindlessness and mystification on a potentially revolutionary populace," he wrote in 1986. "The success of the films is only comprehensible when one assumes a widespread desire for regression to infantilism, a populace who wants to be constructed as mock children" (165). This is underpinned by a loose psychoanalytic rationale: we want to regress to the lost breast of cinematic origins, hence the attractiveness of the films under fire (*Star Wars* and *E.T.*) which, Wood suggests, offer pleasurable nostalgia instead of innovation and difficulty. Another form of childlike consumption—repeat viewing, a practice which children could indulge privately in the post-VCR age—is cited as a global key to box office domination. It is return visits to repeat the pleasure of films such as *Raiders of the Lost Ark* and *E.T.* which fueled their extraordinary box office success, and here Wood conflates a childish reading practice with what the film does to viewers of all ages: "Rereading is tolerated in children. The category of children's films has of course always existed. The 80s variant is the curious and disturbing phenomenon of children's films conceived and marketed largely for adults—films that construct the adult spectator as a child, or, more precisely, as a childish adult, an adult who would like to be a child. The child loses him/herself in fantasy, accepting the illusion; the childish adult both does and does not, simultaneously" (163–164).

Why, given Pauline Kael's blissful pleasure in *E.T.*, this is a problem is because it supposedly enforces aesthetic uniformity—the ubiquity of the family blockbuster makes it hard, Wood argues, for other kinds of films to be made. Originally a champion of Spielberg around the successes of *Jaws* and *Close Encounters*, Kael reinforced her "infantilization" charge with a similar line a year earlier: "Why are movies so bad?" she asked in the *Los Angeles Times* in 1985. "One hates to say it comes down to the success of Steven Spielberg, but. . . . It's not so much what Spielberg has done as what he has encouraged. Everyone else has imitated his fantasies, and the result is an infantilization of the culture" (Rosenfield 1985). Spielberg's films are therefore not merely deemed infantilizing in and of themselves. They trample over cinematic distinction like big fat baby bullies.

The charge is that this Peter Pan has made lost boys of us all, forcing us to journey only to the Neverland of cinematic infancy. Even the director himself seemed to prefigure this 1980s critical turn in an astonishing 1978 lament about his own apoliticism. Discussing his early breakthrough short film *Amblin'*, he reports that he "can't look at it now. It really proved how apathetic I was during the Sixties. When I look back at that film, I can easily say, 'No wonder I didn't go to Kent State' or 'No wonder I didn't go to Vietnam or I wasn't protesting when all my friends were carrying signs and getting clubbed in Century City.' I was off making movies, and *Amblin'* is the slick by-product of a kid immersed up to his nose in film" (Tuchman 1978 51). *Amblin'* is of course a youth-drenched film, a brief poetic essay on young people with no adult responsibilities, made by a rookie director. It may not have the mass-market escapism of the *Indiana Jones* franchise, but here even Spielberg himself reads his own low-budget film as a symptom of cinematic and personal conservatism.

This self-castigation prefigures the 1980s critical turn against him, pitching "maturity" as the preferred term of politically challenging cinema against "immaturity" as the countervailing quality of entertainment films, devoid of seriousness while replete with childishness. Britton's unrestrained essay is perhaps the most stark version of this: entertainment films inhibit innovation or challenge, and instead promote "the pleasurable obviousness of feelings" (1986, 7), with Spielberg as Britton's exhibit A. The wider conflation of eulogistic paeans to extreme youth with superlatives about extreme profit becomes a morally inflected commonplace after the first *Indiana Jones* success and the failure of *1941* (though significantly not after *Jaws* or *Close Encounters*, both also hugely successful but at the time considered the works of a youthful genius rather than a dumbing-down mogul). In the late 1970s the currency was not yet deemed to be debased. Spielberg's chagrin at *E.T.*'s Oscar disappointment is laid at the door of its financial success. "There's always a backlash against anything that makes more than $50 million in film rentals," he said in 1983. "The tendency is for important films to win over popcorn entertainment. History is more weighty than popcorn" (Pollock 1981, 1). This is the cinematic "princeling," as he was called in 1981, an oversuccessful filmmaker likened to a child "playing with very expensive toys" (Moss 1981, 12, 14). Indeed, the link between failing to put away childish things and amassing extreme profit is repeatedly forged in reception materials, here by George Anthony in 1982: "It's the kid in Spielberg who'd play Asteroids from dusk till dawn if you let him. But it's the whiz kid in him who has signed a deal to design video games for Atari." Watching *Indiana Jones and the Temple of Doom* in 1984 was, for Vincent Canby, "like spending a day at an amusement park" (1984, C21). Following the release of *Raiders of the Lost Ark* and *E.T.*, Spielberg was reported as "personally netting $1 million a day."[21] Around this time Richard Corliss cast his *Time* magazine meditation titled "The New Hollywood: Dead or Alive?" as a whodunit: Who killed old Hollywood, the corpse of which "sprawls over the business and entertainment pages of daily newspapers"? (1981, 66). "The prime suspect," he argues, "is the Hot Young Director" (67), citing Spielberg among his contemporaries, and linking gargantuan success to the youth of directors and the audiences they appease ("When a studio executive does get down on his knees, he prays to the young" [68]). Youth therefore multiply signifies. It marks out the director as unnaturally overachieving, but also commercially in touch with an audience that is getting younger all the time.

Yet Spielberg also manages to emerge as a nice guy, somehow removed from the essential commercialism of his business by virtue of qualities such as untouched wonder and humility; he is not one of Corliss's film history murderers ("We can be thankful, then," gushes Michael Ventura in 1982, "for his essential modesty and gentleness. As manifest in his work, they are the elements that imbue all his colors and characters with a childlike hue of wonder. . . . [He is a] slight man whom you wouldn't notice in a crowd, and who looks even younger than he is" [10]). Young and powerful, profitable, commercially prescient yet also wondering, modest, innocuous—somehow he manages to be, contrarily, both just like the moguls he has replaced *and* like the kids he represents.[22] Let us call this figure Nice Steven (we will meet Nasty Steven in a moment).[23]

Of course Kael, Britton, Woods et al. raise the question of how much this complex of enforced youth underpinned by a colossal commercial machine has served to determine audience response in a particular way. Spielberg is a wunderkind, and his characters have "a childlike hue of wonder," but do we inevitably watch Spielberg with that same "childlike wonder"? This is Kael's "bliss-out"; it also fuels the backlash. How do the content and tone of the films themselves reinforce the auteurial profile of their director and encourage a pattern of youth-valuing validation across the marketplace? Such questions remain pertinent decades after these debates first played out in the mid-1980s, even though they are often pinned to the baby boomer generation that raised them. Has Spielberg's transformative impact on the industry as director, producer, and mogul repositioned cinematic consumers and reprogrammed mass taste toward the childish? So noisy were the champions of maturity who challenged perceived infantilization, they drowned out alternative views. We have accepted that this is what occurred because the savage rhetoric of this critical history determined it so, blinding us to the disturbing darkness of many of Spielberg's films and images. The 1980s-era critics threw out the baby, and the bathwater went with it.

More recent critical engagement has begun to show that the very films to which cultural decline was formerly attributed are more complex and ambivalent—that Nice Steven is the flip side of Nasty Steven. James Kendrick persuasively argues that it is not just the post–*Schindler's List* films that display darkness—it has always been there: "Kael's euphoria over *E.T.*'s innocence and warmth blinded her to the fact that there is darkness in the bliss-out" (2014, 3). What happens, then, when, far from empowering a supposed wave of infantilization, children do the opposite, performing the antithesis of childishness? This unsettling child, often the least childish element in a movie, is a key counterbalance to the critical charge of infantilization. It is in performances such as Christian Bale's in *Empire of the Sun*, which oscillates between child, childish, grown-up-too-soon, and "adultish." Other terms of approbation—"sentiment," "innocence," "sincerity"—have been deployed to a level of blinding ubiquity but also require further scrutiny. These key terms mobilize serious critical prejudice.

The Child Is Father to the Man

Of course the version of the Peter Pan syndrome at work here functions to position Spielberg in the marketplace as attractive and relevant to his generational peers and their children, both key components of his audience. Familial discourse characterizes public pronouncements on his production atmosphere, claiming a family atmosphere both on sets that include children and in the working environment of Amblin. As "just a big kid," the buddy-director bonds with his child performers by playing video games with them between takes. While the child (actor, representation, psychic cipher) is my central focus, he (for he is usually male) is commonly discussed with reference to parents and siblings, and wider uses of familial models and metaphors in the purported extended family of Spielberg production.

The next phase of the director's age positioning was equally symptomatic. While he was teetering on middle age, the Peter Pan discourse began increasingly to be supplemented by a story about growing up, with the two threads maintained, sometimes in contradiction, simultaneously. Long before *Hook*, Peter Pan alternates with full-grown manhood in a way that is unique to this cultural figure. Dale Pollock begins a profile titled "The Graying of a Crapshooter": "Steven Spielberg is growing up. The Wunderkind director . . . is 33 now, his face minus its boyish fat, his view of the world a little less wide-eyed" (1981, 1). But then he quotes Spielberg as saying, "All of us are going through our Peter Pan stage of trying to hold on to whatever vestiges of our childhood are left." By 1983, Spielberg reports that the *Twilight Zone* movie scandal (which saw two child extras killed on the set of a film he produced) "has made me grow up a little more" (Pollock 1983a), while in "Spielberg at 40," written five years later, Forsberg says: "From *Close Encounters of the Third Kind* and *E.T.* to *Back to the Future*, *Gremlins*, and *Goonies*, Mr. Spielberg has spun stories featuring children and teenagers that appealed to both the young and the young at heart. But while many of these movies reaped high praise and huge grosses, critics started wondering when the Wunderkind was going to finally grow up" (2000,126).

Yet around the same time that critics such as Kael and Wood were lamenting the infantilization of the marketplace, Spielberg was layering on another familial narrative in press material to account for a new direction in his work, a new perspective on his relationship to the Pan story. The birth of his first son, Max, prompted a family-inspired sea change in his public-facing persona: quoting the director, Ann Bayer wrote in *Life* magazine in 1986 that Max "provided his dad with 'a completely different career—fatherhood,' and Hollywood's aging wunderkind (he's 38) is giving it everything he's got" (148). McBride quotes Spielberg as saying in 1985, "Before I had Max I made films about kids; now that I have one, I'll probably start making films about adults" (2010, 359). This was around the release of *The Color Purple*, in the wake of two *Indiana Jones* films, *E.T.* , and *The Twilight Zone*; his next project was to be *Empire of the Sun*. This book argues that these "films about adults" are nevertheless films about childhood too—girlhood and Black history in *The Color Purple*, and the wartime coming-of-age drama that is *Empire*. Despite many variations on this quote appearing in Spielberg's publicity from the mid-1980s onward, the consistent line was that fatherhood made him reframe his on-screen approach to the child. However, this was also the time when he officially cried off adapting *Peter Pan*, which had long been in development, most particularly since obtaining the rights to the story from Great Ormond Street Hospital in 1985. In 1988 it was reported that he had permanently abandoned this project, while he simultaneously admitted that directing children on-screen had been a kind of surrogate parenthood: "I am up to here with 'I don't want to grow up' . . . I want to stop having kids on the screen and have them in real life" (Forsberg 2000, 131). In the promotion of *Empire of the Sun*, Spielberg used directing a child in darker scenarios as a growing-up strategy for himself. "I'm trying to grow up in increments," he said and then continued:

> I don't want to come up to the surface so quickly that I'm going to have a terrible case of the bends. I'm trying very gently to step up to a different kind of movie. . . . And I felt that *Empire*, which was emotionally the most difficult film I've made, still had a boy in it to help with that transition to a kind of genre I would like to play around with—that all my friends are saying, "Come on, this is fun. Play with the grown-ups for a while. There will always be children's stories, but this is real good for you." (131–132)

Here, then, the child functions as midwife, "birthing" the director into the next stage of his career. This child, to paraphrase Wordsworth, is a curious on-screen father to the behind-the-camera man.

Shortly after this, the on-off *Pan* project was back on again, and predictably the Pan discourse reaches a crescendo with the film *Hook*, itself heralded as the summation of a career and the apotheosis of a brand. The meeting of Spielberg and Barrie's creation delivers Peter Pan as the consummate baby boomer. But Pan is also negatively invoked: "I couldn't be Peter Pan any more," the director said on the release of *Hook*. "I had to be his father. . . . My son took my childhood away from me. But he also gave it back to me" (Bahiana 1992, 13). Bloated and profligate as *Hook* was and is in production and form (at the time it was one of the most expensive films ever made, with critics lobbing insults, particularly at the conjunction of rich spending frenzy and poor reception), as ever the marketing strategy hung on personal obsession. Few directors publicize their films with such regular reference to biography. Sometimes this is as epochal as reconciliation with Jewish identity (*Schindler's List*), or paying homage to the World War II heroism of his father's generation (*Saving Private Ryan*; even *1941*), or as personal as his own fascination with planes (*Empire of the Sun*; *Always*). Sometimes it identifies the motivation for a film through his most private feelings about his immediate family (*E.T.*; *The Fabelmans*). In 1980 he was arguing that immersion in moviemaking was precisely what had prevented him from growing up: "Life . . . has finally caught up with me. I've spent so many years hiding from pain and fear behind a camera. I avoided all the growing-up pains by being too busy making movies. . . . So right now, in my early thirties, I'm experiencing delayed adolescence. I suffer like I'm sixteen. It's a miracle I haven't sprouted acne again." The writer of this profile, Leo Janos, comments, "Growing up in Hollywood is never easy for youngsters. For a thirty-two-year old movie director of renown, it is more difficult by ten" (1980, 237). The discourse of the boy wonder aging in public prevailed even into the 1990s. By 1994 (following success with the resolutely adult *Schindler's List*), he was saying that his children wanted him to grow up: "My kids don't *want* me to be a kid. *They* want to be a kid, and in a sense they have directed me to be more of an adult than I probably ever could do for myself" (McBride 2010, 379). Of course *Hook* addresses precisely this scenario, thinking about Peter Pan grown up and having to "grow down" before he can properly be a father: "I've always been Peter Pan" he said in a promotion. "That's why I wanted to do this movie. In a way, it's typecasting for me to do this, because I've always felt an affinity for the character" (Yule 1996, 266).

As these rich reception materials show, Spielberg (who often appears to be oversharing) plays the interviewers' game—and makes them play his—by delivering the tools and terms by which critics and audiences are then encouraged to read the film through telling biographical detail cut perfectly to the measure of the film. In films about children, and which feature children, the childness of the director provides a perfect publicity angle through a neat marketing self-fulfillment that has worked effectively for decades, as the framework within which the film is presented back to the world through his own story. Childhood is at the heart of Spielberg's auteur identity, and it greases the engine of this biographically sourced branding. Indeed, beyond the journalistic world that primarily circulates the child-man image, the lure of the biographical also shapes most books on Spielberg, even the few relatively serious or academic studies that have appeared in this century. "No other filmmaker has mined his childhood more obsessively or profitably," declares biographer McBride. "Spielberg . . . has said that he 'can always trace a movie idea back to my childhood'" (2010, 16). Yet profiles rarely delve beyond the reiteration of this simple biohistorical fact. The man himself has (to my knowledge) never granted an interview to anyone writing a sustained critical or scholarly study of him—why favor any publication that one does not control? Thus in augmenting the baby boom Pan-ism with a specifically psychological form of narcissistic child obsession, even academic writers take their cue from Spielberg's own marketing discourses: Spielberg is enthralled "by the cosmic resonances not only of childhood in general but of his childhood in particular" (Bahiana 1992, 151).

This common critical connection between the work and the life, has—as far as children are concerned—also affected discussion around later life and was still a focus around the twentieth anniversary rerelease of *E.T.*. "I didn't have children back in the early eighties and suddenly, on set, I was becoming a father" he reflected later. "Every single day, I felt like I was a father to Drew, Henry, and Robert. I felt good. I think I have a big family now because it felt pretty good having three kids back then" (Sunshine 2012, 90). Indeed, few books on Spielberg pass up the opportunity to analyze the biographical tidbit planted in the public arena by the director: parental divorce, initial shame at Judaism and "feeling like an alien," relationship with mother and sisters, bullying by peers. These elements are so present in press books, interviews, and marketing statements, as well as in the surface narratives of his films, one need not dig very far—they hardly constitute a Spielbergian repressed requiring complex analytic work. If Pan-ism is a symptom of being psychologically stuck, of failing to let go of one's own origins, then critics and scholars are also part of—stuck in—this circulating process. This use of the biographical when tied to the promotional generates a particular marketplace incarnation of the auteur.

Much more recently, Spielberg has gone further than these musings on the child as terminator of the adult's childhood, or as midwife of the adult's passing into true adulthood. This post-Pan phase (if we can use such a phrase for Spielberg's work since the mid-1990s) also hinges on the place of the child in public-biographical discourse. With the post-*Schindler* development of his work in Jewish historic remembrance that became the Shoah Foundation, he further reflected on the growing up of parenthood as also a growing into morality—the child's intervention then enacting a shift toward ethical being:

> It's not that after making *E.T.* and *Indiana Jones*, I suddenly decided to settle down and make more serious, more adult pictures. We don't just grow up overnight. But we do often have children, as I did, and through that experience I gained a deeper love for life and a belief in the need to contribute meaningfully to others' lives. Sure, I also had a fear of getting older, as we all do—but it was during those ten years after *E.T.*—in my personal life with *The Color Purple*, *Empire of the Sun*, and *Always*, and my personal foray into fatherhood—that I got a good grip on the idea of morality. (Spielberg 2014, x)

Later in this same document, written for the USC Shoah Foundation publication *Testimony: The Legacy of* Schindler's List *and the USC Shoah Foundation*, he puts it even more bluntly: "I really hadn't seen God until my first child was born" (USC Shoah Foundation 2014, 10). This places a huge responsibility on the child as a fictional, historical, and biographical signifier and mobilizer, the driver of Spielberg's compass and one of the engines of his Jewish awakening. I will say more about this in chapter 7. Across the range of promotional interviews from the 1970s to today, and across the many disparate genres, stories, and stars Spielberg deploys and promotes, this insistence on the child as redeemer, avatar, and surrogate remains constant.

The Sentimental Auteur

The critical reviling (or revulsion) weathered by Spielberg in the mid-1980s came at a time when he seemed to be directing less personal films, distinct from the kind of movies "created by a single filmmaker with a steadfast vision," which he told Dale Pollock in 1983 was the kind of classic auteur filmmaker he particularly admired. Pollock adds that this quality appeals to Spielberg "because that's how he sees himself" (1983b, 1). While there was something hiply mystical about Kael's "bliss-out" (an oceanic trip of filmic response, woven from boomer transcendentalism), in the early to mid-1980s a more embodied "feelingfulness" was also sniffed out in Spielberg's work that energized negative critical reaction: sentimentality. Though a vogueish aesthetic practice in the mid-nineteenth century, by the mid-twentieth century sentimentality was simply not cool.

Perhaps because of this, it is only in the twenty-first century that Spielberg has begun seriously to be analyzed as an auteur figure. Critical attention began to turn in the 1990s; scholarly attention was slow to follow. Auteurist coronations are usually predicated on the identification of a cluster of common motifs or themes amounting to a singular vision; so-called vulgar auteurism casts the net wider to include recent action directors marked by a particular kinetic style. Commercial he may be, the question was whether he was also a "single filmmaker with a steadfast vision." Both are selective practices ascribing critical credibility and coherence at the same time as they disallow unfavorable traits. Sentimentality and an adjacent identification with children and childhood lack the perceived seriousness of more familiar director hallmarks (Alfred Hitchcock's voyeurism, Tim Burton's gothic, David Cronenberg's body horror). So while all things child-focused were identified with Spielberg enough to be deployed as terms of regular critique, they were not credited as elements of a serious director's "steadfast vision." In anyone else's profile such a repeated return to a consistent set of thematic and imagistic concerns would denote instant auteur status. But because this is Spielberg, and because the auteur threads circle children and the family, this creative apotheosis was withheld.

To be clear, I do not believe that auteur status is the prime guarantor of filmmaking success; debates around the politics and usefulness of it as theory and organizing principle have cast serious doubt on this since the 1960s. I am most interested in the terms under which a prolific and consistent director would be denied such a profile.[24] Perceived as both too emotional and too popular, Spielberg became auteur-as-brand but not auteur-as-artist. Children and childhood seemed to make sense as elements of commercial identity but not as canvases for creative exploration. The serious formation of auteurism as a critical category and mode of practice denoted and deployed from the 1960s onward was forged in limited terms, and—however consistent his vision—Spielberg was just too associated with children and feelings to seem sufficiently serious. There is something curiously feminist about this. In her rich study of the child in visual culture, *Pictures of Innocence: The History and Crisis of Ideal Childhood*, Anne Higonnet argues that in art history the sentimentalized child was viewed as "faintly feminine": after Romanticism, "The subject of childhood became intellectually marginal.... Childhood became a subject for women, a subject about women" (1998, 39).[25] It may then not be regarded as a subject for serious but mainstream filmmaking: childhood may be approached if framed by a sufficiently "serious" (male? austere? art-cinematic?) view (as in the numerous European art films with child protagonists discussed in Karen Lury's 2010 study), but if inflected with feeling that spills over to the audience it risks pejorative charges of frivolity or mawkishness. This is also reminiscent of the critical denigration of melodrama itself which, Laura Mulvey reminds us, is the genre of domesticity; early critical neglect of its content has often been attributed to male critics' lack of interest in "women's pictures" (1994, 122). And to bring this full circle, Spielberg said in 1974 (just a few years after directing Joan Crawford), "I'd like to make a woman's picture because the motion picture industry has systematically shied away from the woman's movie and there are few major roles in the works for the self-realized woman" (Bobrow 1974, 34).[26] The film-historical inaccuracy of this notwithstanding (as Crawford's mid-century career attests), and aside from *The Color Purple* (more of which later), Spielberg has not made a woman's picture, nor have women or girls led his films in great numbers. But children have, and perhaps the "never not made a melodrama" director signals in this statement from 1974 that the turn to melodrama for the age of New Hollywood would be one of his pioneering angles.

Auteurism is then—among other things—a matter of taste. This habitual focus on children made Spielberg's chances of being taken critically seriously slim. Only once he began consistently to make more films with fewer children, and to focus on world-historical themes, did he become an auteurist contender. The protracted feud in discussions around Spielberg's films pitched between those who deem him arch-agent of mawkishness (e.g., Mark Anderson's "Adult human beings are sometimes hard to find in Spielberg's mawkish oeuvre" [2007, 105], or "Steven Spielberg's E.T. . . . is so mawkish I can barely manage to write about it" [Grenier 1991, 62]), and those who celebrate either the director himself or a given film as a font of innocence/childlikeness/purity of heart really hinges on the questionability of sentimentality. In short, one can seal one's historical auteurist significance with a deep-focus image of a child's sled on fire in a warehouse of ephemera, but not with the tearful face of a child saying goodbye to his extraterrestrial friend. At their most political, critics of Spielberg cast themselves as opponents in a cultural-ideological war of commercial-emotional coercion.[27] Accusations of sentimentality function to prove one's own immunity from sentiment. It was a brave critic who—beyond about 1984—celebrated spectacles of tearful innocence; Kael's "bliss-out" from 1982 was largely an attempt to articulate a certain kind of nonsexual visual pleasure without resorting to pseudomoral language, but it marked an end point in positive responses to Spielbergian emotional "sincerity." Andrew Sarris was chief prosecutor in this, deeming the response to *E.T.* as "the closest thing we have to a universal religion" while finding the film itself "an excess of self-pitying escape" (1982b, 47, 48).

Somewhere between these battle lines lay (or raged) sentiment as a key aesthetic specter. Perhaps second only to "infantile" as a term of critical abuse, occurrences of the term "sentimental" in writing around Spielberg are too numerous to count. "Bliss-out" attempts to name a heady but spiritual reverie in cinematic affect; "sentimentality" is bliss-out's more common and more tearful sister, provoking an overwhelming visceral feeling. Cognitive psychological approaches to filmic sentiment distinguish an emotional response by the viewer from the content of the viewed, between "sentimentality in the stimulus and sentimentality in the recipient. . . . The former is a representation of fictional affects in a fictional character, whereas the latter is a psychological state in an empirical individual" (Tan and Frijda 1999, 52–53). Clearly, the first does not invariably provoke the second, or Spielberg's critics would not be able so successfully to establish their scornful distance from sentimental material. However, Ed Tan and Nico Frijda acknowledge that "tears of sentiment are contagious, as all tears are. . . . sentimental emotion is even more contagious than sorrow" (53). Empathy is central here, connecting viewer to representation: "Pity's action tendency is to care for, protect, and help the other. Sentiment turns this into an urge to feel into the protagonist's state of distress and share the suffering" (64). The tear is a highly potent sign in this process, passing feeling from actor to audience, from text or film to reader or viewer, in a process of cross-contagious feeling.

Sentiment as a form also has a longer history than melodrama, and, (as Lea Jacobs makes clear in her brilliant study *The Decline of Sentiment: American Film in the 1920s* [2008, 227]), while many melodramas are sentimental, the two are not the same. The history of sentimental culture started with the term accruing more positive connotations. Writing about nineteenth-century slave narratives, Karen Sánchez-Eppler underlines sentiment's intimate role in instigating bodily and emotional response, whereby in sentimental fiction "two versions of *sentire* blend as the eyes of readers take in the printed word and blur it with tears. Reading sentimental fiction is thus a bodily act, and the success of a story is gauged, in part, by its ability to translate words into pulse beats and sobs" (1992, 99–100). I stated in the introduction that tears are the body fluid of melodrama. They are also the staining evidence of "debased"—often (in Spielberg's case) infantile—feeling. They are a contagious giveaway that, however secretly, something has hit its mark.

Throughout its long history, sentimental culture has consistently privileged emotional response rooted in the body over reasoned judgment rooted in the mind. The *Oxford English Dictionary* defines "sentiment" as a "refined and tender emotion; exercise or manifestation of 'sensibility'; emotional reflection or meditation; appeal to the tender emotions in literature or art." Its origins as a cultural term acknowledge the semantic connections made first in eighteenth-century moral philosophy between terms with psychological, ethical and bodily connotations such as sensitive, sensibility, sentiment, sentimental and feeling. Yet sentiment and particularly sentimentality have survived as commonplace terms (usually of approbation), while sensibility as a discrete term has waned. Fred Kaplan claims in his study of nineteenth-century sentimentality that Victorian sentimentality is "a subject that many talk of though few speak well or sensibly about" (1987, 5). The same might be said of Spielbergian sentimentality.[28] Underpinned by the eighteenth-century philosophies of David Hulme and Adam Smith, for whom "an access of feeling cannot be an excess of feeling" (19), nineteenth-century sentimentality as evidenced in Charles Dickens and William Makepeace Thackeray was more overtly linked to morality: feeling was evidence of the innate good of humanity.[29] Winfried Herget simply asserts that sentimental fictions were "meant to generate feelings" (1991, 10). They were also an audience leveler, on both sides of the Atlantic: "Sentimentality is literally at the heart of nineteenth-century American culture," writes Shirley Samuels. "As a set of cultural practices designed to evoke a certain form of emotional response, usually empathy, in the reader or viewer, sentimentality produces or reproduces spectacles that cross race, class, and gender boundaries" (1992, 4–5).

This is sentimental culture as blockbuster. As we will see in the next chapter, which looks closely at the way that lachrymose responses to *E.T.* made critics focus as much on the audience as on the film, tears became tangible evidence of a certain form of success seen across diverse audiences (if not cooler critics). Sentimental filmmaking triggers tearfully wet responses. Tears shed by and for children become inextricably identified with "the Spielbergian" and are so contagious that they threaten to drown *all* audiences, across the globe. An empathic contagion of pleasurable tears thus underpins the sheer popularity of these cultural objects. Tears are of course as culturally coded as any other response, but they are also one common form of manifest affect that global audiences learned—inherited—from nineteenth-century reader responses, which fed into silent cinema through melodrama. Of course, popular visual culture has a long-standing association with sentiment, from nineteenth-century theater, early proto-cinematic shows, and vaudeville through silent film and the development of melodrama as a film genre, to television soap opera. Spielberg's deployment of tears, particularly children's tears and tears shed for children, reaches back to a long tradition of the crying and cried-for child in all manifestations of blockbusting sentimental culture, from the deaths of Dickens's Nell Trent and Paul Dombey to Harriet Beecher Stowe's Little Eva.

So why did a late twentieth-century cinematic version of this cascade of affect provoke such critical ire? When did this emotional contagion become so unpopular? And—given the pleasures of cathartic crying—why did Spielberg's uncanny ability to make cry babies of his audiences inflame such a backlash? Popular culture, as Kaplan further notes, "kept its heart beating with the blood of sentimentality," but high culture took a starker path, "stigmatizing sentimentality as the refuge of philistinism and small minds" (1987, 18). Jacobs (2008) traces the effect of the literary "culture wars" in the 1910s and 1920s, as what was formerly considered the acme of cultural achievement (3) became revalued as "mush for the multitude" (5). Her account pinpoints "the crucial development in Hollywood filmmaking in the 1920s: the emergence of a preference for a laconic and understated style (275), accompanied by a shift away from sentiment and a 'growing distaste for 'bunk' or 'hokum'" (276). This turn—revulsion instigating a new ascetic purity—also occurred in literary culture around the ascetic high-water mark of modernism. It was, as Jacobs shows, to be replicated in film a little later.

But a further reverberation of anti-sentiment occurred in American film (and its criticism) through the 1960s, through the purist second wave represented by some gritty films, affecting but rinsed free of mawkishness. This turn to irony and politicized claims to seriousness underpinned what came to be known as the American renaissance, which coincided with the early part of Spielberg's career. This, I would argue, replayed literary modernism's own reactive "seriousness" in the early twentieth century against the kind of venerated nineteenth-century feeling described earlier by Kaplan. Just as Spielberg was finding his place in popular television production, the work of "renaissance" directors of the period 1967–1975 (which *Jaws* is said to have curtailed),[30] marked by a tonal veneration of anti-sentiment, were revered as politically astute, difficult, taboo-busting, edgy, and above all auteur-led and *adult*-focused. What chance, then, that a director who would go on to collect Norman Rockwell paintings and develop an identification with tearful child-eye stories could also be deemed serious? Spielberg shaped his feelingful craft at a time when displayed emotion on-screen and "caught" emotion in the audience were debased signs, at least among cineastes (if not the popular audiences of his blockbusters).

Of course this did not stop him from becoming the most successful filmmaker of all time, but he could never be cool. While usually attributed to his mass-market popularity, his mogul position as producer linchpin working across a number of studios, and his command of vast budgets, sentiment is also a mobilizer. American auteurs of the late 1960s and early 1970s in particular, consecrated in an atmosphere of high adult pretension, could not be branded through childishness and feeling (though they were of course deeply associated with countercultural youth). Indeed, Spielberg himself was not at first branded a sentimentalist. His career on the world stage was launched by the adrenalin rush of *Duel*, the equivocal, antiheroic *The Sugarland Express*, and the horror-inflected cinema of attractions that is *Jaws*, each film garnering critical acclaim in proportion to its anti-sentiment. As he said of *Sugarland*, it was never about the baby (Tuchman 1978, 53). There is a sense, post-*E.T.*, post–*Close Encounters*, post–*Indiana Jones*, that critics felt they had been cheated: the originally edgy wunderkind had gone soft. As the budgets for his productions grew larger, and the closer his films stuck to children and child culture, the dumber he was accused of being. He dared to dabble in emotionality in an era that felt it had partly outgrown the pleasures of crying like a baby. Yet critical opprobrium may say more about the critic than the subject—a need to keep the faith with cooler dissociated values, and to protest (too much) immunity from the contagion of tears. Thus, however consistently Spielberg returned to a given set of concerns and genres, an association with mass-market emotion prevented him from securing the serious respect of auteur identification. There is also a question about the appropriateness of feeling as a moral indicator in the late twentieth century. Spielberg's challenge continues to raise the question of the role of sentimentality after the ravages of World War II, including the Holocaust. This, of course, he confronted in the 1990s, with the injection of tearful affect into the heart of trauma, particularly through an occasional use of the child in *Schindler's List* and *Saving Private Ryan*—and not without critical consequence, as we shall see.

Sentiment is also capable of reaching from the sublime to the ridiculous. Tan and Frijda situate it as a letting-go to helplessness while connecting with "idealized, paradisiac childhood memories of being completely accepted or being part of some absolute, uncorrupted purity, or at least to desires for such a state" (1999, 63). Put this way, the rather elevated and oceanic feeling of being overwhelmed by feeling, perhaps accompanied by tears is not so far from Kael's bliss-out (who could resist?). Carl Plantinga gives a rather more negative reading of this, identifying sympathetic narratives that "encourage 'closeness' to central characters and put those characters into unpleasant and sometimes catastrophic situations . . . capable of eliciting very powerful negative emotions that quite literally move spectators to shuddering, tears and/or sobbing" (2009, 170–171). He cites the conclusions of many Spielberg films, but particularly *E.T.*, *Schindler's List*, and *Saving Private Ryan*, as prime examples of cathartic psychological manipulation engineered through character identification (173). Sentiment is also often castigated as an excessive response, weighed down by gratuitousness. Yet, as Kaplan explains, neither "sentimental" nor "sentimentality" had pejorative connotations in Dickens's time; it was only later that "sentimentality as insincerity, as false feeling, even as hypocrisy" (1987, 17) became a dominant view.[31] Critiques of sentimentality are then partly judgments of taste, but they also elicit the sense that artworks that deploy sentimentality are trying somehow to bypass more "authentic" means of generating feeling, preferring to go straight for the tear tap[32]—literally jerking tears from the eyes of viewers (we forget what a violent and quasi-sexual term "tearjerker" is). This is clearly evident in Spielberg criticism across the 1980s, when critical opprobrium particularly spotlit "inauthentic" emotion (as if, after the Frankfurt School, such a thing were a given).

Tears have, then, luminously served the critical case against Spielberg as a serious filmmaker, with children as mobilizers. Representing the feelings of children, representing feeling *through* children, forcing adults to feelingfully identify with those children through a contagion of tears are all at the heart of Spielberg's ongoing popular success and his past critical failures. The release of *E.T.* is a crucial historical switch point here and a celebrated high-water mark of Spielberg's craft. It enabled multiple readings and encouraged those bliss-out indulgences; its lachrymosity was also deemed highly suspicious. In the next chapter we will see how the emotional incontinence whipped up by *E.T.* was fueled first by its central child actor's performance. Here I am interested in how the tears (often first engendered by children in a child's own story) function historically in critical responses to Spielberg. Before (and around) the moment of *E.T.*'s release Spielbergian tears could be blissful, cathartic, unifying. After it, they were manipulative and infantile.

So in the period after *E.T.* but particularly between the releases of *The Color Purple* and *Hook* (1985 to 1991), the director slipped from Midas-fingered genius to saccharine mainstream mogul. This was most acutely articulated through a connection between pathos and profit, as if the sound of dripping tears were chiming with the brassy noise of the box office cash register. Richard Corliss's eulogistic profile that celebrated the simultaneous release of both *E.T.* and *Poltergeist* in the same heady week cites a "professional cynic" who "emerged from a Manhattan screening [of *E.T.*] last week and confidently announced, '$350 million.' But the gleam of moisture in his eye said something else" (1982). Or did it? Perhaps the "gleam of moisture" was not evidence that the body gauges value in other ways (sincere feeling undermining the professional's cynicism) but suggested that tears would helpfully lubricate the generation of that $350 million.[33]

But not everyone enjoys a good cry. Charges of mawkishness also distance a critic from that "gleam of moisture." The *Oxford English Dictionary* acknowledges that "sentimental" was originally used "in favourable sense," but it continues its definition of sentiment with "chiefly in derisive use, conveying an imputation of either insincerity or mawkishness," becoming associated with insincerity and even—in the twentieth century—schmaltz.[34] Increased use of the word "mawkish" against Spielberg reinforces those negative connotations, since, for his critics, if there is anything worse than moral sentimentality it is mawkish sentimentality, with its connotations of a good thing gone rotten: "mawkish" derives from the Late Middle English and also the Old Norse words for maggot. Mawkishness is, then, a nauseating form of sentimetality (which might suggest that there is another—better—kind that *does not* make you sick). I would suggest, though, that while one might feel sentimental (or even go on a sentimental journey courtesy of numerous love songs unafraid of the word), one never *feels* mawkish, even if one can be sickened by mawkish things. Only a representation or an object can be mawkish. I have suggested that the turn against Spielberg as sentimentalist is partly bound up with his relationship to recent American film history and brilliantly timed mistiming that put him out of place with countercultural, and even high-cultural judgments. However, acknowledging the bad rap that sentiment has received more widely, Plantinga utilizes cognitive psychology to identify helplessness once again as the issue. Emotional contagion is the process through which we "catch" the emotions of those around us or those we observe (and it seems that the cinema screen is no barrier to this process; it amplifies empathy through the focus of the close-up). But this is only partially under our conscious control, so we despise it at the same time: "This is why spectators can both cry in response to the plight of a character and disdain their own crying. Emotional contagion elicits crying, but the conscious recognition of the film's manipulation resents it" (Plantinga 2009, 129). By the 1980s, Spielberg was astonishingly adept at manipulating emotional contagion; his critics became equally adept at resenting it.

Steven Spielberg is a showman of epic proportions, with his feet rooted not just in the classical Hollywood and midcentury TV traditions he cites as his coparents but in the virtuoso affect-jerking spectacles of the vaudevillian tradition that Henry Jenkins describes in *The Wow Climax: Tracing the Emotional Impact of Popular Culture* (2007), which in part finds the ancestry of "wow" moments in the early "cinema of attractions" live antecedents. Spielberg also wants his audiences to be "wowed," but not (only) through the breaching of a giant shark or a mammoth close encounter with the mothership. His star turns are not (only) the multimillion-dollar special effects he commands but the tear taps he turns on, first in his actors and then in his audiences. The bombastic relationship of affect that connects child performance to audience reception (with a little help from John Williams's scoring) is Spielberg at his most Cinema of Attractions. Throughout this book I make the link between text (readings of performance) and reception (evidence of reaction) via the child across multiple examples. Chapter 2 will explore this, partly through thinking about children as highly effective, and affective, tearjerkers.

2

The Lemonade Stand of Cinema

Spielberg's Performing Children

The 2017 film *The Post*—a largely adult-featured production—included one small but significant child role. *Washington Post* editor Ben Bradlee (Tom Hanks) convenes an intense editorial meeting in his family's living room at which frenzied journalists pour over the Pentagon Papers. In the midst of these grown-up goings-on, Bradlee's daughter Marina (Austyn Johnson) weaves through the crowd of reporters selling her home-made lemonade (figure 3). Indeed, even as the contraband papers were previously entering the house, we glimpse Marina at her sidewalk lemonade stand. This inclusion was read by critics as a Spielbergian injection, as if it were impossible for him to make a film devoid of child actors messaging auteurial significance.[1] In fact, this was not (only) a gesture to situate the child once again as personally and nationally talismanic: the daughter of Bradlee and his then wife, Antoinette "Tony" Pinchot Bradlee (Sarah Paulson), *did* have a real-life lemonade stand, and Spielberg uses this to position her—albeit briefly—at the heart of a historical story that eloquently addresses Trump-era questions of political culpability and freedom of the press.

But Marina is not only an emblem of hope for a free future, at risk if the Pentagon Papers are suppressed. She is also an image of the working child. Selling lemonade on the street is synonymous with American childhood: "Summertime and sunny skies can only mean one thing for the nation's youngest business

FIGURE 3 Lemonade labor: Marina Bradlee (Austyn Johnson) sells refreshment in *The Post*.

owners: lemonade stands" (Campisi and Ahmed 2018). Through this resonant icon of "the irrepressibility of American idealism" (Weeks 2011), *The Post* is able to conflate freedom of the press with a laboring child's "freedom" to make money: the stand represents "capitalism and leisure, refreshment and resourcefulness, enterprise and summer skies all squeezed together . . . and sold by the glass for whatever the market will bear."[2] Marina's brief foray through the adult throng holds more significance than her mother, Tony's, parallel circulation with a platter of sandwiches: busy journalists locked in with a story need sustenance, but while nurturing Tony gives the food away for free, the lemonade must be paid for. The child here is a figure of canny entrepreneurism. There are, of course, parallels between businesslike Marina and the working woman newspaper owner into which Kay Graham (Meryl Streep) evolves, earning her money in the world of adult men, but in the case of Marina the merchandise is as self-created as the marketing is self-orchestrated. In the context of *The Post*, this use of the child as image of and for America is somewhat out of proportion to her screen time (rather like the brief journey of *Schindler's List*'s metonymic "girl in the red coat," standing for the wholesale horror of the Holocaust).[3] As a figure for the working child, Marina initiates some key threads for this chapter on cinema's child actors in the world of adult screen work.

Childhood is central to the emotional and sentimental focus of Spielberg's films, in their reception, and beyond the arena of child as theme—bearing out innocence, exploitation, play, monstrosity—and also beyond childhood's function in the director's own profile. Spielberg is part inventor of the family adventure film (see Krämer 1998; N. Brown 2012, 145–189), a genre that often requires the central participation of actor children. His best-known star children perform in child-point-of-view narratives, which necessitate hiring children to bear out the story: he is a key employer of child actors, facilitating star-making roles but also needing children in smaller roles and as supporting players, filling out filmic families and peer groups. Spielberg's children—employed creative laborers—are not simply the images within his films but, as we shall see, the active coauthors of those images.

Dark Stardom: The Child Actor

The notion of a "stolen childhood" (a cherished and innocent state from which the child is forcibly wrenched) is commonly used in relation to abuse victims, underage laborers—and child actors. The history of the performing child as characterized by a rhetoric of victimage extends back to even before the travesty of little Jackie Coogan's stolen money. This sorry tale at least resulted in a partially positive outcome for the working child actor: Coogan was a hugely successful child star of the silent era whose fortune was squandered by his mother and stepfather before he came of age, resulting in the pioneering California Child Actor's Bill (universally known as the "Coogan Act," first constituted in 1939 and updated since), which requires that a portion of a child's earnings must be put in trust (a "Coogan Account") for the child. It also lays out terms limiting the child's working hours and enforcing on-set schooling and rest breaks.[4] However, legal protection differs from state to state and nation to nation, and liberties are still taken. In my conversations with filmmakers and those involved in casting children both in and outside of studio production, I have been told (invariably off the record) that in order to work with child actors and make the film on schedule and on budget, one must sometimes bend if not break the rules of employing children. I do not suggest here that Spielberg or Amblin/DreamWorks sidesteps protective legislation, and the publicity spotlight shone on bigger-budget productions may be additionally protective. But any employment of children needs to be read in the context of historical instances of poor practice. It is a given that any child employed on a film set is on some level actually or potentially at risk. These risks are multifarious and may include—in addition to the physical hazards of sets as workplaces—interrupting or altering education patterns and quality, exposing the child to a level of public scrutiny they may live to regret, or requiring them to become emotionally involved or upset in pursuit of the finished film.

In her sociological study of child stars, Jane O'Connor argues that because the perception of risk of and for the child performer is a contemporary phenomenon, the very conception of a child star (the definition of which is closely bound to risky practices) is anachronistic, arising from "an earlier time when the welfare of the child was not a priority and childhood as a special period of education and security was not seen as the right of all children" (2008, 8).[5] Of course the child star in the way we now understand it could only exist in the age of mass entertainment practices; the "child star era" in cinema was the period in the 1920s and 1930s when young stars reached an unprecedented level of fame within the Hollywood star system. As children's employment in media industries has grown, so have child protection laws, though employment of the child and protection of the child have often failed to keep pace with each other (child star casualties are probably the clearest sign of this). Questions of consent, who can give it, for what, and on whose behalf haunt the history of children in popular entertainment. Sociologists of childhood have drawn a distinction between "child work" and "child labor," which does not simply assume that "work contradicts the very essence of childhood," but also that children have the right "not only to protection, but also to participation," and that work may be good for children (economically and socially) in some circumscribed circumstances (A. James, Jenks, and Prout 1998, 106, 107). Viviana Zelizer's book on transformations in the relative valuing of children in the United States between the late nineteenth century and the mid-twentieth century posits a transition whereby a family's children became increasingly emotionally "priceless" as they became decreasingly economically valuable. In the past the birth of a child, particularly in rural communities, was "welcomed as the arrival of a future laborer and as security for parents later in life" (1994, 5). Children's sentimental worth rose as they worked less and less to contribute to the family coffers. Sentiment is here not a vague attribution that has fared better or worse according to fluctuating judgments of cultural taste. Zelizer is precise in her use of the term "sentimentalization" to describe the process in early twentieth-century America whereby "the economically useful child became both numerically and culturally an exception" (6), child labor became taboo, and making a profit from children was, as Felix Adler put it in 1905, to "touch profanely a sacred thing" (quoted by Zelizer 1994, 6).

Sentiment thus begins to have numbers attached to it: the more the child is valued in one way (sentimentally), the less they can be in another (economically). This switch from the child as economically viable to sentimentally cherished happened—ironically—at exactly the moment when child stars in Hollywood began to earn huge sums fleshing out idealized images of the child. Against this, as Zelizer notes, "Money-making children, such as child actors or models," are considered "an uncomfortable exception in our society; their parents are often suspected of callousness or greed" (4). Doubly ironic, then, is Spielberg's employment of the child to express the "sacred thing" of childhood, a late twentieth-century extension of the theatrical development whereby child actors emerged as laborers, whose lives were often hazardous and unprotected, who were then "paid to represent the new, sentimentalized view of children" (95).

The dangers and difficulties of this form of employment for minors are well rehearsed. Movie sets are risky places: in the making of the portmanteau film *Twilight Zone: The Movie* in 1983, on which Spielberg was coproducer and contributed a directorial segment, two children actually lost their lives, a dark story to which I will return at the close of this chapter. Until recently the child performer was inflected through notorious popular cultural cases describing a publicly celebrated early life in the spotlight followed by a fall into adulthood, unemployment, and sometimes tragedy: as O'Connor boldly states, "The term 'child star' has become synonymous with a particularly deviant type of childhood" (2008, 1). Historically, few successful child performers parlayed their talents into lifelong careers, with a typical popular narrative arc running from success to failure, from fame to has-been. Adult-penned, adult-ghosted or adult-spoken memoirs of former child stars tend to fall into one of two camps: those that flirt with confessional memoir genres and those that deliberately *refuse* narratives of stolen childhood by insisting that life on set was always a game. The first is undoubtedly the most compelling aspect of the popular culture of the child star, animated by public-private tales of cruel stage mothers, predatory studio heads, and the wholesale denial of childhood experiences to those whose stock-in-trade is the performance of a childhood the star never had. Even if they are resoundingly successful as an adult in some other field, the grown-up actor may be eternally defined as a "former child star."

The very fact of growing up therefore becomes the child star's enemy, resulting in what Marsha Orgeron calls "an unnaturally prolonged imposition of childhood" (2007, 4).[6] Given that these performers are defined by a childishness that, since they are not actually Peter Pan, will pass, the pattern suggests they are haunted by the immanent prospect of a kind of death—the death of their careers, the public passing of youth as employment ends. Diana Serra Cary (aka the silent-era performer Baby Peggy) said in an interview in 2007, "I didn't realize that [my parents] not seeking my long-term interests wasn't normal. My parents never even thought about my adult life. There was no adult life for me ahead, as far as they were concerned, which is so hard to understand. But child stars don't grow up to be something" (Orgeron 2007, 10).[7] Others have stressed that children were not solely victims of their underage laboring. Those who tell happier stories—Shirley Temple Black is perhaps the most famous of these—do so by way of record-straightening, as if all too aware that the common tenor of personal narratives is of exploitation and mental damage. Nevertheless, Temple's account contains some difficult anecdotes, including discovering on her twelfth birthday that it was really her thirteenth.[8] More scandalous tabloid stories of adolescent crash-and-burn have proliferated in recent celebrity culture (from the benign "Potter Class Graduates with No Child Actor Woes" to a Lindsay Lohan blog titled "Child Star . . . Doomed from the Start?").[9]

Against this can be set more recent examples of young stars developing successful adult acting careers, in the context of an industry regulated by tighter protection practices. The term "child star" is no longer synonymous with falling into adult obscurity. The arc of children employed by Spielberg instead traces a shift in child actor history from celebrity casualty to trained lifelong performer with a honed professional pedigree. Contemporary media reports now more frequently emphasize those child stars—better managed, more securely protected by industry-tested legislation—who have been able to parlay short-term opportunities into long-term careers: "'Child star' is no longer a taboo term, a résumé red flag," reported one article in 2013, suggesting that in "the list of who's hot in Hollywood right now, almost half seem to have started their careers as kids" (O. Barker 2013). A *New York Times* discussion of teen actor Emily Osment (Haley Joel Osment's sister) discussed young performers' efforts "to adjust to a new Hollywood" in which child stars "are courted by top talent agents who once ignored them, but now see viable careers into adulthood" (Navarro 2007). Comparisons are still rife, of course. Haley Joel Osment said in 2015 that one of the drawbacks of a successful childhood career "is that the image of you as a child is burned into people's minds for a long time" (Hiscock 2015). Nevertheless, predicating a grown-up career on a child star foundation is now "perceived as a really good thing" in terms of professional advantage and skills in a risk-averse industry: studio executives "like products that are tried and true. They figure if it worked once, it's going to work again" (O. Barker 2013), even when the star makes a significant effort to rebrand themselves as they reach adulthood (Miley Cyrus, Daniel Radcliffe, Justin Timberlake). This is quantified in an article on a financial website titled "30 Former Child Stars Striking Hollywood Gold" (with the strapline "Here's how much famous child actors and stars are worth now" [Olya 2019]), which includes Spielberg child performers Drew Barrymore, Christian Bale, and Dakota Fanning. The "former child star" label no longer predicts the end of a career and social/personal crisis but may promise lasting success courtesy of better legal protection, career mentoring, media know-how, and family support from an early age.[10] Aside from Barrymore (more of whom later), Spielberg's children are not celebrity cautionary tales; safeguarding structures seem to have ensured their well-being (the Amblin compound includes a children's center).[11] Jon Mooallem argues in an article around the release of *The BFG* that Spielberg wants to steer his young actors "toward a safe resolution" and quotes the director as saying:

> In my own experience directing children, I've seen kids sacrifice childhood for a professional place in the world. . . . Suddenly you become a professional actor. You're not playing with your friends. You're on location—you're being taught by a studio teacher, and your childhood is something you reminisce about. If you stay in the business, the memories wither very quickly. . . . I'm always mindful that a young person, innocent to our world, will never be innocent again after starring in a movie. And I always emphasize to the parents: You need to keep your kid safe. When this is all over, they have to be normal. They have to go back to real life. They have to keep their friends, stay in school. Don't get seduced by what people may offer you in the future. (2016)[12]

Some of his young actors have embraced nonperforming adult careers: Ariana Richards (Lex in *Jurassic Park*) is a portrait artist, Charlie Korsmo (Jack in *Hook*) is a law professor, and Carey Guffey, who played the toddler Barry in *Close Encounters of the Third Kind*, grew up to be a financial adviser in Birmingham,

Alabama (Constance White [2001] quotes him as saying, "'I don't want the greatest thing I do in life to be something I did when I was 4 years old,' . . . whilst holding the tiny shirt which he wore in *Close Encounters*. 'I am trying to grow and develop all my gifts and talents, not trying to grow into a shirt that is too small for me'").[13] Others have continued to act: Henry Thomas has graduated to a respectable and fully employed adult career; Haley Joel Osment studied experimental theater at New York University before relaunching his career through diverse roles.[14] His mild foray into criminality (a drunk-driving conviction at age eighteen) is hardly evidence of the old legacy of child stardom (his father denied that the incident was "a pitfall of being young and successful in the entertainment industry," normalizing the incident by adding that it was "was a pitfall of being 18" [Navarro 2007]). For Joseph Mazzello (Tim in *Jurassic Park*), working with Spielberg was life-changing: interviewed in 2013 when he was twenty-nine with an already long acting résumé to his name, he reported that filming with Spielberg was "the greatest time of my life," which "affected where I wanted to go to school and what I wanted to do with my life" (Chi 2013). He continued to work as a child actor, then studied film and television production at the University of Southern California, and has since secured significant roles (*The Social Network*, *Bohemian Rhapsody*, *Unexpected*). Bale is of course one of the most successful screen actors in contemporary Hollywood, though this is despite his distress at sudden fame; while he relished acting, fame and promotion duties were more difficult:

> It was horrific. I was almost crying in interviews and running away during press conferences, pretending I was going to the bathroom and just disappearing. . . . I enjoyed making it [*Empire of the Sun*], but I was shocked when I received all the attention when I got home to Bournemouth. Girls were all over me, boys wanted to fight me, and I was being asked to open local fêtes when all I wanted to do was ride my BMX bike in the woods. I told my parents I wasn't interested in doing anything again because the attention ruined it. (Stevens 2017)

Harrison Cheung and Nicola Pittam's popular biography of Bale begins with an extended account of the boy's horror at the *Empire of the Sun* press junkets, his father's fear that the young Bale might be "embarrassing Steven," and the "incredible amount of pressure riding on his small shoulders" (2012, 7). It cites Bale as later saying, "Before we started, my dad told me: 'This could be a fantastic experience, but it could also be the worst thing that could happen to you.' There have been moments when I've wished it had never happened. . . . You know, when you're a teenager, you just want to be normal" (9). As these statements evidence, more significant than the circumstances of the role itself are the wider contexts of celebrity, family, and education unbalanced by shooting schedules, and alienation from peers. Bale's issues were not with the demands of the shoot but with sudden celebrity,[15] to the extent that he was reluctant to return to acting afterward ("I just don't think it is a good thing for somebody that age to have it happen to them. I had gone from being able to walk about with nobody knowing me, to somebody people pointed at in the streets. It just freaked me out. I didn't leave the house for almost a year after that" [16]). Bale was even pleased to escape an Oscar nomination for *Empire of the Sun* (for which he was tipped) because he felt he was not ready for the recognition (12). Spielberg encourages his young actors to continue mainstream schooling rather than or in addition to studio tutoring, and most of his performers have completed their education, some to a high level (Bale found returning to school difficult). As a young adult Osment reflected on his relative "normality": "the schedule of my career" has been designed "to give me the maximum possible time in a normal schooling environment. I went to a public school until the 6th Grade, and went to a regular High School in my neighborhood from 7th Grade to my senior year of High School" (Chia n.d.). Indeed, in the roster of prized qualities for a child actor, "normal" is both genuinely protective of long-term sanity and a key branding hallmark deployed to present a star as a regular person. This even extends to judgment on Osment's physical appearance. In an industry that prizes "cuteness" in the child (in similar measures to beauty or sexiness in adults), Osment was described as "cute, yes. But not classic cute. Not Culkin Clone. A singular face, not borrowed from anyone else" (Copel 2001). Seemingly a magical combination of regularity and individuality (almost the definition of the star, who must be like us but also charismatically unique) is the prized quality of maintaining a balance between the irregularity of stardom and work schedules and the "normalizing" force of school, friends, and family.

Drew Barrymore is interesting here, as one of Spielberg's youngest child performers with a biography that bears out some key moments in the child star arc, from child/adolescent scandal (her post-*E.T.* life exemplifies that "fallen child star" story) to recovery and respected relaunch of career as an adult (Gabrielle Olya's article "30 Former Child Stars Striking Hollywood Gold" from 2019 cites Barrymore as then worth $125 million due to her long-standing producing as well as her acting work). Yet Barrymore's trajectory after *E.T.* is still shocking. Though her first role as a tiny child was in Ken Russell's *Altered States*, she was made famous as the cute Gertie in *E.T.*—originally a small production (albeit by Spielberg) that did not necessarily promise megastardom to its actors. However, both Robert MacNaughton (who played her older brother Mike) and Barrymore herself tell the story of the three lead children (including Henry Thomas) staying in a hotel around the film's premier, going to bed as relative unknowns, and waking up "as the most famous kids in America" (Ellis and Sutherland 2003, 33), with no guidance on how to manage it. Barrymore reports in her autobiography, *Little Girl Lost*, cowritten with Todd Gold when she was just fourteen:

> There was absolutely no way to prepare for what happened to me—to all of us—from the morning after *E.T.* came out . . . it was like walking into a

> thunderstorm without warning or protection. . . . When we walked downstairs the next morning, the place went wild. Absolutely wild. The movie had been out one day and people all around were whispering, "Check them out. It's the kids from *E.T.* . . ." Everyplace we went, we were followed. People asked for autographs. They stared. They knew my name. They wanted to talk to me. They wanted to touch me. . . . I thought it was insane. I didn't know how to deal with it, and that frightened me. (1990, 66–67)

The legacy of this is something that Barrymore has returned to repeatedly in more recent press. "I grew up under the microscope," she said in 2014 (Lipworth 2014), though this was not primarily because she was part of the famous Barrymore Hollywood acting dynasty but because the dissonance between Gertie in *E.T.* and the notorious celebrity of her later childhood was so marked. In *Little Girl Lost* she writes of being waved into adult nightclubs as a child: "Even if they didn't know my face they'd say, 'Aren't you the little girl from *E.T.*?' It was instant acceptance. I was part of the hip crowd" (1990, 106). As the daughter of a single-parent mother whose own acting career was floundering, it became clear (post-*E.T.*) that the child was capable of earning far more than the parent. So Drew took on the breadwinner role, effectively supporting her mother, enabling her mother to give up work and support her as her manager: "I viewed my mom as the ruthless taskmaster, convinced she no longer cared about being my mother. All she wanted from me, I believed, was the money I earned" (142). Barrymore's subsequent childhood descent into alcoholism and drug abuse is well documented. As a recovered and apparently well-balanced adult she has maintained that she is "not someone who is ashamed of my past. I'm actually really proud."[16] She even merits a volume telling her story as one of a series of popular biographies with the imprint "Overcoming Adversity" (Aronson 2000). Nevertheless, a toxic combination of unstable parenting, extreme fame, and personal insecurity led her—via addiction, scandal, and a reported suicide attempt—to rehab treatment beginning at age thirteen. At fifteen she submitted a petition to be legally emancipated from her parents, which was granted, making her an adult in the eyes of the law and therefore enabling her to work the long hours of an adult without child labor restrictions (Ellis and Sutherland 2003, 118). Despite some fallow periods (particularly when she grew up from little cute Gertie to older childhood, and then again when her addiction problems made her a potential liability to hire), Barrymore continued to act. The impact of the emancipation was that her graduation to adult roles could take place earlier than for other young actors—her breakthrough adult role was at just sixteen, playing femme fatale Ivy in Katt Shea Ruben's *Poison Ivy*, a role that included nudity and sex scenes.[17] This, however, translated into something of a gray area for the film's distribution, and Barrymore—numerically a child, legally an adult because of the emancipation—was replaced by a body double in the final edit.[18]

This history is rarely attributed to the impact of the actor's early role in Spielberg's film, despite her own words attesting to the shock of sudden global fame. As it happens, Spielberg became her godfather and is discussed as a positive force in a fatherless life (John Barrymore Jr. was largely absent, and was himself an addict). Drew said in 2009 that Spielberg has "been a very important mentor. He was the first stable male figure in my life. The best attribute a parent can have is consistency. . . . I didn't have that. When he said he would be there at three o'clock, he was there. That meant more to me than anything."[19] After *E.T.*, he guided her toward some work in an *Amazing Stories* series episode while she was unemployed in 1985 and famously sent her the gift of a quilt to cover herself up when as a young adult she posed naked for *Playboy*. There are many family formations running throughout this book, and here we must also consider the film set as family—a particularly intense, temporary form of family from which the child often finds it hard to separate at the conclusion of a shoot. In the absence of family stability at home, Barrymore found the surrogate family fostered by Spielberg to be a good substitute: in *Little Girl Lost* she writes that filming is "a lot like being in a family, a big extended family" (1990, 43), and by adulthood she was reflecting that "*ET* was the best thing that ever happened to me because it changed the course of my life. I didn't have family and home and structure, so the world of film gave me that framework" (Lipworth 2014). Her costar Robert MacNaughton (Mike) said (in response to the interview prompt "It must be weird to be a seven-year-old and be on the set shooting a film that would become a global phenomenon"), "She was the focus of attention back then. It had to be a great experience for her while it was happening, but then it must have also been terrible when it ended, because we really were like a family, and she really thought E.T. was real. So when it ended it had to be horrible for her" (Avila 2017).

In what looks like a spectacular Hollywoodized version of the British documentary *Seven Up!*,[20] Barrymore, Thomas, and MacNaughton have continued to promote *E.T.* on its various rereleases in regular reunions (even as Barrymore's star has risen beyond that of her male costars, particularly after *Charlie's Angels*). They present themselves first through young adulthood and then into middle age alongside an increasingly aging father figure Spielberg, for comparison with their fresh-faced originals (this comparative process is a regular element of features on former child stars—see, for instance, the *People* magazine volume *Child Stars, Then and Now* [Durkee 2008]). In 2018 Henry Thomas quipped about still being asked about *E.T.* at the age of forty-seven, "It's the longest promo tour you'll ever do" (Watson 2018). Photoshoots at reissue gatherings look like happy family reunions, but there is also some acknowledgment of the strangeness of it all, even if the memories are positive. In 2017 MacNaughton discussed the dissonance between his memories of making *E.T.* (as a fourteen-year-old) and Barrymore's, who has had to fill in the memory gaps. He recalls Spielberg saying to Barrymore, "I feel so sorry for you because you're not going to remember any of this," to which MacNaughton adds,

> I thought about it, and it's true. I don't remember anything from when I was six or seven. We've done interviews together with her [Barrymore], including a reunion on one of the DVD releases. And they're talking to Drew, and she's remembering things, and you can see Henry and I looking at each other like, "What is she talking about?" (Laughs) She has sort of . . . made-up memories of what happened on set. We're not going to tell her they didn't happen. It must have been sort of a dreamlike experience for her, making the movie.[21]

Of course, Barrymore does report vivid memories of the shoot, and that being in the film changed her life. By contrast, Cary Guffey, who was a toddler when *Close Encounters* was shot, remembers nothing of it, though clearly the experience affected him deeply. A souvenir program produced around the time of the film's release states that after the shoot had concluded and Cary returned home, he "would ask his mother daily if they could all move to California so he could 'see Steven'";[22] a small child cannot withdraw from an intense set-bound relationship as readily as an adult. There are, then, indefinable ethical questions around consent underpinning employing children before they can have any conception of what they are doing or the skills to maintain perspective on the kinds of relationships that develop in such conditions. The question remains of why we are not anxious about subjecting children to *any* experience they are unlikely to remember. Though it may be impossible to answer this, the specter of something uncomfortable inflects the space between Barrymore/Gertie then and Barrymore now.

The Nature of Play: "Real" Child Performances

Repeatedly drawn to writing and commissioning child-protagonist narratives means that Spielberg has an ongoing need for child performers. Child's point-of-view stories and the child actor are therefore intimately bound together in Spielberg's work. This specific narrative focus on the view of (and from) the child runs across genres. *E.T.*, *Ready Player One*, and *The BFG* are all examples of the child's point-of-view film geared to attracting child (and family) audiences. *A.I.* and *Empire of the Sun* are adult-focused child's point-of-view films, with children excluded or discouraged from the audience by classification and dark subject matter. Even when Spielberg's protagonist is adult, he regularly imagines the child's experience within an adult scenario—Barry in *Close Encounters*, or Sean Brody (Jay Mello) mimicking his father at the *Jaws* dinner table, or Roy Neary's children upset by their father's growing derangement also in *Close Encounters*. Within these adult frames Spielberg sometimes gives the child the space to improvise. Studies of children's cinema pinpoint different narrative strategies to focus the child as protagonist or storyteller, though few think about the child as a singular agent within the creative work. This has been a more developed area in recent research, from writings focused on the child actor within cinema (Lury

2010; Lawrence and Smith 2012) to wider discussions of children actively determining their own cultures. Addressing how childhood studies has "made the child disappear," Henry Jenkins laments those accounts that have focused "almost exclusively on the exercise of adult authority over children, leaving little space for thinking about children's own desires, fantasies, and agendas" (1998, 24). His collection *The Children's Culture Reader* (1998) strives instead to showcase scholarship that "acknowledges the ways children resist, transform, or redefine adult prerogatives, making their own uses of cultural materials and enacting their own fantasies through play" (27).

The actors I discuss here are literally playing—playing roles, playacting, and playing out. Indeed, "play" is the most frequently deployed term for Spielberg's directorial approach to children. The verb "play" (frolicking, game-playing) is the earliest version of this word in English, appearing around 1200, and quite early in its etymological history it was pitched against labor, with play understood as the opposite of work. It was some two centuries later that the noun form of "play," meaning a dramatic work of art, came into the language. The idea that directing children (in those dramatic works of art) should also be a question of play (having fun, larking around) was crystallized for film studies in Béla Balázs's seminal midcentury *Theory of the Film: Character and Growth of a New Art*, specifically in the notorious short section "Children and Savages," which grounds the idea that children do not act, they just are: "The acting of children is always natural, for make-believe is a natural thing to them. They do not want to 'register' this or that, like an actor; they just pretend that they are not what they are but something else and that they are not in the situation in which they are but in some other. This is not acting—it is a natural manifestation of youthful consciousness and it can be observed not only in the human young but in the young of other species as well" (1970, 80). Here, then, children are not what "we" were or who we may still be, and so are entirely othered by this adult voice. Children are just one remove from playful animals. This is also an Orientalist "we": Balázs continues (albeit with a backward glance at the writer's own blindness): "The same can be observed in savages or primitives. The close-up often reveals unusual gestures and mimicry—unusual, that is, from the white man's viewpoint. . . . [I]t often happens that we fail to understand them" (81).

The distinction between (rational) adult and (savage) child is centuries old, as is the scrutiny of othered "primitives" in "the white man's viewpoint." Yet whatever the patent flaws with this argument, the idea of tapping into children's playfulness as a way of directing them continues to hold currency, and Balázs's is a foundational text for the widespread idea that children do not possess acting skill like adults but rather must be harnessed or tricked into a "natural" semblance of what the adult filmmaker requires them to do. Liz Czach's essay on acting in amateur films cites a 1959 text titled *Eumig's Manual for Better Home Movies*, which argues that to capture "children as they really are" the director or cameraman must distract the child with toys so that they forget that the camera is there. The assumption is that natural children have a capacity for unselfconsciousness, and real response rather than skill (2012, 156).

And yet the opposite may also be true—that children's playful creativity brings something else to the table, something the filmmaker can capitalize on and capture. Even if this does not describe the astonishingly sophisticated skill of a Haley Joel Osment or a Henry Thomas extrapolated across a leading role, the very idea that the act of make-believe is a component of filming children at least partially credits the child's creative agency. The insistence on the "natural" also skews the language of children's acting toward a "jargon of authenticity," as Theodor Adorno would describe it. An ideal of "real performance" that is both curiously consistent and highly contradictory is frequently deployed by the child actors (in press and interviews) and by Spielberg himself. In her autobiography *Wildflower*, Barrymore wrote, "Steven never let us fake anything. Tears or joy or sarcasm. He made us be real!" (2015, 62). Promoting *The BGF*, Spielberg said, "I've worked with kids my entire career and parented seven children. I know that kids can't fake the truth," around which Mooallem glosses "Good performances are often only extensions of a child's genuine feeling in the moment" (2016). But what does this mean? On the one hand, it suggests an almost Method-acted process of—in Drew Barrymore's words—*being* the character rather than *acting* the character.[23] Of course Barrymore had a special relationship with the Method: with Anna Strasberg as her godmother, she describes having the lessons of the Strasberg Institute as part of her toolkit even as a four-year-old (Barrymore 2015, 103–108).

On the other hand, "keeping it real" harks back to the idea that children only present a semblance of performance and need to be prodded into "real" reactions instead. Discussing directing the very young Cary Guffey in *Close Encounters of the Third Kind*, Spielberg reports that he "had to do a lot of tricks to get him to react—like opening up presents in front of him so his eyes would sparkle and flash" (Breznican 2012; he adds—with a wicked flash of the "Nasty Steven" we encountered earlier—"And of course I gave him the presents after. I didn't, like, *take them back*. I gave them to him," raising the prospect that he *might not*). Henry Thomas also appreciated a human connection when emoting his way through the final sequence of *E.T.*: "The thing that made the emotional investment payoff for me was that Steven had hired a mime that did all of the hand acting for E.T. She was always laying underneath the frame in between E.T. and myself so her hands could work. But it was really nice to have a human connection there. That was really a masterstroke of the direction. It really helped out the performances" (T. Cook 2012). A similar strategy was used to help Ruby Barnhill's work in *The BFG*: Spielberg "knew immediately . . . that Ruby was going to need as much authenticity as we could create for her"; that is, she would not be able to perform in the contextlessness of a CGI setup and would need another actor (Mark Rylance as the Giant) to perform against. Still, this limitation of experience and skill ("No normal child can be expected to carry on poignant conversations with a clay maquette or a tennis ball hanging in front of green screen") is also parlayed into a "keeping it real" message in the film's promotion: "I knew that if Mark could always see Ruby's eyes when he was acting, and Ruby could always see Mark's eyes, that they would find companionship and authenticity" (Mooallem 2016; note that here the eye contact is as important for adult Rylance's ability to deliver a credible performance as it is for child Barnhill's). Though we might think that the younger the child the more authentic their performance would be, there is a directorial sliding scale at one end of which (for the small child) a reaction has to be provoked, while at the other end (with the older child) a performance can be creative and self-directed (though sometimes this needs help). The language of the real, the opposition to "fakery," runs across both—and this is a common discourse across child actors as a group, with few age distinctions.

Onto this is placed the notion of child's play as a directorial tool and opportunity, which Balázs also endorses: "All those who have worked with children on the stage or in films will know that children should not be 'directed,' they must be played with. It is not their acting which is natural—their nature is play-acting" (1970, 80–81). While the second sentence here speaks to the adult's fantasy of the child, the first has been crystallized into a method that is cited and celebrated but rarely analyzed by director and cast alike in promotional materials. Yet as a tool within the creative work of making a film, this kind of "play" must be understood as primarily enabling the *labor* of filmmaking. Spielberg's young actors are not playing in the sense that sociologists read children's play as a space outside of adult control or jurisdiction.[24] Rather, they are led into a form of work that mediates between make-believe and playacting and this "being the character."[25] This is directed play, manipulated in the space between the adult director and the child actor, in service of the film. That said, it can also be a means of unlocking and enabling creative input, with children mutually participating in the play-work of the production.

Marina Warner's meditation on child's-eye texts (literary, filmic, fabled), from Henry James's novel *What Maisie Knew* (1897) to recent films, sees the child's point-of-view story as a ready vehicle for adult longing, critique, or nostalgia of and for childhood. Warner reads *Maisie* as a birth-of-cinema-era novel (it was published in 1897); it is also a foundational story of specifically American childhood (viz., *Adventures of Huckleberry Finn* or *Little Women)*, and this is one reason Robin Wood cites it in his analysis of children in American film (2006, 200). Warner reads Maisie's parents as like "phantoms dancing on a screen . . . as if in a magic lantern" (Warner 1993, 37), but for her "it's not the world, but rather the child who is the screen on which the phantoms are projected."[26] Though Spielberg is not often seen as heir to Henry James in American culture (have the two ever been seriously compared?), Elliott in *E.T.*, Jim in *Empire of the Sun*, or David in *A.I.* are also screens on which the phantoms of adulthood are projected. But they are equally projections of childhood by the actor onto the performed child image. The child actor projects childhood onto the screens of self and cinema. To continue the James/Warner analogy, this child is lantern, slide, and projection, all in one.

Historically, when children have been considered at all, it has been on the assumption that the director is the primary "projectionist," but in the range of information about how Spielberg operates on set that circulates in the public realm there is evidence that the child actor also has some creative hand in the image-making. The relatively new field of child star studies has raised some questions around how far adult culture determines the limits of child representations, or whether children coauthor child images in cultural circulation. This builds on the contemporary focus in the new sociology of childhood, which argues that children are "active in determining their own lives and the lives of those around them"; children are not "passive receptacles of adult teaching . . . Relations between adults and children can instead be depicted as a form of interaction, with the young having their own culture or succession of cultures" (Heywood 2001, 4). These questions of authority, input, and impotence form a context for this chapter's understanding of the child performer's agency in narratives of childhood. Thomas's, Bale's, and Osment's are among the most praised child performances of all time. Osment was nominated for an Oscar for *The Sixth Sense* in 2000, a performance that Lib Copel (2001) called "seminal for modern-day child actors . . . at least some critics have suggested he should be nominated again" for *A.I.*[27] Chapter by chapter and film by film, this book considers the active creative input of Spielberg's children through case studies built through production and reception information as well as textual focus. These show that children's work in Spielberg's films makes them at the very least coauthors of the images the films bear out. I maintain a balance between reading the child in Spielberg's films as a creative component in the storytelling process and reading childhood in these film texts as a repeated but diverse focus. Though the twin foci of creative labor and authorship commonly involve different methodologies (production studies and auteurism), thinking about Spielberg as employer and architect of filmic childhood requires both. However, he is not this book's sole auteur; the child performer shares credit throughout as corresponding and complementary creator of screen "childness."

Directing and Coauthoring

Historical accounts of the child actor as victim of their own family's greed or ambition place the filmmaker's need for the child as a secondary level of potential exploitation. Yet if the history of the child performer has had its dark passages, the history of child *performance* is rather different: children have excelled in a range of roles, triumphant and tragic, but this history is only now being seriously researched and written. The young actors Spielberg has employed never publicly criticize their director or the experience of working with him, instead stressing the fun of moviemaking. This has made it particularly difficult to find specific details about what happens on set. Of course, he is a hugely powerful figure in world cinema, and it may not be expedient for career longevity to be publicly negative (should there be anything negative to report). Therefore, information about how Spielberg directs his young actors is piecemeal and often presented in the context of film promotion. However, what does exist is also curiously consistent, with a repeated emphasis on a directorial approach focused around collaborative conversation. While promoting the 2012 reissue of *E.T.*, Spielberg said, "What I decided to do was just talk to them [his child cast] like people and not to treat them like children. So [that's] my approach—which for me was the most natural way to talk to anybody" (Breznican 2012). At a tribute evening held a year earlier at an event for the Directors Guild of America he had stressed the importance of "not talking down to them," but also of using the experience of directing them to become "a kid yourself." That long history of identifying Spielberg with childhood has a bearing on how he articulates his directing style as well as his director branding: "Kids can't look at you like you're a teacher or like you're a principal; kids have to look at you like you're with them in communion on every subject. Kids have to respect the fact that you're a kid yourself in order for kids to really be able to trust you enough to give you what they are when the cameras aren't around."[28]

The words "play" and "freedom" are used consistently when describing Spielberg's method, underpinning the idea that great performances come from treating the work as play and from playing with the children during breaks. Barrymore described him as "the biggest kid of all, the most playful, the most unpatronizing leader" ("We didn't love him because it was our job. We loved him because he was like Peter Pan" [2015, 61]). Robert MacNaughton has said, "On the set with Spielberg, it was kind of a jokey type atmosphere. He was sort of like a teenager" (Avila 2017), whereas Spielberg's long-standing producer colleague Frank Marshall said when promoting *The BFG*, "He's able to make them [children] trust him and relax, and deliver these incredible performances—often with barely any training, like Ruby [Barnhill]. . . . . He becomes a kid himself" (quoted by Mooallem 2016). Clearly, film sets are environments of work, not play, and they are bound by stringent scheduling, safety, and employment constraints rather than an ethic of freedom, so the consistent use of these terms promotes the idea that a particular channel between the director and the actor opens up to enable performed "naturalness" in the midst of highly artificial workplace surroundings. Spielberg, writes Mooallem, "freed [Ruby Barnhill] to improvise dialog and doted on her, constantly checking if she needed a break. It relaxed her, made her feel less powerless in that otherwise disorienting, regimented environment. ('You can't release a kid to be themselves if you have strict rules,' Spielberg says)." Complicating this—and as a supplement to Truffaut's statement to Spielberg on the set of *Close Encounters* ("I like you with *keeds*, you are wonderful with *keeds*, you must do a movie with *keeds*"), Philip Taylor reports that the

French director also advised that children are ideal actors because they are so keen to please (1992, 130), raising a wider question concerning the relationship between desire to please and vulnerability to exploitation. Spielberg has also said that with Henry Thomas he oscillated from best friend to schoolteacher in the young actor's mind (Sunshine 2012, 107). Thomas himself has suggested that Spielberg gets such excellent performances from children not because he plays with them but because he is very precise: "He was really good at directing. He was very specific in his notes. When you're a kid, and you don't have a lot of work under your belt, you need to feel confident about what you're doing and whether or not the people in charge like what you're doing. Steven was really good at explaining scenes in a way that kids could grasp a hold of it and give him what he wanted out of it" (Schrodt 2012).

But there is also much evidence that the director has drawn artistic energy from his actors. Carl Gottlieb, who acted in *Jaws* as well as cowriting the screenplay, reports that "Steven's inclination is to let actors have their way with dialogue in rehearsals, allowing characters to improvise entire scenes. This process leads director and writer to a more natural sound" (2005, 56). This also extends to children, who have contributed performance ideas tantamount to coauthoring their characters. Haley Joel Osment has described the actor's "drilling down" method on his side of the creative equation, which developed in childhood: "As an actor, the only thing you can do in that situation is just focus on the reality of the character. It would be easy to be carried away by that enormity of the context in which that performance belongs, but just by focusing on that one individual character's interactions with the other characters in the story, I think, it's what allowed me to do the best that I could in that situation" (Chia n.d.). He was nineteen when he said this; when he filmed *A.I.* at age twelve, however, the message was remarkably similar: "There's nothing too intense about what's happened to my life. . . . It's all about being able to imagine" (Copel 2001).

This co-creation process is particularly borne out by the creative triumvirate central to *E.T.*'s production process—that of director Spielberg, writer Melissa Mathison, and the three lead children. Spielberg told Martin Amis in 1982, "If you over-rehearse kids, you risk a bad case of the cutes. We shot *E.T.* chronologically, with plenty of improvisation. I let the kids feel their way into the scenes" (Amis 1987, 153). As an adult, MacNaughton reported Spielberg "was constantly asking us [the young actors in the film] for our ideas on what we would do in this situation or that. Between him and Melissa Mathison, who wrote the script, we were always asked for our input." And just as the notion of the director's childlikeness is vaunted as a hallmark of authenticity, so Mathison is described by MacNaughton as "really the heart and soul of the kid characters in the movie" (all quotes by Avila 2017). However, Mathison further hybridizes the vision of the child: "Steven and I shared our imagination on this story; we both brought our own memories and strengths. In 1982 I was not yet a parent, but was a stepmother, and had been a consummate babysitter and an older sister. The kids in

'E.T.' can be directly linked to kids I knew. I even stole some of my little friends' best lines: i.e. 'penis breath.' What adult woman could have thought of that?" (Sragow 2012).

If children outside of the cast have input into the film's dialogue and set pieces, those within its creative melting pot do so even more. Spielberg described the script as being kept alive by a process of eavesdropping within the fabric of the shoot: "Melissa Mathison was on the set everyday, and she'd hear them talking in between takes. She always carried this notepad everywhere with her, and she'd go into a corner and write down what she heard. . . . . Melissa was able to listen to their patterns of behavior and be able to rewrite some of the dialogue for the next day" (Breznican 2012). This resulted in some lines the children expressed making it wholesale into the finished film—Barrymore seems to have been particularly vocal here ("I don't like his [E.T.'s] feet" was hers). These comments are the reflections of adults reunited to promote a reissue of the film, but as reflecting on a child/adult process they are still invaluable insights albeit refracted by memory. Creative collaboration is sometimes described as dialogue or exchange: as Spielberg said in 2012, "With Henry, we would just have conversations about the scene: where the camera was going to go, what I was hoping Henry would do in the scene. But we would just talk. I wouldn't call it directing actors. I think it was just called guiding people to discover for themselves what needs to be discovered . . . rather than spoiling everything by making a discovery and then having them act the discovery. . . . And I would just roll the camera, and Henry would do what he felt that he needed to do" (Breznican 2012).

This is sometimes articulated as an actor-led approach and sometimes as a process of "guiding people" to get to where the director wants them to be, as borne out by Sam Robards during the *A.I.* shoot. Spielberg leads the actor, whether adult or child, toward a marker while at the same time encouraging them to feel that they got there by themselves: the director "knows what he wants, but he allows you the time to find it" (Schruers 2001, 107). Dustin Hoffman echoed this collaboration/control dynamic in relation to working on *Hook* (where he had been accused of directing himself): "Steven listens to everybody. We not only felt free to make suggestions, he actively asked us what we thought. But there was never any doubt whose movie this is, or who made the decisions at the end of the day" (Docherty 1992, 5). Of the direction of the *Close Encounters* cast the director has said, "I would rather let the actors inspire me . . . and begin making visual choices after I've watched a rehearsal. After . . . the actors move where they feel they should move. . . . Then [I] introduce the camera and film it" (quoted by Morton 2007, 177). One would think that with children this process would be different, but what happened with Barrymore as Gertie, after an audition that saw her improvising stories, was even more actor-led, as Spielberg connected with her real-life facility for make-believe and then unlocked her improvisations. "All of us were free to offer input," Barrymore reports in *Little Girl Lost*, "but he especially seemed to like the silly things the kids came up with" (1990, 58). Denise Chamian, the casting director who worked on *Saving Private Ryan* and *Minority Report*, notes that while Spielberg has a tight method for casting, he still invites some improvisation (within a particular remit): "He's not locked into exactly what's in the script. He's very open and very collaborative and that allows him to paint a much deeper landscape. . . . He's like a playful kid and his enthusiasm washes over an actor" (Kondazian 2000, 67).

The Spielbergian child discourse is then blended into a directorial method. This partly informed his decision to shoot *E.T.* in continuity order so as to give the children a stronger narrative context, abandoning his customary use of storyboards: "I had the feeling the boards might force the child actors into stiff, unnatural attitudes and I didn't want that. . . . I wanted them to be so spontaneous that if something natural did come up—something that was a gift from the gods—then we'd be able to use it without the boards saying we couldn't" (Ellis and Sutherland 2003, 26). Henry Thomas famously improvised the scene in which he introduces E.T. to his toys, real toys to which he was already attached. Mathison confirmed the improvisational process, stating that it was "best for the writer to stay out of the way at that point—on set, improvisation is personal, between actor and director." (Sragow 2012). At her audition for *Poltergeist* (for a part she did not get but which showcased her to Spielberg ahead of the *E.T.* casting), Barrymore told fabricated stories so well that Spielberg called her back. Her flights of fancy encouraged him to think, "I can use that imagination in this picture, she can help me make my movie better" (Ellis and Sutherland 2003, 22), and the actor remembers him saying to her, "Let's combine ideas" (Barrymore 1990, 58). The retort "Give me a break!" in response to Elliott telling her that only kids can see the alien is attributed to Barrymore, though Mathison describes a process that was somewhere in between Spielberg, the script, and the actor: "I'm not sure if Steven urged her, steered her, or just lapped up the joy of Drew's wackiness" (Sragow 2012).

Casting and "Claiming the Role"

Before all this collaboration comes the casting process, over which the child only has the control of a virtuoso audition. Later I will look in detail at how this played out for Henry Thomas auditioning for Elliott, but first I want to consider some wider questions. Casting in the sense of an actor landing a role is obviously the starting point for any creative relationship between a film's personnel, but because of questions around child actors both as playing themselves and as freakishly talented, the link between self and role is even firmer. The casting of starring children is often lengthy (though Spielberg often avoids established stars: "The play's the thing," he told Amis. "In every movie I have made, the movie is the star" [1987, 151]). Casting complete unknowns or little-known jobbing actors is itself often the subject of a "search for Scarlett O'Hara"–style prepublicity drive, especially with high-profile, presold adaptations such as *Empire of the Sun* and

The BFG. Nine months was spent considering 4,000 applicants before Christian Bale was picked for *Empire of the Sun*, and *The BFG* was also promoted with stories such as Spielberg spending months "searching for a young actress with just the right balance of innocence, ingenuity and feistiness to embody Sophie" prior to finding Barnhill (Woods 2016). J. G. Ballard, who wrote the novel on which *Empire of the Sun* is based, called Bale's performance "the best by a child in the history of the cinema" (Petley 1988), while Spielberg invoked the spirit of *The BFG*'s author to endorse the choice of Barnhill: "After a lengthy search, I feel Roald Dahl himself would have found Ruby every bit as marvelous as we do" (*Business Wire* 2014). Barrymore was called back for repeated auditions and in the final one was required to scream very loudly in a sound room ("I screamed so loud I broke the device and the tape stopped" [Barrymore 2015, 58]). As would be the case with Ariana Richards's audition for *Jurassic Park*, screaming is, it seems, a prized performance skill in a girl. Barrymore's ability to perform fear was as important as her quixotic storytelling qualities. Denise Chamian reports that besides Spielberg liking to showcase relative unknowns ("We wanted to find new faces . . . We didn't want any baggage"), he also has particular practical methods that initially delegate much responsibility to the casting staff: "Steven likes to see everyone on tape first and that gives me a tremendous amount of freedom. I can experiment, I can see a bunch of people and decide who I think he should see. Once he decided who he wanted, he would have a little meeting with them. . . . So really, it's Steven's ability to look at someone. He can watch someone read three of four lines of something and know that's who he wants" (Kondazian 2000, 67).

Having the casting director as filter is particularly important when the director is as powerful as Spielberg, which is why he now usually requires actors to submit tapes (later in this book Ariana Richards reflects on this process). When asked whether he ever directs actors during his meetings, Chamian replies, "They don't read in front of him. He has done that only on very few occasions. He doesn't like to do that because he realizes that it makes actors nervous. So for the most part, if he's seen somebody on tape, he just wants to talk to them" (67). There can be few children now, up for a possible role in a Spielberg film, who, like Ke Huy Quan prior to and during the filming of *Indiana Jones and the Temple of Doom*, have never heard of the director. Spielberg's awareness of his own star status and employment clout is a significant point of negotiation with the child.[29]

This is true of both adult actors and children. But casting children is also often determined by two priorities: casting directors specializing in child actors stress the importance of casting not just the child but the family, with a particular emphasis on the parents as (variously) supportive, pushy, possibly more interested in film work than the child actually is, and knowledgeable of what they may be signing their child up for.[30] Spielberg has said that his actors' parents must be able to "take better care of their kids" after the experience of making a film: "I always try to let people know that reality begins and ends at home. The reality cannot be sustained in the world I live in, which is the world of make-believe" (Mooallem 2016). But this is also a high-stakes world of work, which makes specific demands on the child—the stresses are based not only on the disparity between creative fictionalizing and the hard reality beyond the shoot. Particularly for the starring child, on whose shoulders and through whose performance proficiency the entire production rests (including the employment and prestige of the whole crew and all the other actors), there is a daunting responsibility.[31] Reviewing *Empire of the Sun*, Janet Maslin notes that not only was Bale "eminently able to handle an ambitious and demanding role," but he was "in virtually every frame" (1987, C25). So parents are not just responsible for ensuring the child's "normalizing" transition after they exit the world of paid make-believe back into the world of friendships and school. They need to be able to manage the stress of production itself and any potential fallout after the shoot, the disparate realities across which the child swings. This is important for ongoing well-being, for the child's future employment, and—longer term—to avoid any potential "former child star" aftereffects. Osment attributes his "safe arrival into adulthood" to the "stabilizing role of his family": "Even today, Osment uses 'we' when discussing the decisions that he and his family made in those years, as though his career's trajectory had been guided by a benign collective" (Parkin 2014).[32] Bale was bullied on returning to his Bournemouth school and was held solely responsible by his peers for the relative underperformance of *Empire of the Sun*, which was used as schoolyard ammunition: "I walked down corridors with people going: 'Oh look, it's the has-been.' Fourteen-year-old boys would quote me box-office numbers. It was weird how much they wanted the movie to fail" (Cheung and Pittam 2012, 15).

Second, for the reasons described by Balázs (the pervasive belief that children *are* more than they *do*), there is a governing principle that the child must come ready to "fit" the role. This is far more the case for children than is so for adult actors, for whom the skill of turning themselves *into* the role is most prized. The child already in some sense must inhabit the character in order to be allowed to perform that character. Spielberg told Barrymore's mother, "Never give your daughter any acting lessons. She is the most naturally gifted actress I have ever seen. She has the stardust magic" (Ellis and Sutherland 2003, 27), and this "it" quality is often cited as a key component in casting children, as well as reinforcing the thread of the idealized natural child running through Spielberg's work. In the context of casting Henry Thomas as Elliott, the producer Kathleen Kennedy said: "I think, in a funny way, with children, you almost know the minute they walk into the room whether you're in fact looking at the character, because they do come in and claim the role in some way. Usually that's because you're casting some element of their existing personality" (Sunshine 2012, 37). Despite the sense of agency suggested by the reference here to children claiming the role, a special unique something over which the child may have no control is, then, more important than well-trained skill. This has tended to inflect judgment of performance, read as real expression rather than talent.

Of course, the truth lies somewhere in between; Osment and Thomas were employed for skill as well as individual preexisting qualities. Still, the sense in which we are watching not just young Jim Graham but also thirteen-year-old Christian Bale informs how we read the creation of that character by an actor inputting "some element of their existing personality" into the fleshed-out role. One of my arguments throughout this book challenges the view that children's culture is wholly a question of adults fantasizing what it is to be a child and using a child to sell that image back to child consumers. The child performer's acting brings to the work a certain creative control over meaning. Unless we see the child actor as a mere puppet maneuvered by the adult director, we must ascribe agency to performance, with the child actor as coauthor.[33] Certainly, to some extent the director "authors" the child's authorship of their performance, but the child still has meaningful input. To paraphrase but also to counter Jacqueline Rose, all of Spielberg's child actors "give us the child," but these children are, at least sometimes, insiders to the process of film, and part of cinema's denotation of meaning around what it is to be a child. This close affiliation between performance and the real haunts the child at every turn, and I now want to focus on one particular element of this. Melodrama and its prime body fluid—the tear—are once again .pertinent. For all his family-friendliness, Spielberg makes films that *make children cry*, that move their bodies to receptive and resonant grief responses. If the child's off-screen life can sometimes be a vale of tears, the performance of tears on-screen also makes us ask what it is to make a child cry for entertainment. Children are both recipients and engineers of these tears.

Making Children Cry: The Tears of Henry Thomas

Henry Thomas's audition tape for the lead role of Elliott in *E.T.* has become a YouTube favorite and a much-watched DVD extra,[34] and it raises questions about how we distinguish between the "real" of tears and the performance of pain. It is Thomas's tears that Spielberg is most interested in seeing evidenced, not whether he can act drunk or feisty or joyous or any of the other emotional states he would have to demonstrate if offered the role. As would be true of the film itself, in the improvised audition scene the tears flow in a dramatic arc that is utterly touching, with the casting director Mike Fenton functioning as the boy's off-camera foil. Fenton's role is that of a "man from the government" who insistently claims he has the power to take away the boy's alien friend. Against this Thomas first protests; then portrays fear, anger, and loneliness; and finally produces a narrative arc of tears that well up and brim over before falling fast and full down his cheeks (figure 4). As the brief but heartbreaking scene concludes, an off-camera Spielberg can be heard to say, "OK kid, you got the job." The

FIGURE 4 "OK kid, you got the job": Henry Thomas auditioning for Elliott in *E.T.*

audition tears are a clear sign of things to come: on this film production, "It was easier for Henry Thomas to cry than to laugh" (Sunshine 2012, 134).

"Gushers" have long been the most prized of child performers, from the nineteenth-century theatrical child star craze to contemporary cinema and television work: the ability to cry at will is a cornerstone of many actors' repertoire. Cary Guffey got the role of the toddler in *Close Encounters of the Third Kind* because "He could laugh or cry on cue," according to the film's casting team (Delano 1978). This places him and Spielberg's other young gushers in a long tradition. Tracing the origins of the child star in Victorian theater, Diana Serra Cary observes that children were especially needed for the rush of stage adaptations of Dickens in the middle to late nineteenth century (1979, 8).[35] These commonly featured workhouse-destined waifs in narratives contextualized by Dickens's wider campaign against child labor. The irony, of course, is that the very productions that exposed the plight of exploited working children themselves employed child performers for long, late hours with no regulation. Little Cordelia Howard, who debuted in *Oliver Twist* at New York's Purdy's National Theatre in 1852, set the pattern "for generations of stage families yet unborn," according to Cary (8). Her unrehearsed sobs and ad-libbed predictions of her untimely death made the four-year-old an instant stage sensation.[36]

Spontaneous tears thus became the authentic currency of theatrical children, as they would in turn be for cinematic ones. Cinematic tears of course have a higher premium and are both rewarded and demanded by the close-up shot. The close-up enabled the human stories of early (and subsequent) cinema to be told more precisely than ever and made the minute dramas of the human face the common building block of cinematic grammar. It could reveal in pristine detail the quantities and qualities of tears—how they glistened as they caught the light (and the audience's breath), but particularly how authentically they flowed. Not even the best front-row seat for a live performance delivers the forensic view of the cinematic close-up. Technologies of artifice developed: glycerin drops when tears failed to flow, onions, tear blowers or sticks—menthol crystal vapor blown into or held near the eye just before shooting. Theater does not have the luxury of breaks between takes when these can be applied—live performers either cry or do not (but at least their excretions are not viewed as under a microscope). But while glycerin may trickle fairly authentically, pristine choker close-ups may reveal that it does not flow readily from the tear ducts. Nor does it absorb ultraviolet light like real tears, so glycerin tears look more solid—real tears contain molecules that make them subtly fluoresce in ultraviolet. Of course glycerin, and particularly Hollywood melodrama's copious use of it, came to be a synonym for fakery and mawkish sentimentality (that stick with which Spielberg has so often been beaten, hence the urgent requirement for real tears). As well as pontificating on film children, savages, and play, Béla Balázs has been called "the poet laureate of the close-up" (Stam 2000, 61), and he reads tearing up as an emotional story in itself: "We cannot use glycerine tears in a close-up. What makes a deep impression is not a fat, oily tear rolling down a face—what moves is to see the glance growing misty, and moisture gathering in the corner of the eye—moisture that as yet is scarcely a tear. This is moving, because this cannot be faked" (Balázs 1970, 77). Classical Hollywood produced some prodigiously lachrymose children, the most well known of which were girls.[37] Because of this, boys' tears may be even more prized than girls'.[38] Bobs Watson was one of nine performing children in a Hollywood family who were all able to cry on cue, but Bobs's talent was the most copious and precisely engineered: when asked if he found it easy to cry he said in an interview conducted later in life, "Oh yeah. You just tell me what you wanted. . . . I said to Uncle Norman [Norman Taurog, the director of *Men of Boys Town*] . . . 'Do you want halfway down tears or all the way down tears?'" (Goldrup and Goldrup 2002, 308).

So what does it mean for an adult to make a child cry for the camera? The child's ability to cry on cue is often so spectacular that it overrides any question of the adult's manipulation of those tears. In the long gestation of *A.I.* through the developing relationship between Spielberg and Stanley Kubrick, Kubrick would quiz Spielberg on his (more commercially successful) techniques, including asking, "Gee, how did you get that kid to cry that way? Did you have to threaten to kill his dog?" (Abramowitz 2001). In James Kendrick's memorable phrase, "Childhood is not a place of safety in Spielberg's films" (2014, 193). When we watch Thomas's audition tape, we are perhaps so overwhelmed by contagious sorrow that we pay little attention to the knife-twisting of the adult voice—the adult who seems, to paraphrase Henry James, to be turning the screw of affect. In an article from around the release of *A.I.*, Lib Copel reports on watching Haley Joel Osment in *The Sixth Sense* and being "almost worried for him" in a way that bleeds beyond the story and into its production: "Who was this terrified child, and what had the director done to him?" (2001). Susan King (1999) reports that the intensity of the script and material made *The Sixth Sense* director M. Night Shyamalan concerned about auditioning young actors, though "it never entered my mind with him."

So what are the implications of provoking simulations of fear, distress, and pain fit to generate this manifest distress? Manipulative trickery is often used to elicit fear and upset responses, because children are not trusted (nor do they trust themselves) simply to "act" them. If the child effects what seems like real grief, the adult must be being "really" cruel. But is this not exactly what adults are *not* supposed to do to children—upset them, for entertainment? The image of the child actor as either victim or freak has marked many individual biographies, but crying performance extrapolates this through focused if tiny tragic moments. Almost as commonplace is the act of eliciting a "real" performance of tears for the camera by telling a child something upsetting; particularly choice examples are reported by Cary, including Jackie Coogan's father's famous promise that "if he didn't [cry], we'd take him away from the studio and *really* send him to the workhouse" (Cary 1979, 59; emphasis mine). Andrea Darvi also reports a stage mother making her small child cry by saying that if she cannot act it, "we'll call in your sister and she can come in and do the job" (1983, 20). Here real/fake scenarios (Coogan's real fear of the poorhouse intensifying his fictional fear of it in *The Kid*) and real/fake tears build up a crescendo of response. Even in the allegedly benign world of Spielbergian performance-play, Henry Thomas (bearing out Kubrick's question) thought of his dead dog during the audition—better than remaining dry when the cameras roll, or losing the job. Christian Bale reported, "I'd think of something sad, or something that makes me angry . . . but I'd only need to do that the first time. After that it would just come" (I. Davies 1988, 12). On the conclusion of the *E.T.* shoot, to compensate for the breakup of the production "family," Spielberg gave Drew Barrymore a kitten, which she called Gertie. It ran away, and the lost animal became the thought the little girl deployed for crying performances in subsequent films. The work of *E.T.*, and Spielberg's influence, thus continued to hold her through future roles.

Extreme performances also play with our sense of the child's age, or render the child perhaps unnaturally "adultish." If Spielberg is often described as a child in a man's body, skilled child actors are commonly described as adults masquerading as children. Spielberg calls Thomas "an adult actor, not a nine-year-old" (Royal 1982, 20), while the *Washington Post* called Osment "only sort of a child": "In terms of years, he was a minor, but by other measures he was more like an intense little man"; he looks "like a real kid, like your neighbor's son, not some coveted star who gets his lips Vaselined before photo shoots. . . . . No hint—till he speaks—of the man trapped inside" [Copel 2001]). Though Shia LaBeouf was twenty-one when he was featured in *Indiana Jones and the Kingdom of the Crystal Skull*, he was a veteran child performer, and this child star discourse inflects Harrison Ford's promotion of his costar: "He's young but he's an old soul. He's been an actor most of his life, so he knows what he's doing" (Hiscock 2008, 25). Another interviewer around the time of *A.I.*'s release conjectured that Osment was "possessed by the soul of a 35-year-old . . . generations-older colleagues, which include

Bruce Willis and Kevin Spacey, never use the word 'child' in their praise of the pint-size actor" (Kim 2001).

Clearly, this is intended to be highly complementary, but it only complicates the conundrum of the child performer considered freakish if too "methody," who cannot be allowed to be both a child and a great actor—greatness can only come from a form of perceived "adultization." Barrymore's mother recalls, "Steven Spielberg once told me that my daughter is an old soul, and I have to agree with him. One minute Drew's a playful nine-year-old talking to her dolls and stuffed animals, and the next she's twenty-nine or an old woman of seventy-five" (quoted in Ellis and Sutherland 2003, 50). There is also the risk that the child will slip too quickly from the much-prized "cute" to what Robin Wood characterizes as a harder formation—"the 'smart kid,' the premature adult, a figure denied both childhood and maturity" (2006, 200). Some children even torture themselves physically. Osment (who was only required to cry at one precise moment in *A.I.*) had already engaged in a form of self-harm to ensure the right quality of fear on *The Sixth Sense* shoot: "On the set, to conjure the sense of trauma he needed for a certain frustrating scene, Haley threw himself against a stage wall over and over, until he felt sufficiently shook up. In his next film, 'Pay It Forward,' Haley asked the actress playing his mother, Helen Hunt, to forgo a stage slap and really make contact. So he could feel the shock" (Copel 2001). On *The Sixth Sense* his technique was to "work himself into a state of terror" by believing he was actually the character he played (King 1999).

Despite his skill in directing children, Spielberg was not confident enough when he shot *E.T.* to think he could rely on skill-generated performance, so he pressed his actors into a wash of real sadness by making the shoot a version of their lives. He admits to playing tricks on his actors "to keep them spontaneous and fresh," though claims that he played "no mean tricks, never mean tricks, never on kids" (Royal 1982, 20). Despite the fact that reports from ex-Spielberg cast members are almost universally positive regarding his working methods, *Close Encounters* producer Julia Phillips alleged that Spielberg was not beyond such tactics, and Andrew Yule writes: "During the shoot he'd made Gary [*sic*] Guffey, the movie's littlest hero, his best buddy—all in the interest of getting the best performance possible out of the kid. After failing to get the required emotional wallop from Guffey for one crucial scene, Spielberg took the boy aside and told him that the movie was finished, that he wasn't going to see either him or the rest of his friends any more. That piece of calculated, some would say callous intelligence, produced the tears Spielberg sought" (1996, 80).[39]

Bale reported in the *Empire of the Sun* publicity that when a servant had to slap him in the film, it was rehearsed with a fake slap, and "that's how they told me it would be. But Steven told her when it came to the take to slap me hard so that my shock would look real. Well, it certainly did" (I. Davies 1988, 12). Barrymore reports that her upset about the *E.T.* shoot coming to an end was mitigated when she heard they needed one more day: "The idea that this would not all be ending as soon as I thought cheered me up so much, Steven came over and told me that I needed to be upset! Not happy!" (2015, 62). Against this, Spielberg's particular care is cited as part of a more positive story of his affinity with childhood: "Spielberg seems to feel an almost chastening responsibility to keep his young stars feeling . . . free and safe. He understands that they're still guileless, with a thinner buffer between themselves and their characters than veteran, grown-up actors, and that he, as their director, is forced to manipulate volatile emotions that these children are only beginning to understand and control" (Mooallem 2016).

He also wanted the *E.T.* children to believe, as well as to act. The team of technicians that mobilized the mechanical model of the eponymous alien via multiple cables was screened from the actors to enhance the sense that E.T. was a real being, moving all by himself. Shooting in continuity order maximized Spielberg's chances of getting authentic reactions such as horror and grief out of them—often they simply did not know what was coming next. The director has said in a "making of" publicity documentary, "Every day was a surprise until finally when ET began to die [the kids] . . . really believed that this was happening to their lives. . . . And I think their acting couldn't even be called acting at that point—it was just reacting. It was reacting to their best friend in the universe who was going away and leaving them."[40] Barrymore testifies that she thought the alien was really being hurt, and that this sense of the real, which the children tapped into (and which also implicated Spielberg so much that he felt like he was a father to the children), was key to how involved the audience felt: "The chemistry between all of us was so real that we really did feel like a family. . . . When the film came out, it seemed it was hitting people the same way it had hit all of us when we were making it" (Sunshine 2012, 90). The leave-taking scene was shot right at the end with Spielberg playing it as a last goodbye for the children. "All the kids were trying to hold it together," he says. "And if I did three, four, five takes the kids fell apart on each take because they knew they weren't going to see ET again."[41] There is of course a contradiction here: performing repeatedly across multiple takes is not the same as a real last goodbye. Spielberg has also said, "The final days of shooting were the saddest I've ever experienced on a film set" (P. M. Taylor 1992, 133), returning to the language of "real performance": "I wanted the kids to be caught up *as themselves and as their characters* so that, by the time they say goodbye to E.T., their emotions are genuine" (Sunshine 2012, 146; emphasis mine).[42] Even as adults, the former child actors continue to report in interviews that they thought ET was real, that their grief was real: "I don't think tears have ever been that readily available to me in my entire life," Barrymore has said (132).

The tears of the "affected" child actors in turn charge up the tears of the viewers who "catch" them. Universal expected the movie would be squarely a small-scale children's film (and limited its budget accordingly), but it became one of the first of New Hollywood's crossover family films with equal adult and child appeal. The wash of response engendered by Thomas's audition tears and the film's lachrymose conclusion are not unlike the vaudevillian's provocation of the "wow climax" as analyzed by Henry Jenkins, here quoting the theater critic Walter De Leon from 1925: "The natural, at least customary, reserve of an American audience is comparable to the cement work damming a river. If the performer can open a sluice gate or spillway the tide of applause will rush out—we hope—in a strong compact stream. If through lack of fitting climax or showmanship no outlet for the pent enthusiasm is provided, it is very apt to trickle thinly over the top of the dam or swash around weakly in backwater bayous" (2007, 5). Of course there is another form of acted bodily response that elicits such climactic "wows": sexual response in the performance of pornography. The child who can cry on cue is uncomfortably close to the pornographic actor who traverses the unclear line of real/performance through sexual arousal when the cameras roll. Both forms of acting, which make the body do something biologically "real" for fictional reasons, risk similar charges of unnaturalness and manipulation. Just as sexual response is available to seasoned pornographic performers, so is it possible to produce tears without emotional instigation or physical irritation of the eyes.

A tearful "wow climax," in which audience joins actor in a wash of tears, also charges the audience in a mimicry of acted feeling. Joan Copjec memorably proposes that public, excessive crying—indeed crying per se—"was an invention of the late eighteenth century" (1999, 249).[43] The deployment of children's tears in *E.T.* is a late twentieth-century filmic version of the mid-nineteenth-century theatrically crying child, rendered via cinematic rather than dramatic melodrama. Tears are the prime body fluid of melodrama—crying is melodrama's money shot. And for all its science fiction trappings, *E.T.* is nothing if not a melodrama (remember Spielberg's "I don't think I've ever *not* made a melodrama" [Friedman and Notbohm 2000, 65]). It is when the audience "catches" crying that we know the actor's tears have worked their magic in a form of emotional contagion. Jenkins deems the "wow" response as causing the audience to lose control over their emotions, maybe even over their bodily functions. This too is the child actor's goal, as he or she is directed to initiate a viral outbreak of emotion that does not recognize the cinema screen as a barrier. In his review of *Empire of the Sun*, William Marshall wrote, "Christian's performance . . . made me actually weep—great wet wracking globby tears, there in the dark, blundering out into the daylight embarrassed and shaken" (1988, 17). At the London premiere of *E.T.*, Princess Diana had to make an early exit to fix her makeup before being seen by the crowds because she had been crying so much.[44] Martin Amis wrote of an audience reaction in Los Angeles: "Towards the end of *E.T.*, barely able to support my own grief and bewilderment, I turned and looked down the aisle at my fellow sufferers: executive, black dude, Japanese businessman, punk, hippie, mother, teenager, child. Each face was a mask of tears. Staggering out, through a tundra of sodden hankies, I felt drained, pooped, squeezed dry" (1987, 147).

Leaving aside the almost postcoital catharsis evoked by this last sentence, it seems that unprecedented box office is not enough to evidence the appeal of this originally small film to wide audiences: the spectacle of communal tears seals its success. Indeed, this has become one of the most discussed issues in the reception of *E.T.*: who cries, and how much, in an ostensibly cross-class and cross-generational public shedding of body fluid.[45] The claim to universality is strong too. Andrew Gordon begins his analysis of the film as a fairy tale with an account of a family of Cambodian refugees taken to see it in the United States: "Towards the end of the movie, tears were running down the cheeks of their seven-year-old son. Yet he didn't understand a word of English. That's cinematic power: a movie that doesn't really need language to communicate, that's as strong as a silent Griffith or Chaplin. E.T.'s death scene may be the contemporary equivalent of the death of Dickens's Little Nell: millions weep" (2008, 75).

We return to the acute Dickensian melodrama that gave birth to the child star. The "ouch" moment is, for Thomas Sutcliffe, where "even the most resistant viewer will finally surrender" (2002, 1).[46] Yet the bodily facts of affect have overwhelmed questions around why it makes people cry, and what the child's role is in this. Since Peter Brooks's foundational 1995 work, melodramatic excess has been read as a symptom of repression or prohibition. But at the same time that academic film critics were decoding these signs in classical Hollywood through psychoanalysis and semiotics, popular film critics were reinscribing them as sentiment, counter to the preferred terms of irony, restraint, and the "cool" codings of auteurism. It is, then, perhaps surprising that this tear-fest of a film would be so universally loved, given the prevailing critical wind. This is not just because critics are often out of step with popular audiences. I put this down to the three central child performances, forms of "unaffected" affect that save their director from another attack on perceived emotional excess.

As we saw earlier, Spielberg is commonly accused of making children of his audiences—Ilsa J. Bick, for example, writes, "Instead of simply invoking the memories and associations of childhood, Spielberg consistently aims to infantilize the viewer" (1992, 26). Yet Amis's tirade of tears goes further: "And we weren't crying for the little extra-terrestrial, nor for little Elliott, nor for little Gertie. We were crying for our lost selves. This is the primal genius of Spielberg." (1987, 147). In this formulation, Elliott is the child we no longer are (adult tears shed for the lost child within—a very *Hook*-ish sentiment). Spielberg knows well enough that a particularly skilled child actor has the ability to attract adult as well as child audience identification, which is what makes the child such an affecting all-round protagonist. How Thomas's performance "caught" the adult crew—how they "caught" the emotion—was of course crucial: as Spielberg testified about the audition, "Everybody in the room was in tears." Osment also had a reputation even before he came to *A.I.* for affecting the crew in the audition room, promising a similar reaction from the audience. When Osment went up for the role of Cole in *The Sixth Sense*, the director M. Night Shyamalan had already auditioned many children, but, he recalled, "It was like I had never heard the dialogue before.... He finished the scene and he was crying and I was crying. I could not believe it. I said: 'Oh my God: Who are you?'" (Parkin 2014). Tears immediately parlay emotion: the contagion that floods forth from the child's tears first infects those on set, then penetrates the screen to wash across the audience. The affecting narratives the child tells themself (Thomas's dead dog, Barrymore's lost kitten, Coogan's fear of the workhouse) are just the first stage in the affective story through which viewers multiply identify. I would then complicate Amis's position and say that adult viewers of *E.T. are* Elliott, as well as knowing that they are *no longer* Elliott, and at the same time they want to protect the weeping Elliott.

And what of child viewers of child actors? Children also cry at *E.T.* Jon Mooallem writes, "It was a movie about childhood that was too real for many children to watch. There were reports, in that summer of 1982, of kids becoming ill in the theater during the last scene, when E.T. lifts off and leaves Elliott behind."[47] In light of the lively research culture focused on children as being negatively affected by entertainment culture, how do we read the responsive tears of children to fantasy melodrama? Are they the same as other melodrama-engendered reactions—for adult women, for instance? We should now move on from circular assertions about Spielberg infantilizing his audience (for good or ill) to discuss how his audience is "melodrama-ed" into shedding tears, which may not be age-specific. The image of the beautifully suffering child is ubiquitous; their suffering infects surrounding adults. Children's performed pain is aestheticized through the tear and is left unresolved in contradictory family scenarios. Weeping *at* movies in response to weeping *in* movies is then curiously sadomasochistic (and is unlike weeping in other quarters, since it can be turned off when the movie ends): viewers may also want Elliott's/Thomas's pain to continue for a little longer so that the sad pleasure of his tears can be vicariously indulged. Children make this pleasure more acute than any other class of performer.

But it is not *just* Thomas welling up that makes us do so in turn. The improvised dialogue in the audition sequence—with Fenton threatening to take away Elliott's friend, even suggesting that he has the power of the president on his side, before finally claiming the power to give the alien back to the now-mute child—plays out in miniature the narrative of the final third of the movie, from the moment the adults enter the child/alien enclave of the suburban house. At first this seems to be a narrative of conventionally ascribed power and impotence. The exchange articulates the positions of desperation and loneliness on the one (child's) hand and assured omnipotence on the other (adult's) hand. However, it is the sad-angry tears that gain the upper hand and become most potent. If Thomas's performance across the whole of *E.T.* is manipulation or exploitation, it is self-inflicted and self-engineered as much as it is Spielberg-directed. When the audition concludes, Thomas briefly smiles, even as he brushes away a tear, reminding us of the performance at play here: the tears are real, the anguish seems real, even though we know it is all a performance of the real. Clearly, he has acute emotional control over his apparent lack of control, which then in turn controls both his diegetic interrogator (Fenton in the audition tape) and his audience (the crew, the viewers). The control raises questions of intention and conscious action, which are valued in adult actors but in children raise suspicion about "manipulation" and "knowingness"—though why pejorative terms for forms of control would be used in relation to a child's skill but not an adult's is interesting. In the language of the sadomasochistic contract, Thomas controls the other's control, developing a potent rhetoric of powerlessness that ends with him just nodding and brimming over—as if he cannot trust himself to speak. This is most affecting of all. For Spielberg, Thomas is "a very controlled, methodical performer who measures what he does and feels what he does and yet broadcasts it in a totally subtle way. His performance is so controlled, unlike most kid performers, who seem to be giving you 150 percent on every shot. Henry's performance is just a bread crumb at a time, but he takes you in a wonderful direction to a very, very rousing catharsis" (Royal 1982, 20). "Just a bread crumb at a time" reminds us of Elliott enticing E.T. with the Reese's Pieces. We follow the trail and are trapped by our own response.

This is a physical performance with a similar narrative (shared between actor, director, and audience) to the vaudevillian's "bits of business" of early cinema. Their sometimes freakish skills, displayed first onstage in variety acts, then on the short spectacles of early film, would become as much a part of the cinema of attractions as more disembodied spectacle. Henry Jenkins cites Lev Kuleshov's fascination with "monsters"—performers "who could exert extraordinary control over their bodies" (2007, 6), and here the parallels with the "freakishness" of the skilled child actor are clear, as are comparisons with Spielberg as both a master of a neo–cinema of attractions delivered through visual effects and of the older variety of physical and emotional performance. Henry Thomas's skill and demonstration here are acutely emotional *because* they are focused through the physical, and—like the vaudevillian performer—the actor's "economic livelihood depended on the ability to shape and control an audience's emotional trajectory through the performance in the hopes of hitting a crescendo at the moment that really mattered" (5). This link between physical performance, emotional affect, employability, and boyhood will thread through the next two chapters—on boy's bodies (human, alien, cyborgian) and on (primarily) two popular Spielberg films that, rather than endorsing a notion of childhood as a cozily familiar if lost fantasy for the adult, instead suggests childhood as a strange and sometimes alien state. The performances of Henry Thomas and Haley Joel Osment are at the fore, but they are joined by a cast of smaller performances and brought into comparison also with the children of *Close Encounters of the Third Kind* and of *Ready Player One*.

I want to conclude this discussion of child performers with a brief meditation on *The Twilight Zone: The Movie*. For all this child-friendly identification,

Spielberg is also associated with the worst single event involving child performers in postwar Hollywood history. "Performers" is perhaps an exulted word: the two small children who were killed on the set of one of the segments of the portmanteau film of *The Twilight Zone* were supporting players employed ad hoc and illegally, with none of the protection of work permits or guardians on set. Spielberg coproduced this film with John Landis, who was responsible for directing the segment on which the deaths occurred. The one unfounded allegation that Spielberg was present at the accident has been discredited, and writers take pains to stress that he could not be placed at the scene of the filming.[48] Two books published in 1988 in the wake of the trial provide clear journalistic accounts of the events from before the accident through to the aftermath of the resulting litigation, spotlighting the actions, inaction, and culpability of various crew members and Landis: Stephen Farber and Marc Green's *Outrageous Conduct: Art, Ego, and the* Twilight Zone *Case* and Ron LaBrecque's *Special Effects Disaster at "Twilight Zone": The Tragedy and the Trial*. There is, then, no need to rehearse this terrible episode in great detail, especially given that my focus here is a through line analyzing Spielberg's directorial work rather than his copious enterprises as a producer; I do not want to court inconsistency by discussing at length a scandal that took place in part of the film produced by Spielberg but directed by someone else (Landis). Spielberg did also direct a segment of *Twilight Zone* (entitled *Kick the Can*), which I will discuss later in a rather different context. However, in a book about children and childhood itself it would be remiss to omit discussion of the moment when children actually died on one of Spielberg's productions. And in a chapter on child performers, the case illuminates the fatal riskiness of locations and sets as workplaces for children, and the casual callousness of the U.S. film industry when out of control or flouting regulation, at its litigious extreme.

In brief, this appalling story runs thus: Spielberg—a longtime fan of Rod Serling's *Twilight Zone* television series—developed a portmanteau film, one element of which would be directed by him, all of which would be coproduced by him and Landis. Landis's segment (*Time Out*) told the story of a racist bigot (Vic Morrow) who—in a typical *Twilight Zone* ironic reversal—finds himself a victim of the Nazis, then of the Ku Klux Klan, and finally of U.S. troops in Vietnam, as he slips through time and conflict zones only to be repeatedly identified as the non-white enemy. Warner Bros., which produced the film, asked that a final sequence be shot that would partially redeem Morrow's character, so a sequence in which he rescues two Vietnamese children whose village is under attack was planned. The children would not have been on set and put in danger had Warners not wanted a slightly softer—even more family friendly—conclusion to the tale. Landis planned an extravagantly violent night shoot, but Californian labor laws prevented children being on the location at night, and in such a dangerous situation. Dolls or small-stature adults were considered as substitutes for children, but rejected, so the clandestine employment of two child supporting players went ahead; the children were then concealed from anyone on set who may have protested their presence. They were paid with a check for $2,000, split between the two families across two nights of shooting, which was signed by Spielberg's long-standing collaborator Frank Marshall and paid through Spielberg's office. This is far higher than the usual daily rate of $90 for children hired legally under the auspices of the Screen Extras Guild (see LaBrecque 1988, 13–16, for an account of the hiring process in this case). Their parents—who were not briefed about the danger six-year-old Renee Shin-Yi Chen and seven-year-old Myca Dinh Le would be in—functioned as unwitting chaperones. The children were not professional child actors but were the children of friends-of-friends; both sets of parents were approached privately and agreed because they felt it would be an interesting and enhancing cultural experience for Renee and Myca. They did not know that permits were needed or how dangerous the set would be. The children were chosen on grounds of their particularly small stature (two other, bigger, children were rejected), and Landis "wanted 'adorable' kids" (16). The brief was "2 Vietnamese kids Boy/Girl (Chinese or Korean Thai 2 nights)."[49] Myca and Renee were deemed to fit this generalized brief of East Asian/South Asian children: Renee was from a Chinese family, Myca had been born in Saigon before his parents fled Vietnam in 1975. Essentially, the children functioned primarily as props in the story of the redemption of Vic Morrow's character. Landis orchestrated a battlefield scene of extremity: explosives detonated near the children destabilized a helicopter flying low overhead, which fell, crushing Renee and decapitating Myca and Vic Morrow. Despite this, and the lengthy court case that followed in which Landis and four others were tried for manslaughter, the segment remains part of the released film, minus footage of the children. Spielberg's contribution to the portmanteau—*Kick the Can*, in which elderly adults are performed by children—comes directly after *Time Out* in the sequence of the *Twilight Zone* movie. It is hard to watch *Time Out* without interpolating the story's missing children.

Given the potentially seismic influence of the developing case on the industry, *Variety* followed it on a daily basis. Civil compensation claims by the parents were settled ahead of the criminal trial; everyone charged was eventually acquitted of manslaughter. Thomas Budds, the Los Angeles Police Department detective detailed with leading the investigation, was convinced that "at the very least, he possessed the foundation of a child-endangerment case" (LaBrecque 1988, 62), but this did not develop. And no one was ever charged with the one clear-cut crime that was committed in the chaos of incompetence, aggrandizement, and accident: that of the illegal employment of minors. This may seem like a lesser issue given the deaths, but illegal employment in an entertainment context was the very condition that put the children in danger in the first place. This illegality, if proven, would have had a major impact on Warners' ability to hire children in the future. Spielberg has largely refused to speak about the event, aside from one interview with Dale Pollock in 1983 in which he describes the previous year as one of "ecstasy and grief": "It has mixed the best, the success of *E.T.*, with the worst, the *Twilight Zone* tragedy," but these then became part of the director's developmental biography: "It has made me grow up a little more" (Pollock 1983a, 1). Interviewers since have had their slots with Spielberg cut short when they have broached the subject. His only official contribution went unquestioned and was unchallenged in the legal fallout. A simple statement was sent to the National Transportation Safety Board, which initially was investigating the case; it read, "In response to your request, I was never at the Indian Dunes location of *Twilight Zone* on the night of the accident or at any other time. I declare under penalty of perjury that the foregoing is true and correct, executed at Los Angeles, California, this first day of December, 1982" (Robb 1982b). This signed declaration, distancing him from the incident, has gone so unchallenged that the story has shifted from potential culpability to the accusation that some people in Hollywood are above the law. Landis has continued to work on films with little interest in child performers, but the stakes are particularly high for a director wanting to continue to employ children. Anyone involved on any level with a prosecution for the illegal employment of minors, or being party to hiring children in this way, would lose their permit to work with children and could no longer make films centered on childhood.

Avoiding the risk of legal culpability through refusing to make any further statements (even of sorrow or apology) veers close to callousness. Spielberg said to Pollock "No movie is worth dying for," and shifted the onus of responsibility by advocating that the less-powerful challenge the too-powerful—directors and writers "who ask too much": "If something isn't safe, it's the right and responsibility of every actor or crew member to yell, 'Cut!'" (Pollock 1983a, 1). His own alibi was ignorance: he was not there, he did not know. Frank Marshall, as Farber and Green put it, had "slipped away and stayed away until the case was closed" (1988, 245). But, to continue with Farber and Green's argument, "*shouldn't* Spielberg have known that his associates were planning to violate the child labor laws? Whether Spielberg intentionally turned a blind eye to the illegal hiring of children or was too busy to keep himself informed, his behavior did not reflect well on him" (244). One defense argument even suggested that Spielberg's very attachment to this project lent hiring child actors a veil of legitimacy: Surely with this coproducer, all child involvement must be assumed (by those crew not responsible for the subterfuge) to be entirely above board? Even worse was the response Spielberg's attorneys made to the wrongful death suit filed by the children's parents: "Spielberg is informed and believes and thereon alleges that at the time and place of the events complained of, plaintiffs [the Chen and Le families] . . . were not exercising ordinary care, caution or prudence to prevent the injuries sustained . . . and that, therefore, the injuries alleged were proximately caused by the negligence or comparative negligence of the plaintiffs" (quoted by McBride 2010, 347–348). Though this accusation that the parents were to blame did not succeed, even more astonishing is the further rebuttal made by Warner Bros. (which also did not succeed): "If the plaintiffs suffered or sustained any loss, damage or injury . . . the risk, if any risk there was, was knowingly assumed by the decedent, Renee Shin-Yi Chen" (quoted by McBride, 348). This bears reiteration in plain English: Warners is here claiming that six-year-old Renee was responsible for her own death on set and knowingly took the risk.

Spielberg is generally a squeaky-clean figure who keeps Hollywood scandal at arm's length. When we think of the outrages of 1980s cinema, it is narratives of excess such as the *Heaven's Gate* or *Bonfire of the Vanities* stories we remember, or tales of individual extremity, triumph, or hubris such as Julia Phillips's or Don Simpson's personal and production excesses. The *Twilight Zone* story has none of the rock-and-roll glamour of these volcanic failures, even given the larger-than-life figure of Landis at its center. It is shocking and sordid, and the death of Morrow usually overshadows that of these two obscure children. It is, nevertheless, an important context for those more successful and famous child performers, and child-focused narratives, discussed in this book. Risk—at its mildest and its deadliest—remains a significant framework for understanding the work of children in film. Every gesture, utterance, and luminous screen look borne out and played out by these child actors must still be read in the context of high-end filmmaking as a high-stakes industrial process within which adults will push working lives as hard as they can, compromising the safety of those who cannot consent.

3

Boyhood and the Child's Alien Body

E.T. the Extra-Terrestrial and *Close Encounters of the Third Kind*

Steven Spielberg is an intensely embodied filmmaker. Bodies feature centrally in his exploitation-tinged visceral universe. They are threatened, celebrated, and damaged as malleable puppets of narrative invention and spectacle. Spielberg is a director of somatic as well as sentimental pain—and pleasure—though his public profile is of a family-friendly populist, pulling the strings of heart and soul. But more than this, his films think about morality via the body, and the spiritual/soulful/mindful self's relationship to its body. This chapter and chapter 4 will explore how Spielberg's corporeal focus is largely staged across children's bodies, most frequently boys' bodies. Therefore, since boy characters are central to these popular stories, it is boy actors who are most employed. Sometimes Spielberg's characters find themselves in the wrong body (the child-adult, for instance, or the nonhuman child), but that is for discussion later. Here I am most interested in children who have almost come to epitomize Spielberg's discourse on ideal and also troubled childhoods. Two boys in particular, one organic-"real," the other cyber-robotic, play out the multiple resonances of idea-rich cinematic bodies: David (from *A.I. Artificial Intelligence*) and Elliott (from *E.T. the Extra-Terrestrial*) articulate the contradictions of children's fleshly identities to mass audiences. Then there is E.T. him-/itself, a 900-year-old (possibly agendered) alien whose bodily relationship with a boy also helps to tell Spielberg's child story.

These chapters ask, what is a boy, as envisaged by Spielberg's films? Like the puppet Pinocchio, robot David's quest is to become a "real boy," while the working title for *E.T.* right through casting and early production was *A Boy's Life*.[1] Through these films Spielberg negotiates, thinks through, and sometimes idealizes what "boyness" might mean for popular contemporary cinema. Both *E.T.* and *A.I.* are commonly read as humanistic parables, but these films also present children as the focus of acute corporeal-emotive anxieties. Sentiment is visceral, but it is also surprisingly often sidestepped by a rather darker filmmaker (that Nasty Stephen we encountered previously) not afraid to threaten children or make them suffer. The tangible physicality of tears within and without Spielberg's hybrid melodramas is evidence of a (not-so-debased) strain of sentiment—a highly viscerally affective sentiment—that runs through his work like mineral veins through rock.

Tears, then, are prime evidence that despite moving away from the "adult" schlock-thrill of *Duel* and *Jaws*, bodily response and its insistent fluids continue to betray Spielberg as a full-blooded shock director, milking responses from actors and audiences. As I have argued elsewhere (Williams 2020), *Jaws* dangles its children (again, primarily boys) as juicy bait, and—at least for the first half of the film—it is the potential for the child to be physically dismembered, even eaten, that drives its visceral thrills. From the get-go Spielberg was using children to tell stories of all sorts of bodily undoing, from physical threat to emotional incontinence. One British newspaper made the link quite clear in 1982 in the wake of *E.T.*: "Having scared the pants off a few million people with a plastic shark in *Jaws*, Steven Spielberg set himself the task of reducing a few million more to red-eyed wrecks blubbing into hankies over the fate of a small bug-eyed foam rubber creation from outer space" (Thirkell 1982, 18). In *Close Encounters of the Third Kind* and *E.T.*—the primary subjects of this chapter—it is children who set this in motion: they have particularly leaky bodies, and we have already found Spielberg's actors to be seasoned weepers. Their eyes are not so much windows to the soul as orifices of feelingful performance.

Close Encounters and *E.T.* also press the audience's bodily buttons just as, for *Time* magazine's 1977 report on the director, *Jaws* had "mercilessly attack[ed] . . . the audience's nerves, quickly establish[ing] its director as the reigning boy genius of American cinema" (Rich 1977, 34). As well as shredded nerves, gallons of tears would be shed in the wake of *Close Encounters* and *E.T.* These films present childhood through a variety of guises, asking questions of the body's limits, of its humanity (or not), and of children's relationships to their own bodies. The boy child's bodies in *E.T.* and *A.I.* are both transformed and transformational, target and creation of idealization, power, and desire. But they are also "fleshed out" by boy performers pushing their acting to formulate partially self-authored visions of boyhood. I will turn to artificial children in chapter 4, thinking about David the robot boy alongside the organic children of *Ready Player One*, who become digital avatars in the narrative's gaming landscape. In this chapter, however, I will analyze the child in relation to the alien and *as* alien, folding into the discussion young Barry Guiler (Cary Guffey) in *Close Encounters*, as well as the six-year-old girls who performed the aliens at that film's epic conclusion. *E.T.* and *Close Encounters* are foundational films in definitions of childhood in contemporary cinema. Affective responses and supposedly innate qualities such as wonder, innocence, and guilelessness are attached to the child image and the child's perceived ability to experience and touch realities inaccessible to (most) adults. This chapter discusses boyhood according to Spielberg, and the curious defamiliarization of what we think we know about the Spielbergian child through his unsettling alignment of child with alien.

Wonder Boys (and Girls) in *Close Encounters of the Third Kind*

Recall Spielberg telling Gene Siskel that the vision of Barry in *Close Encounters* is his career "signature image": the little boy "opening the door and standing in that beautiful yet awful light, just like fire coming through the doorway. And he's very small, and it's a very large door" (Ebert and Siskel 1991, 72). As performed by four-year-old Cary Guffey, Barry epitomizes vulnerable childhood, an image and trope that are repeated across a number of films: very young children, toddlers, or preschoolers, exquisitely framed and acutely idealized, emblematizing wondrousness. A lot of symbolic work is achieved through these usually supporting or background small roles. Some are iconically "Spielbergian": Sean Brody (Jay Mello) singing to himself on the beach of *Jaws* amid the panic as Alex Kintner (Jeffrey Voorhees) is consumed, or the girl in the red coat in *Schindler's List* (Oliwia Dabrowska). The child wanders through a baffling landscape, its diminutive frame rendering the danger swirling around them ever more menacing, the alien stranger and the adult world more alien. This might be characterized as innocence (that contested term) in relief, with the child held separate at a moment before darkness descends. It is more accurately a form of distance marked by incomprehension. But this also works in reverse: in *Close Encounters*, proximity to the alien also serves to make the child strange.

Close Encounters of the Third Kind tells the story of benign aliens visiting earth. People are abducted: young Barry is enticed from his house by the initially menacing alien light (which he finds playful) and seems forever lost; family man Roy Neary (Richard Dreyfuss) encounters the aliens too, becoming obsessed with what he has seen. Neary's incredulous family leaves him, but he pursues the alien promise, eventually participating in a grandiose "close encounter" set-piece in which a gargantuan mothership lands, returns its abducted human specimens (including Barry), and takes Roy away to unknown universal adventures with childlike (and child-performed) aliens. The wondrous child—the actual child

Barry, and Neary as child-adult—is, then, the perfect playmate for the alien. In chapter 8 I will discuss Neary as monstrously rather than awesomely infantilized by this alien affinity. Roy and Barry converge in the "encounter" tableau wher curious humans confront (in Vivian Sobchack's terms) aliens presented as benign, redeeming child figures (1991, 16–17). The human narrative pathway to this galactic meeting is, then, through two routes: the male child as innate innocent, and the radicalized adult male rediscovering his inner child through alien-endowed "innocence." *Close Encounters* is an adult-focused film featuring an adult as neo-child, and a child going where adults fear to tread. By contrast—as we will see—*E.T.* is a child-sized film featuring a child as parent to an alien innocent, and a child-alien as parent to the "true" child.

Let us not forget that Spielberg initially responds to Siskel's question (asking which film, which image, would be saved if all the others were thrown out) with "It's kind of like saying, 'Which of your four kids do you like the most?'" (1991, 72). Films are children too. The apposite linking of child with light in the "master image" statement has been extensively cited, for example, by James Kendrick, who in *Darkness in the Bliss-Out* reads the door-opening as part of "the invasion of science fiction by the horror genre" (2014, 59). But the force of Spielberg's words to Siskel equally apprehends scale: the diminutive child encountering not just the very large house door but the monumental alien array. The mothership (when we finally see it at the film's climax) was designed to appear a mile wide, all the better to dwarf the aliens who made it; it references all-too-human landscapes—the lights of Manhattan, the array of the San Fernando Valley as seen from the crest of Mulholland Drive. The "beautiful yet awful light" may be a signal statement, but here I am more interested in that addendum, "And he's very small." The child framework has persisted as part of the promotional story since the film's original release—the press notes state, "'Close Encounters of the Third Kind' was filmed under the leadership of a talented team of experienced artists with major successes to their credit, yet characterized for the most part by a surprising youthfulness."[2]

This has persisted as the primary mode of understanding the film's work, its production, meanings, and legacy. In the promotional interview *Steven Spielberg: 30 Years of Close Encounters*, the director said of everybody involved in the film (except for the military personnel), "We *were* kids, and we made this picture in the spirit of childhood and believing in things that don't make sense, that only children believe in because it doesn't have to make sense for a child to deeply believe in something."[3] This partly justifies Barry's impulse to follow the aliens, but there is also the question of his mother's pull back into the domestic. Elsewhere (Williams 2017) I have discussed Jillian Guiler's (Melinda Dillon's) failure to keep her small son safe, in an analysis of the uneasy dysfunctional and recalcitrant mothers across Spielberg's films. Jillian cannot keep her house secure, and—to frame his loss in the terms of Emma Wilson's incisive 2003 study—Barry becomes one of cinema's missing children.[4] In a rerun of the statement to

Gene Siskel describing his "master image," articulated afresh in this 2007 documentary, Spielberg interprets Barry's escape as submission to an irresistible, playful magnetism (see figure 1 in the introduction). This, then, is an optimistic curiosity, which is both era-specific and politically loaded:

> The image that I've always taken sort of to bed with me at night, if I ever flash on an image, from *Close Encounters*—I don't have to think of it—it thinks of itself. And the image that always comes into my mind is when the little boy opens the door. And all that orange light, yellow light, poured across him, when I designed the shot and when I wrote it in the script. For me that was very symbolic of what only a child can do [which] is to trust the light. You know, open a door, when an adult would run and hide and say don't open the door—lock the door, there's things outside we don't understand, things that could kill us or change us. But the optimism of childhood in opening that door. And light being the presence of everything . . . that light was something that that boy wanted to know more about. And so for me thematically *Close Encounters* is all about children opening the doors, onto beautiful sources of light. 2007—twenty-first century—sadly people have a different interpretation of opening doors. But back in the seventies, to open the door to a curiosity was a safe experience.[5]

This is a huge cultural burden to place on the small shoulders of Barry. Political idealism, a questing spirit (a literalization of "enlightenment"), and indeed door-opening in its widest sense all converge on "true" children and their adult imitators. Of course, this was still a moment when deploying a child to tell such a story could be a radical rather than a reactionary maneuver. As we saw in chapter 1, the trajectory from 1970s celebration to 1980s denigration can be traced through critical attitudes toward the image of the child and the director-as-child, articulated most clearly by Pauline Kael, who said in 1985 that Spielberg was responsible for "an infantilization of the culture" (Rosenfield 1985) though previously it had been precisely on childish terms that she lauded *Close Encounters* in 1977. For that earlier Kael, *Close Encounters* was "the most innocent of all technological-marvel movies":

> This film has retained some of the wonder and bafflement we feel when we first go into a planetarium: we ooh and aah at the vastness, and at the beauty of the mystery. The film doesn't overawe us, though, because it has a child's playfulness and love of surprises. . . . This vision would be *too* warm and soul-satisfying if it weren't for the writer-director Steven Spielberg's sceptical, let's-try-it-on spirit. . . . The immense charm of *Close Encounters* comes from the fact that, for all its scale and expense (nineteen million dollars), this is a young man's movie—Spielberg is still under thirty—and there's not a sour thought in it. (1977, 174)

Frank Rich in *Time* similarly lauded the "sweet" *Close Encounters* as a celebration "of children's dreams": "When the earthlings and the visitors at last communicate in the film, bellowing 'Hello' to each other in bursts of light and music, it is like hearing a child speak for the first time. . . . [A]t the end of *Close Encounters*, the audience is sitting with him in the lap of the universe" (1977, 36). What is remarkable here is not just the wholesale marriage of childlike director to child-identified subject matter, but that the very terms that convey praise here would later become key terms of criticism: "innocence," "play," "warmth." Kael's conclusion, rendered as a compliment (Spielberg "may be the only director with technical virtuosity ever to make a transcendentally sweet movie" [1977, 181]) could by 1982 have been repeated almost word for word as condemnation, as the connotation of "sweet" acquired an era-specific cultural poison.

"Play" is another term that shifts and warps depending on who is doing it, and when. "Playfulness" was lauded as a keynote of the director's signature style in the mid-1970s, denoting a fresh and inventive creativity. Even Spielberg's relationship to his production equipment was articulated through play early on. An article in *American Cinematographer* from 1978 features an image of Spielberg and Dreyfuss poring over the film's train set,[6] but it echoes that anxiety referenced earlier that here is a boy director having fun with some very expensive kit: "Looking about twelve years old . . . Spielberg himself favors bigger toys—such as the largest interior set ever constructed" (Lightman 1978, 41). There is, then, a conflation of playfulness between the story itself (Barry's child's play, the playful aliens, Neary's toy trains and model-making) and the work of a boy director playing with awesomely powerful filmmaking kit.[7] The film was almost universally reviewed as the work of the thirty-year-old (sometimes twenty-nine-year-old) "wonder boy who directed *Jaws*" (F. Barker 1978; see also Miller 1977; Hinton 1977; Coleman 1978).

Playfulness matched by attention to the apparatus of play runs through *Close Encounters* and is first identified within the story through little Barry. Spielberg's films spend a lot of time in toy-strewn bedrooms: *E.T.* is largely staged inside bedrooms and their adjacent toy closet, while *A.I.* and *Empire of the Sun* also develop their stories inside boys' private play spaces. Toys seem to come alive before Barry does: the first view of him is of his beatific sleeping face. Spielberg is not alone in this. The sleeping child is widely reified as the epitome of innocence across numerous cultural idealizations of childhood, as if unconsciousness had assuaged the soul of sin associated with awareness. This is a child whose capacity for mischief has been immobilized. It is hard to resist the notion that here the most innocent-looking child is the child who appears dead. As Barry sleeps, the toys wake up, risking association with another kind of film (more *Child's Play* than *Toy Story*). First his monkey performs by bashing cymbals (as if to prefigure Cary Guffey "performing" Barry), then everything else with a motor or a battery or clockwork innards comes alive. Barry, who soon awakens, responds to this not as nursery horror but with grave curiosity. Guffey's performance is enacted in staged steps—a look, a smile, a reaction—as if he is being pulled by the director's strings behind the camera (he is). Karen Lury discusses the prevailing notion that children cannot act but can only react, and this premise founds Spielberg's direction of Guffey: "I'd play tricks on him, as all directors would. I had large presents that I would slowly open off camera, one ribbon at a time, I'd take the paper off slowly, then take the lid off the box, then take the cellophane wrapper and spread it back, and reach my hand in and pull out a police car, with the siren going. He would react to that, and I'd take that close-up and patch it into the shot where he's reacting to the sky opening up" (Powers 1978, 50).

In his illuminating book on the experience of acting in *Close Encounters*, Bob Balaban (who plays the interpreter David Laughlin) confirms that the director staged things for the boy to look at and react to off-camera, including having the makeup man "dress up in a giant bear costume and wait to surprise Cary at the bottom of the stairs" (2002, 68). Knowing this, the more one looks at Guffey's performance, the more it seems to be knitted together from unconnected reactions, though Spielberg's account of this, in which he is also dressed as the Easter Bunny, stresses—confusingly—that though the dressing up "was a trick" to elicit a visible emotional attitude from the boy, "the reaction was pure and honest" (McBride 2010, 285). Occasionally, Spielberg claims that Cary "brought most of that performance to the movie himself" (Powers 1978, 50) and that this "didn't come from playing a trick on him. I told him what was on the other side of the door, and what it looked like. That all came out of Cary imagining how he would react to seeing something like that" (51). By this account, then, Guffey is both an active and a reactive actor, but these moments still appear as part of a patchwork of tableau and response. The strategy of befriending also comes into play: when asked in 1978 how he got the boy to react so well, Spielberg replied, "By adopting him; we were inseparable for three months. I knew what he liked and didn't and how to get him to smile. I would describe what he was reacting to and he would make pictures from my words and react to those pictures" (Heathwood 1978, 379). Barry, then, is more symbol than character, while Guffey is more an animated presenter of elemental "childness" than an active author of his own performance, as Spielberg's older child stars were later to become.[8] What exactly, then, is Cary's agency in this performance? Where does Spielberg end and Cary begin?

Two small boys were initially auditioned for the role, and both played out this first scene to help Spielberg make a choice (Morton 2007, 136). The boy who did not get the role was a "willful, rambunctious tot who refused to do anything anyone told him to" (183), not a good "fit" for direction. By contrast Cary was, in the words of Melinda Dillon, "this wondrous, quiet, soft, attentive, *listening* child" (183). The character of Barry is of course more independent than this: he follows the aliens rather than listening to his mother. Cary, then, obeys direction to mimic Barry's willfulness, and he ventures downstairs, taking the first step toward dangerous freedom. The aliens outside have messed things up inside; domesticity has come awry while the mother sleeps upstairs—the fridge has emptied itself onto the floor, the dog door swings. When Jillian is finally awakened by Barry's toys invading her room, she—too late—sees him running away across the lawn, giggling. For me, this image of the illuminated house, fixed to the earth as the tiny boy runs into darkness and "lostness" under the wheeling stars, is as iconic as the big door/small child frame "master" shot. Barry is then figured in various perilous situations: running down a dark lane (like Dorothy on the yellow brick road), meeting a feral family with their oddly passive children, nearly being hit by a car. Jillian pursues, but Barry continues to worm out of her grasp, shouting simple greetings to the aliens flying down the road ("Hello—I'm here," and "Ice Cream!" to the cone-shaped spacecraft). The sequences in which the aliens seduce Barry into following them are unsettling because (at this stage in the film) they might yet signify menace: Barry giggles at frankly threatening cloud formations foaming across the sky and dances in delight as their awful light fingers its way into the house.

When the aliens return to entice Barry away for a second time, Jillian again fails to keep him safe. Frantic about the invasion, she is powerless to stop it: despite incessant door- and window-locking, the leaky house conspires against any attempt to hold the child. At this stage in the film Barry's freedom to delight in and face the strange seems itself alien and casts an othering shadow across the wayward child. The boy is finally successfully abducted through the dog door, with Cary being pulled in two different directions as the aliens (in reality, members of the film crew) draw him out while Jillian/Melinda tries to claw him back in. Watching the scene (which "really looks scary, even without music and editing"), Bob Balaban sees "something out there" yanking the child hard through the door: "Sweat pours from Melinda's forehead as she desperately pulls on Cary, and whatever is outside just keeps pulling harder. 'Try harder, Melinda,' Steven quietly urges from off-camera. Little Cary's body is being pulled in both directions like a piece of taffy" (2002, 68). This is an intense scene for child actor and character alike. Barry's special qualities make him a choice specimen for abduction, and the snatching methods are relentless. Eventually—and for the shooting of scene—Jillian must let go as her house (vacuum cleaner, cooker, fireplace) conspires against her and the aliens win: Barry is gone.

The film then shifts focus to Neary's family, and later to Neary leaving his children and pairing up with Jillian, the mother now in pursuit of her lost child: a quest ensues that takes narrative precedence. Astonishingly, the original script did not include the child snatching, since Barry seemingly "served no purpose"; Spielberg even "toyed briefly with the idea of cutting him" (Morton 2007, 150). The writers Hal Barwood and Matthew Robbins suggested to Spielberg that abduction would both strengthen the mother's role and also "give the film an incredible emotional kick in the final sequence . . . and mother and child have a tear-filled reunion" (150–151).[9] When Barry toddles out of the mothership at the film's climax, he does so accompanied by a surge of John Williams's most melodramatic scoring. A child of limited vocabulary, Barry waves and says "Goodbye!" as the ship takes off. Indeed, his inarticulacy is one of the keys to his "innocence": of casting Guffey, Spielberg said, "I wanted a boy about two years shy of being able to tell his parents what he experiences in the privacy of his growing up. So I needed someone with bright, wonderous eyes and a beatific look" (Powers 1978, 50). It seems to me that we focus on the look in one way (Barry as image; innocence signified), but not in the other—what Barry himself is presumed to see. Of course, on one level we cannot know this. But is Spielberg casting children whom he believes convey an inner child life, perhaps even something he does not understand within the "privacy of his growing up"? Is this another nuance of the child taking (back) agency over the role—even if Barry does not articulate it and Cary never remembers it? Barry's is the last human face seen in the film and the last human voice heard (he calls "Bye!" to the mothership)—as if Spielberg was determined to give the child the final word.

Of course there are other children in *Close Encounters*, but none as emblematic as little Barry. Roy Neary's three children perform the agonized heart of their crumbling family, as I will discuss later in relation to their father's breakdown and redemption. But other key child performers in *Close Encounters* have been specifically overlooked and yet are entirely central. Three different types of aliens appear in the film's climactic scene. A spindly limbed alien first emerges from the mothership, raising its arms in what might yet be a horror image. Some of the human onlookers run away, but those who remain steady meet the next visitors: a group of child-sized aliens with long, tapered fingers, who walk from the ship in a sequence edited choppily as if interrupted by the shutter of a still camera (Jillian is indeed taking Instamatic photos from the sidelines). These aliens mill around and stand in a rather untidy group encountering the humans, child-coded in both their physical uncertainty and their otherworldliness. Roy is led into the mothership by a crowd of them (an inverted Pied Piper image), while Barry, now back with his mother, simply looks on, with matching shots continuing to maintain an equivalence between the small boy and the alien child figures. Finally, a larger alien appears, exchanging hand signals with the human über-scientist Claude Lacombe (François Truffaut).

Some of these aliens were performed by children. Spielberg wanted the extraterrestrials to match first-person accounts of those who claim close encounter experiences, in which the visitors are described almost universally as small humanoids (Morton 2007, 143). The director toyed with using trained apes, or adults of small stature, but in the end the only people able to provide the "sleek, tapered look mentioned in most encounter reports" were "delicate and petite" children. A group of six- and seven-year-old girls from dancing schools local to Mobile, Alabama (where the film was location shooting), were hired for their age and size, and were paid twenty-five dollars per day. As Spielberg put it, "The kids in leotards were mostly little black girls. Boys are tough and stand stiffly, but girls are much more poised and graceful" (Powers 1978, 48). The age here is quite

FIGURE 5 Young girl dancers perform as higher beings in *Close Encounters of the Third Kind.*

precise: whereas Guffey needed to be young enough to emblematize "beatific" semi-preverbality, these alien performers had to be both old enough to take direction and small enough to fit into ready-made and uniform-sized tiny costumes (Balaban 2002, 46). Early in preproduction Spielberg was casting young girls to roller-skate through the final scene as floating extraterrestrials, shot from the ankles upward (33); they were also hoisted on wires in order to hover and fly like Peter Pan in a pantomime. Both ideas were eventually dropped; in the final film, the children just totter down a ramp.

Crucially, they needed to be visually interpretable as aliens, not minors. Separate from human adults in stature and wondrous ambience, these are the inquisitive outriders of a sophisticated advanced species, and therefore perhaps as culturally removed as it is possible to be from the (disempowered) small children of color who are actually inside the costumes. This is achieved by them wearing heads that, as Balaban puts it, "look like giant fetuses and are really quite frightening; some kids start crying as soon as they see them" (46). Heavier heads contained radio-controlled eyes, but these could only be worn by bigger children (five boys were cast) who were thought to be strong enough to support tech-intense prosthetics (61, 106). However, it is primarily girls in the finished film; the boys sporting the bigger heads got too tired and were dropped.[10] Still, as the released film stands (even in its many rerelease incarnations), the girl/aliens are unidentifiable as gendered, or indeed as differentiated individuals (figure 5). Kael posits that these extraterrestrials "appear to have evolved beyond sex" (1977, 174). In a cultural universe in which femininity is identified as sex-specific and masculinity as neutral (males are just people, just as white is coded neutral while Black is racially othered), there is something heartening about the fact that here young Black females perform universal, postgendered, higher beings, even if their all-too-earthly child realities fall short of this.

Not so the slightly larger mechanical alien with which Lacombe exchanges hand gestures, which was designed by Carlo Rambaldi and used for the final encounter. This being has a visibly moving Adam's apple,[11] and since this biological feature is more prominent in men, one must read this singular, communicative alien as male. It is also called Puck in some interview materials (though not named as such in the film), the more familiar name of Robin Goodfellow, Shakespeare's mischievous fairy from *A Midsummer Night's Dream* who until recently was invariably performed by a male actor.[12] Spielberg explicitly infantilized this figure, stating: "It had musculature operating under a pliable substance that's like baby skin. I kissed it on the cheek, and it was like kissing an infant. We had to study the facial reactions of a child smiling and then pull the right levers in the right sequence to allow the extraterrestrial to smile in a posthuman way. That took a week" (Powers 1978, 48). Were the film made at a more advanced stage of CGI effects (such as *A.I.*'s later production, with its entirely digital future mecha), the aliens would not necessarily be gendered at all or sensorily babyish. Nor would they be human performances, or mechanical child replicas, but instead would be replaced by the performance of digital design. *Ready Player One* would later give an even more radical iteration of child-as-digital-idealization.

Spielberg felt that the audience for *Close Encounters* needed an on-screen surrogate to help them read these strange beings "appropriately." He did this by deploying an adult actor's fondness for children. The viewer's way in to perceiving the aliens as benign superchildren was to be explicitly carried through Truffaut's character—and it was of course Truffaut who had said, "You are wonderful with *keeds*, you must do a movie with *keeds* . . . You are the child." (Sragow 2000, 113). Spielberg effectively replied to this in his tribute following Truffaut's death: "There was a child inside François Truffaut" (Spielberg 1985, 40; in publicity in 1978 he had already argued that Truffaut was "as innocent as his films" [Powers 1978, 51]). This child-brokered rapport between adults extended to Spielberg's direction: as Balaban reported from the set, "He knows how Truffaut likes little children," so extrapolated that "the audience's reactions to the extraterrestrials will be largely determined by Truffaut's reactions. He wants Truffaut to think of the extraterrestrials as little children" (2002, 55). Of course they *are* little children, and accounts suggest that Truffaut was as interested in the dancer-actors as his character is by the idea of childlike E.T.'s. In Truffaut's obituary, Spielberg wrote of the French filmmaker's child focus on Puck (whom Truffaut named), of directing Truffaut as he would a child actor, and (without any sense of the potentially strange connotations of what he was reporting) of Truffaut's fascination with the girl performers.[13] As Spielberg described it, "He would come on to the set just to watch the 50 little kids put on their extraterrestrial costumes and have their e.t. heads put on" (1985, 41). In the midst of this idealization of the child form as a higher being and of superconsciousness as "innocent" or even post-evil, Spielberg manages, for the moment, to escape any charge in popular reception that he is utilizing the child figure sentimentally.

There were also considerable discomforts for the young performers. Ray Morton reports that one hundred were initially recruited, but soon fifty had dropped out because conditions were "rough on the little girls" (2007, 189). By the end of the alien shoot only thirty-five were left: those heads that Truffaut took such delight in watching them don were unventilated, and crew had to "cut holes into the mouths so the children could breathe."[14] Because the eyeholes were in the wrong place, the children kept bumping into each other and had to look out through the nostrils. Mobile, Alabama, in summertime is a tough location for regulating temperature; in June and July 1976 it was punishingly hot, even more so on the set, and hotter again inside the mothership, so that Spielberg worried that the children would "get baked," as Balaban inimitably puts it (2002, 62). The masks could only be worn for ten minutes at a time. And not only were the costumes made before the actors were cast, but they also failed to make it easy for the children to go to the toilet while wearing them; regular bathroom breaks interrupted takes.[15] It is not surprising, then, that, unlike the "quiet, soft, attentive, *listening*" Cary Guffey, the troupe of girl aliens constantly misbehaved—throwing food around, disco hustling in mid-take, and pulling off their rubber alien hands to use as weapons (67, 63). Watching the ethereal end sequence of *Close Encounters* with knowledge of these mischievous girls in mind is rather like watching Dorothy being greeted by the Lullaby League once one knows about the Munchkin actors' raucous romping. That said, the girls eventually learned to take direction and shaped up into honed professionals.[16] *Close Encounters* thus utilizes child performances iconically but does not present seminal examples of the child actor's craft, as would later films featuring children and alien encounters.

Elliott/E.T. in *E.T. the Extra-Terrestrial*

The next film in which Spielberg posited an equivalence between child and alien came five years later, developing some of the same questions, using some of the same alien designers and crew, and containing one of the most celebrated child performances in film history. *E.T. the Extra-Terrestrial* remains hugely successful by any account and was one of the highest-grossing films of the 1980s. The plentiful press materials it generated hang their analyses on three hooks: tears and sentiment, the director's youth, and the film's unprecedented profitability (box office and merchandise). But the film is also (and perhaps despite these hooks) still critically celebrated, regularly cropping up on "greatest movie" polls. Both versions of the American Film Institute's 100 best American movies lists (originally titled *100 Years . . . 100 Movies*, published in 1998 and 2007) contained more films by Spielberg than by any other director (five films in each list), with *E.T.* twenty-fifth in 1998 and twenty-fourth in 2007. When the British filmmaker Mark Cousins showed a sample of five films to the children of an Iraqi village who had never before been to the cinema, *E.T.* was the only English-language film chosen (see *The First Movie*, UK 2009). *The New York Times Essential Library: Children's Movies* states boldly, "This may be the greatest children's movie ever made" (Nichols 2003, 90).

E.T. begins with the small, scuttling shape of the extraterrestrial lost in the woods like so many fairy-tale children before him, as his parent-mothership departs with all his alien kin. It then presents ten-year-old Elliott in the thick of squabbling family life, the middle child who cannot join in the games of his teen brother, Mike (Robert MacNaughton), and friends, and is equally shut out of the dyad of mother Mary (Dee Wallace) and younger sister Gertie (Drew Barrymore). Uneasy boy power games (which we will see again in *A.I.*) send Elliott out into the garden running errands for the older children, where he meets the feral alien. Child and alien befriend each other: as the lonely child of separated parents, Elliott finds in E.T.—according to a wealth of critical interpretations ever since—a surrogate father, buddy, and angel/savior all in one. But these are also mutual relationships. E.T. is no doubt also a child figure, diminutive and infantile even if "he" is also advanced and ancient, as well as an offspring surrogate whom Elliott can parent. How, then, does this reflection reframe the child that is Elliott *as* alien, and what might this mean?

E.T. is first and foremost a child's-point-of-view film told from Elliott's perspective. This is an important form and location for cultural fantasies for and about children and is a genre delineator for Cary Bazalgette and Terry Staples, who write: "Children's films can be defined as offering mainly or entirely a child's point of view" (1995, 96). This may make them consequently rare; as Phillip Lopate puts it in a 1997 meditation titled "When the 'I' in a Film Is a Child's," "Serious narratives about the inner lives of children tend to be rare on-screen, for obvious commercial reasons. Studios shy away from projects without marquee names, and the days of the child star are over." In *E.T.* Spielberg was able to negotiate these commercial concerns by being willing to work with a small budget to minimize risk; this was also one of his first films starring mostly relatively unknown actors, or those with a less than starry working profile. Marina Warner sees the child's-point-of-view film as celebrating "the child's superior wisdom"; through a higher "vantage point of innocence and the greater access to fantasy," the child's privileged view causes adult viewers "to see their own absurdity and hardness" (1993, 43–44). While this provides ample opportunity for comedic/cute scenes of secrecy, learning, and friendship, the premise in *E.T.* is an extreme version of Warner's model: here a child is the first person on planet earth to have such intimate contact with an intergalactic being, and that child is E.T.'s prime example of the human race. Few stories set out the child as "superiorly wise" quite as expertly as *E.T.*; Elliott and later his siblings leapfrog over adult humans while reaching for the stars. As the story unfolds, Elliott's inability to keep E.T.'s existence secret only shores up his power: his emotional and epistemological superiority first elevates him above older children and then above adults. His brother Mike and his friends must defer to Elliott's knowledge and secrets, accepting him as a kind of leader. Before revealing E.T. to Mike, Elliott makes his brother and sometime tormenter swear that Elliott has "absolute power."

Children are, then, unevenly wise/ignorant or privileged/disempowered: all the children get to know E.T. before any adults glimpse him, but it is Elliott who is most endearingly wise and knowledgeable of the king-children. Romantic child philosophy might have determined growing up through childhood as a sliding scale of fallenness, but here the younger Gertie and the older Mike are less powerful than Elliott, whose ten years seem to make him a perfect balance of capability/tenaciousness and wonder/openness. *E.T.* does not then subscribe to the common Romantic view that the closer one gets to adulthood, the less insightful one becomes. Adults also defer to Elliott: when E.T. is finally discovered by the scientific-military authorities, a benign (human) father figure emerges who comes to complete the family group: Keys (Peter Coyote) aligns himself with Elliott ("He came to me too. I've been wishing for this since I was ten years old") but acknowledges that this young boy "did the best that anybody could do. I'm glad he met you first." Throughout the story Elliott, as focus of point of view and child authority, is privileged over all adults, including his mother, his father (entirely absent for the whole story), and this sensitive, usurping surrogate father (Keys).

But the film requires not merely identification with Elliott's emotional state or narrative predicament—it goes further than Warner's model in actualizing the child's point of view in a number of ways. Sharing point of view usually involves a leap of identification that reinforces a relationship of "likeness" between viewer and player/character. That the to-be-identified-with protagonist is a boy means that all non-boy viewers (adults; non-males) must cross-identify if Elliott is to "be" them on-screen, as their fantasy representative or surrogate. That Elliott has an extraordinary adventure simply makes the leap of identificatory faith a little wilder, as with all fantasy scenarios. However, as the eulogistic reception materials evidence, few were able to resist the lure of walking in Elliott's shoes and entering the story through the lens of his boy's eyes. Still, Spielberg goes further, taking point of view seriously cinematographically. Of course, literal point of view is rare in cinema—1940s film noir experimented with it, particularly with *Lady in the Lake* (1947), in which the camera perspective is entirely that of the protagonist/narrator Philip Marlowe (played by Robert Montgomery, who is only seen when caught in mirror reflections), or the first part of *Dark Passage* (1947), prior to the revelation that the "first-person" eyes through which we see and with which we move are Humphrey Bogart's. Far more common, of course, are the everyday point-of-view shots that align viewers with characters via over-the-shoulder camera positions. *E.T.* takes a more wholeheartedly child-centered approach. Typically, camera height and the level of shots in Western cinema are gauged to capture the upper bodies and faces of adults. Spielberg wanted to immerse his viewers inside the (shorter) world of children, so he had his director of photography Allen Daviau lower the camera to make the whole world of the film Elliott-high. In direct point-of-view shots (from Elliott's eyes), over-the-shoulder shots, and reverse shots from the perspective of the similarly diminutive E.T. or other children, the camera stays at child-height level. The shooting of *E.T.* is then determined by the size of the performer Henry Thomas. This is in marked contrast to the iconic shot of little Barry in *Close Encounters*, dwarfed by the doorframe and diminished by the dazzling bright light beyond him, when adult-gauged cinematography serves to make the child look affectingly tiny.

This cinematographic stricture is not so constrained as to render *E.T.* an art film, though adults are seldom seen clearly, particularly for the first two-thirds of the film, when the only visible adult face is that of Mary, who is sometimes seen through more conventional, adult-gauged framing and more often in family contexts in wide shots that incorporate all the children. Other adults are cut off, with the higher-than-children parts of their upper bodies lost beyond the top of the frame. Spielberg has said, "I never wanted to show grown-ups in the movie until the very end. I wanted to suggest them like in a *Tom & Jerry* cartoon where, when the mom comes in, you only see her from the waist down. . . . I didn't want that world contaminated with anything beyond a young teenager's point of view" (Sunshine 2012, 15). Occasionally Mary—who has been read as a disempowered, childlike figure herself—maneuvers to child level, such as when she reads Gertie a bedtime story. As *E.T.* reaches its endgame, the alien sickens, and biohazard-protection-clad adults (the military, scientists, probably also the FBI, though the film fudges their identities into a totalized adult "them") invade. The film reframes to capture the full-grown dominance of adult power, with diminutive E.T. and his symbiotically sick human twin, Elliott, shrunken on small beds. But when E.T. rises from the dead and the children mastermind his escape and bid to rejoin his people, once more the film reframes its scale back down to child proportions, following the bike-riding troupe of teens and preteens taking E.T., carried in a basket like a pet, to a rendezvous with his mothership.

The Symbiotic Body

As a lavishly physical filmmaker who is not averse to using exploitation techniques in the family adventure film, Spielberg is well-grounded in the politics and aesthetics of the popular cinematic body.[17] In *E.T.* and across his wider child stories, children's bodies are used as somatic emotional expressers as well as vehicles of fantasy, often both together. His interest in souls or emotions inside bodies has long been a focus of critical revulsion; tears have shown us that this is no less visceral than body horror. The physicality of those bodies, in performance, speaks to mass audiences and acute cultural anxieties about flesh, minority, and emotion, with children as the focus of corporeal-emotive complexes here. In *E.T.* this is expressed in Elliott's visceral connection to the alien's body—he sickens when E.T. fades, and as E.T. departs, he touches Elliott, proclaiming he will be "right here." In the wash of tears commonly provoked by the film's conclusion, it is easy to forget quite how strangely—corporeally—literal this is.

As we will see later, in *A.I.* identification with David is intensified by his limited understanding of why adult humans let him down so badly. Vivian

Sobchack has argued that *Close Encounters* "valorizes the bourgeois myth of the little, innocent, vulnerable child and transcodes it as a myth of the little, innocent, and benevolent alien—who, however poignantly scrawny, is also awesomely powerful and invulnerable" (1991, 15). *E.T.* and *A.I.* also make the nonhuman stand in for the child, and the child stand in for the nonhuman, though we should ask whether this may be more in service of—surprisingly for Spielberg—an anti-humanism or posthumanism rather than the bourgeois myth of the child. Both films figure the child as a way of framing and addressing those marginalized groups that have appropriated the political sympathies of the science fiction film: cyborgs, aliens, robots. They hierarchize children/aliens against adults, and mecha (*A.I.*'s robots) against orga (*A.I.*'s humans), prioritizing the first as more "authentic" than the second. These other figures are also minors in that, like children, they lack rights and are "less than." "Minor" is then read in relation to the adult's/human's "majority." If a child is deemed to have not *yet* arrived at the moment of legal or sexual responsibility, these nonhuman outsiders will (like Peter Pan) never reach that moment. They are both irresponsible and a-responsible, and available to adult/human whims. This makes them acutely vulnerable: David in *A.I.* is cast into the dark forest and threatened with physical dismemberment and destruction; *E.T.* is strapped onto a high-tech gurney and forensically scrutinized by adult scientists threatening vivisection. The child—traditionally designated less than human, even if sanctified for special qualities—provides a ready pathway to the nonhuman in these most mainstream of popular fictions. So through his exploration of the child, humanist Spielberg does seem surprisingly posthumanist. Or, more likely, a more Spielbergian humanist view would be to say that these are films that, in reading aliens, robots, and children as ultimate formations of the humane, work to subhumanize adults just as they superhumanize children and their alien kin.

Though *E.T.* is a firm and "safe" family favorite, its aesthetic styling and emotive strategies are rooted in horror, and a close look at this almost too-well-known film shows that its alignment of Elliott with the alien does as much to make the boy strange as it does to make the alien familiar. The film's hybrid genre form of melo/sci-fi pivots on the splicing of (lonely/tearful/abandoned) boy and (hyperintelligent/weird/abandoned) alien. Spielberg has an easier time defining (and enjoying/revisiting) cinematic boyhood than girlhood, and *E.T.* establishes a key evocation of boy culture according to Spielberg—primarily the positive, caring version of boyhood borne out by Elliott, though there are also meaner boys here. E.T. becomes incorporated into boy culture in numerous ways: cinematographically through those downscaling shots; induction into human life through play and TV; inhabitation of the toy cupboard, the latter of which had lucrative implications for marketing merchandise to its child audience (quite simply, E.T. looks like a toy, and then becomes one). But the connection between boy and alien also has a surprising somatic focus: Elliott's body is constantly figured in the mise-en-scène as mirroring the alien's, and the two are symbiotically connected (through intoxication and illness). When E.T.'s body is endangered, Elliott feels it. The film's press notes tell us that E.T. jumps when the phone rings, not because he is startled but because Elliott's heart missed a beat.[18] This symbiosis in turn has interesting gender implications: we come to think that E.T. is male partly because we know that Elliott is a boy.

I am, then, most interested in thinking about how this film describes what it is to be a boy child in contemporary America through the alien it/himself (and its/his body). On its original release, spiritual and moral questions became the keynote for much critical reception and academic discussion. However, in the extensive production- and fan-based discussions the body is at the fore. One popular book that provides useful information is *E.T. the Extra-Terrestrial: from Concept to Classic* (Sunshine 2012), a "making of" production history published as part of the film's twentieth-anniversary release, which includes transcriptions of memos and exchanges from the original shooting schedule, including cast and crew reflecting with hindsight on the filmmaking experience. Like other fan-focused publications, the book provides a wealth of production detail. By far the most effort was expended on making the figure of E.T. credible as the living, emoting body of a life-form that is at the same time alien, ancient, and childlike. Because Henry Thomas's virtuoso performance as Elliott needed to be matched by something equally believable as his alien friend, preproduction energies and $1 million of the $10 million budget focused on making E.T. look convincingly alive—the foundation on which the somatic/psychotelepathic relationship between Elliott and E.T. would be built. If David in *A.I.* would be a fleshly boy actor rendered into a simulated boy by makeup and performance, E.T. is a simulation of a life-form rendered credibly fleshly by clever mechanics, costumes, and performance in a predigital moment of practical effects. Fascination with the alien's body in popular discourse generated lively public discussion, ranging from promotional releases hinting at the construction of the E.T. models and costumes, to leaks and secrecy surrounding the character's "look" before the film was released, to mass-produced versions of E.T. sold as toys that then become part of the fantasy lives of children. E.T., then, has many bodies, discussed in various registers. Promotional articles featured extensive discussions of how the alien was made, how much he cost, who controls him (see, for example, Gray 1982; Davis 1982; Wigmore 1982). Yet the "whole" E.T. that audiences came to believe in was a patchwork of differently constructed bodies, some incomplete yet knitted into conviction. Spielberg guided the production illustrator Ed Verreaux through this body-part collage: looking through a pile of books, "He would say, those are neat eyes, that's a neat mouth" (Sunshine 2012, 19). These needed to add up to something that was more than the sum of its parts, as Spielberg makes clear: "I didn't want anybody to think that E.T. was anything other than an actual extraterrestrial. Therefore, it couldn't look like there was somebody in a suit" (19).

Of course there *was* sometimes someone in a suit—two people of short stature "wore" E.T. for some walking shots, as did a child actor born with no legs. A production photograph includes twelve-year-old Matthew De Meritt in a group of the more famous cast members, as part of the "family" of child-performer talent,[19] though more often the "E.T. children" are cited as just the Thomas/Barrymore/MacNaughton triptych.[20] In a profile of De Meritt in *Boy's Life* (the youth magazine for the Boy Scouts of America, of which De Meritt was a member), the actor describes what he brought to the performance, including E.T.'s iconic wobbly walk, which was partly the result of De Meritt having to walk on his hands but also an exaggeration he developed for the role. De Meritt plays E.T. in the ghost costume; E.T. unnoticed by Mary in the "fridge scene"; and the famously drunk E.T., of which he says, "At first Steven wanted me to walk straight . . . but when I swayed back and forth and kicked the beer cans across the floor, he liked it."[21] This may not have the emotional scope of Thomas's tears, but the paired/shared symbiotic drunkenness takes on an even closer tone if read as a relationship between two child actors.

Other actors were also inside E.T. In a moving essay that links watching *E.T.* to the experience of her mother's death, Dodie Bellamy counts all of the unknown inhabitants of the alien suit, taking Elliott's "we are sick" as her cue to read the character as multiple (2009, 102). E.T. is a collective performance and also includes another child actor without legs, Tina Palmer. In her memoir *Wildflower*, Drew Barrymore includes De Meritt and Palmer in her description of the *E.T.* child family as "part of the gang" and "super cool," calling De Meritt "a total badass": "The tone was that they were like capable superhero circus performers, and so there was no somber attitude" (2015, 60). Other adult actors of short stature—Pat Bilon, Tamara De Treaux, and Nancy MacLean—were able to withstand the heavy E.T. head for longer than young De Meritt, while a further actor (Caprice Rothe, a mime artist) performed E.T.'s hands for close shots that required a more organic dexterity. Spielberg describes Rothe's involvement as a literal embodiment—an animation: "She really brought E.T. to life in that moment. He was alive. Completely alive. Nobody was running him. There were no wires. There were no servers running. E.T. was really an organism from somewhere else" (Sunshine 2012, 26). In addition to this, a mechanical model and a remote-controlled electronic model were used to perform the character, the first operated by twelve men (including four animating the face). Spielberg—in an appropriately sentimental/somatic gesture—referred to this technical team as "E.T.'s Twelve Hearts" (33).

E.T. is, then, a fragmented being with a particular connection to childhood and sometimes performed by children, sometimes by adults.[22] His production body is intimately connected to the engineers who worked him and the actors who inhabited and performed him. There may be nothing especially remarkable about this: most special effects–heavy productions require diverse human involvement and bodily fabrication on a complex scale. But as scholarship into body horror has often shown, constructing biological fantasies is far more than just a question of latex and offal. E.T. is not merely a cute fabrication conveying sentimental meanings and reproduced a million times over in merchandise form. He/it has many bodies, all of which are intimately connected to Elliott's, and these multiple animated physical forms are part of the story of corporeality and embodied childhood that this tale is also telling.

Even more viscerally indicative is the attention taken to construct the alien's insides—not just the wiring and electronic control that made him move and emote but the illusion of physical interiority integral to a compelling image. Two memos from the producer Kathleen Kennedy dated first July 1 and then August 26, 1981, detail Spielberg's visceral concerns. First, he had "always emphasized that the heart light should be organic"; then he was exercised about the quality of the mouth interior: E.T.'s gums must "have a very fleshy, gooey consistency similar to a human mouth" (Sunshine 2012, 27). This of course is squarely the territory of the abject locations of body horror: places on the body where inside and outside meet, and where biofluids should be either expelled or held in. The mouth is a particularly sensitive location for policing (or failing to police) a clear distinction between inside and outside. E.T.'s rather reptilian mouth is based on images of very old people and must be made to look credible as he does some of the customary things humanoids do with their mouths—primarily talking (which Elliott and Gertie teach him) and eating (he mostly consumes child-focused junk food, with the singular exception of beer). He never uses his mouth to kiss, though he does mediate when Elliott kisses the "Pretty Girl"; he also allows Gertie to kiss him in the finale, and his finger passes from heart to lips in the famous "ouch" gesture that describes separation from Elliott in the film's extravagantly emotional conclusion. Though Gertie identifies him as an abject form of organic life ("Is he a pig? He sure eats like one"), E.T.'s consumption is one of the key signs of the "higher" connection between him and Elliott, a "twinning" read as telepathic or feelingful but symptomatized through food and drink. Generally E.T. has well-trained orifices—if he is a child formation, it is a child who has grown enough to mostly maintain control of these functions that police the borders of abjection: he drools and dribbles when he ventures into the adult consumption of alcohol (popping cans of beer from the fridge like a briefly bad parent),[23] causing both himself and Elliott, who "catches" drunkenness across space in his school classroom, to burp loudly.

While the mouth should properly keep the outside out and the inside in, E.T.'s torso displays an even more spectacular transgression. Pushing ever further into medical veracity—or perhaps body horror gross-out—is Verreaux's memo to the artistic consultant Craig Reardon on July 31, 1981, concerning what that famous heart light should illuminate:

> While E.T.'s skin is not totally transparent in the heart light area, we should be able to see some internal organ activity (always movement) when the light is

> on. The pulsing of the heart (two-three hearts?), intestinal contraction, changes in the density of viscera, lung expansions and contractions. The rib cage will block out light but the skin should be diffuse enough to allow some light to bleed through. Also, we should be able to see some vein activity in front of the light radiating out toward the limbs, not necessarily with bubbles of E.T.'s blood pumping through, but some lines to indicate blood vessels. (Sunshine 2012, 33)

Of the numerous E.T. toys and action figures still available for sale as vintage items online, only a few feature light-up hearts (usually a simple red light in the chest and a finger, or a stain on the chest, as if he has been wounded). None seem to show this level of fleshly detail, which would certainly turn E.T. into a rather more grotesque category of toy. Yet clearly the filmmakers felt it entirely necessary to support the conviction of organic life—the drive to veracity involves obsessive interior attention bordering on horror. It contributes to the sense that though Spielberg and screenwriter Melissa Mathison originally conceived of E.T. as a form of plant life,[24] the film suggests he is more animal than vegetable or mineral.[25] Most of all, the visible vessels suggest he is vulnerably fleshly, delicately damageable. Many plants, of course, are also vascular: in animals the vascular system transports blood, while in higher plants it transports water and nutrients. The "vein activity" to which Reardon refers would then be more xylem and phloem than artery. Yet we do not read E.T.'s red stain as vegetable sap—it clearly signifies animal blood, and its fading augurs death. Spielberg and the designer Carlo Rambaldi visited neonatal units when designing the alien's look, measuring newborn babies' features (N. Morris 2007, 86). Premature infants and neonates are also the only viable human forms for whom the skin has yet to become fully opaque: like E.T., a very young baby's skin is so thin it is still translucent, and one might trace the blood pumping through. Human skin becomes opaque around the normal term of forty weeks' gestation, as fat is laid down and the skin thickens. Like these young babies, ultrasensitive E.T. is literally thin-skinned.

All of which suggests he is more child than man. Of course, how the alien is named, and how he relates to "his" boy, is more than a question of bodily veracity. Ell-i-ott (as E.T. calls him) is an extrapolation of the name "E.T."; E.T. is a contraction of "Elliott" in so many ways. E.T. becomes the object of an intense identification process, with the children in the film making several key statements that serve to identify what kind of embodied life he is. Gertie asks some perceptive questions, and the answers she gets initially situate him in a fairy-tale framework. His arrival coincides with Mary reading Gertie the section in *Peter Pan* that requires one to clap one's hands if one believes in fairies, in order to revive the ailing Tinkerbell. Elliott tells his sister, "Grown-ups can't see him," which proves to be true: Mary fails to see E.T. even when she looks. For ordinary suburban adults he is rather like the mythological creatures of some cultures, who can only be seen by the privileged or the gifted. There is some cinematic magical thinking here, but this is also a question of scale. I noted earlier that the film is shot through a child-sized frame, but narratively and cinematographically it also follows E.T.'s need: because he is physically small, he must ally himself with bodily matches (children) in order to conceal himself. In form and story the film is cut to the cloth of E.T.'s (as well as Elliott's/Thomas's) stature, which in turn reinforces its status as a child's-point-of-view narrative: the alien/child fact at its heart physically shapes it into a small-scale film (which became a colossal hit). Mathison has said that she and Spielberg "didn't want to have any adults mucking up the works" (Sunshine 2012, :15) (though of course both she and he are adults, as are the crew and production team). This is partly to denote power to Elliott rather than to parents/scientists, but it is also because E.T. relates to bodies with the stature of children. In *Close Encounters* the abducted specimens are primarily adult-sized—Barry appears to be the only child returned to earth at the conclusion. In *E.T.* Spielberg goes one further. "The earth that he experiences is small and filled with little people his own size," Mathison says. "When he returned to his planet, he would be reporting on a planet that was populated by children, which we thought was a poetic idea" (Sunshine 2012, 15).

However, when E.T. sickens and scientists arrive with the might of the military, this veneer of make-believe is blasted away: suddenly grown-ups *can* see him, and they do overpower him. They answer the question of what he is with the bald definition "He's got DNA," a statement of connectedness (to earthly life forms) and separation (he is categorized). If Elliott's body is pretty much left alone in the film, his alien twin is the source of significant somatic prodding. "They'll give it a lobotomy or do experiments on it or something," Elliott worries, and when E.T. seems to have died he laments, "You're just going to cut him all up." As if we needed further evidence of their physical/spiritual pairing, the medical sequence places Elliott side by side with his sickening twin, pinpointing their sameness through mirrored electroencephalogram traces. A scientist's voice intones, "EEG analysis shows complete coherence and synchronization of brain-wave activity between both subjects" over an image of two tracks of identical vital signs blipping across a green digital display, in parallel and in unison, one labeled "ELLIOTT" and the other labeled "E.T." Earlier, brother Mike had commented that E.T. "doesn't look too good anymore," to which Elliot responds, "Don't say that—we're fine." By the time E.T. sickens, which coincides with the adult invasion, Elliott has lost all sense of his own separateness—unsurprisingly, as the alien fades the boy weakens, until he finally admits, "We're sick—I think we're dying." And then, of course, as the resurrected E.T. departs for home he touches Elliott's head, proclaiming that he will be "right *here*" (not "*there*"), as if he is addressing his own body.

The film has been read both Oedipally and socially in terms of family structure and dynamics: E.T. is both parent and child to Elliott, the lonely offspring of a suburban broken home (like Spielberg), who does not fit in and finds in the alien someone to nurture and be nurtured by. Spielberg himself has suggested that making the film was tantamount to therapy, and that it is deeply autobiographical (as he would later say of *The Fabelmans*). Psychoanalytic interpretation has had a strong impact on science fiction studies, finding family structures and particularly parenting surrogates in character and relationship. So here E.T. could occupy the role of absent father: Vivian Sobchack, for example, reads him as a transformed father (1991, 20), Nigel Morris sees him as a surrogate father "socializing him by teaching consideration and setting responsibilities" (2007, 87), while Heung (1983) also deems the unit Elliott forms with E.T. as a surrogate family. Bick goes further in psychoanalyzing the very "ideological premise of the film as process" (1992,27).

However, a more compelling model presents an alignment between child and alien as both vulnerable outsiders (yet curiously omnipotent)—a dominant thread in Spielberg's discourse on the child: E.T. is "someone who didn't belong. . . . I always felt E.T. was a minority story . . . that stands for every minority in this country" (Spielberg in McBride 2010, 325; see also Breskin 1985). Elliott is of course also an outsider and, as a child, is a literal minor. Through their name mirroring and other ways, E.T. and Elliott are more often than not presented as peers: the alien certainly instructs and ushers the otherwise friendless boy into new experiences, but equally the boy helps the alien in multiple ways. Benign and wise though he is, E.T. is not a powerful father figure such as the patrician Klaatu from *The Day the Earth Stood Still* (though, like Klaatu, he has also been read as a formation of Christ). We have seen how E.T.'s body is something of a collage of parts, including very young and very old people. Colin Brady, the animation supervisor on the 2002 reissue of the film, has said, "Sometimes we would describe him as a baby crossed with an old man" (Sunshine 2012, 178). Just as his body recalls a range of physical forms, so he is multiply identifiable in a variety of roles for Elliott. Robin Wood interprets this as part of the movie's outright manipulativeness: the use of E.T., he writes, is "shamelessly opportunistic. From scene to scene, almost moment to moment, he represents whatever is convenient to Spielberg, and to Elliott: helpless/potent, mental/intellectual giant, child figure/father figure" (1986, 178). This makes E.T. the perfect psychic floating signifier: just as his body parts are collaged, so his multiple representational resonances are available to a number of interpretations. Nigel Morris says this in another way when rehearsing the Christian analysis: "As paternal figure himself, as infant requiring nurturing and protection, and as inspirer of positive telempathic feelings that negate individual difference [E.T.] is at once Father, Son and Holy Spirit" (2007, 94). Why, then, should the child identification be the most compelling? The connection with Elliott—and E.T. as a replication of Elliott—is key. Even on the issue of religious symbolism, readings slide from seeing E.T. as Christ to reading Elliott as a kind of Christ figure too: after all, it is Elliott who is the son of Mary. What, then, makes the figure of E.T. so important for the understanding of childhood in Spielberg?

For Elliott, E.T. is, most important, *a boy*—not just a male (as a father figure might be) but a male child, albeit not human. E.T. must be a boy in order to fulfill Elliott's need for a best friend, and narratively his "boyness" is definitively established in response to another good question from Gertie. After the monumental scream she expels on first sight, her immediate question is—appropriate to a six-year-old child—"Is he a boy or a girl?" Elliott absolutely insists on E.T.'s maleness as a condition of their twinning. At his age, friendships are commonly focused on same-sex peer groups: Elliott needs E.T. to be male, enabling the physical symbiosis of boy and alien to be predicated on common gender. Here language denotes gender from the start: Gertie's very question is a gendering designation, though it is Elliott whose insistence that "he's a boy" ensures that everyone else falls into line—and this chapter has also fallen into line with its sole use of male pronouns for the creature. As for sex, there is no genital or chromosomal case; E.T. is a plant, seemingly asexual, but still the child story fails to contradict or qualify Elliott's view. A key stage in E.T.'s human language acquisition is when he watches *Sesame Street* with Gertie: his first clear utterance is repeating the letter *B* as "B for Boy" appears on the TV screen (causing Gertie to claim that she taught him to speak). This is soon followed by Gertie's attempt to feminize him by dressing him in her own clothes as a girl. That this is characterized as a comic moment (as was more true of male-to-female cross-dressing than the reverse in the 1980s) suggests that the rhetoric of the film also presupposes E.T.'s gender as male, causing the presentation of male-in-drag to be played as ridiculous. Elliott is certainly horrified.

That *Elliott* is a boy the film is sure of: although the working title *A Boy's Life* was a production smokescreen, it is still curiously apposite. Spielberg has called this "a movie about boyhood wonders" (Sragow 2011). Recent discussions of boyhood in culture customarily justify the need to specify the qualities of the male-gendered child against a prevailing view that boyhood is as resistantly transparent as whiteness or adult maleness. Girlhood as a formation of difference may require definition and specification; boyhood is somehow the universalization of childhood itself (e.g., Nodelman 2002, 1–14). As Murray Pomerance and Frances Gateward write in their introduction to *Where the Boys Are: Cinemas of Masculinity and Youth*, "It is as though nothing needs to be said about what boys are, or about what makes the category of boys distinct and discrete. Stories in print and onscreen have presented boyhood to us in the guise of an obvious and natural, perduring, matter-of-fact, and taken-for-granted reality. Boys, it seems, are simply there" (2005, 1). One of the primary agendas for boy studies has been to identify the contradictions in cultural representations: fictional preadult males have borne out adult masculine stereotypes, with boyhood read as prototype manhood, a transitional state building the path to a full-grown muscularity, toughness, and aggression and also disruptive or resistant representations such as "sensitive" or feminized males.[26] As an exemplary boy of 1980s cinema, Elliott is a mixture of conventional and unconventional boy motifs.

Henry Thomas was chosen from 300 boys who auditioned for the role; we have already seen evidence of his crying ability. He is thoughtful, empathic, inward: there is little sense that Elliott will grow up to be a jock, though he does become leader of the "jockish" older boys in Michael's peer group. Perry notes Thomas's "solemn, controlled gravitas, unusual for a ten-year-old" (1998, 49); once again, here is the child performer as perfect conveyor of childlike qualities precisely because he is—unnaturally—not quite a child. This makes him the perfect autobiographical figure for Spielberg, an adult who has said that conceiving of *E.T.* meant imagining himself as "ten years old again—where I've sort of been for thirty-four years anyway" (McBride 2010, 323). One crucial element of Elliott's character is his isolation: he has no friends of his own until E.T. becomes his friend. Alienation from human peers primes Elliott to align himself with the alien—he becomes positively alien-ated. Against the multiple readings that interpret E.T. as a father figure, the focus on play positions him as peer to Elliott. Even if the Reese's Pieces are initially a lure, essentially the first thing Elliott does is to share his sweets with his new friend. Having introduced himself as "Me—Human. Boy," he then makes it his job to show E.T. how one must operate as such in his culture. Elliott's tutoring takes the shape of a hilarious, touching journey (semi-improvised by Thomas) around a toy collection characteristic of the period and his age: *Star Wars* action figures Greedo, Walrus Man, Hammerhead, Snaggletooth, Lando Calrissian, and Boba Fett (the first four introduced by Palitoy in 1979, the last two in 1980) are highlights of Elliott's toy-studded soliloquy as if they were recent real-time acquisitions still exciting to a boy in 1982 ("And look, they can even have wars!" he exults).[27] Also mixed into the breathless listing is Coca-Cola, a peanut-shaped money box, and his live goldfish pets (opportunity for a *Jaws* reference), all stops on a grand tour of boyhood paraphernalia through which the child guides his visitor. Elliott comes into being, as a boy and for the film, in the process of passing boyhood on.

Child/Alien

Elliott, then, *is* a boy, albeit a "sensitive" one, and so it follows that his friend E.T. is referenced as male. But if E.T. is associated with boyness, is the opposite also true? How does the film also visually identify Elliott with the alien and *as* alien? Nigel Morris's reading (2007, 84–94) suggests that the connectedness of the pair emanates from E.T.'s powers of "telempathy," as if the channel of communication were beamed one way from alien to human, and were solely psychic and emotional. But some of *E.T.*'s most memorable moments show that the connection is both more somatic and more reciprocal, opening a manifestly visceral channel between human and alien. Spielberg has said that the seeds of *E.T.* were sown in the utopianism of *Close Encounters of the Third Kind*'s conclusion: What would happen if the benign contact at the culmination of that film were extended? The definition of close encounter three is taken one step further in

E.T.: though nonsexual, the interpenetration of E.T. and Elliott is astonishingly intimate—E.T. is not just *any* friend. Michael responds to the scientist's question "Elliott thinks his thoughts?" with the answer, "No. Elliott feels his feelings," but neither of these quite goes far enough. Elliott and E.T. are far more physically implicated in each other. The film's visual vocabulary bears this out in its repeated framing of the two bodies as mirroring each other. Gaylyn Studlar discusses adult masculine embodiment in silent cinema (in an analysis of Drew's grandfather, John Barrymore; Studlar 1996) and the teen male body in 1980s cinema (Tom Cruise; Studlar 2001), citing and contesting Marjorie Garber's formation that "embodiment *itself* is a form of feminization" (1993, 372). In *E.T.* the male child body is alien-ized through identification. The pair are similar heights and are mostly positioned as each other's physical equivalent, though this is challenged in a sweet scene, deleted for the original release but reinstated in the 2002 reissue, in which the two stand in front of a mirror and compare heights, with Elliott vying for tallness until E.T. trumps him by extending his monstrously snaky neck. We have seen great care was taken to give E.T.'s throbbing heart exactly the right quality of visible viscerality. Elliott's chest is opaque, but Spielberg matches the redness of the heart with costume: Elliott often dons his red sweatshirt, which visually echoes the alien's glowing heart. Repeated two-shots connect them through palette—the common redness suggests an intimate cross-transplantation, as if E.T. has part of Elliott held within him, and vice versa.

The two comedic moments that show Elliott symptomatizing on behalf of E.T., his body externally exhibiting the signs of what the alien has inwardly digested, bear this out. Across the space from home (where E.T. has been left to spend the day quietly, but cannot) to school (where Elliott tries to concentrate on his work, but cannot), somatic connections are made. This is not just a telepathic communication of thought or feeling but a chemical contagion. E.T. consumes beer, and in his distant classroom Elliott shows signs of drunkenness. E.T. channel surfs on the TV—another form of consumption—and happens upon a clip where John Wayne seduces Maureen O'Hara in *The Quiet Man*. Simultaneously, Elliott plucks up the courage romantically to sweep an admired girl off her feet.[28] (This is the only time we see Elliott meaningfully interacting with another child who is not a sibling or his brother's friends, as if E.T. were inaugurating Elliott into the wider world of friendship.) Desire is transferred (though it is not clear whether E.T. as mediator also feels it). Here the Elliott/E.T. physical symbiosis catalyzes Elliott into some more adult experiences of pleasure—E.T.'s consumption (with mouth and eyes) initiates more-than-childish behavior, including tentative steps into adult sexuality. Morris reads this as a psychoanalytic figuration of cinematic identification: "One becomes drunk as the other drinks, or acts out fantasies the other observes on television, figur[ing] the spectator's Imaginary relationship to the Other on-screen" (2007, 90). This suggests that E.T. is spectacle and Elliott is audience. However, the physical interimplication of the relationship is closer than this, even if the distance between them belies it: consumption is key here. Crucially, where Elliott has had his difference from other boys confirmed through his sameness with E.T., here E.T. initiates a kind of separation by launching the boy into a human—adult—activity. Elliott is on the cusp of adolescence: when conveying sexual confidence to him, E.T. ushers him tentatively over the brink of childhood (another early working title for this film was, according to Douglas Brode, *Growing Up*).[29] Spielberg has said of Elliott, "He's at that stage where he's just bored with everything around him. He watches a lot of television, doesn't read, is starting to look at girls. Older girls, eleven or twelve. And he's starting to have those feelings like I had when I was ten or eleven. Elliott's not me, but he's the closest thing to my experiences in my life" (Brode 1995, 115).

This identification of Elliott with Spielberg is familiar, but the director has also been identified with and as his alien: both figures are autobiographically intermingled as child-Steven formations. A number of statements Spielberg made about the genesis of the idea reinforce the equivalence of the characters and present them as peers rather than hierarchized family stand-ins: "I remember saying to myself, 'What I really need is a friend I can talk to—somebody who can give me all the answers.' . . . I began concocting this imaginary creature . . . and what if he needed me as much as I needed him? Wouldn't that be a great love story?" (McBride 2010, 323). Though those two working titles—*A Boy's Life*, *Growing Up*—were primarily in place as part of the secrecy machine set up around a film (suggesting to press and public that this is a mere story of childhood in the suburbs), they are still resonant of its various thematic emphases, of boyhood and childhood in transition. A further working title was *E.T. and Me*, which stresses the double act of child and alien—promotional materials were even struck under this title. The abandonment of all these alternatives in favor of *E.T. the Extra-Terrestrial* suggests a sidelining of Elliott and a foregrounding of the alien.[30] However, while promoting E.T. as star certainly makes merchandising sense, there is little question that he exists narratively entirely in relation to Elliott, and he is indeed a function of Elliott's desire. Although much of the pleasure of *E.T.* for children lies with its representation of childhood from the child's point of view, the meaningfulness of the alien for children extends beyond the film. In the early to mid-1980s, many children already had a relationship with E.T. in toy form even before they saw the movie, and this is central to the ongoing life of the film: the alien's body is also something to play with, extending the film's wider reception and its peripheral life. E.T. has a materiality that stretches from screen to auditorium to child's bedroom (perhaps very similar to Elliott's own). Of course, a child could enjoy and engage with their own cuddly toy E.T. without ever actually seeing the film, so successful was the character paracinematically (though Dodie Bellamy reports her students' "fear," with one stating that "*E.T.* was the scariest movie ever made" and another that though he had an E.T. doll, "It was too creepy . . . I never played with it" [2009, 96]). This rather different approach to bodily form bridges the symbolic and the material, as children in the audience engage with the body on-screen not as a visual mechanical wonder or a performed mask but as an entity that exists within their fantasy lives via purchased merchandise. E.T. on-screen is thus a formation of the toy in their bedrooms at home, as more or less than "the real one" that is theirs. Among the "several hundred" different *E.T.* products licensed by MCA Inc., which owned the rights to E.T. merchandise, 10 million E.T. dolls were sold for $15 each around Christmas 1982; the *New York Times* reported that "E.T. products could easily generate more than double the $300 million earned so far by the film."[31] By 2007, *E.T.* tie-in merchandise had earned at least $1 billion, of which Spielberg received 10 percent (Jackson 2007, 36); Morris reports that from 1982 to 1983, Spielberg was earning $1 million a day from the film.

The syndrome of dissociation between experiencing the toy and experiencing the film has become more prevalent as merchandise has increasingly been marketed to children too young to see movies, which have been certified for an older demographic—a direct relationship between film experience and promotional object may not be necessary. So the scene in which Elliott shows E.T. his merch treasures speaks to many concerns at the heart of this book. It is an exemplary child's-point-of-view sequence: nonsequitous to adults but driven by a compelling child logic, with E.T. established in his customary position—a child equal, yet absorbing (almost as a researcher might) all the earth-specific information Elliott is pouring out, as if *Star Wars* characters were as crucial for an intergalactic scientific investigator as the structure of earth-borne DNA. E.T.'s gaze is both cosmic and child-eyed. Furthermore, it exposes the symbolic force of material and consumer objects, on which Spielberg—and contemporary cinema—has capitalized so lucratively, but which also extends our understanding, in the popular sphere, of people's totemistic relationship to things. The sequence is not (just) a mendaciously cynical paean to (Spielberg's friend, George Lucas's) merchandise, an apology that uses an individual child's fictionalized but oh-so-real pleasure to justify a billion-dollar profit. Spielberg's films can play around in their own merchandise stalls, to the extent that the monsters take over (and destroy) the mart at the end of *Jurassic Park*. They know that the toys are part of the story. Yet toys also make cinema active, extending the scope of cinematic pleasure into the bedrooms of child viewers and activating the fantasy lives of child audiences. Clearly, this can be read as a dark sphere of influence: toys parlay the film product into the wider life of the child, and vice versa. However, there are other, more active readings of this relationship. The afterlife of merchandise also hands movie characters over to their audiences for imaginative recycling and rewriting, and forms an important thread in the material life of cinema from the audience's point of view, beyond the screen itself.

Melodrama, Tears, and the Family Adventure Film

E.T. was a crossover film like none other: as we saw in chapter 2, it squeezed a lake of tears from adults as well as children, and from a wide social and international demographic. Between 1977 and 1982, Spielberg made science fiction a child-friendly genre once again, after decades in which it was more closely associated with exploitation movies (drive-ins and cult audiences) or art cinema (from future-dystopian visions to Stanley Kubrick). His first step was with *Firelight*, made when he was a teenager, which formed a blueprint for *Close Encounters*; his second was *Close Encounters* itself, which, though not primarily a children's film, is certainly a childhood film. Wholehearted child-friendliness came with *E.T.* in 1982. *Jaws* ostensibly invented the summer blockbuster, but *Raiders of the Lost Ark*, the film Spielberg made directly prior to *E.T.*, developed the family audience on which *E.T.* capitalized. However, its reach was older—teen audiences and thrill-seeking adults—due to its dark and sometimes violent content, and its protagonist was an adult. *E.T.* strove to exclude adults on-screen while earnestly soliciting their attention in the audience. George Perry calls *E.T.* "the most popular family film of all time" (1998, 51). The family film, or family adventure film, as Peter Krämer has defined it (1998, 2006), is particularly identified with post–classical Hollywood production as an industry-wide phenomenon more than a genre, and the two films under discussion in this chapter played a major part in its evolution. This distinct form has dominated Hollywood cinema since the mid-1970s, the lucrative love child of Spielberg and Lucas. So although *E.T.* contains many of the qualities of the children's film, as we saw earlier, that is a more limited category. While some family adventure films may be children's films, not all children's films are family adventure films. Bazalgette and Staples deem the family film as "essentially American" against the children's film as "essentially, but no longer exclusively, European" (1995, 94–95). Noel Brown calls *Close Encounters* one of the first "'kidult'-inflected mainstream products of the 'New Hollywood,'" which, along with franchises, including the *Indiana Jones* films, represent "a new paradigm in Hollywood family entertainment. Possessing genuine cross-cultural, cross-demographic mass appeal, this new paradigm was founded upon largely undifferentiated audience address."

As Brown makes clear, key titles that have come to define the family adventure film were not initially marketed as "family" entertainment at all (2012, 156–157). *Close Encounters* and *E.T.* are particular cases here: the first, substantially budgeted because of its spectacular effects and developed in the wake of the phenomenal success of *Jaws*, needed to reach maximum audiences. It did this through its promise of unprecedented spectacle, but given the limitations of the children's film (about children, and for children only), it could not press any closer to a limited child's-eye view. Instead, an intergalactic story hooked around adult children (Roy Neary) and universal children (Barry; the child aliens) spoke to a baby boomer cultural moment that resoundingly venerated the inner child and "authentic" childhood. This was a film for adults of the "Peter Pan syndrome" generation, and for the teen audiences at the same time returning to science fiction through *Star Wars*.

But though driven by child-inflected narratives and aesthetics, both *Close Encounters* and *E.T.* were watched by adults in huge numbers. *Close Encounters* was not marketed to younger children; *E.T.* captured audiences of all ages. On many levels *E.T.* presents as a children's film, and indeed it started life as one: Columbia Studio's marketing and research department ran a demographic survey on Mathison's script and concluded that "it had limited commercial potential" and would appeal only to juvenile audiences (McBride 2010, 326). Given the enormous success of *Jaws* and *Close Encounters*, this is an astonishing film-historical twist—one of those lost opportunities of cultural history, rather like Decca Records refusing to sign the Beatles ("Guitar groups are on the way out, Mr. Epstein"). McBride reports that Spielberg was furious, and the film passed to Universal, which put *E.T.* into production as a (then, for Spielberg) low-budget film ($10 million) predicated on its child's-eye focus. Spielberg himself thought of it as a small, autobiographical story, with the children's performances as his special effects.

E.T.'s emotionalism brought audiences into theaters in the same way that special effects had brought audiences into *Close Encounters*. *Close Encounters* succeeded as a huge family film because of its combination of vast spectacle and "childness" (as distinct from "child's point of view"). *E.T.* succeeded as an even bigger family film because the performances of its children parlayed audience sympathies toward the alien. If Truffaut was the means by which audiences of *Close Encounters* would read the climactic child aliens as benign and lovable, child actors themselves would have to do that for E.T. in *E.T.* However, though children may have long been easily "spectacularized" consumables for adult audiences (as with Graham Greene's notorious view that Shirley Temple attracted middle-aged male viewers who appreciated her body as well as her mature emotional display,[32] or those pitiful waifs of early cinema), it is an industry truism that child actors can be hard to identify with as protagonist-surrogate unless one is a child oneself or the subject matter is particularly serious (as in the European art films discussed by Noel Brown and Karen Lury). Even as an autobiographical film about divorce and minorities, *E.T.* would have no trouble speaking to child audiences, especially with the lure of merchandise greasing the path to the box office. But it also touched adults, who, as repeat viewers and through frenzied word of mouth, also contributed to its gargantuan success.

Child's-point-of-view films succeed with adults when the viewing experience both adopts the child's perspective and simultaneously stands at a critical remove from it, as with, for instance, films that portray historical events, when the child's ignorance of or isolation from context is part of the drama filled in by adult viewers who both see with the child and flesh out what the child cannot see. This is not the strategy of *E.T.*, which as we have seen keeps all viewers inside the bubble of the child's world and the culture of the children's bedrooms, so much so that at times there seems to be simply no "outside" to or of this. Thus the experience of *E.T.* is not just "small," but intense.

What, then, brought adult audiences to it in such large numbers? This can be answered not just through performance but also once again through the way in which performance inflects genre. *E.T.* is a science fiction film, but it is also a children's film, a family adventure film, and—perhaps most supremely—a melodrama, its "weepie" qualities most acutely enacted when family members gather around a trauma, music swells, and children (not women) cry. This description might also characterize the ending of *Close Encounters*, which becomes most melodramatic (literally *melos* [music] + *drame* [drama]) at its most spectacular and musical, as on-screen characters encourage us to cry with them. Spielberg gives full credit to John Williams for his "melo" part in the melodrama cocktail, and he specifically asked for music that would not evoke a science fiction ambience. He wanted "something emotional and sort of theatrically old-fashioned" (Austin 1977, 29; in the press notes he says that Williams "can take a moment and just uplift it, like he can take a tear that's just forming in your eye and cause it to drip." *Close Encounters* chooses to edit Melinda Dillon's concluding tears against images of Neary departing onto the mothership, giving the impression that she is crying at his loss (the response of a heroine in classic melodrama) rather than "catching" the tears of the child (the response of anyone in Spielbergian melo/sci-fi). However, here Cary Guffey began spontaneously to cry as he was directed to wave goodbye to the aliens, and Dillon's tears are in turn infected by the small boy's, according to Balaban (2002, 127). We saw in chapter 2 how Henry Thomas's audition tears infected the crew and were in turn "caught" by the audience, but this truly reached epidemic proportions as the film made its way around the world. Certainly, we see a woman cry in *E.T.*—Mary cries, but only as she watches her son's emotion (and then only when the scientists have invaded, not in the film's finale). Both Gertie and Mike cry, too, as E.T. departs, but in a kind of lachrymose alliance with and echo of their brother. It is the children's tears that flow out and then "pass on"; it is the children's tears that sear the science fictionality of *E.T.* to melodramatic conclusions. Spielberg uses children's tears as glue to weld adult genres to melodrama.

Crucially, for all their bodily symbiosis, E.T. does not cry even when Elliott floods. Perhaps Spielberg felt that no audience could take the spectacle of glycerin rolling down those wizened cheeks. Just as drunkenness is passed from E.T. to Elliott but with E.T. doing the drinking for both of them, so Elliott seems to be doing all of E.T.'s crying for him. As he repeats E.T.'s "ouch" gesture back to him (a finger traced from heart to lips to the space between them), Elliott's voice catches on the tears, as if catching the alien's low growl. But—though by now generous tears held in Thomas's eyes have spilled over and are rolling down his cheeks—it is the almost inaudible voice that is most affecting, that is the mark of active suffering, speaking the unspeakableness of the pain of loss anticipated.

This chapter has focused on the embodied and the visceral contagion of feeling, and on character symbiosis. But there is a further physical contagion that passes into the auditorium. The fact that most people watching this film were neither child nor alien did not stop the "caught" emotions here from infecting beyond the screen. If E.T. did not catch Elliott's tears, audiences made up for this, and this huge crossover appeal accounts for the film's extraordinary success. The *New York Times* ran a headline on December 30, 1982, that simply read, "Adults Lured Back to Films by *E.T.*," a stark historical shift underpinned by Andrew Sarris's scathing account of what adults wanted from the experience: "E.T. is the teddy bear we crush forever to our bleeding hearts. E.T. is every childish fantasy we never outgrew. E.T. is the eternal child in all of us" (Sarris 1982, 59). Again and again, the child's presence causes a reinflection and a reinterpretation of genre in Spielberg's work. Horror affect melds with melodrama in the war stories *War of the Worlds*, *Saving Private Ryan*, and *Empire of the Sun*, but horror techniques are also readily deployed in *E.T.* and *A.I.*, though to different ends; in both films adult humans become monstrous. Focus on the child refracts science fiction in a particular (melodramatic) direction, with splashes of horror-inflected child peril. The child cries, and we cry. The child suffers, and we squirm. The child feels, and we catch it. This is of course exactly what happens between E.T. and Elliott, a relationship that therefore might be read as also embodying the character-audience relationship of affective provocation. The manifestation of audience feeling is borne out in a plenitude of reception materials attesting to a visceral response to these very somatic stories. A year after E.T.'s release the collection *Letters to E.T.*, with an introduction by Spielberg, was published, containing numerous testimonies to the alien's affect, many from children but a significant number from adults. Seventy-three-year-old Vera Binder writes to the director that he had "pushed [her] cry button," and this meant she lost her contact lenses (she asks him to replace the cost). A mother of a twenty-year-old autistic man writes that *E.T.* had made him come "out of himself. He screamed—he clapped—he laughed . . . and then—yes—Tommy cried. Real tears . . . *E.T.* has changed Tommy's life."[33] Spielberg as exploitation showman deploys the affective tricks of popular storytelling and will use the child to meld science fiction to tear-jerking. His omnivorous approach to genre thus becomes a method for maximizing audience affect, and the child is a key tool in his kit.

4

Real Boys and Synthetic Children

A.I. Artificial Intelligence and *Ready Player One*

Steven Spielberg's 2001 science fiction melodrama *A.I. Artificial Intelligence*, in which a robot child yearns to be a real child, is a much darker film than *E.T. the Extra-Terrestrial* or *Close Encounters of the Third Kind*, but, like *E.T.*, it also rests on the virtuoso performance of a child. The 2018 teen adventure *Ready Player One*, in which real children adopt cyber personae within a digital realm, is, by contrast, lighter and squarely family-focused. Its central character is closely supported by an ensemble of young actors who switch between the live-action "real" and digital performance capture throughout. *E.T.* is a child-identified film that reached out to all audiences (including children), and *Ready Player One* targeted a similar demographic; *A.I.*, however, is an adult-oriented film with a child actor/protagonist and a less certain audience demographic. Its diminutive hero, David (Haley Joel Osment), is an android who is ejected from an organic family that was never his, making *A.I.* at least as concerned as *E.T.* with fleshly and embodied childhood, and the parented (and orphaned) child. Here Spielberg's interest in childhood is rendered through the nonhuman performed by a human, predicated still on some very familiar formations of boyhood. *Ready Player One*, which will be threaded through this discussion of *A.I.*, features children and young adults adventuring with and without fleshly bodies, relating to each other first through self-fabricated digital avatars. Their actorly performances therefore require a mixed skill set, with naturalistic live-action screen acting limited to the spaces around the edges of the CGI set pieces, where they perform their artificial personae. Robot David, by contrast, is (like most organic children) stuck with the body denoted by his creator, and the actor performing David must present to the tune of the character's limitations and abilities. Both films consider children and young people as embodied and disembodied, dreaming of more idealized selves; both films push the concept of the developing self through and beyond biology, enabling young actors to grapple with performative circumstances at the interface of childhood and digital identity. Across this chapter runs the question of the negative child: the child as not physically, not emotionally, not "really" a child at all (but still read as one). This is manifest through passing and masquerade: of the digital being who passes as and for something other (machine as human, child as adult, female as male). Negative definition hems in these acts, and performances, of robotic, digital, and "real" childhood.

Digital Difference

In *A.I.* Spielberg returns again to melodrama-inflected science fiction to articulate childhood agonies and continue his exploration of boyhood. Though critically misunderstood on its release, it is a remarkable film exploring posthumanism through a Pinocchio-inflected tale of a tragic robot aspiring to childhood. The story was first developed by Stanley Kubrick before Spielberg took over as director and brought it to the screen following Kubrick's death, a collaboration that enabled critics to accuse Spielberg of "adding some sugar to Kubrick's wine" (in the words of the science fiction writer Brian Aldiss [2001], on whose short story *A.I.* was based). The suspicion of mass-market Spielberg that historically has marked critical responses to his work was nowhere more apparent that in the writing around this film, and is addressed head-on in the press notes accompanying its release. [1] This suggests that the "Spielberg or Kubrick?" question was both a marketable angle and a source of anxiety—febrile territory, since Spielberg is rarely considered an auteur in the Kubrickian sense. While the story was initiated by one of the world's most revered "serious" directors, the screenplay was sole-authored and the film singly directed by one of its most commercially successful moguls. Accusations of Spielbergian sentiment are sharpened by Kubrickian origins: "Trust Spielberg to keep softening the blows that Kubrick inflicts," wrote Peter Travers in *Rolling Stone* (2001), attributing the film's irony and nihilism to Kubrick, its emotion and sentiment to Spielberg.

However, as Spielberg takes pains to point out in publicity, the "so-called sentimental" ideas were all Kubrick's and the darker elements were Spielberg's. Spielberg's producer Bonnie Curtis joked that the film was the work of "Stevely Kuberg. It's a complete meld of both of them" (Abramowitz 2001). V. Alan White even suggests that the film itself is a child—the child of two fathers (2008, 210). This may be what makes it such an interesting case, and—as we will see later—parental metaphors around the "dark" father passing on a legacy to, and being resisted by, the "lighter" son only proliferate around this contradiction. Of course, although capitalizing on the Kubrick conception, Spielberg must also show it to be very much his own film (or else risk an authorship question like that of *Poltergeist*, with Spielberg in the Tobe Hooper role). While utilizing the Kubrickian seal of authenticity, the press notes stress Spielberg's claim as primary auteur: the screenplay is his credit alone, and "everything, in a sense, had to be designed, fabricated and invented by Steven." So is this hybrid authorship or a singular focus of control that capitalizes on deploying the Kubrick brand when expedient? Alongside and connected to the questions of the child, *A.I.* is a particularly interesting episode in the story of critical suspicion of Spielberg that I am telling throughout this book.

A.I. is, then, a child's-point-of-view story that is too upsetting for children to watch. Though classified at PG-13 in the United States and 12 in the United Kingdom, it is not a children's film like *E.T.* or *The Adventures of Tintin* or even *Ready Player One*. This was evident from early in development: when the story collaborator Ian Watson proposed that David's companion should be a male hooker, Kubrick replied, "Okay, we've lost the kiddie market" (Harlan and Struthers 2009, 14), and later *Variety* reported some confusion when marketing relied too much on the film having a child star, "leading auds to expect a kinder, gentler picture" (Diorio 2001, 8). It is also a child's-point-of-view film that may not even have a child as its point of view.

In a future world of climate disaster–generated scarcity in which sexual reproduction is controlled, mecha (mechanical humanoids and other creatures) have become an indispensable social and economic resource. They are manufactured to meet the needs of the orga (organic or biological humans) as service workers, sex workers, and toys. Professor Hobby (William Hurt), the head of the Cybertronics corporation, develops a mecha child with the capacity to love, a service and product for childless orga. Once its proposed parent takes it through an imprinting ritual, the mecha child will love that parent to the end of its (near-eternal, eternally infantile) existence. So the family drama of *A.I.* begins, focusing on the plight of Monica and Henry Swinton (Frances O'Connor and Sam Robards). With their biological son, Martin, languishing in a cryogenic coma pending a cure for his illness, Henry (a Cybertronics employee) persuades Monica to take on Hobby's mecha child prototype David. To Henry and Hobby, the relationship will be experimental, a means of testing out the emotional imprinting process, apparently without consequence. But to Monica and David, it is agonizingly affecting: this being a fairy tale, of course, as soon as Monica has irrevocably made David her own, Martin recovers and returns home. David's obsessive devotion to his mother causes Oedipal friction with father Henry and sibling jealousy with Martin. The robot child is a misfit in the human family, reviled and tricked by his spiteful brother and peer group (Spielberg can render children as nasty as they are charmed and charming), giving the family the excuse they need to cast David off. At first it is proposed that he simply be returned to the factory for destruction, as one might do with any faulty household appliance. Instead, in a gesture that is equal parts hopeful and heartless, Monica casts David out into the woods, leaving him with few social skills to face the multiple horrors of this dystopian future, eternally to pine for the mother who rejected him.

The lost mecha child then sets off on a quest to become a "real boy" (Pinocchio the wooden puppet's dream) so that his mother might indeed finally love him. He is befriended by a group of cast-off mecha (more empathic than any orga, even though they have not gone through the love-eliciting imprinting ritual of child to mother), some of whom end up being publicly executed at a disturbing "flesh fair"—a carnivalesque entertainment event at which working-class orga humans take ghoulish revenge on the mecha who have replaced them in menial roles. Mecha sex worker Gigolo Joe (Jude Law) helps David on his way, becoming a better parent than the orga predecessors Hobby, Monica, or Henry. When David finds his way back to his "original" father, Hobby, toward the end of the film, he discovers that he is the image of Hobby's dead (orga) child David, and that he is the first in a production line of identical Davids and Darlenes (the girl version that has since been developed). This is the child as pattern, signifying primarily for its non-uniqueness, a template only for future industrial reproduction. In delivering such a consumer commodity into the marketplace, Hobby exposes the worst excesses of bad parenting, creating emoting, sophisticated products that become victims of family desire and technical innovation.

David's quest then appears to end when he and his toy Teddy (his "Jiminy Cricket" companion mecha) sink to the bottom of the ocean, where they wait, frozen, for two thousand years. They are revived by a civilization of super-mecha, successors to the film's mecha and the long-dead human race, who nurture David as the last remaining witness to human existence (as Sue Short scathingly puts it, David is "an archive of our most sentimental values" [2011, 208]). Of course, this means that David is a mere resource twice over—first giving "childness" to the empty parents, then evidencing humanity in the future devoid of it for the super-mecha. They in return do at least reward him, perhaps because they genuinely feel for him, perhaps as a kind of fee paid in exchange for the archaeological information he provides: David is given a cloned (but more loving) fabricated version of Monica to enjoy. However, their technology only enables one (perfect) day of dreamlike, amnesiac family pleasure. In an interview some years after its release, Spielberg called this his darkest film, darker even than *Schindler's List*: "It is the most tragic . . . because somehow *A.I.* is about the end of the entire human race" (Windolf 2008). However, since *A.I.* has presented humans as mendacious, cruel, and selfish, it is unclear whether their demise really does constitute an unhappy ending.

By contrast, *Ready Player One* returns to a family adventure format and was compared to *E.T.* in reviews—for its ensemble cast, its science fiction quest story driven by young adventurers, and its nostalgic view of 1980s popular culture.[2]

The story, set in the year 2045, is initially focused on a nerdy youth, Wade Watts (played by Tye Sheridan, and in this performance a dead ringer for a young Spielberg), an orphan who lives with his aunt and her abusive partner in a vertical trailer park (the Stacks) in Columbus, Ohio. Like most others in this future dystopia, Wade escapes the everyday into the virtual reality of the OASIS (the acronym for "ontologically anthropocentric sensory immersive simulation"), an alternative realm of pleasure and excitement contrasting the drudgery, poverty, and ecological crisis of real life. The OASIS was built by the now-deceased digital genius James Halliday (Mark Rylance), whose legacy is not only this other world itself but a highly competitive and hitherto unwinnable immersive gaming competition that promises as its prize to the winner total control and ownership of the OASIS. Wade—in the guise of his sleeker, dynamic avatar Parzival—focuses his considerable skills on this quest, aided by his best friend, Aech, whose avatar form is a powerful man of color: a superhero-proportioned builder and fixer of fantasy machines in the digital realm. Parzival and Aech have only ever met in the OASIS, never as their fleshly human selves in the grittier Columbus. The same is true of the female competitor Art3mis (whose Columbus/real-world name is Samantha, played by Olivia Cooke), initially a rival to Parzival in the competition but soon to become his girlfriend in both Columbus and the OASIS. The three join forces together with their other young friends Daito and Sho, battling as a team (the High-5s) through the rounds of the game, advancing toward the final Easter Egg that unlocks ownership of the OASIS, all the time pursued and challenged by the henchmen of Innovative Online Industries (IOI), a corporate monster seeking control of the OASIS for profit. Of course the High-5s—a winning collaboration of youthful skill and sure moral instinct—secure the prize, sharing control of OASIS, and closing it for two days each week to ensure that everyone is also invested in their real physical world.

As Matthew Leggatt astutely argues, OASIS is a space of nostalgia and escapism that serves to degrade the dystopian reality of 2045 America, with the whole film turning in on itself to become "essentially a homage to [Spielberg's] own work" (2021, 184). The key to winning the game comes when Parzival visits a hologrammatic archive of the dead Halliday's life, which—through a simulation of the past—can be interrogated in three dimensions, as if one were walking around an interactive theater of memory. Scenes from Halliday's boyhood and youth, including his 1980s childhood bedroom replete with Spielbergian cultural references that echo Elliott's in *E.T.*, provide crucial puzzle pieces. So a young man (Wade) uses his avatar Parzival to find answers in the cultural fabric of another young man's distant childhood memories, vicariously visiting a decade dominated by Spielberg as cultural touchstone for representations of boyhood in Western cinema.

Part of their journey to this film's happy ending takes place not in the OASIS but in violent, dangerous Columbus, which frames the film's considerable identity shifts. Spielberg, as we have seen, is not afraid of posing complex questions of selfhood, which often circulate around the child. *Ready Player One*'s future realism builds these questions on what has become, in the world of the film (and the novel on which it is based), the by now ordinary reality of avatar selves, played out in a worldwide digital realm. But when Wade/Parzival meets his friends in the flesh, what he finds is something of a parallel to the realities of the child actor. In a triple-reveal sequence, Parzival's best friend, Aech, turns out to be *not* the mature, powerfully large male of her alternative self but a woman of color, Helen Harris (played by thirty-four-year-old Lena Waithe). Sho—a tall, adult-presenting ninja figure—emerges as an eleven-year-old boy named Zhou (played by Chinese American child actor Philip Zhao). Wade calls him "the world's most badass eleven-year-old ever," but Zhou reiterates the wisdom of performing older, adultlike, and tougher (as Helen had done in gender terms): "Do I have to wear a sign saying 'I am eleven years old—shoot me first'?" Like the young actor trying to extend the reach of their performance range and "playing age," some avatars here "play" older/taller, while others play younger. This may also be a more generalized signifier for the actor in a role, who becomes unrecognizable as their real self by virtue of their utter immersion in their fictional/performed self.

This is, then, a story dominated by a troupe of sometimes older-presenting young people. Only Zhou is actually a child performer, though Sheridan was only nineteen when filming commenced, and therefore still a minor in some U.S. states (he had been a teen actor for six years before this). Nevertheless the High-5 group functions as the ensemble "children" of the film, which both gives them the moral high ground and enables them to relate to the youth in Halliday enough to crack the clues. Again Spielberg has cast a young, relatively unknown ensemble; as the producer Donald De Line notes, "What was unique about this is that the leads . . . of the movie, the High-5, are all young for the most part. They're 18 to 20 years old. So it wasn't going to be big movie stars because they haven't reached that point in their career yet."[3] I will say more about how the film negotiates these gaming identity shifts, the possibility of being both/and one's "real" and alternative self, and the impact of this on its vision of young identities shortly. The High-5s both are and are not "real boys," men, and women, and are also differently real, at the same time.

The Cookie-Cutter Child

Online identities are universal in the 2045 world of *Ready Player One*, and inhabiting an avatar, albeit temporarily, is a universal practice. The young (or young-presenting) protagonists slip between their physical and digital identities with a meritocratic ease. In *A.I.*, a far darker film, it is not so simple. David's struggle is to be something he is not and never can be. So who or what is David, and why must Spielberg use a child to flesh out this drama of human and nonhuman selves? Would an adult not do just as well at articulating this bleak story of the death of the human race? Is David even a child—and, if so, how does the story persuade us of this? What does it mean for a director who is so "wonderful with *keeds*" to champion artificial kids?[4]

Before venturing further into the film itself, I want to pause on its main promotional image, which boldly asks what it is to be a child in the very act of advertising itself. The widely disseminated film's poster is designed around a replicated boy surrounded by teasing text. Though essentially a series of statements, cumulatively these pose the question of what David is even before one has seen the film. The most striking element of the poster's core visual image, which is at the same time both picture and letters, announces many of the film's key questions of identity and attachment, embodied boyhood, self-definition, and consciousness. The outline of a boy has been cut out, like a silhouette in a paper chain, but the figure has escaped from his frame stepping out of the letter A to form the letter I of the title. The suggestion is that there is a template for "boyness," which could be used for mass production. Or perhaps the opposite of this—that *this* boy is individual, and has escaped the *A* to become an *I*. Where the boy's (negative) shape (chopped in half) forms the absences that constitute the holes in the letter *A* for "Artificial," (and also "A" as indefinite article), he is the presence that stands upright as the letter *I* (the sovereign subject). Though this is literally *I* for "Intelligence," it also, of course, suggests the *I* of the *cogito*. Though silhouetted, he is clearly looking upward—wondering, questioning—as if seeking answers from the stars, as his predecessors Barry (in *Close Encounters*) and Elliott (in *E.T.*) had done. It is a smart and eminently readable image, which resonates with many of the film's questions: Is the child a cookie-cutter, production line commodity? Is he (also?) imbued with free will to step out of line? Surely this is a heavy philosophical burden for a child to bear, and these are unusually complex questions for a popular cinematic poster to pose. Yet the film bears them out: as he is pulled to his doom, Gigolo Joe's legacy statement to his mecha child David is "I am. I was."[5]

Of course, the authorship of a poster as a promotional object with a separate production origin to a film (here, Warners' marketing division) raises questions about its meaningfulness for the story of "Spielbergian" childhood this book is telling. I have also tried to highlight throughout that these meanings emerge both from Spielberg as a uniquely powerful, controlling presence, and as part of the composite collective enterprise that is film production, sometimes claiming complete control, sometimes promoting collaboration.[6] Nevertheless, as a first step toward the film, the poster proves remarkably enticing. The image of the boy is visually preceded by an extensive tagline—actually formed of six sentences set above the A.I./ wondering boy image. Cumulatively, they announce the ordinariness of his outward body, as well as the impossibility of him-self. The first four sentences detail David's physical characteristics:

David is 11 years old.
He weighs 60 pounds.

He is 4 feet, 6 inches tall.
He has brown hair.

Then there is a graphic gap, before the final two sentences complete the thought:

His love is real.
But he is not.

The first four sentences are designed to suggest ordinariness by drawing attention to his apparent everyday physicality, but there is marked dissonance between these two sets of statements, focusing on the "seemingness" of David's body. The possibility that David both is and is not real is a signal question for the film: Julian Rice cites the finished script as containing the word "real" forty-six times (2017, 46). This insistence is based on an existential uncertainty hanging on the way *A.I.* sets up the mecha/orga difference, with children placed in both camps, and the film's questions of human/posthuman identity posed in a familial frame. The issue of whether David is "real" comes down to whether he is conscious in the human sense of the term (and recalling Alan Turing's famous test):[7] he is intelligent (if artificially so), he has emotional responses (if forced by humans), and he will never be made of organic flesh.[8] All of these are in keeping with his high-end mecha origins, and also the reason he must sink to being a lowly fugitive. In his influential essay "Issues of Difference: *Alien* and *Blade Runner*," Steve Neale shows how differences such as human/monstrous often interact with or stand in for "sexual and racial categories of difference" in fantasy and science fiction (1989, 222). The racist responses to *Blade Runner*'s "skin jobs" (termed "replicants" rather than "mecha" in that film and franchise) effectively others/feminizes them; the film codes them as both socially subordinated and morally superior. Mecha are *A.I.*'s "skin jobs."

Indeed, the very first mecha that we see is presented in the context of how she looks rather than what she does, her body being central to how her "reality" is understood by the mecha herself, by diegetic others (both mecha and orga), and by the film's audience. This has a feminist dimension while pressing the question of how the outside relates to the inside. The opening scene finds Hobby addressing his technical and creative team by way of an industry showcase, in which he turns to a female colleague (Sheila) in the midst of the group of employees and first reveals her mecha status by stabbing her hand, then by ordering her to undress. It is a shocking setup: the question of her interiority and consent (Does she feel pain or shame? Is she a nonconscious machine or a conscious slave?) is answered by Hobby literally showcasing her insides for his audience, like the neurologist Jean-Martin Charcot displaying symptomatizing hysterical women patients for his students and colleagues at the Salpêtrière clinic in nineteenth-century Paris. Pushing a button inside her mouth and another on her back, Hobby causes her face to split open and reveal a constructed android interior hiding behind the convincing skin simulation. The inside is foregrounded but with a scrutiny that might, in body horror, be reserved for visceral gloop, yet here the nonorganic is pristine if still abject. Even in genre films, the abject need not be wet or "icky": Sheila's "real" face underneath does not ooze body fluids but reveals her to be a body without a soul—one of Julia Kristeva and Barbara Creed's definitions of the abject corpse, though Sheila has never lived. The mecha's fabricated "inside" undermines as well as underpins the too perfectly simulated "outside," with the inside revealed almost as soon as we are fooled by the outside, an outside that evokes an othering discourse predicated on invisible threat: on the outside "they" look "just like us," and "we," as well as the film's orga, cannot tell the difference.

So though it culminates in a lachrymose conclusion that establishes emotional connection as the stamp of one's most authentic self, like Spielberg's other visceral works (*Jaws*, *Duel*, *Jurassic Park*), *A.I.* initially foregrounds embodied threat and physical vulnerability. The Sheila revelation sets the scene for the arrival of David, at first presented as a simulation of a boy just as Sheila simulates a working woman. Like Pinocchio, it is the nature (or unnaturalness) of David's body that underpins the problem of how real he is, and which prompts Monica's first othering question, "Inside he's just like all the rest?" Henry, the excluded father, never understands the permutations of "inside" in Spielberg's landscape, so can only answer, "A hundred miles of fiber." On this the film is also ambivalent, showcasing viscera while also ultimately arguing that some have "truer" insides (the personhood, or soul, of David), while others do not (Sheila's physical and spiritual abjection).

Perhaps the most stark exposé of David's physical interior comes when he tries to eat spinach one mealtime, fusing his wiring, since eating—along with other orga bodily functions—is something he cannot do. The scene halts abruptly as David's mistake becomes clear: his face droops as if afflicted by a cyber-stroke, and he just *stops*. Surgery fixes him, surgery that has the theater of an operation but is really the mechanical fixing of the workshop. Where two years earlier *The Matrix* had envisaged humans as an energy source for an ever-consuming race of self-interested artificial beings, *A.I.* presents a drowned world of scarcity in which its android beings—in the words of the opening voice-over—"were never hungry and did not consume resources." Joining in with the materiality of family life (i.e., trying to eat as other humans eat) provokes this dire abjection: David should not (has no right to) consume, in any way. While the child's interior is opened, incised, he remains fully conscious, with his mother holding his hand while watching the welding in his open stomach cavity. As children protect their parents, so David reassures her that "it doesn't hurt," and Monica rushes away. If witnessing visceral surgery on one's son were not bad enough, why would it be better for Monica if it *did* hurt? Sue Short takes the machine's inability to cry as a baseline robotic definition (2011, x–xi). But this child-robot is also curiously clean: nothing that decomposes should or can go in or out of him. David's abjection is then "purely" physical: the spinach revolts, but this largely humanist film asserts another unalloyed "inner self."

A fairy-tale transition comes when Monica leaves her babe in the woods to fend for himself, loading the moral hierarchy of the rest of the film by advising him, "Only mecha are safe." Here David becomes a lost boy; Lester Friedman has noted that Spielberg's crowds of "psychologically and emotionally lost boys" are lost because of the "sheer number of missing, consumed, distant, or malevolent father figures" who have let them down (2006, 34). Spielberg's mothers may be dysfunctional (Williams 2017), but they rarely abandon. However, this one does: Scott Loren (2008) reads Monica's act as attempted infanticide. But is it? Why is it worse to discard the "hundred miles of fiber" David in the woods than it would be to abandon the very car in which Monica drives away, should it break down? David's status as a true *child* rightfully belonging in the nuclear family depends not only on whether it is possible to forget that he is not organic but on whether we can come to believe, as the film seems to, that the very presence of love in a creature's heart overrides such radical differences of bodily composition and mode of creation. Two aspects of *A.I.* in particular effect a shift of perspectives, refashioning David from a figure of monstrosity to one of sympathy, both rooted in his body. First, Haley Joel Osment's performance style changes radically after Monica has imprinted herself on him, and once again Spielberg sets up sympathy for the child as engendered through the physical performance of childhood by the child actor. Second, the impact of threat and risk to David's body within the developing story ratchets up the affect and effectively overrides the "hundred miles of fiber" qualification to his claim on authentic childness. I initially want to explore the second of these—how the threat of dismemberment, of radical bodily damage, pursues David—in conjunction with a wider set of questions the film poses about the body, before turning to Osment's performance.

Bodies of/in Peril and Pleasure

Underpinning many of *A.I.*'s questions from that poster onward is that of the "nature" of David's body: the film's representation and explanation of the child's flesh. The digital bodies of *Ready Player One* are accepted universal modes of social exchange; switching between different appearances and abilities, online and offline, is commonplace. The metaphors of bodies and embodiment in digital identity do not get close to what David must do: in virtual reality (VR) one might be said to "wear" a body like a costume, but David must *be* his body—he is trapped in the body of his maker's technological imagination. Even though the place where such bodies are destroyed is called the Flesh Fair, this is not regular flesh.

Following his abandonment, David joins a debased collective of mecha who have pleasured or serviced orga before being exiled or going on the run. They are routinely gathered up, tortured, and destroyed in the gladiatorial public spectacles of the Flesh Fairs Monica warns David about. "We are alive, and this is a celebration of life," boasts the master of ceremonies Lord Johnson-Johnson (Brendan Gleeson) at one such fair, as boiling oil is poured over and melts a kindly FemMecha Nanny (Clara Bellar), the only "person" who has offered David maternal kindness since Monica's abandonment. Here he also meets Gigolo Joe (Jude Law), a mecha sex worker who becomes his best father figure. Joe articulates the film's most acute statements of difference and shows that it is his (and David's) physical perfection that provokes their owners/clients most violently—it is one of the reasons David is unlovable.[9] Key to the orga's hostility toward the mecha is mecha physical superiority, whereas the young protagonists of *Ready Player One* can inhabit what they perceive as a "better" digital body (younger or older, stronger, bigger or smaller) but also can choose to slip back into their physically embodied forms. In *A.I.* the division is between types of beings, not physical manifestations of and in a single being. This enables the racial violence of orga against mecha, particularly prompted by orga's need for mecha. As Joe puts it: "They made us too smart, too quick, and too many. We are suffering for the mistakes they made because when the end comes, all that will be left is us. That's why they hate us, and that is why you must stay here, with me."

What, then, are the mecha experiencing as they are violated in the Flesh Fair spectacle? The avatars of *Ready Player One* "die" in the OASIS as one might in any gaming scenario, but what is lost is only the resources of online lives. The Flesh Fair dispatches artificial beings in a darker and more permanent way, and if this is not simply the wanton destruction of household gadgets, then it is a spectacle of death. Note Joe's acknowledgment that "we are suffering" in that previous quote: pain and death are embedded in the mecha's understanding of the struggle of inequality they endure. They care for each other and turn off each other's pain receptors before facing torture; one of them asks the existential question "Is my time over so soon?" as he faces his executioners. So why do the wanton humans only stop when a child robot is paraded? As David and Joe are readied for destruction, the crowd's baying turns to protest, with the spectacle of a child (or even the realistic simulation of a child) being destroyed for pleasure exceeding a limit of revenge and its accompanying sadistic frenzy both for the diegetic audience and as entertainment spectacle for Spielberg. Crucially, the Holocaust-inflected Flesh Fair, one of the film's darkest sequences, was Spielberg's conception. In his protracted script development, Kubrick explicitly aligned David's trauma with that of Holocaust victims, but it was Spielberg who put this to work in the Flesh Fair: "I'm the guy who did the dark center of the movie, with the Flesh Fair and everything else. That's why [Kubrick] wanted me to make the movie in the first place" (McBride 2010, 484). At this point David stands for the Jewish boy who "passes" as Aryan, until his mecha traits are technologically outed by an X-ray sensor. He does of course look almost archetypically Aryan, an interesting visual choice in the context of Spielberg's historical agenda.[10]

The Flesh Fair is not the only place where the film worries over physical composition and reframes it as threat. There is a pervasive anxiety around robotic genitalia—a place Spielberg would not venture toward if David were a real boy. Vivian Sobchack (1990) has explored the asexuality of male astronauts in science fiction cinema that is orchestrated around an absence of women and sex, but perhaps the worry of *A.I.* is not too little sex but too much. After Pris, the "standard pleasure model" in *Blade Runner*, *A.I.* presents an established sex industry serviced by mecha and based in the carnivalesque Rouge City. Sheila succinctly articulates her role through the performance of a range of physical signs: "Love is first widening my eyes a little bit and quickening my breathing a little and warming my skin and touching." When Hobby proposes the child creation to his colleagues as the next stage on from the "sensory toys" that do so well as responsive sexual partners, the link between adult mecha sex worker like Sheila and child as emotional toy for would-be parents is plain. David is more than a "sensuality simulator," but the limits of his body are a source of prime curiosity in the film. His genitalia are alluded to twice in the film: first, obliquely, when Monica refuses to put his pajamas on for him on his first night under their roof. She has engaged reasonably well in the parenting activities that lead up to this, but the film suggests that donning nightwear is too intimate. We have seen that boys' bedrooms are a staple of Spielberg's child landscapes: Martin's bedroom is replete with toys, including near-future gadgets that did double service across the line between child actor and child character—the press notes state that Osment and Jake Thomas (Martin) "spent many hours of their lunch periods playing with the many toys in Martin's bedroom." David does a fair job of performing the child-at-play, though we do not know if this is also play as pleasure for the character (as it is for the actor). The "tucking in" ritual is part of this performance: since David cannot sleep, who is this for? Perhaps, just to get his strangeness out of the way as respite for the parents? (He says, "I can never go to sleep. But I can lay quietly and not make a peep.") Later, after Martin comes home, the penile fascination returns. Crowding around him, the orga boys stroke his skin and wonder at how genuine it feels, the othering "right to touch" a subordinate being masked by boys' admiration for impressive technology. The boys also know that just as David cannot eat, so he cannot urinate, manhandling him with a symptomatic statement of mutual presence and absence: "Let's see what you can't pee with." It really is there, even if it does not function for real. The latent homoeroticism of this bullying moment before it all goes wrong for David (one of the boys stabs him) foregrounds a taboo anxiety about childhood sexuality per se that haunts this film, and Spielberg's work more widely.

David is, then, a toy boy, but—despite this penile fascination—he is not a sex toy. A conscious but manufactured commodity, he is more like a slave created to the measure of adult obsession, owned rather than parented, and both product for and victim of a heady complex of anxieties fueled by family desire, commercial innovation, and AI phobia. The Pinocchio precedent also places him in a long history of puppets in culture, beings who are directly controlled by a puppet master or who break free of their strings and find the ability to learn independently through a picaresque journey. It emerges that David's journey through a dangerous world is an accidental experiment in the development of emotion-based experience, overseen by his creator—who may still then be seen as a puppet master.[11] David slots uneasily into a world where children function primarily as the playthings of adults, eternally available and to be deployed at will. Indeed, Spielberg's screenplay explicitly refers to him as Monica's toy: Henry says as much, though Monica corrects the word to "gift." While this connotes generous or even miraculous bestowing on Monica as lucky recipient, the prematurely "gifted" David is only a gift as long as she chooses to view him in that way (David's "gifts" are exactly the reason his parents give him back).

"Gift" in the context of consumer culture also prefigures the rows of Davids and Darlenes that are later seen lined up in a robo-child production line at Hobby's headquarters, boxed and ready to ship like so many Christmas presents for a lucky elite, like any other identikit household commodity. They are literal "white goods." This powerful scene, with David confronted by dozens of copies of himself and despairing at his lack of uniqueness, recalls a wonderful example of postmodernism-for-kids in *Toy Story 2* (1999), when Buzz Lightyear finds himself on a massive store shelf with hundreds of other identical Buzzes, proclaiming that he is the "real" one. We may all be Spartacus (at least since Kubrick's eponymous 1960 film that created the iconic "I am Spartacus" moment), but the individualistic humanism of both *Toy Story 2* and *A.I.* means that all the others *cannot* be Buzzes and Davids. Both films support a notion of particular and unique individuals, borne out through characters proclaiming in their own ways (like Joe) "I am—I was." The Cartesianism of this suggests human consciousness, or rather a singularity that stands in for the human, but—with their conscious (and consciously constructed) beings—these films also reach to a model for humanism in the posthuman.

The *Toy Story* franchise also asks what happens to the toy when the child tires of and discards it, but in *A.I.* it is parents who get rid of "children" as they might abandon pet animals. As Scott Loren (2008) argues, David is a particular type of luxury consumer object, activated by the mother's need and able to reflect his owner's desire back onto her. Consumerism in *A.I.* is then interrogated through a scenario in which children are expendable accessories in their parents' lives; the film asks how adults use children, and it frames parenting as consumption. Anything that can be bought can also be thrown away. In his meditation on *A.I.*, originally written for *Sight and Sound* in 2001, J. Hoberman reads David, manufactured to fill the mother's gap, as "a sort of emotional prosthetic device, the Frankenstein monster of love" (2003, 77). But consumption is also somatically revealing. David heals Monica's grief for Martin, a grief that a doctor diagnoses as having gone "undigested"; he is the appliance that promises digestion of grief. Of course Martin then returns, so the grief is passed on to David (and reflected back to the mother), who can no more digest it than he can digest food. The implication is that in "having" children (generating them, or using them), parents must experience consumption as power and pain.

The sales tag inscribed on the rows of David and Darlene boxes reads, "At last a love of your own," which echoes the marketing of sex dolls, fabricated humanoids cut to the measure of a different adult human desire. David fulfills one domestic function for orga, but the "sensuality simulators" do too. One of these, Gigolo Joe, eventually parents David, bringing him closer to the exchange world of overt bodily labor. And just as Martin's friends want to see what David cannot pee with, so the question of how far the male prostitute Joe goes with his body is also an issue when we first see him, with a nervous female orga client raising the question of what kind of abnormal appendage he might have been fitted with to ply his trade, and whether penetrative sex might hurt: "I'm afraid of what you've got under there," she says. "May I see what it looks like first?" Spielberg, ever coy at sex scenes and mindful of the target age classification, implies but does not show. Joe wields his member as a sex toy, which is presumably its only function: since the more sophisticated one-off child model David cannot pee, no doubt the production-line sex worker cannot either, raising a series of further bodily questions: Does Joe ejaculate? How convincing is sex with a mecha? And if mecha feel pain, do they also feel orgasmic pleasure as part of the purchased "show"? It matters to David's display of filial love that he must, once imprinted, feel love himself (this is his tragedy).[12] Does Joe's pleasure equally matter? Does the mecha's pleasure underpin and determine the orga's? Do mecha have recreational sex with each other for the sheer android pleasure of it? This may be something of a "how many children had Lady Macbeth" question (in L. C. Knights's famous formulation), but the limitations and abilities of mecha are finely worked in this long-gestating film, and these Kubergian/Spielbrickian entities often and deliberately seem to supersede their factory settings. The interdependence of mecha and orga underpins the violence done to and done by, respectively, an awful tangle in which the robo-child is caught. Of course Joe does not just wield a sex toy appendage for his clients; his whole body is entirely sold as a romantic prosthetic, complete with a soundtrack of love songs. We never know if he also serves male orga, but "gigolo" suggests a younger man purchased by older women, originally as a dance partner, and Jude Law performs Joe with a lightness of foot modeled on a classical Hollywood song and dance man. Gigolo Joe also makes it clear that young robo sex workers do exist in his world: as he says to a car full of youths intent on a spring break–style pleasure trip, "There are girls your age that are just like me." The sex industry has long been an early adopter of new technologies: young mecha sex workers are, it seems, a more urgent manufacturing priority than loving mecha children.

As the prime articulator of the class/race battle that he finds himself losing (but which the film as a whole has the mecha finally winning), Joe is also able to address what sex work feels like as labor (emotional as well as physical): "We are the guiltless pleasures of the lonely human being. You're not going to get us pregnant. . . . We work under you, we work on you and we work for you. Man made us better at what we do than was ever humanly possible." Again, uncanny physical perfection provokes violence, but this conflict in turn seems to engender the development of "true" feeling, and perhaps an unconscious, in the beleaguered mecha underclass; Joe has been politicized by his work, but there is more. When later he returns to this theme in an explanation for why David has been cast out by his mother, he tells him: "She loves what you do for her, as my customers love what it is I do for them. But she does not love you, David. She cannot love you. You are neither flesh, nor blood. You are not a dog, a cat, or a canary. You were designed and built specific, like the rest of us. And you are alone now only because they tired of you, or replaced you with a younger model, or were displeased with something you said, or broke." Though overtly a statement of mecha inequality, read another way this becomes a more generalized critique of the selfish parenting of objectified children. All mecha are thus infantilized through use, but they are also the children of this story's future, in that they outlive the orga who created them. To extend this image, when developing the Pinocchio project that became *A.I.* in Spielberg's hands, Kubrick thought of future AI beings as his great-grandchildren (Rice 2017, 183).

Here, then, is a direct challenge to the film's own tagline, and further elaboration on the film's understanding of the real: "His love is real. He is not." *A.I.* fully considers David real, and not just because David is so poignantly performed by a human. The film argues—more psychoanalytically than sentimentally—that love makes the lover real. And, like *Blade Runner*'s replicants, whose implanted memories are no less real for being belated or originally someone else's, David's implanted feelings suggest that *all* feelings are more or less implanted, enabled by chemistry and fostered by familial nurturing. Here all bodies are "real" bodies, all emotions "real" too. It is as if Spielberg has finally looked in the eye those who have used the word "sentimental" as a weapon of critique and, emboldened by Kubrick as ghostly collaborator, has called their bluff. Humanist Spielberg acknowledges that body chemistry may differ between orga and mecha, but—with a strangely proto-Marxist flourish—there is the suggestion that it is the subservience of the mecha that fosters their feelings, their compassion, and a hyperawareness of pain elicited through exploitation. This is supported by a framework of authenticity that characterizes many humanist fictions focused on children. That these feelings are grounded in cyber-circuitry rather than fleshly synapses matters nothing. In this fable the moral distinction is not new: just as children have been celebrated as innocent or castigated as demons throughout cultural history, so the cyborg/replicant/robot has been polarized as better than us or worse than us since at least the early twentieth century—a utopian ideal, a moral touchstone, or else a dangerous, amoral monster. That both *A.I.* and *E.T.* are child's-point-of-view films (blurring distinctions between other/child/android) already aligns our belief and sympathy with the alien other.

It is, then, entirely appropriate that the focus of mecha consciousness and noble subordination should be a disenfranchised child, though it is also interesting that he is seconded by a sex worker politicized by inequality. And, as the "2000 years into the future" final sequence evidences, history is on the mecha's side. This elevation of mecha is prefigured by Donna Haraway's cyborg manifesto (originally published in 1985), in which machines make better "animals" than biological bodies do, and the distinction between animal-human and machine is a "leaky" one: "Late-twentieth-century machines have made thoroughly ambiguous the difference between natural and artificial, mind and body, self-developing and externally designed, and many other distinctions that used to apply to organisms and machines. Our machines are disturbingly lively, and we ourselves are frighteningly inert" (2004, 11). *A.I.* goes further than simply suggesting that we are David and David is us: he is one view of the future, and orga are stuck in the past. In an essay on Kubrick and philosophy, Jason T. Eberl asks, "Can an artificially created being possess the qualities that define a *person*—a being who merits a fundamental respect and bears certain inalienable rights?" (2007, 235). Spielberg's *A.I.* concludes that the human is a state of mind rather than a bodily condition, while also allowing for vestiges of the organic human to survive digitally. Current discussion about the ethics of developing artificial intelligence (AI) already focuses on issues such as encoding empathy responses that may bring AI machines closer to born humans. As I write, in the first quarter of the twenty-first century, we already use AI robots in care for the elderly, including those with dementia; Alexa and Siri read bedtime stories to children. What would Spielberg's film look like if posed the other way around, positing an AI parent raising an orga child? I now want to turn to what Osment brings to these questions, through a physical and emotive performance that carries the film.

Acting Natural: Laughter and Tears in Haley Joel Osment's Performance

A.I. is highly lachrymose. David is of course one of Spielberg's most acute figures of melodrama, one of those children who functions to "melodrama" (understood as a verb) the overarching genre (science fiction) in which he appears. Osment's performance, as well as David's predicament, was praised for its tear-jerking qualities, even though he himself is not required to produce the consummate "evidence" of authentic performance, that hallmark of thespian skill—actual tears. Yet in the round of discussions of this film that I have participated in at various universities and film festivals and with my students, I have lost count of how many people have testified to their tears, which often articulate their position as child or parent or both: one woman, pregnant at her time of viewing, told me, "I cried so much I got leg cramps."[13] This embodied cinema that provokes a (leaky, abject) response from its audience is somehow too much, yet predicated on a performance that is strangely too little, but brilliantly so. David cannot cry, cannot blink, cannot sleep. In contrast to Henry Thomas as Elliott in *E.T.*, Osment does not have to perform tears to get the job or to elicit them in his audience, but while as a real human child he must sleep and blink, in character he must perform the unblinking eternally awake other. David is, then, defined by what he cannot do, by what he is not; Osment's excellence rests on an ability to bear forth these inabilities, this "notness."

But Osment does not solely perform one note; this dramatic showcase won him the Saturn Award for the Best Performance by a Younger Actor in 2001. When Monica initiates the imprinting process, the child's acting style changes, becoming more humanly natural, less angularly android. He never loses the grave studied look, but once it is underpinned by love and fear, it becomes more fluid, like that of a guarded animal. Clearly the question of what a "natural" human is (and how it must appropriately behave) is central to the subtle negotiation Osment makes. I have discussed throughout this book what it means to consider childhood as an element in the director's reworking of genre. Spielberg himself has offered as the "master image" that sums up his career the moment in *Close Encounters* when the boy opens the door to the blast of UFO light, "that beautiful but awful light, just like fire coming through the doorway. And he's very small, and it's a very large door, and there's a lot of promise or danger outside that door" (Ebert and Siskel 1991, 72). The child in Spielberg's films functions to skew or mobilize genre: like women, children bring melodrama straight into the heart of those genres in which Spielberg specializes (fantasy and science fiction, the war film and action-adventure); we recall that in 1988 he said, "In my work everything is melodrama. I don't think I've ever *not* made a melodrama" (Spielberg 1988, 14). The child performing the child rewrites whatever genre it finds itself in on its own terms, inscribing this Spielbergian discourse of childhood for the film, but also writing it in its own language.

In David's/Osment's case this is not primarily materialized through tears, but through the behavior that is often seen as tears' opposite, laughter—another natural reaction that David has trouble *doing*, but Osment shows considerable acting chops *playing*. If one were a Frankensteinian robot maker like Hobby, with apparently endless resources dedicated to manufacturing an artificial human indistinguishable in look from a real human, one might place the ability to laugh convincingly and in context as a key desirable attribute (along with the need for each child to be unique, which makes the cookie-cutter Davids and Darlenes all the more puzzling as a credible commercial proposition). In order for the synthetic humanoid boy to "pass" as a child human, he must demonstrate laughter. David laughs in only two sequences in the whole story (then again, he does not have much to laugh about). Neither of these moments is particularly funny: though characters around him are "infected," it is hard to imagine audiences joining in. In one incongruous dinner table scene before imprinting, Osment performs the reaction deliberately to look fake. But within the scene, the artificial child's

FIGURE 6 Dinner table Oedipal triptych in *A.I. Artificial Intelligence.*

artificial laughter provokes "genuine" laughter in his parents that—though of course also performed by actors (O'Connor and Robards)—looks spontaneous and mirthful. In this wordless scene a chain of laughter circulates between mecha son and orga parents, which dances between real and faked, humored and cheerless.

This short sequence takes place as Henry and Monica are getting used to the strange presence of the stilted boy, who Osment performs as prehuman, overly mechanical, and yet unable to "pass" as a human in movement, speech, and behavior. The scene begins with a striking overhead shot, framing David through a hoop-shaped pendulum lampshade (figure 6) that both haloes him and separates him from his parents, who are ranged to his left (mother) and right (father). As the (Jewish) Freud might have pointed out, and the (Jewish) Spielberg (or Kubrick) cannot fail to have noticed, such Oedipal triptychs evoke the holy family of Christian iconography, a familiar storytelling trope across Western cinema, regardless of religious belief. Though David has, at this point in the film, not yet stepped forward to claim his place as its protagonist, the axis of action here runs from mother to father with child at the center: though the table is oval, the child is framed at its "head"—he also references Leonardo da Vinci's Christ presiding over the Last Supper. Only Monica and Henry are eating here: David has a place set for him, but his bowl is empty. Regular establishing shots also suggest a place set at the opposite side of the table (a breadbasket does service for the missing son Martin's absent presence). Having commenced, then, with a visual disconnection (the funky overhead light holding the image of David's face separate), the meal continues to reinforce David's difference. The conventions of continuity editing form the familiar grammar of the scene, with shots ping-ponging over each parent's shoulders, to those establishing shots framing David at the center, to close-ups of individual faces.

Regular and simply orchestrated though it is, this is a turning point in the film. David scrutinizes every forkful raised to the mouth—like many children, he stares when it is inappropriate to do so (his robot errors are really child errors). In the near silence David mimics the physicality of eating with dining implements, as might a toddler learning to feed himself independently: he raises his empty glass to his lips, winds imaginary spaghetti onto his empty fork.[14] Then, quite suddenly, David/Osment explodes with laughter, and everyone jumps. It is incongruous, exaggerated, shocking—the very definition of "bursting out." He booms a regular, repeated noise that has none of the cadence or unpredictability of a recognizably human peal of laughter. Instead it is a shouted performance of ha, ha, ha's. Instantly, Monica jumps and screams; perhaps Spielberg slyly instructed his twelve-year-old actor to shock the adults for real as they do not seem to know precisely when the burst is coming. The laughter initially seems inappropriate, but it is a response to a stray strand of spaghetti dangling from Monica's mouth, which she then plays with to extend the joke as she herself begins to laugh.

This aspect of David's laughter is, indeed, "true": William Hazlitt's famous line on laughter and humanity runs, "Man is the only animal that laughs and weeps, for he is the only animal that is struck with the difference between what things are, and what they ought to be" (2004, 410). While this might evoke David's seeming/being, it is Monica who springs the joke. She ought to eat cleanly, but she eats messily. Philosophers have long diagnosed laughter as a superiority response—in the seventeenth century Hobbes described that moment of "sudden glory" when the laugher rises above the laughed-at.[15] However, what David "feels" in response to this remains a mystery because his laughter sounds so alien and extends into ever stranger and falser territory—a booming cascade of ha's followed by an almost inaudible cackle, changes in cadence that mimic the ebbs and flows of real human laughter but here do it *too much*. It is quite monstrous and evokes the strange dark, horrifying child of cultural history from the Middle Ages onward.[16] David's/Osment's face is also set into an expression that could do double service as fear (figure 7)—without the audio track, he might be screaming (of course the phrase "screaming with laughter" is another way of expressing extremity of response).

Strange as Osment's laughter style is, it is gauged within the story for its contagiousness, demonstrating that even the synthetic mode of the android can be as contagious as that which sounds authentic or familiar. First the adults laugh at their own shock, but this does not die down once the adrenaline has subsided: Monica and Henry are quickly overcome and perform at least two different forms of laughter that play out a slightly hysterical exchange, a wordless conversation of sounds. David ejects bursts of sound mimicking the natural; the parents are

FIGURE 7 Screaming with laughter: Haley Joel Osment performing *A.I.*'s uncanny robot child David.

twisted by spontaneous paroxysms. David's laughter is from the neck up, delivered with a spooky-child expression of open mouth and fixed, shining eyes. The parents, by contrast, symptomatize a range of laughing styles that present them as creatures of individuality. The edit shows, in shot-countershot, the adults' whole upper bodies given over to a pantomime of happy helplessness—hands covering mouths, then opening up in gestures of delirious surrender, faces looking this way and that as if seeking rescue from uncontrolled hilarity, wrinkled noses and foreheads and eyes that close, then connect, then look around for further confirmation of the shared situation.

In short, the adults lose control, but the child does not. While their laughter starts as the effervescence of shock, it quickly runs away with itself, becoming funnier the longer it continues. Laughter breeds laughter: like a disease carrier who feels no symptoms, David (another species) has contaminated them with a reaction that he himself does not seem to feel, and it circulates. The philosopher Henri Bergson, speaking from a wider model valorizing animism, would argue that the laughter here continues because "*we laugh every time a person gives us the impression of being a thing*" (2008, 33). For Bergson, the comical is the stilted—a human mimicking an object. The valued aspects of life and being are movement, flexibility, and agility, and for Bergson the comic is the opposite of this: "THE ATTITUDES, GESTURES AND MOVEMENTS OF THE HUMAN BODY ARE LAUGHABLE IN EXACT PROPORTION AS THAT BODY REMINDS US OF A MACHINE" (24; uppercase in original). Of course, David *is* a machine, and laughs like a thing. In his analysis of *A.I.*, Sidney Perkowitz even refers to David consistently as "it" rather than "he" (2010, 148–149); Roger Ebert read the story as a failed drama about "a very advanced gadget" (2001; see also Ebert 2011, where he later revises his view of the film). Osment must play out that "thingness," even if this is not the film's final rendition of the boy. E.T. cannot laugh, but he is never an "it," even if, as we saw earlier, his gender identity is more fluid than the pronoun Elliott insists upon would suggest. Monica may at first be the cause of David's Hobbesian "sudden glory," but she is humorously agile enough to get in on the joke. However, while Bergson would argue that it is David who then becomes the object—with Monica and Henry turning the laughter around onto his strangeness—what actually happens in the performance is that they lose themselves in laughing at laughter itself. David's involvement in this somehow makes him more lovable, as it is this sequence that precipitates the imprinting to come.

The merriment prevails even though David injects another jolt of strangeness: in the midst of this three-way laugh-in, he stops as instantly as he started, as if a switch has been flicked. Robot laughter can be turned off like a faucet, but human laughter must trickle to a stop: as Monica and Henry slow down, they betray an awkwardness that suggests it is *their* continuing laughter that is now inappropriate, with David fixedly observing them as they put on the brakes. The ensuing meaningful glances exchanged between the parents is evidence that something of real emotional significance has taken place. Perhaps, artificial though the robot child might be, he has managed to provoke "real" responses in the would-be parents? Though short and wordless, the scene is an important narrative juncture in David's story, since—despite his strangeness, made even more manifest by Osment's baying—it signals a new acceptance of the cuckoo child. Straight after this, Monica is able to tuck him into bed for the first time, and the next day she imprints him as her own. *A.I.* as a whole mostly charts David's appalling impotence, but here at least Osment's curiously freakish performance shows him leading and then terminating the strange laughter party.

If David has difficulty laughing convincingly, it may also be because he is from a long line of melancholy robots and paranoid androids. Eric Wilson sees the android as imbued with existential sadness because he expresses his maker's relationship to loss: like Professor Hobby, the fashioners of automatons and artificial beings in cultural history have put their inventions in the place of an absence; we learn that Hobby has made mecha David in the image of his own dead son, David. In Spielberg's curiously philosophical screenplay, Hobby conjectures that creating the potential to love will be the catalyst for the formation of a true inner life, the means "by which [the loving, mecha child will] acquire a kind of subconscious . . . an inner world of metaphor, of intuition, of self-motivated reasoning, of dreams." For Wilson, such robotic self-consciousness is a contagious response to the melancholy of its maker: "Humanoid machines reflect forms of melancholia that have resulted from what human beings have perennially called 'the fall'" (E. G. Wilson 2006, 2).[17] But, having created a being in the image of their loss, the maker of automatons all too frequently casts off its progeny into a hostile world of which the creature must then make some awful, incomplete sense. David does not acquire self-consciousness from love itself but from the pain that knots around unresolved love, just as Joe achieves emotional and political consciousness through his experience of unequal labor. Joe replicates a fantasy of romantic desire; David stands in for the absent child but can never be the thing he simulates, neither Hobby's dead doppelgänger son nor Monica's living one. No wonder laughter does not come easily to him, nor to his mechanized kin. No wonder laughter is so rare in *A.I.*

But David's laugh in this early sequence is startling not just because robots see nothing to laugh about. Sometimes they simply *cannot* laugh convincingly, and laughter becomes a touchstone of their artifice. Of course, there is a substantial history of fleshly automatons in visual culture—creatures who, by dint of their elastic, muscular mouths, may indeed have the technical ability to smile: David is one of these.[18] He does not look like a robot—his ability later to convincingly "pass" as a human child pitches him into trouble as well as (occasionally) saving him. Laughter is one moment when we "tell" the difference, a "telling" addressed by Frances McDonald, who reads cyber-laughter as usually threatening: "representations of laughter in SF serve the therapeutic function of propping open the increasingly negligible gap between human and machine. In SF, natural laughter is coded as being a signal of authenticity and sentience; artificial laughter is the synthetic being's 'tell'" (2012, 116). It is, then, entirely genre-appropriate that Osment so skillfully performs David as a "bad" laugher, and it raises the entangled question of how an unnatural child (one who cannot fulfill the dictum of spontaneous joy) reveals assumptions about passable humanity. What, the performance asks, is natural laughter, and why is it so welded to our fantasies of the happy child? David's uncanny laughter—more than his inability to blink or cry—magnifies his more generalized unnaturalness. Indeed, before David is switched on to bond with Monica, he is a less convincing simulation than after, and Osment's performance, as noted earlier, reflects this: this early laughter must not look natural, since at this stage he is a doll-child that mimics childishness but does not inhabit it.

This is a sophisticated distinction for a twelve-year-old actor to negotiate. In an interview he discusses some basic principles of playing a mecha, such as never blinking.[19] The laughter is more subtly different, performed as out of place rather than wrong. It reveals not an underlying mirth but a programming that tells him to exude such signs and sounds when confronted with particular stimuli. Osment does not perform the scene as if David genuinely "feels" something funny but rather as if, having recognized that it *should* be funny, he must perform an adult-pleasing display through appropriate-seeming behavior. And what human child has not done this? David's/Osment's is, then, the essence of hollow laughter, but not in the way we usually understand it (to mean laughter tinged with blackness or bleakness, laughter fringed with darkness), but because it emanates from *knowing* something to be funny but not "finding" it funny—the very opposite of the spontaneous child. What Osment performs looks like forced laughter—the laughter associated with "humoring" someone (a child telling an unfunny joke, perhaps, or someone who needs their comic aspirations to be flattered). Here he precisely does not "lose it." Before and after this telling laugh, Osment must obviously finely judge his performance: before imprinting, he smiles on cue and displays a too-bright desire to please. After imprinting he is increasingly grave, wary, and from thereon in, a mixture of afraid, panicked, and distressed. Of course, Osment was by this point no stranger to dark roles or to an actor's immersion in character: we saw in chapter 2 his propensity for embracing painful extremes in order to "method" his way into a role. His performance in *The Sixth Sense* ("a raw, exposed nerve during the entire film") involved him "getting scared all day," which, he told journalist Susan King, he never tired of. Though worried about a child inhabiting such disturbing material, the director M. Night Shyamalan saw Osment as an adult actor: "Because the material was so intense, Shyamalan was concerned for the kids auditioning. 'But it never entered my mind with him,' the director said. 'He had such an understanding of the material. I asked him my usual question: "Did you read the scenes or did you just get handed them by your agent right now?" He said, "I read the script twice." He had a thorough understanding of the character and the movie. I treated him exactly the way I treated all of the other actors" (King 1999). Once more we encounter the paradox of the child actor: if he is good, and the material is "serious," and he behaves like a professional, he will be viewed as an honorary adult rather than a child with particular and focused talents.[20]

David does not laugh again until the concluding sequence of the story, when, 2,000 years into the future, an advanced civilization of mecha is able to create a clone of Monica for him to play with for one perfect day only (*this* Monica will not abandon him, though she will die at the end of the day, but for that one day she will love him unconditionally). The clone convincingly passes as his mother (O'Connor performing a kinder semblance of Monica), and, after his long learning journey, David looks like a happy child. This time Osment performs a form of laughter that does not "tell" of its difference but nudges the humanoid toward the human (with David and the simulated mother as the only images of humanity left). Where Osment's earlier android laughter was directed outward, at the object David's programming told him to find funny, the conclusion's "real boy laughter" is a shared experience of play.

Of course it is not really Monica with whom David spends his perfect day at the end of the film but his fantasy of her: *she* now becomes the plaything, the toy. After 2,000 years in frozen limbo, David's Freudian unconscious is manifest, for the film ends with the astonishing Oedipal wish fulfillment of the son in bed with his mother. This follows a montage in which, like a young patient in Kleinian child analysis, David paints naive pictures narrating a version of his picaresque tribulations for the clone Monica, who has no understanding or memory of his experience. Kubrick observed in his notes for the film, referring to Ian Watson's story treatment, "David wants to become a real boy, which is impossible, but he manages to turn Monica into an android" (quoted in Harlan and Struthers 2009, 20). David has first served a woman (Monica, who needed something to perform "childness" for her), and the parallel with Gigolo Joe is made clear by Vivian Sobchack, who notes that they both "enact performative desire for a woman" (2008, 2). Later it is the woman who fulfills his need.

But more than this, the creation of clone Monica suggests a queerer notion, of the boy as life giver. Just as Elliott nurtures E.T., so David brings forth life: the (boy) child is father to the mother. This is a strange inversion of both Oedipus and conventions of parenting: the boy not only is nonorganic but also is (too) young, while also being 2,000 years old, and the "son" of the woman he bears and fantasizes. As discovered at multiple points in this book, semblances of family form themselves in Spielberg's family melodramas in a variety of nonstandard ways. This may beg the question of why their shared laughter, at the end, sounds so natural, since both beings are now artificial. Perhaps it reveals that what was wrong with David's laughter at the beginning was not that it "told" on his artificiality, but that David laughed in a foreign register to that of his parents: David has finally learned to laugh like his mother. Would he have been, or have sounded, as happy if the fantasy had turned the tables, fulfilling Kubrick's note, and Monica had instead learned to laugh like David? For the first (and last) time, mother and son laugh the same laugh. That it is underpinned by a shared mirth is more evident of the existence of an android unconscious than anything else in this remarkable posthuman yet Oedipal story.

By contrast, *Ready Player One* does not seem to recognize the same difference between physical/fleshly and digital selves. Its young characters slip easily between their limited organic selves and their powerful fantasy avatars, rendering these constructed digital identities as an ever-shifting fulfillment of each player's desire. But the film's conclusion—the closure of the OASIS online realm for two days of the week—suggests that "real life" has its benefits too, and Spielberg's direction and editing choices ultimately privilege the real. While Wade slips into Parzival, and Samantha slips into Art3mis with the quick donning of a diegetic VR suit, for actors Tye Sheridan and Olivia Cooke to morph into the online parts of their roles, a panoply of motion capture skills and digital technology must be deployed. Cooke said in interview that she enjoyed her performance capture work because it enabled her to bring more to the role—"it was liberating . . . uninhibited in a wonderful way": "You're in this white box with 150 sensors and cameras around; you're wearing these funny suits and you have this head camera on with four cameras attached to capture your facial expressions. But you were just forced to live in your imagination and forget all that; because there were no sets or camera angles, you could just do these long sequences without stopping" (Lambie 2018). While Spielberg seems once again to welcome the creative input of his young performers in authoring their double characters,[21] of course what Cooke conveys may be true of any motion capture performance. The release of the film was accompanied by fanfares around Spielberg's innovative use of VR technology to inform the actors' understanding of the settings their avatars inhabited: VR headsets enabled the actors to orientate themselves around the digital world of the avatar-led action-adventure story, a canvas for character creation. But while continuing to describe himself as a technical pioneer, Spielberg also promoted the film through the idea that technology must serve emotional connection, and (like children's tears in *E.T.*) the actors' young fleshly faces are his prime special effect here. The overabundant digital world within which these actors play out imagined lives, and the visual spectacle this presents to audiences are not, then, underpinned by or created in service of a belief in an unfettered freedom of identity above all else. *Variety* reported the virtual production supervisor Gary Roberts as saying, "Getting the performances right was very important to Steven. . . . He was cutting back and forth between the avatar and the live-action actor, so the audience would be able to make comparisons directly." Actors' actual facial expressions were then anchors for the storytelling across and between the real and the virtual world; as Grady Cofer, the Industrial Light & Magic visual effects supervisor, has said, "When it came to the avatar animations, Spielberg scrutinized facial performance 'to the nth degree'" (all quotes by Parisi 2019). So while the young characters in the story may choose avatars that augment or supplant their physicality or age, Spielberg wanted the virtual to be regularly—and finally—anchored to the reality of their human characters and their performing selves. Pinocchio may yearn to be a real boy, and may indeed imagine he has become one, but (as *A.I.* suggests and Guillermo del Toro's *Pinocchio* [2022] confirms), his wooden body remains the story's material reference point.

On Not Growing Up: David, Peter Pan, and Pinocchio

Both *A.I.* and *Ready Player One* are coming-of-age films predicated on the child or youth changing through learning—to love, to problem-solve, to find family outside of biology. Wade and Samantha change in and out of their avatars, young people in both guises, but always fixed and referenced back to their "real" selves. They will never entirely "be" their virtual characters, but the humanistic conclusion shows that they do not want to be. In this sense Spielberg's *Ready Player One* is a reverse Pinocchio story, with the selves starting in the real, returning to it, and preserving all of its power and problems. David inhabits a strange physical unchangingness that is central both to his emblematic childness and to his connected but contradictory inability to ever be a real child. In this sense his tragedy is the opposite of the (all-too-quickly-changing) child actor who fleshes him out—and who, at twelve years of age and with an Oscar nomination behind him, was nevertheless on the brink of obsolescence *as a child*. When Professor Hobby refers to the perfect child android as "caught in a freeze-frame, always loving, never ill, never changing," he may as well be describing the typecast child actor, or the dream of a child star, never to change and always to work.

Though a preternaturally talented child actor (and like Henry Thomas before him), as an adult Osment has so far sustained an acting career but has not matched his early career plaudits. Growing up takes away as well as gives; the ghost of Peter Pan once again haunts this story of boys and their performance.

I want to conclude with origins. Warners secured the rights to Ernest Cline's novel *Ready Player One* in 2011, and though Spielberg did not become attached to the film until 2015 (Kroll 2015), in many ways this seems the consummate Spielberg product, with its 1980s nostalgia, its gaming pleasures, and heartwarming teamwork by its young ensemble cast set against massive scale digital special effects landscapes. Its release was accompanied by energetic comparisons between a (beloved and reviled in equal measures) fiction source and its adaptation by a studio behemoth. *Ready Player One*'s young adult target demographic made it cut to the measure of Spielberg's favored family adventure film template. *A.I.* is a rather different case, with critically predetermined views about its cultural parentage. How we read the child in this film, initially a Kubrick project, pivots on competing views of *A.I.* as the manifestation of Kubrick's or Spielberg's vision, often read—as we have seen—as mutually exclusive, with that dominant critical perspective deeming Spielberg as himself too popular to be a fit collaborator for the more serious Kubrick. Eberl, for instance, reads *A.I.* as an entirely Kubrickian vision, with David as a sympathetic angel set against *2001*'s diabolical HAL; Kubrick even "handpicked Spielberg" (2007, 245). Teresa Heffernan calls the project a "collaboration between the cerebral director of *2001: A Space Odyssey* . . . and the sentimental director of *E.T. the Extra-Terrestrial* (1982)" (2018, 11). Tim Kreider (2003, 33) even deems the part of the film that is emotionally "manipulative" a children's film, while its more complex qualities (Kubrick's) are the "adult film" in the mix. In the preface to his coedited book on *A.I.*, the film's producer (and Kubrick's brother-in-law) Jan Harlan writes that Spielberg's involvement was "authorized by Stanley himself" (Harlan and Struthers 2009, 8). Harlan's afterword to the same book seems to reinstate some kind of equality in its subtitle "The Two Masters" but notes that "Stanley's vision was too black and cynical for an expensive film that had to appeal to a broad family audience. Steven had the ability to lighten the tone without changing the substance" (148). In light of repeated deployment of "lightness" as a term of critique across Spielberg's reception, set against the supposedly "serious" and culturally revered qualities of dark cynicism, this reads like damning with faint praise. More devastating is Peter Bradshaw, reviewing the film on its UK release: "In theory, Kubrick should play the salty Lennon to Spielberg's sucrose McCartney. . . . AI winds up with Kubrick's empathy and Spielberg's intellectual muscle. It's a lethal combination" (2001). The balance of power and priority between the directors—cerebral or sentimental, serious or popular, salty or sucrose, Lennon or McCartney—widely characterized journalistic film criticism on the film's release.

This chapter shows Spielberg's intellectual muscle, as writer as well as director, to be a significant cultural force (and I will refrain here from commenting on Kubrick's capacity for empathy); knee-jerk critical spite does him (and Paul McCartney) a disservice. The development of *A.I.* from Kubrick's blueprint has continuing implications for Spielberg's director image, as articulated and mediated by the child. Parental resonances abound in the two filmmakers' relationship, with accounts of their friendship inevitably invoking a father-son dyad: Andrew Gordon sees the partnership as one of a series of mentor relationships Spielberg entered into throughout his life with older Jewish men as father figures (2008, 228), but the surrogate parenting also extends beyond the death of the father and the creative survival of the "child" who is haunted by the father's overbearing post-mortem presence: Spielberg reports that, as his screenplay developed, "I felt like I was being coached by a ghost!" (Abramowitz 2001). There is also a purely practical element to the question of who was capable of what in its genesis. A key trait that has made Spielberg a consummate director of children is—post-*Jaws* at least—his efficiency in keeping to a tight production schedule. This became particularly important when he took over *A.I.* from Kubrick, who was originally going to direct it, with Spielberg as producer and long-standing collaborator. Over the decades that he worked on it, Kubrick did not refer to the project as "A.I." but as "Pinocchio" (Feeley 1999). But though Spielberg himself adhered to the Pinocchio legacy, Peter Pan is also evident: David is a Peter Pan character because, since he is not alive, he cannot grow up.

"Real" children are of course in a constant process of change, which is exactly the child star's problem for career longevity. Sameness is the signal element of David's image, and the impact on the production of the central character being a "fixed" child was therefore salient to its production story. Because typically Kubrick's production development runs across several years, casting a child actor who would change (by virtue of being a child) was problematic, so Kubrick explored the possibility of developing a robot performer or a lifelike puppet that would not have the aging problems of a "real boy." Following some initial discussion around developing a robot actor with Mitsubishi, then at the cutting edge of convincing humanoid robotics, Kubrick turned to Industrial Light and Magic, which started to develop a live-action/practical effects puppet with a "genderless, mannequinlike visage" (Schruers 2001, 53; see also Seabrook 2003). Kubrick also enlisted Chris Cunningham, at the time an animatronic artist, to create a silicone child in the likeness of the director's own five-year-old grandson (a strange echo of Hobby's re-creation of his David) (Fordham 2001, 70; McBride [2010, 479] reports that Kubrick's *nephew* was the model). Under Kubrick's direction, the boy performer would not be "real." Though these technical developments proved unfeasible,[22] even more difficult for Kubrick was the prospect of getting a live performing child to stay developmentally "still" (as David must) across his customary long production schedules. With a speedier approach to principal photography, Spielberg took the project on, better placed to represent a child who is frozen in sameness. Working with Osment for just a few months in late 2000, he showed that alacrity can capture eternity better than the most carefully crafted long-term productions. David knows that however organic he looks and acts, love will only come with a body that changes and, paradoxically, moves him beyond boyhood.

Yet for the child actor the opposite is true. To be a real boy is to be capable of mutation (aging)—in other words, to be not a boy for very long. Every child actor works in the shadow of their own obsolescence. The casting director Mark Brandon, responsible for casting children between age ten and twelve in the stage production of *The Lion King*, says, "We're also challenged because at that age, the kids get too big in about twelve seconds" (Kondazian 2000, 39). Spielberg aged David up from Kubrick's five-year-old boy to the eleven-year-old we see (Argent 2001, 52)—presumably in order to tackle scenarios particular to the older child, and because an older child's working day can be longer. But of course the question of robots or real boys, of technological puppetry or child actors, hinges around that of Stanley or Steven (though Stan Winston did also try to "talk Steven into letting us construct a complete robotic version of Haley Joel Osment," which Spielberg resisted [Fordham 2001, 70]). Authorial imprint and collaboration are illuminated by the child, and the child image is manipulated across this.

Layering into the more Spielbergian *Peter Pan*, *Pinocchio* becomes a fascinating source for a visceral melodramaturgist like Spielberg, and even more so for Kubrick, who envisioned the *A.I.* story as a far closer adaptation. Of course Spielberg had previously referenced Disney's film *Pinocchio*, released in 1940 (six years before the director was born), in *Close Encounters of the Third Kind*. Here Roy Neary proposes taking his children to a rerun of the film that he "grew up with," and when he later ascends into the alien ship at the film's conclusion, Ned Washington and Leigh Harline's song "When You Wish upon a Star"—the signal tune and message of the Disney film—is referenced and interpellated into John Williams's score, enabling Spielberg to convey, as he put it, Neary "los[ing] his strings" (quoted in McBride 2010, 283). Carlo Collodi's serialized *The Story of a Puppet* (1881; later consolidated as the 1883 book *The Adventures of Pinocchio*) tells of a fabricated wooden puppet who aspires to becoming a human fleshly boy. It is a moral tale that consolidates the father-son relationship through the emotional and physical journey of the child. In *A.I.* we see Monica reading the tale to a revived Martin, at his (malicious) instigation (hoping it will upset David). Throughout *A.I.*'s long gestation, in which Kubrick worked with, and rejected, numerous collaborators, the writer Sara Maitland—exasperated at the Pinocchio insistence—objected, "You just can't load two and a half thousand millenniums onto the poor little Pinocchio story" (Feeley 1999). But load he did, only for Spielberg to add in a poor little Peter Pan story to leaven (or enrich) the mix of European antecedents.

This hybrid Pinocchio/Pan story is not just a function of the main character and his relationships with family, but of the whole protracted production. *A.I.* is a transnational Pinocchio/Pan: a U.S. movie recalling a European fairy tale and children's story/play, mediated by a British science fiction writer (Aldiss), yet also the movie child of an American (Kubrick) who left the United States for the United Kingdom in 1961, and passed the directorial baton on to Spielberg because of his track record in crossing family fare with science fiction, as well as working with children. Though Kubrick initiated Pinocchio as a way of thinking about AI and human identity, Spielberg folded Peter Pan into the development as a way of articulating childhood. But Spielberg himself has also been seen as a Pinocchio figure, and this once again pertains to his auteurial public image and the "seriousness" of his corpus: "If the tale of an entertainer who yearns to be an artist sounds a bit like the story of a puppet—or an android—who yearns to be a boy," wrote Rachel Abramowitz on the release of *A.I.*, "it's not surprising that 'Pinocchio' is one of Spielberg's favorite fairy tales" (2001).[23] One overt Pan reference—a stanza from W. B. Yeats's *The Lost Child*—is carved into Professor Hobby's gate and ushers David into the final act of his quest. Yeats's poem itself is referenced in the title of chapter 3 of Barrie's *Peter Pan and Wendy* ("Come Away, Come Away!"), but there are other strange echoes here that also link J. M. Barrie to Spielberg's David. Marjorie Garber makes much of the autobiographical resonances of Peter Pan, much as Spielberg critics often do of the director. The play that preceded *Peter Pan and Wendy* (a novelization for children that came later) was called *Peter Pan or, The Boy Who Wouldn't Grow Up*. Garber reads the boy who did not grow up as Barrie's brother—strangely also called David—who died at age thirteen. For Barrie, "boyhood begins with loss," writes Garber,

> with not being the right boy, the boy who should have been the boy eternal. . . . His mother apparently never fully recovered from this blow [the death of David]. . . . Then aged six, . . . [J. M.] was urged by his sister to go into his mother's darkened room and remind her that she still had another boy. From the dark his mother called out, "Is that you?," and, as Barrie remembers, he "thought it was the dead boy she was speaking to, and I said in a lonely little voice, 'No, it's no' him, it's just me.'" (1993, 169)

J. M. learns to imitate his dead brother, but he cannot imitate the brother's failure to grow up: "When I became a man . . . he was still a boy of thirteen."[24] Professor Hobby's loss and Barrie's own are strangely entwined in these echoing Davids who never make it to adulthood. The philosopher René Descartes also provides a strange precedent for Hobby's child replication. As Gaby Wood discusses in her cultural history of mechanical dolls and artificial beings, the philosopher had lost his daughter Francine, aged five, and replaced her with a mechanical Francine he constructed (2002, 3–4). None of these dead or mechanical children will ever grow up: David is also a replacement child for grieving parents (Hobby, Monica), but he is too fixed to fit.

So we return to Peter Pan, linked to the Yeats poem, which, as James Kendrick (2014, 182) reminds us, is about an Irish fairy who lures children into an immortal life of perpetual childhood. Yet changelessness is there at the origin of the story but not in its more recent execution. Women, in performances akin to pantomime boy roles, usually play Peter Pan on stage: Barrie originally wanted a boy child for the role, but child labor laws prevented this, so the thirty-seven-year-old Nina Boucicault became the first to perform Pan (Tuite 2009, 109). Garber's comment on productions of Barrie's play—"Why is Peter Pan played by a woman?" (1993, 168)—is therefore historically answered through issues of legislation around child performance. Garber's actual answer—"Because a woman will never grow up to be a man"—has of course been radically challenged by the changing landscape of trans possibility and identity politics in the decades since her book. For a director so fixated on formations of boyhood (and the next chapter will ask whether and how his girls can pose such resounding identity questions), Garber's quip about cross-performing does not quite capture the play on Pan variations. Spielberg's Peter Pans (Banning in *Hook*, for instance) are resolutely cis male; Banning does become a man (an adult to the boy), which is the signal message of that film. However, the cultural legacy of performed Peters is more complex. Teresa Jones (2009) writes eloquently of the power of watching a forty-one-year-old Mary Martin play the role in the U.S. network telecast of 1955 (following the 1954 Broadway production); Martin's is perhaps the most famous of the many Pan incarnations. Though (to my knowledge) Spielberg has not publicly discussed this production, it first aired when he was nine, and was an influential cornerstone of U.S. entertainment culture for decades (the 1960 telecast was repeatedly rebroadcast), so it is hard to believe that he never saw it. Martin's catchphrase "Never gonna be a man, catch me if you can," is of course particularly resonant because a year after *A.I.*, Spielberg released the film *Catch Me If You Can* (for Dan Callahan [2003] this is "a perfect Spielberg title," though Spielberg has merely taken the title of his source book, Frank Abagnale's semi-autobiography of 1980). In Martin's hands, Peter Pan becomes, for Jones, "a boy who looks like a girl played by a girl who looks like a boy" (2009, 244). This gender switch was so embedded in American cultural memory in the second half of the twentieth century that it became a news story when Spielberg announced his new *Pan* project in 1984, reported by the *L.A. Herald-Examiner* as "the first time that a male will play Peter in a major production in this country" (Swertlow 1984).[25]

David will also never grow up to be a man, or anything. His uncanniness, as expertly performed by Osment, is most acutely "unnatural" in the form of the mechanical eternal boy figure. Parents may mourn the loss of childhood in their children, but "owning" one who cannot change is far worse. For the immortal David, dying (as may be happening to him in the film's fantasy conclusion) would be "an awfully big adventure" (a line repeated by Peter in Barrie's book and play). Two elements thus make David monstrous: his inorganic doll body is one issue of difference (the mecha as Pinocchio puppet), but so too is the deathlessness and permanence of the fixed child. These combine to make David a supremely unlovable monster child, a figure of taboo just as the unloved child is a figure of melodrama. When David's conception is proposed at the start of the film, one of Hobby's colleagues argues that the problem is not getting a robot to love but getting humans to love it.[26] *Ready Player One* takes an easier emotional route. It enables its young avatars to befriend each other in the digital realm, and even to fall in love there, but it squarely advocates the real of the orga/fleshly/human Columbus, Ohio, and Wade/Samantha rather than Parzival/Art3mis, who finally and fully connect as their original human selves. While never excluding the digital as a realm of bad faith, it chooses to favor "real life" as a more authentic relationship space. By contrast, *A.I.* is bolder, and bleaker. But it has also offered at least one writer a queerer hero/heroine: Eileen Myles takes the promotional strapline of the film—where this chapter began—as an LGBT call to arms in a think piece titled "Our love is real, but we are not." This finds David to be a "girl boy" who "just looks and acts like [a boy]. It's a performance." David emerges as "our first butch lesbian hero": "His unshakable belief in his true self and his search to rectify the family's error through fantasy make *A.I.* the lesbian legend that it is. David is a story, like the one I'm telling; he doesn't have a birthday, he has a build day. Once upon a time he began. . . . *A.I.* is a toy version of the puberty of gay kids" (Myles 2001, 43).

So while both films are examples of Spielberg's dominant interest in boys, Myles's *A.I.* provides an apposite transition to the next chapter, on girls. Peter Rubin argues that the Spielberg of *Ready Player One* "wants you to feel like a kid again" (quoted by Leggatt 2021, 183). But who is this "you"? Halliday is dead and leaves behind a fortune and a bank of digitally pickled memories specific to his generation, but not that of the young Gunters, who experience a dream of the 1980s only vicariously. More important for the work of the next two chapters, this "you" rarely includes girls. Karen Mann, in her fine reading of *Minority Report*, wonders "how *AI* would play if David were replaced not by a biological son but by a biological daughter" (2005, 000). Would Darlene's story have been any different? I want to approach these questions next, investigating some of Spielberg's (rarer) representations of girlhood, and his employment of female actors to bear out those images.

5

Girl/Daughter

War of the Worlds and *The BFG*

With a few singular exceptions, Spielberg has given less screen space to girlhood and narratives articulated from girl children's points of view than he has to boys. He is of course a renowned architect of cinematic boyhood: no film has awarded a girl character or actor the same privileged exposition as Elliott in *E.T.*, David in *A.I.*, and Jim in *Empire of the Sun*. This chapter and chapter 6 will focus on representations of girlhood, though with child actors who fundamentally share screen space as costars (even if they sometimes steal the limelight). In chapter 6, I will look closer at two films (*Jurassic Park* and *The Color Purple*) where girls function as sisters to brothers or other girls, and as carers, their identities established through their relative positions within a family structure that is both protective and perilous. In this chapter I will examine those who have costarred as younger characters with older men, and as young early career actors with highly celebrated male stars. Dakota Fanning performs Rachel, daughter to Ray (Tom Cruise) in *War of the Worlds*, and Ruby Barnhill performs Sophie, the young girl who befriends a giant who, though older and in every way "bigger," is more buddy than father figure (Mark Rylance in the title role of *The BFG*). These stories feature girls in relational roles; seldom are girls the primary articulation of the story. By contrast, there is hardly a scene in *E.T.* or *Empire of the Sun* in which the boy stars do not feature as defining subjects, even if surrounded by family or surrogate family. Boys are simply less relational and more singular, and they are allowed to occupy their narrative landscape as fuller subjectivities, which effectively gives boy actors more to do. The relational positioning of girl to man is revealing, both in terms of relative thespian reputations and because both Cruise and Rylance have, like Tom Hanks, served as Spielberg's muses, unusually starring in more than one film and clearly functioning as half of an enriching creative relationship—which makes for a particularly challenging setup for a relatively unknown girl to join.

The overall performing landscape is also arguably a little more positive for girls. Christian Bale excepted, Spielberg's girl performers have perhaps graduated to more successful adult careers than his boys: Drew Barrymore and Dakota Fanning have sustained A-list profiles, contrasting Henry Thomas's or Haley Joel Osment's supporting player adult careers. Though girl audiences more readily identify with boy characters than is true the other way around, girls on-screen in family adventure films may more securely capture the specific attention of girl audience members. Spielberg does give some of his girl performers rare action-cinema opportunities: Kelly (Vanessa Lee Chester) takes out a velociraptor with her gymnastic skills in *The Lost World*, and Lex is resourceful in evading dinosaur attacks in *Jurassic Park*. However, ultimately both are rather eclipsed by digital dinosaurs (indeed, in the case of *The Lost World*, by *child* dinosaurs). If adult actors—to return to W. C. Fields's memorable formulation—should never work with children or animals, perhaps children should never work with CGI animals. But it is girl children who risk being eclipsed most of all, even by such a child-focused director.

Nevertheless, Genia ("the girl in the red coat") in *Schindler's List* is one of Spielberg's most resonant images, and is perhaps all the more emblematic of vulnerability because of her gender. I will be addressing Genia (and Oliwia Dabrowska, who performs her) alongside Danka Dressner (and Anna Mucha, who performs her), another significant character from *Schindler's List*, in chapter 7, on children in war. More widely, girls do drive the genre direction of the films in which they feature even when they only costar: Fanning, Arianna Richards, and Barnhill are all girls playing girls in differently genred vehicles: horror/sci-fi (*War of the Worlds*), action-adventure family film (*Jurassic Park*), and children's film (*The BFG*), respectively.[1] Other girl characters are threaded through Spielberg's films with less to do except fulfill a basic narrative function: Emilie (Celine Buckens) in *War Horse* is a passive figure of impotent femininity caught in a war scenario, whose death ultimately means that Joey the horse can be returned to his rightful young (male) owner. Ben Bradlee's daughter Marina (Austyn Johnson) is only fleetingly present in *The Post*, but her lemonade-selling turn positions her as an initiative-driven girl who foreshadows the developing corporate power of adult newspaper owner Kay Graham (Meryl Streep). Kay's growing authority over the major brand she has inherited (the *Washington Post*, referenced in the title) is the film's primary developmental arc, but this is also told through the brief appearance of the confident girl, already bearing out a sense of entrepreneurial entitlement. Tom Hanks as Bradlee and Streep as Graham—titans of contemporary American film acting—dominate the screen (eclipsing even their starry director as the name[s] above the title), but this small child role works hard to underline the link between their characters.

Another female character who features prominently in the film is Kay's adult daughter, Lally (Alison Brie), used as a sounding board and support system for her mother's journey. One telling scene, set in a darkened bedroom with Lally's small daughters asleep in a shared bed, features Lally and Kay discussing the future of the newspaper while the youngest generation sleeps on. This recalls a bedtime tucking-in moment in *Empire of the Sun* (itself modeled on a Norman Rockwell painting) in which adults hover over their sleepy son (I will discuss this in some detail in chapter 7). In both films—as well as in *E.T.* and *A.I.* and numerous other Spielberg moments—the bedroom (usually the boy's bedroom) is both sanctuary and play space, with the (usually) boy child at the center of that space. This is somewhat at odds with Catherine Driscoll, a theorist of girlhood, who argues, "Private spaces and domestic cultures, rather than public space and sub-cultural styles understood as self-expression, seem to structure girls lives. . . . While boys as much as girls might participate in bedroom culture, girls' association with this space belongs to preexisting discourses on girls' lives" (2002, 260). By this account, girls lives are far more focused on interiors and the domestic. Kay and her daughter in *The Post*—mothers and their children—can speak openly because they are enabled by this locked-down quiet space, in a film otherwise dominated by public spaces: newsrooms, restaurants, streets. While the children here are literally marginalized by unconsciousness, they are no less symbolically present; the quiet, sleepy space is the stage on which the older parent and older (adult) child connect. Of course, this is an adult-oriented historical drama into which children are sprinkled for symbolic resonance, so the child's-eye view is marginal. The girl/woman's view only becomes central as the story develops: Streep's Oscar-nominated performance is a significant female role for Spielberg, with her name alongside Hanks's as the primary promotional driver. Other roles for women in *The Post* are few and far between. This may be more widely symptomatic: it is only from *Jurassic Park* onward that girls gain more screen time, in more dynamic and significant roles. This shift, explored in the next chapter, comes with Spielberg's decision to take the (younger, unskilled) girl character overshadowed by her big brother in Michael Crichton's book and make his filmic Lex older and more of a leader. Aside from *The Color Purple*, all of my readings in these chapters feature the work of a post–*Jurassic Park* Spielberg, in which girls are more confidently able to step forward.

There is no question that this greater center-stage prominence for girls in the films of the most prominent director of the late twentieth and early twenty-first century is to be welcomed, as is the rise of girl studies more widely around the same time, which has shone a remarkable theoretical and cultural spotlight on girls in society and popular culture (e.g., Gateward and Pomerance 2002; Harris 2004; Projansky 2014; Handyside and Taylor-Jones 2016). Yet at least three of the films under discussion here use girls to express and react to horror (*War of the Worlds* and the Spielberg-directed *Jurassic Park* films), and while not horror films, the other two titles (*The BFG* and *The Color Purple*) also show girls in some relationship to fear even if they are genre worlds apart. As I have discussed elsewhere in an analysis of children as bait in Spielberg's exploitation cinema (Williams 2020), the child-friendly Spielberg is nevertheless surprisingly keen to show children threatened or at risk, efficiently visualizing the drama of their distress. He brings an exploitation cinema aesthetic to a family audience, making horror a family-friendly experience by deploying the child in situations of peril. The terrified on-screen child functions as a surrogate for the fear to be passed into the auditorium. While spectacles of violence to adult bodies are common in horror, visible violence to children is rare and taboo in mainstream cinema, and though horror tests the limits of audience tolerance, children's bodies are usually one of those limits. The Flesh Fair scene in *A.I.* offers an analogy: the baying crowd calling for the live public execution of robot service workers hesitate when the target is a seeming child. Children's tears are common across Spielberg's genres, particularly the family adventure melodrama, but the risked child performing peril and abject fear pushes toward horror. The next chapter will focus on particular performances of fear and peril as borne out by girls, most clearly by Richards in *Jurassic Park*, Chester in *The Lost World: Jurassic Park*, and Desreta Jackson in *The Color Purple*. I start this chapter by considering Dakota Fanning's work in *War of the Worlds*. Here it is the child taking on the "scream queen" position usually borne out by young women in exploitation horror who crystallizes narrative tension as women might in other texts, genres, and hands. Spielberg therefore uses the child to shift an adults-only genre away from its typical demographic in order to capitalize on wider markets.

Dakota Fanning's Eyes: The Horrifying/Horror-Bending Girl in *War of the Worlds*

E.T. and *A.I.* are films that, for all their science fiction apparatus, are really about developing boyhood, while—via a very small boy and an unsuccessfully grown up man—*Close Encounters* represents male childness in a science fiction setting. Another major science fiction story by the director centrally features a girl, but *War of the Worlds* is not about developing girlhood; rather, its child focus is refracted by wider issues of paternity and family. Indeed, the first individual human the film spotlights, while Morgan Freeman provides the film's contextualizing introductory voice-over, is a boy child, picked out throwing a baseball in the midst of a montage of nonindividualized swarms of humans going about their ordinary lives. Nevertheless, though she is not primarily essaying girlhood in her performance, the film is such a strong showcase for Dakota Fanning's skills that the ten-year-old gets second billing only to Tom Cruise.

A contemporary reworking of H. G. Wells's 1897 novel of the same name, the story (written by Josh Friedman and David Koepp) features Cruise as Ray

Ferrier, a divorced dockworker from New Jersey whose weekend visit from his two children coincides with a violent, global alien attack. He flees with teenage Robbie (Justin Chatwin) and younger Rachel back to their (and their mother's) abandoned house, then embarks on a further, riskier journey to reach her at the grandparents' home in Boston, where she has fled to. All the while the wanton savagery of the alien attack lays waste to the Eastern Seaboard and thousands of lives. Robbie questions his father's masculinity and departs to join the armed forces—presumably to his death. Ray becomes a better father as he protects Rachel from aliens and deranged humans; Rachel comes to trust him but remains a highly disturbed witness to horror. Not for nothing, then, did the film get widely reviewed as a Spielbergian story of Ray's evolution as a parent, though it is also a story of systematic traumatization: while he is increasingly capable of protecting his daughter, he does not evolve into a macho superhero.

Rachel is the younger child, which is often (as we will see later in *Jurassic Park*) a feminized position, regardless of the child's gender. She is therefore relationally defined as sister and daughter, younger sibling to Chatwin's older brother and youngest child needing protection to Cruise's "proving himself" father. This might seem disempowered, and it is true that, to many viewers' irritation, she is seen (and heard) screaming a lot: there is even a YouTube compilation called "Every Dakota Fanning Scream in War of the Worlds."[2] But she is also resourceful, often drives the narrative, and challenges her father's early attempts at authority. Once Robbie has left to join the defense forces, she is the *only* child, and much of the story is played out through the double-act dynamic of Fanning and Cruise. Ray is initially set up as a feckless single male, eschewing family responsibilities and even the most basic provider duties. His son calls him an asshole, refuses to play ball with him, and makes off with Ray's car. Rachel tries to advise him on how to parent her older brother, only to have Ray remind her of her place with familial positioning: "What are you, your mother or mine?" Ray is initially yet another failing parent in Spielberg's long list of defaulters, and when the impending alien attack creates crazy weather, father meets daughter's fear with exhilaration and is incapable of reassuring her that everything will be OK (the first duty of an empathic parent). Initially he cannot cope with the child's anxiety; only Robbie understands his sister's claustrophobic panic attacks and is able to calm her down. Hers is trauma as a response not just to a world overrun by aliens but also unbounded by a parent who is only slowly able to establish clear protective boundaries. She is detached, dislocated from safety from the outset—a fundamentally distinct position from the emotional state of insecurity.

So Rachel the character becomes unpredictable, and Fanning makes this real, articulating her character between two related positions—the child taking responsibility and the child initially abandoned by adult responsibility. To these roles she adds a more complex inflection, performing a particular form of distracted dislocation with quite realist precision. This is the child under unimaginable stress, and the extreme emotions Fanning must convey

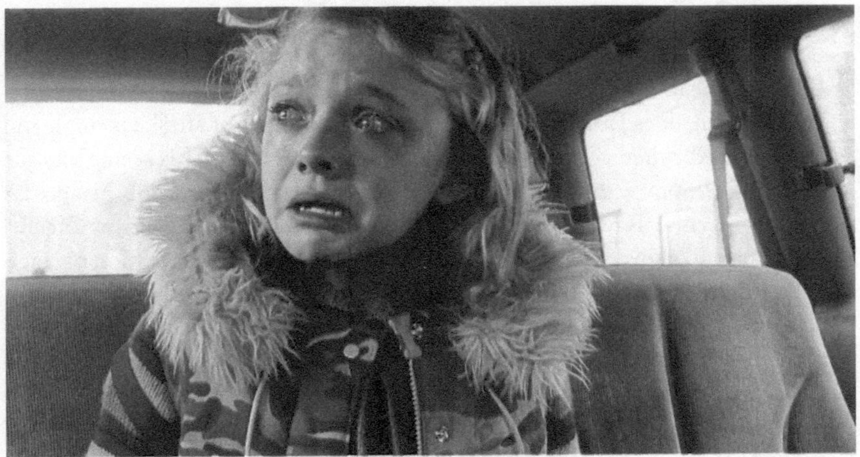

FIGURE 8 Spotlit seeing: Dakota Fanning's transfixed gaze in *War of the Worlds*.

require a leap of imagination from the actor. Like a toy balloon in a weak grip, the unsecured child can (and does) drift away into danger at any time. She often escapes her father's grasp in the most perilous situations, because her father offers little security and as if she is seeking out the danger that so horrifies her, leading the camera to (and through) some sublime set pieces. Spielberg relies on his young performer to provide the surrogate reaction for the audience. When horror is laid out, it is the job of Fanning's face, in particular her saucer eyes, to convey just how horrific it is (figure 8). Though one reviewer called her an "acting prodigy with the face of a medieval madonna" (McCartney 2005, 6), her flossy blonde hair and wide blue eyes are not presented primarily as idealized white girlhood but as spotlit terror. Transfixed in still observation or panic, this face is one of the most iconic images of the film, partly because of its stark whiteness against a grainy, often desaturated noirish terrain.

A landscape of horror spectacle unfolds as the story gets darker: the alien lightning freezes tarmac; a church snaps in half; people are annihilated. After the initial attack Ray returns to his dust-covered children (presumably the ashes of the vaporized people), and Rachel—a post-9/11 child—asks if this is the work of terrorists.[3] But this also revisits the spectacle of ashes from Nazi incinerators, thickening the air of Kraków and falling like dark snow in *Schindler's List*. The primary image of the escaping family as they flee in a stolen car is of Rachel's screaming face (the crazed image of it, as well as the sound), crying for her mom, alone on the back seat but framed by brother and father in yet another Spielbergian family triptych. This initial escape seems to play out like a normal awful family car journey taken to extremes, except that—with Ray unable to parent properly—the children have to keep trying out and trying on roles of responsibility. Earlier, too-young Rachel is "adultized" by responsibility, ordering (healthy) takeout because there is no food in her father's house. Ray's idea of sustenance is dangerous as well as inadequate: he does not even know that Rachel is allergic to peanut butter.

What, then, does Fanning bring to this scenario? First of all, she is small and is often carried, when this is safer or quicker than running. This seems like the ultimate disempowerment, and she does not have the active job her costar performs—Cruise/Ray can take control, move and play out, but Fanning/Rachel must watch and above all react. Acting is often most skillfully a question of reacting; Fanning performs sometimes with stock-still shock, sometimes with frantic panic. As we have seen numerous times, plaudits for a child's talent are mediated through adult compliments. Spielberg says in the press notes that Fanning "has a very wise old soul—it's like she's been around about seven or eight times," while Tim Robbins deploys that old chestnut that we have seen several versions of throughout this book: "Man, this girl's 35 years old."[4] Presenting the ten-year-old Fanning as entirely skilled because and in the context of the fact that she is only ten is clearly not a strong enough promotional message. Ray rescues her from rising terror at the tide of floating bodies on the river by clamping his hands over her eyes, saying, "Stay where I can see you": whereas seeing the horror paralyzes her and he must blind her to protect her from it, seeing *her* gives him a sense of control. As the former ambulance driver Harlan (Robbins), with whom they shelter, says of those that are near to death, it is "the ones that keep their eyes open, keep looking at you . . . they're the ones that survive." The knowledge and power denoted by fixed and active looking is strength within the film, and Fanning is a key focus for this. Rachel's fixed eyes—seeing the danger before others do—secures not only her own survival but her fathers' too.

In chapter 7, also on war, I will discuss how Robbie uses the military scenario of *War of the Worlds* as a conduit in his transformation from boyhood to manhood. In that framing, I read this film as a war film. But it is more complexly genred than that. Though predicated first on the famous science fiction premise of the originary novel, the film shows exactly how multiple genres can cohabit in Spielberg's work. All three central characters actually bear out and occupy different types of film: while Ray belongs in a male-melodrama-action-adventure, Robbie inhabits a war film (he effectively joins up), but Rachel is a character in a horror film—a child in peril, aestheticized through horror framings and performance style. One of the ongoing stories of this book concerns how children function to "melodrama" other genres, yet here it is the girl child who "horrifies" science fiction. Indeed, Rachel-as-daughter does also function to make her father's story a melodrama: in the world-scale apocalypse of the attack (and his initial ineptitude notwithstanding), his primary concern is for his children's welfare, which he realizes through the mission to return them to their mother. Rachel therefore twists her father's primary drive—that of the solitary action hero looking out only for himself—into a relentless, single-minded carer who will kill for his daughter.

However, Fanning's performance keynote is fear. While she might function to activate the father in his own male melodrama, she activates a horror scenario—a child mobilizing in a more adult genre inflection, even if it is limited to a "PG-13 gore factor" (McCarthy 2005). Horror affect is often driven more by the views of victims or witnesses (screaming or struck dumb, eyes wide with shock), and though this may be targeting the teen/family adventure film audience, it is Fanning's most iconic look (awed apprehension rising to confirmed terror) that inflects it toward horror. Mindful of the 12A classification the film got in the United Kingdom (an advisory category, which allows adults to accompany children much younger than this), one British critic warned her readers that "a near-total absence of reassurance in this film . . . means that, although parents [in the United Kingdom] can choose to take children under 12, it is not suitable for a child of an even vaguely nervous disposition" (McCartney 2005, 6). Fanning screams a lot because there is a lot to scream about, and child distress can be as affecting as child tears: as Kenneth Turan writes, "Her look of horror as she faces terror out the back window of a car is the film's emblematic image, the one shot that makes us feel the nightmare in our bones" (2005). This audible and visual spectacle is then deployed and passed on. McCartney continues, "The sheer scale of the frights inflicted upon Fanning will undoubtedly combine to create a series of sleepless, jabbering bedtimes" (2005, 6).

The horror scenario intensifies as the family journeys toward the children's home. But when a plane crashes just outside, blasting a bright light through the window (recalling *Close Encounters of the Third Kind* and also *Poltergeist*, both films where children have a strange affinity to sublime spectacles of fear), it is Robbie and Rachel who must lead their father into the safety of the subterranean boiler room. After the terror of unknown noise and light subsides, Rachel's voice first speaks out: "Are we still alive?" Again, Rachel is protected by her father preventing her from seeing what the adult must bear: Ray takes her through the devastation by urging her to look straight into his face and not look around as curiosity would have it. Safe spaces swiftly become unsafe, and the disjointed family journeys on. At one point Rachel has to stop to pee, and she pauses to look at a New England river, enabling the cinematographer Janusz Kaminski to present an exalted, backlit view—another chapter in the "light story" Spielberg is telling about children. Her uncannily illuminated face, with flickers of river reflection animating it, hovers between horror and the sublime as she watches bodies float through the water, echoing a similar spectacle from *Empire of the Sun*. Then comes Ray's first moment of desperate heroism: the trio are pulled from the car by a frantic crowd (the destitute, pleading families they pass as night falls recall the refugees in Spielberg's more realist war stories, such as *Empire of the Sun*), and he resorts to violence to save his children. As with the terrorized first journey that recalled many normally stressful holiday road trips, the three end up in a diner and look, briefly, like a regular family. But civilization has broken down; Rachel turns to Robbie, not Ray, for comfort, and it is not the little girl or the teenage boy but the grown man (Ray) who cries.

Across his career, Spielberg the exploitation filmmaker has indulged some celebrated moments when people become meat to the monstrous other (*Jaws*, *Jurassic Park*). *War of the Worlds* is not a family adventure film, nor is it a drive-in creature feature, though it shares generic common ground with both these forms. The bleakness of the new moral landscape is underlined when, once Robbie has departed for war, Ray and Rachel take refuge with the lone Harlan, who has retreated into survivalist madness, and it is Harlan's place to remind us of the difference here. "This is not a war any more than there's a war between men and maggots," he says, positioning humans now as the maggots. "This is an extermination." Still Ray cannot be the father Rachel needs: when she asks him to lullaby her with "Hushabye Mountain," it is clear he must have evaded those repeat viewings of *Chitty Chitty Bang Bang* with his daughter, and so must resort to the Beach Boys' anthem to automobiles, "Little Deuce Coupe." Then the basement in which they have taken refuge becomes a trap, on two fronts: an alien probe invades, snaking around in reconnaissance, and is then followed by a group of small biped aliens resembling evil children, poking around in the detritus of human life. But Harlan is worse, sexually and pseudopaternally preying on Rachel ("If anything happens to your daddy I'll take care of you"). As in *Empire of the Sun*'s reluctance to confront the threat of child sexual abuse (and also of child sexuality, only briefly acknowledging Jim's dawning puberty), Harlan's predatory intimation must be quickly stomped out by Ray, who kills him (the question hovers as to whether he should have brought his daughter into the preserve of this man in the first place). Once again Ray must cover Rachel's eyes (with a blindfold this time) and cover her ears (he asks *her* to sing "Hushabye Mountain" this time) as he kills Harlan, off-screen—our view and auditory experience remain with the girl. But another masking is also taking place: as ever, Spielberg hesitates on the threshold of acknowledging the dark danger of children as sexual objects, and then retreats.

In a film about troubled family it would be easy, then, to say that the aliens are not the point. But there are multiple metaphors for invaders in the film, which come to speak for the family in disarray, from the handover message the children's mother leaves about their son having homework (a paper on the French occupation and colonization of Algeria, reminding us that Wells's novel was already a reflection on European colonialism) to the casting of Fanning herself, who was of course already well known to Spielberg, and to audiences, as the human-child alien Allie Keys in *Taken* (aka *Steven Spielberg Presents Taken*), produced by Spielberg for the Sci-Fi Channel in 2002. Like monstrous Cronenbergian fifth columnists, *War of the Worlds*' tripod aliens "came from within"—they were under the ground all along, biding their time across millennia until the moment of attack and conquest came. But it turns out that what defeats them also comes from within: humans are food, but they take with them into the tripod bodies microbes and viruses against which the invaders have no resistance. Rachel could have predicted this: rejecting her father's offer to remove the splinter she gets in her hand, she rationalizes, "When it's ready my body will just push it out." Children and their parents are also exposed as only uneasily fixed in the family, which might, as a structure, push out the unwanted members (divorced fathers) or fail to keep its members in check. The inside/outside story of *War of the Worlds* posits family as only safe, and bounded, through action and effort, not through biology and tradition. We will pick up this thread later in discussion of Spielberg's found or chosen families. The girl's vulnerably hovers here at the border of this precarious and leaky enclosure.

I have argued that Spielberg uses the child to shift an adult-only genre away from its typical demographic in order to capitalize on wider markets. *War of the Worlds* is not H. G. Wells for children; it is a horrific war story that makes the little girl the conduit for (adult) audience identification. Fanning's affect on the genre inflection of *War of the Worlds* is to hybridize science fiction and melodrama with horror. But how does she function as an embodiment of girlhood? While Henry Thomas and Christian Bale might be performing iterations of boyhood—identified with boys' toys and adventure, bearing out a specifically male form of childness—Fanning's Rachel is not a specifically female child. Though she wears pink, this becomes systematically grubbier as the story unfolds. She rarely plays with girls' toys or overtly differentiates herself from the males around her, though the film's costume designer, Joanna Johnston, wanted to give her "something that made her feel safe, some little thing that she could sleep with and put over her face"—a lavender-colored horse purse.[5] When Ray's early parental evasion is replaced by Rachel's evasion of her father's control, she drifts into the tentacles of the tripods themselves. Yet even as potential victim of the invaders, her size and gender do not differentiate her—her panic is that of the pursued human as "maggot," not something specifically feminized. Just as Barry's mother fails to keep him indoors in *Close Encounters*, so Rachel escapes into a trap and is also curiously framed against the light, then pinned by an overhead beam emanating from the belly of the beast (as if she is spotlit on a stage). As the tripod closes its grip on her, she looks up into the awful light, and we look down on her from the alien's point of view. Rachel stares up and does not flinch; her eyes are huge with something approaching awe. Paralyzed with fear, she obligingly enables the alien to whisk her into its cargo of people, who are picked off one by one, to be used as live fuel. The aliens are omnivorous: anyone in their path is fair game. But some people are smaller than others—little girls, for instance, might not "resource" these consumption machines as effectively as muscular men. In *Empire of the Sun*, Jamie must show that he can work as hard as an adult to accrue privileges; in *Schindler's List*, children too small to work are exterminated, and pretending to be older is a matter of survival. The tripods do not distinguish in this most egalitarian of horror shows: all humans are equal as a food source, and small females are merely less useful in this than adult males. Nevertheless, that Rachel occupies the position of "child" or "human" rather than specifically "girl," even up to the point of (near) death, begs a question about the gender specifics across Spielberg's films. One of the most substantial child roles given to a girl performer in his oeuvre is not so gender-defined (all that screaming notwithstanding) as the three substantial child roles occupied by boys that I am considering in this book. If Ray's youngest child were a boy, would the story be different?

Fanning came to *War of the Worlds* as an established child star, having already featured in films and television for adults. Though most of her early films were not children's products, she was nevertheless a child star with a developing child-audience following, through (before *War of the Worlds*) *The Cat in the Hat* and *Uptown Girls* (both 2003), and (after it) *Charlotte's Web* (2006) and *Coraline* (2009). Several short celebrity biographies of Fanning build on this. One trend has been to track the performer's youth to a target readership's age though titles aimed at hooking reluctant young readers into engagement with written text in book format. These include Sarah Tieck's *Dakota Fanning* in the Big Buddy Books Buddy Bios imprint by Abdo Publishing (which also includes titles on former child stars Miley Cyrus, Vanessa Hudgens, and Shia LaBeouf), and Joanne Mattern's title in the Mitchell Lane Robbie Reader series (which also includes biographies of Ashley Tisdale and Emily Osment [Haley Joel's sister and—like many of these former child actors—a Disney Channel stalwart]). Claire Hibbert, a prolific author of nonfiction for young readers, wrote the Fanning title in the Hachette Children's books EDGE—Teen Stars series (which also includes titles on Taylor Momsen, Jaden Smith, and Selena Gomez). Clearly, young celebrity culture has been identified as an encouragement to children to read nonfiction—the Robbie Readers boast "short, easy-to-read non-fiction chapter books for the beginning reader," while the EDGE series promises, "These teen celebrity biographies will appeal to existing fans and those coming into the teen celebrity scene, giving reluctant readers more of what they really want—more facts, biographical snippets and glossy photos."[6] Tieck's, Mattern's, and Hibbert's titles offer little complex analysis of performance development or the processes of working with Spielberg, and given the dark horror of *War of the Worlds*, the writers do not assume that their target readership is familiar with that film. However, they all identify her as a performer with a clear child-culture grounding and (by 2012 onward) a developing adult performance profile. More than for Henry Thomas or Haley Joel Osment, these texts bear out the way in which Fanning has been promoted for her child celebrity as well as hired for her skill, and was able to graduate successfully to adult roles, taking her child viewership and fan base with her as they grow up in parallel.

The BFG's Girl Child Lead

Of the girl-focused films discussed here, only *Jurassic Park* is a family adventure film; *The Color Purple* and *War of the Worlds* are both films for adults, but *The*

BFG is arguably primarily a children's film starring a child (and coproduced by Disney). Though Spielberg has directed many women in substantial costarring roles, *The BFG* (2016) is the only Spielberg film up to the time of writing to feature a girl protagonist—unless we read the infantilized character Goldie Hawn plays in *The Sugarland Express*, as more girl than woman. Of course, while Sophie leads the action, the Big Friendly Giant of the title is the film's primary spectacle, and Barnhill's inexperience is contrasted to Mark Rylance as the giant, who was by this point a multi-award-winning veteran of stage and screen, including Spielberg's previous *Bridge of Spies*.

Spielberg is known frequently to cast (relative) unknowns, and his child actors are no exception, often found through an audition process that then forms one of the promotional stories around the film. *The BFG*'s marketing made copious mention of the production's search for "a young actress with just the right balance of innocence, ingenuity and feistiness to embody Sophie" (Woods 2016). Adjectives used to identify the qualities of the role are then turned into a celebration of what Barnhill brings to it. When an unknown is cast in a high-budget film, it is equally common to surround them with established star talent which will guarantee box office revenue (known in the business as 'meaningful casting'). This is the strategy adopted on *The BFG*. The scale question—inherent in the story as "Roald Dahl's whizzpopping world of outsized ogres and much tinier orphans" (Semlyen 2016)—also dominates discussion of how child Barnhill and adult Rylance made credible their characters' differing statures, with much focus in reception materials on the CGI techniques used to equalize the co-performances and better foster their developing affection.

The literal size differential between child and giant also merits comparison with *E.T.*, in which, of course, the child actors were of a scale with the central fantasy spectacle/special effect—E.T. himself. Comparing the work of that film with *The BFG*, Spielberg said, "There are a lot of opposites, especially in scale. . . . All the kids were E.T.'s giants" (Bentley 2016). Sophie (and her young performer) is by contrast diminished in relation to the giant, who is also diminished as a lesser giant than his bigger-giant foes in the story, so the question of scale is posed the other way around. Perhaps both ultimately are overwhelmed by the story of technological prowess in a way that the *E.T.* stars were not. The relative distinctions of fame and prestige intertwined with those of actual stature are key here: *The BFG*'s set design, its camera perspectives, and above all its innovative CGI work, which enabled the small-girl/unknown-child-actor and the large motion-capture-giant/well-known-thespian to perform equally in the same frame, tell the film's story about scale and power, with the girl at its center.

Ten-year-old Sophie's smallness and isolation are set against a background of a caricatured Dickensian London (though the film is set roughly in the present day), which of course has a particular historical resonance for representations of the neglected child. Indeed, she has been reading Dickens's *Nicholas Nickleby* under her bedcovers with a flashlight—a novel that includes children being sent away to a cruel institution by their parents. In Sophie's own institution, the orphanage staff cast threatening shadows across the floor, as does the BFG outside when he patrols the neighborhood at night, a prelude to Sophie being snatched by the giant and taken to his home. Her smallness then forms the primary contrast to the huge scale of his house in Giant Country (where of course everything is large), so much so that the giant would not seem so giant if it were not for the diminutive girl. But while a girl seems to drive these contrasts better than (larger) boys might, Sophie has already functioned as a giant, when—Alice-like—she peers into the orphanage dollhouse and appears giant-sized from the inside looking out. So when the BFG creates a child-sized bedroom for her in a small corner of his house, it looks to him like the dollhouse Sophie had played with, the implication being that she is now his doll. Of course, as a feisty, capable female hero in the model of recent fiction for girls, Sophie is no one's plaything. The empowered girl has been identified by girl studies as a keystone of popular culture since the 1990s; the girlhood theorist Anita Harris contrasts the "can-do girl" to the "at risk girl"—the former usually white, middle-class, and identified with consumer culture, the latter often working-class and/or nonwhite and from an unstable family background—a cautionary popular cultural example (see Harris 2004, 13–35). Sophie is something of both, and of course much younger than these new female stereotypes, who are frequently teens or adolescents featuring in older girl-focused or young adult literature or TV. Although she emanates from a novel written in 1982, her capable coolness and refusal to give in make her a very 2016 girl heroine.

A wider drama envelops this story of BFG-child friendship: the threat of even bigger giants attacking the BFG (who is then rendered diminutive compared with them), and of children being snatched and eaten. Small Sophie grows into ingenious Sophie, helping to mastermind the plan to enlist the Queen to defeat the giants once and for all. Thus the film plays with scale throughout, with the girl at the pivot of large and small, both physically and through her action and courage. This play with visual scale (figure 9), rendering versions of the child across a cinematic landscape that knits digital and live-action performance, is confident Spielberg territory. Of course "stature" is a question of professional experience as well as of on-screen characterization, and this in turn has a bearing on the child actor. Here a young child "carries" a film (a term rich with implications of weight and strength) alongside a celebrated costar, and a huge budget rests on her competence. Barnhill's happy pleasure in getting the role and negotiating the shoot sounds rather more negative when she says, "I literally felt lost. I was shaking with nerves." The pressure is significant: "She was 4,500 miles away from her home in England. There were 300 people on set. She had her own makeup artist and a driver named Cindy."

Accounting for both the enormous digital infrastructure and the modest ingenue performer, Spielberg said when promoting the film: "Everything was designed—the entire production was designed—for two actors to be constantly

FIGURE 9 The small girl as hero in *The BFG* (Ruby Barnhill as Sophie, Mark Rylance as the Giant).

in eye contact with each other. . . . I knew immediately . . . that Ruby was going to need as much authenticity as we could create for her. . . . I knew that if Mark could always see Ruby's eyes when he was acting, and Ruby could always see Mark's eyes, that they would find companionship and authenticity" (Mooallem 2016). Whereas Fanning's eyes in *War of the Worlds* perform outward to the audience as a communication of terror, eye contact here is a key element in generating credible performances. While celebrating potentially alienating but technologically dynamic advances, Spielberg is still able to deploy affective "truth" (note the repeated use of "authenticity" in this quote) as an emotional storytelling hallmark, all in the service of bringing the girl to the level of the actor of stature. Jon Moallem, the journalist reporting Spielberg's words, notes, "No normal child can be expected to carry on poignant conversations with a clay maquette or a tennis ball hanging in front of green screen to approximate the location of a digital giant's face" (2016). Despite the fact that even adult actors have to acquire these skills, and that the ten-year-old is more likely to be a digital native than the fifty-six-year-old Rylance, it is Barnhill who has to be technologically "lifted" by eye contact with the more senior actor, not veteran-of-stage-and-traditional-acting-skills Rylance himself. This is articulated as part of the pseudo-parental support system put in place to help the child give the performance she has been employed to deliver: "Spielberg freed her to improvise dialog and doted on her, constantly checking if she needed a break," continues Mooallem. "It relaxed her, made her feel less powerless in that otherwise disorienting, regimented environment. ('You can't release a kid to be themselves if you have strict rules,' Spielberg says.) And gradually, Barnhill opened up. . . . She calls him 'a second father.'"

Directing is, then, a form of parenting, according to this promotional line, combining technical wizardry and nurturing coaxing. The producer Frank Marshall reiterates the obvious, with the directorial feat seeming all the more impressive when judged against the actor's unimpressive starter credentials, so that the story of the inexperienced unknown becomes part of the story of directorial skill: "He's able to make them trust him and relax, and deliver these incredible performances—often with barely any training, like Ruby" (all quotes by Mooallem 2016). If children are really the special effects of *E.T.*, *A.I.*, and *The BFG*, as has been said, this only serves to illuminate what the film's promotional message casts as its most effective element—the director's transformational skill. Stories about how brilliant untrained kids are when plucked from open call auditions are also about how brilliant the big guy is in eliciting their performances.

This is not to demean what Barnhill brings to the table, or her approach to this strange and unbalanced workplace. She survives the pressure though concludes at the end of the shoot—according to interviews conducted with Spielberg again around the promotion of the film—that she would far prefer to direct than act, and (like the child filmmaker Spielberg we encountered earlier in this book) makes on-set films around the set with her smartphone.[7] A further reflection on her work and future is even more scaled down (and appropriate to discourses of girls underreaching), stressing the importance of evading the "big-headedness" of fame: "I like the idea of becoming a director but not a famous one like Steven. . . . I'd prefer to do something smaller, like TV or maybe theatre or to become a drama teacher. I want to do something smaller than being a huge Hollywood director" (Grant 2016). Whether this is because the circus of a huge digital production does not seem like much fun or because girls must not be seen to overreach themselves, the young performer is here both setting out her ambition and drawing it in at the same time. However, she is acknowledged for her useful costarring qualities by Rylance: "Pretty much all children are helpful to act with; they lack any guile when they act. . . . Ruby was particularly helpful: very, very present." But the very fact of having a child on set also situates the adult actor back in line with the basics: they must be directed in a way that adults, particularly an adult of Rylance's experience, may not typically be. As he continues: "And you also hear the very useful basic instructions that Steven would never say to Tom Hanks or to me, but he says to her: 'Now concentrate, take your time before we start, just get into character, feel and think what's going on.' I'm doing that anyway, but it's great to be reminded" (Clark 2016). The child actor is, then, both helpful and superfluous to the seasoned performer's craft, who carefully acknowledges the child's importance to the production while reinstating their own significant experience. Yet the girl's presence is central to marketing the film: Barnhill is there with

Rylance on the movie poster; though its title underlines the giant as central spectacle, the strapline emanates from her point of view: "The world is more GIANT than you can IMAGINE" (uppercase in original, emphasizing both scale and the Spielbergian life of the mind/heart). Sophie is the "you" in this iteration, and the two most common images used in the poster design are of the tiny girl sitting on the massive giant's hands or of a full-length Barnhill standing on the giant's feet. The girl hooks in the child viewer and provides the golden child's point of view so central to this strand of Spielberg cinema. Mindful of this girl's centrality in the promotion of the film, a particular narrative must then be deployed by Rylance in selling his participation. As we have seen, adult actors' acknowledgment of the uncanny abilities of their child costars is frequently characterized by a rueful acceptance that the unknown newcomer "acted me off the screen," or else their preternatural talent made them equal to the seasoned actor in the frame. When one has to work with children (if not animals), the most effective way to promote it is through a performance of professional modesty, enabling the inexperienced newbie to rival or eclipse the seasoned actor for as long as the film product needs star endorsement.

These meditations continue to worry away at the child's ambivalent role in the workplace of filmmaking, with perspectives on smallness that are particular to the girl—particularly the girl performing with famous adult male actors. The next chapter will examine girls in the frame of another relational perspective on their roles and performances: the girl in the narrative as sister, as daughter, and—more troublingly—as sexual partner. Though Sophie is buddy to the BFG, as an orphan she also finds a father figure in him. Similarly, Rachel in *War of the Worlds* is defined as daughter to Cruise's Ray. In *The Color Purple*, family relations are confused by sexual violence, while in the Spielberg-directed *Jurassic Park* films, girls become more powerful (and indeed become action stars) in relation to younger siblings. This second-level narrative of girlhood in Spielberg's films is where this story of Spielberg's children goes next.

6

Clever Girls

Resilience and Relational Girlhood in *The Color Purple* and Spielberg's *Jurassic Park* Films

This chapter focuses on the dynamic and diverse performances of girls in Spielberg's films, often placed as protecting elders or protected youngsters, with the family figured as both a safe and a harmful space. Despite the predominance of boy heroes in Spielberg films, the girl—as sister, as playmate, as supporting player or background performer—is also a significant part of the story of Spielberg's filmic children. In earlier chapters we encountered a little sister in the form of Drew Barrymore's most famous early role as six-year-old Gertie in *E.T.* Though it is Henry Thomas who carries the weight of the story, budget, and developing child subjectivity, Gertie (and Mike) substantially feature. Sisters are also figures of power in the Spielberg-directed *Jurassic Park* films and are the sole support systems for each other in the first act of *The Color Purple.* The child actors who carry the opening of this conflicted film, performing the young Celie and her sister Nettie, are fourteen-year old Desreta Jackson and eighteen-year old Akosua Busia; Jackson is later succeeded, for the remainder of the film, by a twenty-nine-year-old Whoopi Goldberg playing Celie from twenty-one to old age. These actors present Black female childhood into adolescence and adulthood through the lens of historic violence and domesticity. *The Color Purple* is a contested film;

though successful at the box office, it has been criticized for "Spielbergizing" Alice Walker's harsher vision of racial inequality (though Jacqueline Bobo [1995] reminds us that Black women have responded positively to it—and as we shall see this is also not without difficulty). The novel is widely read as a key articulation of Walker's "womanism" (distinct from but related to feminism). I will discuss the film's early the girls' perspectives and performances, Bobo's foundational analysis, and Walker's own experience of being attached to the film.

The films discussed here highlight distinct horrors that girls confront, and they show girls to be resilient in the face of fear and violence. The previous chapter spotlit Dakota Fanning's performance as the horror key that twisted the tone of *War of the Worlds*, while Ruby Barnhill led child viewers through the sometimes alarming shocks of *The BFG* (for younger viewers, anyway)—a film for smaller children that may not be a horror film, yet it is still a story about children confronting monsters, as Sophie befriends a figure of fear for younger children (a giant), who is himself afraid of bigger giants. The stories of this chapter are distinct both from this previous discussion and from each other. *The Color Purple*'s Celie and Nettie are African American girls living in the post-slavery United States and confronting real social and sexual horror on a daily basis. I am not proposing that we read this film as a generic horror film in the frame of entertainment exploitation horror, with which the *Jurassic Park* titles and *War of the Worlds* flirt. But in a discussion that focuses on girl stories, visions of the distress and anxiety of girls' fear run through these performances in ways that reinflect the usually male focus of children in Spielberg's films.

Scream Teens and Final Girls: *Jurassic Park* and *The Lost World: Jurassic Park*

The gargantuan *Jurassic Park* media franchise began with Spielberg's 1993 film, inaugurating a series that now extends to multiple titles: the first three appeared within eight years, and then the series went into abeyance until a reboot and franchise consolidation under the *Jurassic World* umbrella from 2015 onward. Spielberg directed only the first two (*Jurassic Park* in 1993, and *The Lost World: Jurassic Park* in 1997), though he maintains an executive producer credit on all subsequent *Jurassic* releases. In keeping with the director frame of this book, this discussion will focus on these first two titles, which also offer girls active performance and narrative opportunities. The first *Jurassic Park*'s children are siblings Lex and Tim Murphy (Ariana Richards and Joseph Mazzello), the grandchildren of the dinosaur-cloning mastermind John Hammond (Richard Attenborough), who visit their grandfather partly to experience his new theme park full of live, cloned dinosaurs prior to its opening, and partly because their parents are getting divorced—a detail that is easily passed over, with one line half buried in an early conversation featuring Hammond's lawyer Donald Gennaro (Martin Ferrero). It could have just as easily been missed out: critics eager to find the biographical in every Spielberg screen act might read this morsel as they had read *E.T.*, with Lex and Tim joining Elliott as symptomatic children of broken families. Why else would they be so eager to become part of a new surrogate family structure, as the film demonstrates? Along with a team of scientists and a lawyer (paleontologist Dr. Alan Grant [Sam Neil], paleobotanist Ellie Sattler [Laura Dern], mathematician Ian Malcolm [Jeff Goldblum] alongside Gennaro), the children tour the island, a storm encroaches, and human villainy intervenes, enabling the animals to rampage into the safe zone, killing people and each other while showcasing state-of-the-art effects technology. As with *Jaws*, here Spielberg brings creature feature exploitation aesthetics to the maximum-budget filmmaking arena, splicing horror with family adventure film formats. And again he uses the child (though not only the child) to intensify the affect of peril. That Lex and Tim combine particular vulnerabilities is no accident: though she is older, she is female; though he is younger, he is male.

However, the first child we see in the film is a foil to showcase Grant's antipathy to fatherhood. On a dig that has just uncovered a complete velociraptor fossil, the esteemed paleontologist lectures the assembled volunteers and assistants about its evolutionary relationship to birds. When a particularly vocal boy (Whit Hertford) scorns the idea, Grant elaborates on how deadly the velociraptors are by ghoulishly narrating an attack on the child, to that child. The speech sets out a number of threads, including the prowess of the velociraptor (prefiguring later set pieces) and the child as bait and prey, as well as Grant's anti-familial stance. The description *is itself* an attack, as well as being *about* an attack: expressed in the present tense, it is articulated with physical gestures mapping out injury to the child's body with the aid of a talon fossil: "He slashes at you with this six-inch retractable claw, like a razor . . . he slashes at you here or here or maybe across the belly, spilling your intestines. . . . [Y]ou are alive when they start to eat you." Spielberg directs the boy to look increasingly uneasy to the point of fear, while Ellie watches, amused but shocked.[1] Later she quips, "If you wanted to scare the kid you could have pulled a gun on him." The child's horror, then, becomes the setting for Ellie and Grant's negotiation of whether to start a family—Ellie wants to; Grant objects that "they're noisy, they're messy, they're expensive, they smell." This has since become the dominant interpretative framework for reading *Jurassic Park*. If *Jaws* is not about a shark (apparently), and is read as a meditation on male bonding and political hierarchies, *Jurassic Park*—with similar bias—is about men reluctant to be fathers who learn to come around to the idea. Just as *War of the Worlds* was popularly interpreted as a story about the Tom Cruise character's developing approach to fatherhood to which the girl's (Dakota Fanning's) star performance was a mere adjunct, so Lex's role is generally framed in the film's reception as a mere tool for this paternal impetus.

However, the production story actually reverses this. The writer David Koepp was brought in to finesse the screenplay, including the formation of Ellie and

Grant, whereby it was thought that the grapple over whether to have children gave their characters more depth. Spielberg, however, wanted children to also be at the center of the story, so the Ellie-Grant parenting question becomes a pretext for the presence of the child over and above the historical fact that Spielberg likes to work with children. "The kids were kind of a challenge," reported Koepp, "because we didn't want it to seem like they were there just to have kids in the movie." He continued: "Steven, in particular, is vulnerable to criticism like that, because he likes to work with kids. He works with kids awfully well, so it's not entirely fair, but the perception is there nonetheless. So our challenge was to find out why these kids were essential to the movie" (Shay and Duncan 1993, 57). This is an interesting twist in the childhood tale: contrary to the notion that *Jurassic Park* is really about men becoming fathers, the narrative balance is actually the other way around, with the father story functioning to place children center stage. In the following I will be framing Lex as a strong narrative presence, driving the story, just as the actor who plays her is part agent of her own performance. Of course, there are kids in the original novel, but their roles were different. Other currents also move children in different directions. The idea of violence to the child enacted twice over, albeit comedically, in this opening sequence (Grant's description and the velociraptor's potential act) suggests that the film's central children are there only as victims and pawns in an adult parenting game. Indeed, suggestions of potential and later actual violence circle the child pervasively and throughout. Soon after this opening velociraptor story, Hammond appears, describing the park and its attractions in ambivalent terms that suggest it will "entertain" its target audience in an extreme way: "There's no doubt our attractions will drive kids out of their minds!" Though only adults actually die, the pervasive threat of violence to children also serves to establish the strong child as survivor and narrative agent.

There is of course another child in the film, who appears even before Lex and Tim arrive. She is part of the explanatory dinosaur science narrative delivered to the visitors, inaugurating a progenerate thread that underpins the film's consideration of natural or unnatural families. This is a dino girl child, born from cloned DNA and grown in an ostrich egg, who cutely chips her way out of her shell to the encouragement of a paternal Hammond ("I insist on being here when they're born"). I further discuss nonhuman children elsewhere in this book, but what interests me here is that these are specifically girl babies, and here it is explained that all of the dinosaurs on the island are female—a strategy to prevent spontaneous breeding among the animal population (which fails). Memorably, when the park warden Muldoon (Bob Peck) hunts and is hunted by a velociraptor, his last words before she strikes—praising lethal skills that outwit his, even to his death—are "Clever girl." Hammond explains that the hatching babies imprint on the first creature they see, at which point child-phobic but science-obsessed Grant insistently points to himself, keen to be daddy to this girl-baby velociraptor, if not to human offspring.

When the (human) kids arrive, it becomes clear that they are also prototypes, this time of commercial consumers—trial-sized versions of the paying customers whom Hammond hopes will buy into the attraction: he introduces them to the scientists first not as his grandchildren but as his "target audience." They are, then, part of a market experiment (and will also become a form of bait), test-driving the attraction's scientific wonders and its family-friendliness as an entertainment spectacle. Metaphors of predation illuminate *Jurassic Park* on many levels: natural (the creatures themselves, the most visually and narratively exciting of which are carnivores), personal (exchanges of human rivalry and weakness, in which the worst will sacrifice children for gain and the best will risk all to save them), and economic (the free-market enterprise of the theme park itself). The diegetic park is a family show not unlike the film that imagines it: as Peter Wollen pointed out in 1993, for all the scorn the screenplay directs at slapping the brand "on a plastic lunchbox," *Jurassic Park* itself simultaneously exploits exactly the same merchandise. There is even a copy of Don Shay and Jody Duncan's *The Making of Jurassic Park*—about the making of the film—playfully placed in the film world's gift shop as if it were a book about the making of the fictional park, not its filmic fabrication.

The children are first seen running toward Hammond through the visitor center attractions (entering, as it were, through the gift shop) and are quickly bundled into a tour car. At first the focus is on Tim, who inveigles himself into Ellie and Grant's car and targets Grant with his dinosaur knowledge (a passion the film attributes to boys, not girls),[2] repeating the skepticism of the first boy we saw but avoiding the threatening riposte (presumably because unlike the child at the dig, this one is grandchild to Hammond, Grant's project-funder; Hammond has greeted the children with open arms, but other adult males are uneasy in child company). As with David at the *A.I.* dinner table, our first clear view of Tim is of him surrounded by would-be mother on the left of the frame and reluctant father on the right: the child of divorcing parents may be looking for a new father, but Grant resists in his body language and dialogue to the point of fleeing the car and then shutting Tim into another car away from him (a move that will ultimately endanger Tim). Lex then confronts him head-on. Ellie, she reports, "said I should ride with you 'cause it'd be good for you." Ellie's raging maternal desire seems to dog Grant's every move, setting in motion a story of refusenik fathers and desperate would-be mothers: no wonder the all-female dinosaurs on the island, when faced with a lack of males with which to breed, find a way of doing it by themselves.[3]

That the children are at risk is evident from the start: children in peril is one of Spielberg's stock-in-trade narrative tropes. The director is not averse to high-end exploitation thrills, and, while even the suggestion of children's bodies being damaged or destroyed is rare in his corpus, children are not exempt from being placed at the center of the occasional but no less relished visceral thrills. As I argue elsewhere (Williams 2020), in *Jaws* they are explicitly offered up as shark bait, are allowed to go unsupervised into shark-infested waters, die in a horrifying spectacle of foaming blood (Alex Kintner's demise), and provide a jangling anxiety of child endangerment that pervades the first two-thirds of the film. So as Hammond the grandfather-entrepreneur watches his gene pool depart in the tour jeep alongside the adult visitors, he audibly delivers an apprehensive gasp expressing *hope* that it will go well but fear that it might not, as he hears of a tropical storm heading their way. Even *Jaws*' Brody seemed genuinely to believe that his son Michael would actually be safe in Amity's lagoon and did not send him there merely *hoping* that the shark would not enter. In *Jurassic Park*, the children's separating parents have dispatched them to the security of the grandfather's care, but his is not a safe pair of hands. Michael Crichton has described the character as a dark Walt Disney, but given the regularity with which critics garland Spielberg himself as Disney's heir, this characterization must also implicate the directorial showman of *Jurassic Park* the film, as well as the fictional showman (who, we are reminded, started as master of a flea circus) of the fictional theme park. Chuck Stephens's rather scatological meditation on *The Lost World* in *Film Comment* pins Spielberg's invention of the franchise back to the biographical ("Spielberg's been taking his Oedipal angst to the bank from *Sugarland Express* on") but pays homage to the director as heir to that primary cinematic child-scarer: "No-one since Walt Disney has so diligently delighted in caring for children by scaring their pants off" (1997).

Disney first and Spielberg second are, then, cinematic child-catchers, trapping them on-screen in order to lure them into the auditorium. In *Jurassic Park* this begins with Hammond, orchestrated by Spielberg (after Crichton), and the children in question are Lex and Tim. It is Lex primarily who oscillates between caution and terror, who loves her grandfather even into the sequel despite the fact that he has used her as a guinea pig, or—in the prey metaphorics of *Jurassic Park*—a tethered steer or goat. If, by the time we get to *The Lost World*, human children are matched with dinosaur offspring, the first film can only figure them as surrogates for the live meat dangled in front of carnivores. Lex senses this from the outset: as the children's jeep proceeds toward the monumental (and closed) park gates, she delivers the first of many lines apprehending danger, not trusting the car to stop: "Are we going to hit that?" A little later, when that live goat is placed in the T-Rex enclosure, she asks, "What's going to happen to the goat?" The question may sound simplistic (Tim can only say, "Excellent!"), but it lays bare a bald truth that speaks to her own vulnerability just as the words test the parameters of the theme park as blood sport: How far will they go, how elastic is a family adventure attraction, and how permissible is it to spell out violent death in a family film?

Lex and Tim also function to make adults question their relationship with children, which is nowhere more luridly rendered than when the generations are trapped together first as tourists and second as prey. Grant asks Malcolm if he has ever had kids, and the response is casual, suggesting he collects them as he does wives, but also that he views those offspring as nonspecific generic children: "Me? Hell, yeah. Three. I love kids." He continues, "Anything at all can and does happen." If Hammond has a worryingly experimental relationship to his grandchildren, Malcolm here suggests that his children's primary function is to test his specialist research area (chaos theory—much of his screen dialogue is spent explaining this to anyone who will listen). However, when the power fails and the two jeeps—one containing Grant and Malcolm, the other Gennaro, Lex, and Tim—fall stranded by the now unprotected T-Rex enclosure, it is Grant who physically checks on the other car but Malcolm as father who asks, "Kids OK?" Grant replies, "I didn't ask—why wouldn't they be?" "Kids get scared," responds Malcolm, himself visibly scared. In a car without children, the children still provide a gauge of fear and a touchstone for adult response and responsibility.

Malcolm is then positioned somewhere between parent and child himself, while marking an ethical boundary between pure science and commodified technology as generationally distinct. When he delivers his set piece ethics speech ("Your scientists were so preoccupied with whether or not they could that they didn't stop to think if they should"), he deploys the metaphor of a child out of control with adult weaponry: "Genetic power's the most awesome force the planet's ever seen but you wield it like a kid that's found his dad's gun." This is not the only time the undisciplined scientist is figured as the wayward child: as the computer technician Ray Arnold (Samuel L. Jackson) tries to fix the first of many systems failures in the control room, the camera lands on, then scans past a photograph pinned to a screen amid the chaos of a working desk: a man poses in front of a blackboard of mathematical formulas, a midcentury photograph embellished by a Post-it reading "Beginning of Baby Boom." The film gives us few clues here; however, the man is the Manhattan Project nuclear scientist Robert Oppenheimer, popularly known as the "father of the atomic bomb." The Post-it draws a comparison between the Oppenheimer-inaugurated atomic era and the coterminous midcentury baby boom (1946–1964), of which Spielberg was a part.

But Oppenheimer's image here, with its enigmatic annotation, also suggests the reproductive peril that is to animate the story—Ellie has discovered that, notwithstanding Hammond's supposedly failsafe single-sex policy, a triceratops is nevertheless pregnant, and so control of—or *failure* to control—the production of offspring becomes one of the film's, and the franchise's, key anxieties. Like Oppenheimer's, Hammond's unethical science releases forces into the world he cannot control, and the park teeters on the brink of a dangerous dino boom courtesy of a female-only population that learns to reproduce through parthenogenesis. Of course, the question remains: If Hammond is so keen to avoid a dino population explosion, why does he make his park all-female rather than all-male? Perhaps to avoid territorialism and aggression? The females are hardly harmless. If the historical Oppenheimer came to regret the death-bringing force of his invention, Hammond's work is dangerous precisely because it is life-bringing.

While he tries to prevent the generation of family outside of his control, ultimately it is family—too much family, and of the wrong kind—that prevails.

When the virtuoso set piece T-Rex attack finally comes, it is prefigured by a reminder (and a nod to *Jaws*) that creature features equalize all humans, young or old, as potential meat. A tethered goat, placed as a lure, is soon replaced by a goatless tether. This instigates the first of many shots of Lex's terrified face, one of the film's key images and, I would argue, as iconic as any dinosaur sequence. The goat's dismembered leg is dropped onto the jeep's sunroof, which frames it like a cinema or tv screen, and the children's peril is ratcheted up by amoral anti-parent Gennaro departing the car and fleeing to the shelter of a toilet. Lex's initial outburst is not in direct fear at the T-Rex but abandonment by the adult: "He left us—he left us!" As the huge beast breaks through the fence and marauds around the stranded jeeps, Grant tells Malcolm to "keep absolutely still—its vision is based on movement," making it crystal clear how bad it is when Lex, resourcefully, finds a flashlight and waves it as an SOS. Courtesy of that obsessive knowledge of dinosaurs, Tim knows what his older sister does not—that darkness and stillness save while light and movement (elements of the cinematic) endanger. Spielberg situates the action alongside the two abandoned children inside the jeep, which the T-Rex toys with like a tin can, yet the spectacle is as much the children's stricken faces as it is the dinosaur. This goes on for what seems like a horribly long time (over two minutes) before the adult men in the other car take action and put themselves in the place of the children, both Grant and Malcolm distracting the beast before it finds abject Gennaro sitting on the toilet, and eats him.

Grant's evolution to father figure is negotiated through his parenting of Lex and Tim, instigated by his response to the hysterical Lex's continued mantra "He left us! He left us!" with an assured adult statement "But that's not what I'm gonna do." In the sequence that follows, in which Grant parents the children back to safety, their different fears, knowledge, and skills come to the fore: Lex is a self-styled computer-obsessed nerd ("I'm a hacker," a status that will give her a heroic edge later), whereas Tim is chatty and (dinosaur) fact-filled. Whereas he can be funny, cheeky, she is utterly straight, seems to have no sense of humor, and is sometimes the butt of the film's jokes. But she is also markedly more physically courageous than her brother, which gives Richards the opportunity for a dynamic performance, climbing trees and fences without fear of injury (it is Tim who hesitates while scaling the perimeter fence, and receives 10,000 volts). As observed in several reviews and interviews, Richards "brought a great sense of adventure and fear to a visually stunning movie" (Patrick 2011). Denoting the active element of a film is rarely granted to women performers, let alone girls—except perhaps horror's "final girls" (who are always women)—so this is welcome.[4] Fear is more usual: in the history of horror, fear often seeps from a film to its audience via its women positioned through vulnerability and victimhood. Lex bears this out too: her screams (in the first T-Rex attack, where they are piercing and relentless), and her performance of stricken horror (throughout) fulfill that function in *Jurassic Park*.

Though a seasoned child actor (earlier she had been in *Tremors* and *Prancer*, and was particularly acclaimed in the TV movie *Switched at Birth*), Richards auditioned for the role via videotape, which was then sent to Spielberg to be viewed alongside many others. Whereas the ability to cry was the quality needed from Henry Thomas, as with Fanning after her, it was Richards's screaming skills that were paramount here: "They just wanted me to be put on tape screaming my head off. So I just kind of let loose." Spielberg reports that he had her "scream for three minutes. . . . I hadn't seen screams like that since Fay Wray was undone at the sacrificial altar by King Kong" (Shay and Duncan 1993, 73). And whereas Thomas's audition needed to also elicit tears from those in the audition room, Richards's screams also infected the Spielberg domestic scene; she reports that Spielberg told her later, "You know, Ariana, when I was looking at those girls screaming that day on tape I sat down on the couch in the evening, and my wife Kate was asleep next to me on the couch. And I went through one girl screaming and then the next one, and then I came to you, and when you started screaming Kate literally flew off the couch and ran into the hallway screaming, 'Steven are the kids OK?'" (*Jurassic Cast Podcast* interview n.d.).

This level of alarm clearly bodes well for a creature feature promising thrills and terror; that it also implicates Spielberg's own children in the adult fear is interesting, as if he needed another's extreme response to confirm the casting. Richards's reports of Spielberg's direction are focused on her performance of fear ("He told me that he enjoyed seeing how much I was doing in the role and how deeply I was getting into the fear"; Patrick 2011). When she is asked by interviewer Seb Patrick, "Your performance in the film is especially remarkable for the sheer sense of genuine terror that you get across throughout—where did that come from?" she responds, "Actually, Steven asked me the same question when filming! When we were filming the scene of the T-rex with the jeep, during the moments between scenes Steven came over to me once and said, 'Ariana, you reach such a deep level of fear and terror—what do you draw from? Were you scared by a clown when you were three? Don't tell me, I don't want to know!' And then he smiled and walked away" (Patrick 2011). This also references another claim, that Spielberg wanted Richards and Mazzello to coauthor their performances, endorsed also by costar Sam Neill, who "didn't really think of them as children; I thought of them as actors" (Shay and Duncan 1993, 72).

The idea of Richards as agent of her performance is, however, something she both affirms and draws away from, "He knew what he wanted," she says in one online interview. "He would ask me and Joey for our input, and we would go for it and get the scene right within no more than a few takes."[5] When asked by one interviewer why Spielberg's young actors "tend to be so good," inviting a response about how Spielberg directs children, Richards both acknowledges the innate skill and "rightness" of the actors ("I think he is very good at casting roles and choosing actors") and then suggests a combination of invisible control and openness to the child's creative input ("As young actors he gave Joey and I the gift of allowing us to be very natural—and directing us without actually directing us, often asking for our input into scenes"; Patrick 2011). However, some of the fear is, as is customary with child actors, genuine. As with *E.T.*, which was filmed in sequence to aid the children's relationship to the developing story but also to bond them to the alien they must be seen to love and lose, Richards and Mazzello only encountered the dinosaur models when actually being attacked by them, with only the sun roof between them and "a full-size tyrannosaurus crashing down on us" ("Steven had it planned out that Joey and I wouldn't have a great deal of exposure to the dinosaurs before we actually encountered them on set so our reactions were the most genuine childlike reactions").[6] Richards's reaction is then important in fueling audience reaction, so to start with it is important that she is afraid herself ("It looked so realistic—it shocked me").[7]

But Lex's/Richards's fear is also performed through the opposite mode—a fixed expression of paralyzed terror that becomes as iconic as the intense screaming. If we discount the entire population of dinosaurs, the only other female in the film—Ellie—is a contrasting portrait of courage. This not only enables Richards's frozen face to emerge as one of the film's signal images but also suggests an interesting method for pinning the audience to the center of the film's perilous action. Since following that first T-Rex attack we know that stillness may save one while movement can seal one's doom, so Lex's survival depends on her ability to hold her body, including her facial expression, motionless for an unusually long time. That face then becomes the remarkably focused center of several action set pieces in *Jurassic Park*—immobility in the midst of "big and loud," the "high-cost, high-tech, high-speed" production (Gross 1995). This of course characterizes one of Spielberg's signature visual tricks—the still glass of water that vibrates with approaching monstrous footfalls; the still spoon of Jell-O that jiggles in Lex's trembling hand; small objects moving minutely, which betray immense threat. These imagistic touchstones might support Gary Arms and Thomas Riley's (2008) framework of the "big-little" film for reading Spielberg—big action spectacles encasing small intimate character stories. Though *Jurassic Park* is not their focus, this is nowhere better exemplified than in the T-Rex attack sequence, a practical and digital effects extravaganza that repeatedly beats back to Richards's young face to intensify the peril and abandonment. Tim is of course there in the beleaguered jeep with her, but it is *her* frenzied, misguided attempts to save them both that drive the heart of the sequence—the iconic mask of terror she holds as she and the monster eyeball each other in the light of the irised flashlight she has unwisely deployed, eyes unblinking and sinews straining even as she hyperventilates.

Arms and Riley use this "big-little" model to drive an argument about distinct father types and moral philosophy, but they also suggest that Spielberg fails to capitalize on the performance potential of Richards (and of Fanning in

War of the Worlds), instead using his girl actors only to "give fathers or father-types an opportunity to save them" (2008, 14). But reading *Jurassic Park* as a child performance artifact rather than a director biography (Arms and Riley once again suggest that all Spielberg stories are narratives of paternal abandonment), it is clear that Richards is doing (and being) much more than this. Her reactions orchestrate audience response. Tim and Lex, bloodied but alive, return to the deserted visitor center, where a buffet had been laid out (to welcome a victorious park tour that went badly wrong) and—in yet another dinner table scene—feast on decadent desserts after their night of terror (the power to eat *anything*, unsupervised by adult instruction, also animates the sequence when Jamie returns home in *Empire of the Sun*, as we shall see). This is one in a series of moments when the children realize they are not safe after all, and is as immersive to the audience as it is to the actor: though Lex/Ariana does not look directly—confrontationally—into the camera, Spielberg's direction of her to stare fixedly at something behind the viewer effectively transfers the terror from protagonist to audience ("Look behind you!"). This is the image Ariana Richards chose to illustrate her experience on the film: after a very successful career (with twenty-six film and TV credits as a child performer), she became a portrait artist, which she describes as "be[ing] my own director in a way, when you get to create these portraits of people on canvas" (Lyus 2011). In repeated interviews she cites a self-portrait she did around the making of the film as crystallizing that working experience ("For me it's more difficult to put something as multi-faceted as the experience of playing Lex into words, and so I decided to paint a watercolor of the 'Jello' scene" [Patrick 2011]).[8] The painting (which she bequeathed to Spielberg at the end of the shoot, and is included in some interviews, including that by Patrick [2011]) follows the film's iconic image of Lex's frozen face staring into the distance somewhere behind the viewer, while her hand holds the trembling spoon (figure 10), but adds the velociraptor just behind her shoulder, rendering her as even more unseeing of the imminent danger coming up behind her.

This moment in the film leads immediately into the velociraptor kitchen scene, in which child Lex becomes leader Lex, masterminding the escape as the more powerful figure of the sibling duo. The scene oscillates between the children's screaming panic and Lex's controlling actions (locking doors, switching off lights, shepherding her brother, deflecting the predators' attention). Chaos in the kitchen has of course characterized moments such as *E.T.*'s drunken exploration, or Jillian's attempt to keep Barry inside as the aliens try to extract him from without in *Close Encounters*. Lex is not so much maternal here in relation to Tim (though she does draw the beasts to attack her so he can escape) as a child in arms against a common enemy; a relationship first seen as testy disaffection becomes that of compadre/comadre, with the sister in the senior role. Michael Crichton's novel featured a younger Lex and an older Tim, but Spielberg chose to reverse the roles, partly because Joseph Mazzello, who looked younger than

FIGURE 10 Ariana Richards performs Lex in *Jurassic Park*.

his age, was already cast, and Spielberg "realized that if I cast Lex younger than Tim, she would look about five years old—which was much too young to put in jeopardy with these dinosaurs. It would have turned the audience against us completely. So I thought it would be best to cast older for the girl" (Shay and Duncan 1993, 73). There is, then, a fine line in terms of just how young, how vulnerable, a child can be before extreme peril is acceptable. The filmmakers report the "bonus" of the rewrite being that Lex would now be old enough to foster a prepubescent crush on Grant, who is simultaneously being set up as a father figure. However, Richards sees the age switch as entirely positive in terms of her character's empowerment: "Steven really gave my character a great deal. When you compare it to the book . . . [where] my character is the younger sister and quite a brat with not very much to offer" (Lyus 2011).

Lex then graduates to the film's primary savior courtesy of her IT skills. In the computer control room the adults are left to physically fend off the beasts, but it is Lex's digital superiority ("It's a UNIX system—I know this!") that enables her to single-handedly make the park safe again, graduating from scream queen to skilled hero in a digital age formation of the final girl who *actually* is a girl (figure 11). The actor was very aware at the time that this was a bold move: "Having the roles reversed and the fact that I was given the computer know-how that was only given to the boy in the book was really extraordinary. I got so many messages from fans about the fact that they got to see a young girl given the chance to be smart and know something about an important topic and save the day" (Lyus 2011). Indeed, the very act of representing a computer geek won Richards the 2018 Reel Women in Technology Award, which recognizes "the best portrayal of leading women in technology from a program (e.g. documentary, TV show, film, YouTube, etc.) who serve as role models for girls and women with computing aspirations while disrupting the stereotypes of female ingenuity in technology fields." As the Reel

FIGURE 11 "It's a UNIX system—I know this!": Lex (Ariana Richards) saves the world in *Jurassic Park*.

Women in Technology Award page tells us, Lex's ability to hack the park's computer system "has inspired countless kids (and probably some adults) to take up careers in science, programming, or computer graphics."[9] In a 2018 interview with Richards, Rachel Leishman notes that "Ariana's Lex was rather revolutionary in her day, and she upended the book's characterization," but the Reel Women in Technology Award suggests that she remains significant. Gender-neutral casting has become a call to arms since 2017's #TimesUp and public debates over equal pay in Hollywood, but Richards argues that Spielberg's gender swap was as significant for children as it was for adult women: "Steven has always been so good in expressing children in their roles and giving women an empowered role" (Lyus 2011). Notwithstanding those arguments that she is only there to support the father story, or the girly adolescent crush inflection, or because a younger girl would not work with the already-cast young boy, Lex/Richards runs with an opportunity even if it is an accident of developing production choices.

However, Lex's resourcefulness was not simply a strike for a feminism already underlined by Ellie's quips about women inheriting the earth and sexism in survival situations. It would also have no small effect on the box office of the film. We have seen repeatedly how the presence of the child on-screen skews genre to incorporate family audiences, and here it is Lex and Tim who finesse an exploitation creature feature toward young viewers: the film got a PG-13 certificate in the United States and a PG certificate in the United Kingdom. The Classification and Rating Administration (CARA), the secretive ratings organization that classifies films on behalf of the Motion Picture Association (MPA—formerly the Motion Picture Association of America [MPAA]), does not provide statements justifying individual decisions; the R (Restricted) rating *does* require a child to be accompanied, but they can still get entrance to the film. The PG-13 rating must therefore be understood as advisory and is currently defined with the loose statement "Parents strongly cautioned: Parents are urged to be cautious. Some material may be inappropriate for pre-teenagers."[10] The British Board of Film Classification (BBFC) is rather more transparent in its processes: it has published justifications for its classification decisions since the turn of the century and focuses decisions around classification boundaries for films such as *Jurassic Park* around questions of age-appropriateness. Given the United Kingdom's cultural history of anxieties around filmic harm to child audiences, the examiner's report is particularly telling here. The definition of a PG classification is that the film is suitable for "general viewing. A PG should generally not unsettle a child aged around eight, although parents and caregivers should be aware that some scenes may be unsuitable for more sensitive children."[11] *Jurassic Park* was tested on child audiences by the BBFC, and the results were considered before a certificate was issued. Clearly worried that a decision to allow *any* child in to see such a frightening film would be controversial, the board issued a full report on the case, which includes the following reflection on the original certification:

> At the time, the Compliance Officers who viewed the film made a clear recommendation for a PG certificate. One argued that the film was part of a long dynasty of "monster movies," such as *King Kong* and *The Lost World*, but that Jurassic Park's "chase scenes are long and realistic and there is a quality of *Alien* about some of them."
>
> The film contains numerous scenes of threat towards the two child characters, Lex and Tim, most notably in the first attack from the tyrannosaurus rex and the extended velociraptor chase in the third act. However, the Compliance Officers recognised a key mitigating factor in how the characters were portrayed, with: "one of the children being resourceful when the other is scared, one pointing out the excitement at a time when the other is fearful." These onscreen reassurances and the balance they provide were crucial aspects in making the classification decision.[12]

Lex's sometimes clear-headed courage, as well as her fearfulness, was then material in *Jurassic Park* reaching the huge UK audience it reaped. A higher rating—for instance, the next one up in the range, 12 (later changed to 12A)—would exclude younger child audience members. Originally introduced as a strict minimum age rating, it was changed to an advisory rating in 2002: "No one younger than 12 may be permitted to attend a 12A cinema screening unless they are accompanied by an adult" runs the current BBFC definition,[13] making the category one that filmmakers and distributors of family adventure films would seek to avoid, given its potential box office–limiting implications. However, *Jurassic Park* was recertificated to the 12A category by the BBFC in 2023, when it was resubmitted by the distributors for the film's thirtieth anniversary. It is unusual to reclassify a film upward, into a more prohibitive classification, which here was due to changing guidelines; there is significant feeling in the industry that it should always have been located in this band of protection.

So does this age switch (older, leading girl) and skill advance (saving the world) mark a shift in Spielberg's relationship to his young female roles from the 1990s onward? It may seem so from the fact that the first *Jurassic Park* sequel—*The Lost World*—features just one primary child role, but this is a twelve-year-old girl. Vanessa Lee Chester is also one of Spielberg's few female-of-color leads (*The Color Purple* and *Amistad*—both Black-focused stories—are exceptions; Rachel Zegler, star of *West Side Story* and eighteen years old when it went into production, also identifies as white Latina). Kelly's/Chester's race is discussed in passing (in relation to the whiteness of her on-screen father, played by Jeff Goldblum), but it is her other minority attributes—as a child and as a girl—that drive the development of her character as protected and vulnerable. Consequently, the role itself is something of a step backward from the original *Jurassic Park* in terms of action and empowerment. Aside from the gymnastic display cited in chapter 5, Kelly/Chester has little to do, and certainly does not function to move the story forward as does Lex in the first film. As the daughter of one of Malcolm's broken relationships, and therefore one of the "three kids" he casually admitted to in *Jurassic Park* (the other two seem to have been forgotten by the time of this sequel), she provides him with an opportunity to put to work all his statements about fatherhood that hung over the first film.

We first see Kelly visiting Malcolm as he prepares to travel to Isla Sorna, which, we are told, was in fact the "factory floor" island where *Jurassic Park*'s dinosaurs were initially bred before being showcased at the theme park of Isla Nublar. All the animals have since escaped and naturalized, and all the humans have fled. Four years later John Hammond is assembling a small team to travel there and observe, ahead of the island being stripped of its treasures, which are destined for a theme park in San Diego. Kelly's function, as another child of a broken relationship, is at first to lecture her part-time father on parenting failures: "I'm your daughter all the time . . . you can't just abandon me whenever opportunity knocks," she opines, and "You like to have kids but you just don't want to be with them, do you?" But this is as far as it goes: whereas boy children of divorce articulate intricate, subjective narratives such as in *E.T.*, girl children of divorce seldom play out the complexities of Spielberg's psychic journey. Given that Malcolm is this sequel's main character and Kelly is less central than the Lex-Tim dyad of the first film, *The Lost World* essentially articulates its divorce story from the father's point of view.

Yet for one moment early on, Kelly promises to be more central than she turns out to be: walking through the workshop where equipment and heavy-duty transportation for the expedition are being assembled, the arc of welder's sparks she traverses recalls the sequence in *Empire of the Sun* when Jim breaks ranks and embraces a Japanese plane in a shower of fire, a moment of remaking for his own self. However, after this moment in *The Lost World*, Kelly is seldom seen (or heard) on her own terms, only ratcheting up the stakes of tension for the adults. Stowing away in the laboratory/accommodation trailer that is taken to the island, she is here on in only the focus of rescue missions and peril, and Chester's performance oscillates between nervous panic and feisty willfulness, though as the story continues she mostly performs needy vulnerability. Once on the island, she essentially functions as Bambi in Chuck Stephens's view of the film: "The Lost World is certainly darker and deadlier than its predecessor. The body count is higher, the 'boo!' factor's been amplified, and as with Bambi—and what is the Jurassic franchise if not Bambi meets Godzilla writ very large?—children are doomed to emotional damage while diligent designers further their careers" (Stephens 1997).

However, *The Lost World* also features two other moments of prime risk focused on less central (and more dispensable) children. Here the aforementioned Nasty Steven peeps out from behind Nice Steven's family entertainment curtain when he throws a small girl and then a young boy to the beasts for black comic effect. In 1993, he had said of Lex and Tim (and their adult compatriots), "The minute their helicopter lands on the island, they aren't safe," describing the first film as "more like Ten Little Indians than it is like Godzilla attacking Tokyo" (Sears 1993, 80), with narrative tension driven by who will die next. If in 1993 he seemed reluctant to put children plainly on the menu, by the opening of the 1997 sequel he is not so cautious. *The Lost World* opens with a privileged English family who have happened upon Isla Sorna in their luxury yacht. They take an excursion to the beach, allowing their small daughter, Cathy (Camilla Belle), to wander off into the jungle with a beef sandwich in her hand. The sequence plays out through a series of darkly comedic edits: finding herself surrounded by a herd of small, apparently cute dinosaurs (of the Compsognathus genus, we later learn—the smallest carnivorous dinosaurs), she feeds them the meat but only as a prelude to becoming meat herself (figure 12). As she is overwhelmed by their sheer numbers, the film cuts brutally to her unsuspecting parents farther up the beach being served roast beef by their staff. The child's screams are heard, but the attack and consumption of her are not shown, though the camera does pause on the spectacle of her mother screaming. However, this is cut short by a comedically heartless edit to another open-mouthed adult: Ian Malcolm in a city subway, not screaming but yawning. It is a breathtakingly funny filmic splice, underlining child peril as risibly tiresome to feckless adults.

Malcolm, it turns out, is traveling to John Hammond's house, where he encounters Lex and Tim, now four years older (and played again by Richards and Mazzello). The substance of their brief cameos is to highlight the danger to come: in response to the question "Is everything OK?," Lex replies "Not exactly." Hammond then reassures Malcolm that the "wee girl" on the beach is now fine (off-screen child death must wait for later in the film), but judging by the mother's reaction we have just witnessed, "fine" is clearly a relative term. Litigation by the parents is the primary consequence of the attack;[14] the child's injuries only signify

FIGURE 12 Cathy (Camilla Belle) succumbs to Isla Sorna's wildlife in *The Lost World*.

because they set in motion the film's underpinning story, which balances pursuit of profit generated by exploiting highly dangerous animals against monstrous consequences when those animals follow their nature, which ultimately affects the bottom line.

If the attack on Cathy bookends Kelly's story at the beginning of the film, toward the film's climax another child meets a darker fate. An adult T-Rex has been shipped to San Diego, but it escapes and hunts for food and drink, settling on a suburban swimming pool for the latter. A kenneled, chained dog barks its objection, and we know from *Jaws* that how Spielberg handles dog death or dog survival will determine the subsequent violence toward children. A sleeping child (Benjamin, played by Colton James) wakes up in his bedroom overlooking the pool, and walks obediently into his parents' room to report on the dinosaur in the yard. Of course they do not believe him, and comic reproach ensues. However, by the time the nuclear family can be persuaded to check Benjamin's bedroom, the dog's chain hangs from the T-Rex's mouth, with its now-empty kennel dangling below. The last time Spielberg featured dog death so blatantly—the unseen demise of Pippet in *Jaws*—his owner (Alex Kintner) was soon to follow. Just as Pippet's floating stick is the seen metonym for his unseen death, so Alex's shredded inflatable raft confirms that he will not be coming back. Nor, it seems, will Benjamin's dog, or its owners.

So much for expendable children. Indeed, this sequel's primary child is not even human. *The Lost World: Jurassic Park* is the wayward baby birthed by parent film *Jurassic Park*: where the increasingly feral dinosaurs of the first film get pregnant, by the second film they have fully procreated and are busy negotiating the politics of family. As Malcolm said in the first film, with kids "Anything at all can and does happen," which turns out to also be true of the baby T-Rex.

Malcolm's girlfriend, the paleontologist Sarah Harding (Julianne Moore), discovers that Isla Sorna's dinosaurs are not only breeding but also form themselves into nuclear families, with both mommy and daddy highly protective of their offspring ("Dinosaurs were characterized very early on as vicious lizards!" she complains, venturing that she will be the first scientist to show them as "nurturing parents"). So the triptych of Malcolm-Sarah-Kelly is mirrored by that of dad-mom-infant T-Rex, the latter becoming a helpless lure, stolen from its nest and held captive as bait to aid big game hunter Roland Tembo (Pete Postlethwaite) in his mission to bag a "buck." The hapless baby is used by villains and saviors alike to manipulate its enraged and protective father ("We're taking the kid!"), so much so that even the intimated slaughter of the suburban San Diegan family and its dog is part of a bigger story of love and instinct, of dinosaur parent and child separated and then reunited across the oceans, one (human) family as expendable collateral damage for the primary (nonhuman) family. However, in the move from *Jurassic Park* to *The Lost World*, the gender story has mutated: all the dinosaurs in the first film were female, but after just four years of naturalization without human intervention, patriarchy will out, and male dinosaurs not only have bred and thrived but now are the heads of their family units and the focus of the film's family story, with the mother T-Rex taking a secondary role. In contrast to the infant velociraptor seen near the start of the first film, here the dino baby is also male. The *Jurassic* girl story is thus lost between the first film and its sequel. Whereas Lex's power develops as she grows through a sibling connection, singleton Kelly functions only within a surrogate nuclear family triptych, in a story that also passes the focus of interest from female to male, and—from the girl perspective—charts her atrophying presence despite her promising action skills.

The Color Purple: Sisters, Contention and Viewing as Authorship

Spielberg's 1985 adaptation of Alice Walker's Pulitzer Prize–winning novel *The Color Purple* approaches girls in families, and girls as survivors, from a radically different perspective. This was his first foray into sometimes harrowing explorations of historical racism. He has said that the experience of *The Color Purple*, as a character-led serious drama, was a directorial stepping stone that enabled him to later tackle *Schindler's List*; some years after that came the slave-era period drama *Amistad*.

The Color Purple opens with an idyllic (and brief) vision of carefree girlhood, before quickly materializing into an adult melodrama underpinned by a story of child abuse. As the opening credits roll, two young sisters laugh, skip, and play childish clapping games through an arcadian field of purple cosmos flowers. The tall plants conceal a troubling truth about one of the girls, Celie: as she emerges into the open field, leaving behind the cloak of petals, she is seen to be pregnant

FIGURE 13 Pregnant young Celie (Desreta Jackson) reveals herself in *The Color Purple.*

(figure 13). This is the image that Spielberg chooses to accompany his name credit, as if to indicate that this child-focused overture does not promise the simple aesthetic pleasures or images of childhood with which the director may have become associated.

Quickly, the film establishes a founding framework of sisterly support and male brutality: Celie labors to birth her daughter, with the baby being caught by her younger sister, Nettie, but the girls' joy is immediately undercut by their father removing the infant for adoption. We learn, through voice-over, that Celie is just fourteen (as is Desreta Jackson, the actor who plays her), and this is the second child she has conceived by a man she believes to be her biological father. Though she has named both babies (Adam and Olivia), she has no chance of mothering them. Her sister Nettie is then preyed upon by a neighbor (Mr. Johnson, known as Mister, played by Danny Glover), who is seeking a housekeeper to take care of both his children and his sexual requirements. Celie's father offers her for this service (since Nettie is deemed too young), though Celie is at first rejected because of the previous paternal rape ("she ain't fresh—she's spoiled"). But Celie does take on the role; though she is but a child herself, and though they throw stones at her, she mothers his children (later complaining that looking after them has been torture). Johnson continues to harass young Nettie, to the point of attempted rape as she walks to school. When she retaliates by hitting him in the crotch with a bag of books, he orders her off his property and out of Celie's life. There is an agonizing struggle when the two girls are forcibly parted by Johnson, which is where Spielberg as an experienced director of children comes most skillfully into play: as they say goodbye, they reprise their clapping game. The girls' pleading is performed with painful desperation, across the arcadian rural setting. Young Celie is left to a grim life of service and brutality, at the hands of men in her close community; the film contentiously spotlights this more than wider racist violence against people of color by whites. At one point she has a chance meeting with the (more affluent, older, and middle-class) Black woman who has adopted her daughter, and she briefly holds the baby—as if the estrangement were not painful enough already. Nettie, it turns out, travels to Africa with a missionary service of which this adoptive mother is a part, and though she is away from her beloved sister for decades, she is able to be an active aunt to the children she helped to birth, and is able to reunite them much later with an older Celie. But this happy ending only comes after considerable trauma, and though girls set the story rolling, it is soon handed over to adults: some thirty minutes into the film, Spielberg elides the years, revealing a twenty-one-year-old but still self-effacing and victimized Celie, played by a twenty-nine-year-old Whoopie Goldberg, who ages with the part through middle age.

Children, then, function in *The Color Purple* to set out some initial threads. Launching the film, they establish a view of girlhood as both risky and resilient. Celie and Nettie are precisely *not* protected by adults; indeed, their vulnerability is exploited by them. But they counter this with a strong sisterly bond, including Nettie teaching Celie to read (Nettie has attended school, Celie has not) by adorning Mister's house with written signs attached to their referent objects: Celie learns (and becomes empowered) through a sibling game laid over a location of oppression. Spielberg has the girls positively dancing through the domestic space of Celie's servitude, declaring the words arrayed around them, in what is now a fun learning place, the schoolhouse she has otherwise been denied. Briefly, Mister's presence is edited out of Celie's oppressive home by her sister's intervention, with Nettie's word games overlaying and rewriting the space. Additionally, as in many Spielberg films, children fill out the ensemble and background landscape around the story of Celie growing older and more powerful, as small part-players such as the children of the main adult characters. Indeed, the mothering of children in *The Color Purple* is often seen as more struggle than ideal: the wedding of Sofia (Oprah Winfrey) to Harpo (Willard Pugh), for instance, contains a church full of children with mothers fighting to hold them in check. Multiple scenes feature the grown Celie surrounded by needy waifs hanging off her, picking at her body and clothes. The desperate desire for physical mothering becomes a form of torment for the children's female carer. In the next chapter I will consider the Jews of *Schindler's List* as infantilized through their oppression, but this is not so marked in the inequalities explored in *The Color Purple*, which takes its cue from the novel with its primary focus on the African American community.

Controversially, Celie's oppression is at the hands of Black men, which brought significant criticism. The screenplay follows the book in this: older Mister advises younger Harpo of his relationship with Sofia, "You ever hit her? . . . Wives is like children—have to let them know who got the upper hand. Nothing can do it better than a good sound beating." Sofia in turn reflects to Celie on how she has had to fight father and uncles and brothers all her life: "Girl child ain't safe in a family of men." One of the respondents in Jacqueline Bobo's pathbreaking qualitative study *Black Women as Cultural Readers* reports that "many people who did not like the film felt it was an airing of black people's dirty laundry" (1995, 126). A widespread charge was that it deflects blame for Black women's oppression from persistent white dominance to other members of the Black community. Layered into this, of course, is anger that this cinematic story is helmed by such a prominent white man.

That white characters are few in a story foregrounding the Black community is, for *The Color Purple*'s Black women viewers studied by Bobo, both a blessing (it gives proper attention and budget to Black women's stories) and a problem (it fails to show the origin of inequality as white oppression). Folding children into consideration of this story complicates this further. Later in this book I will explore infantilized adults—mostly white men—sometimes deified for their "Peter Pan–ish" qualities. However, the third child figure in *The Color Purple* is not a child at all, and here Spielberg infantilizes an adult as a form of critique. The one white character who steps from the margins is the mayor's wife, a vengeful woman who forces Sofia to become her maid, in the process cutting Sofia off from her own children. But the power dynamic between the two women is that of tyrannical but dependent employer and capable but disenfranchised servant, who must step up to being an adult figure to keep the white adult-child (who is really the master) functional. Bobo's study raises a criticism of this excessive white woman as itself pernicious: she is *so* ridiculous that she seems aberrational, and therefore not representative of all white people, who might then evade responsibility for a white-driven racism presented in the film as exceptional (1995, 112). But this is not to say that the film's African Americans are noble "adults" rising above the privileged white adult-children: there is a prevailing contextual sense that disempowerment renders all Back characters infantilized on some level by virtue of limited social and public power. True to Walker's source novel, this is tempered by the terrain of the story being almost entirely that of an African American community in which, as Walker puts it, "black landowners did not dress in rags and could afford wallpaper" (1996, 161): land is farmed successfully, businesses are established and thrive, families function across generations (because of the strength of the women), and within the purview of that community there is some self-determination (albeit, initially, mostly for the men).

Two problems beset the release of *The Color Purple*, affecting its critical response if not its box office. The first was that it was perceived as a sanitized, "Spielbergized" version of a beloved novel with an established passionate readership, complicated by perceptions of the director as someone squarely in the business of converting challenging source material into anodyne mass-market entertainment (the same would be said of *Empire of the Sun*, as we shall see). The second—that he was white and male—compounded the first, to the extent that the film was roundly charged with racism. Many of the films explored here are adaptations of best-sellers or revered source novels,[15] but it is not the role of this book to investigate Spielberg as adaptor, though the field is rich with potential. The question of the most appropriate "fit" between director and source material became particularly acute around *The Color Purple*. The book was a female-authored, feminist (or "womanist," as Walker articulated it) story about the troubled but ultimately triumphant lives of women of color in the early twentieth century, so Walker's decision to approve Spielberg as her novel's adaptor was controversial. The rationale—that such a mainstream filmmaker would draw maximum attention to the issues the book highlights—backfired when critics deemed that it mostly drew attention to how inappropriate he seemed for the task, that a mainstream "Spielbergized" melodrama was essentially rendered down for white audiences (Bobo 1995, 123), and the film was perceived as a serious awards failure.[16]

However, Bobo's important research has spotlighted the fact that, for all this, Spielberg's *Color Purple* itself facilitated Black women viewers' sophisticated and oppositional readings of a film they also knew very well to be flawed, but nevertheless engaged with for the positive recognition of their experience that it managed to deliver somewhat against the grain. Bobo takes both Walker's book and Spielberg's film adaptation as case studies that foreground the active critical work these women carried out as cultural consumers. Against a tide of overwhelming scorn from the critical establishment, including some vociferous Black critics,[17] these viewers effectively "filter[ed] out that which was seen as the standard negative images and . . . recreat[ed] a more satisfactory story" (29). Bobo's reading of Spielberg's film does not pull its punches: set against the novel, she finds it has displaced women from the narrative's center in favor of a redeeming conclusion for Mister, making Celie's happy ending a function of dramatic events rather than her own self-will (68–90). One significant problem Bobo identifies is the repositioning of the novel's strong woman character Shug as someone fighting to get the approval and love of her father. This added-in father is an unnecessary function of making Shug dependent and pathetic (in the film) rather than independent and feisty (in the novel). This serves to infantilize Shug, who is referenced through the need for an adult male rather than her own self-determination (crying at one point, "Children ought to have a pa," by which she means her adult self as the child). These discrepancies notwithstanding, Spielberg's *The Color Purple* proved elastic enough to provide significant visual pleasure for Bobo's respondents, who were generally less critical than those commentators who sought to speak on their behalf. The film also led viewers back to the novel as readers, which Bobo sees as a happy accident that benefited the culture around this revered woman writer (and her contemporaries).

This is not to redeem a film that is at best astonishingly inappropriate in places, at worst deploying racist stereotypes. Instead, it is to suggest that in its racially focused and gender-inflected messiness, *The Color Purple* delivers some surprising representations and performances within an aesthetically oversaturated landscape that managed to facilitate significant pleasures for some Black women viewers. This research is savage in its discussion of Spielberg as controller of the negative images on-screen, but it also manages to displace him as auteur and replace him with the active viewer. To draw this back into the remit of "Spielberg studies," the tenor of my analysis of the director's work suggests that because he is such a powerful filmmaker across multiple roles and with historic successes under his belt (the reason he was given *The Color Purple* to adapt in the first place), his name and presence inevitably dominate both the perceived successes and the failures of his films. This is largely true for global audiences.

Yet Bobo's interviewees view the film and its maker as two separate things, enabling them to blame Spielberg for the flaws of the film, but not credit him for the positive moments.[18] While decrying the lack of women filmmakers with sufficient cultural heft to make this film at that time ("they are viewers who understand that they do not have control over image creation in mainstream media" [96–97]), Bobo's respondents have a ready readerly agency (fully invested in how much "control [they have] over how they will exhibit their responses" [97]). For instance, a dinner table scene in which the four key women are at their most powerful is, for Bobo, undermined by Spielberg's juxtaposition with comic caricature. However, her respondents actively bracket these out, enabling them to fully appreciate the women's strength and largely altering the film's cultural importance: "If a viewer could physically edit the film and remove the comic routines, as it appears that the women I interviewed did mentally, then the sequence featuring the women at the dinner table becomes a pivotal and empowering moment in the film" (106). Thus, these Black women viewers' pleasure is gained despite rather than because of the director.

For her part, Alice Walker was also divided on the film, though far more positive than Bobo. Her memoir *The Same River Twice: Honoring the Difficult*, written ten years after the film's release, meditates on how the adaptation transformed her into more of a public figure than she had been before or was comfortable with, and of weathering the hostility surrounding her association with the film. "Though *The Color Purple* was not what many wished, it is more than many hoped, or had seen on a movie screen before," Walker reflects. "It still moves me after all these years, as I relive the feeling of love that was palpable daily on the set. This does not, however, prevent me from cringing at the same spots in the film that originally seemed bizarre to me" (1996, 40–41). She even describes the film as a gift (43). Countering Bobo's horror at Mister's redemption, Walker felt Spielberg had been harder on him than he deserved: "I still regret that Mister was not as 'forgiven' by Steven as he was by me, and that Shug and Celie don't have the erotic, sensuous relationship they deserve. . . . The ending is moving. But I wanted Mister up on the porch too!" (41; 161). The memoir includes a section consisting of letters from viewers expressing the complex pleasures and contradictory responses they experienced through the film and back to the book, complementing Bobo's study.[19] Indeed, Walker's meditation on the experience of both embracing and resisting the narrative, aesthetic, and political choices made particularly by Spielberg and producer Quincy Jones during the shoot, and of both endorsing and critiquing the final result before confronting the aftermath, echoes the ambivalence of Bobo's respondents, oscillating between passionate pleasure and outright horror.

Spielberg rarely features women in leading roles, and *The Color Purple* is therefore an atypical exception. A more recent example of a leading woman features Rachel Zegler as Maria in *West Side Story*, but since she was eighteen when she performed the role, and that film focuses on older young adults, I won't be discussing it here (even though Tony so memorably sings "I just met a girl named Maria," she is not strictly speaking a girl). Bobo's important study shows women viewers enjoying those representations of women both troubled and triumphant, by virtue of performances such as Goldberg's and Winfrey's, and Walker's source material. This chapter and chapter 5 are not primarily concerned with representations of women; they attempt to address and redress the fact that if female leads are rare in Spielberg, amid the plethora of child actors he deploys, girl leads are even rarer. But those who *do* feature both illuminate and expand popular cultural images of the child, and reinflect girlhood in particular ways. This chapter has featured a number of examples of female authorship around performance and reception—Richards's execution of fear and action, Nettie's rearrangement of oppressive domesticity into a learning space for Celie, and—on the other side of the camera/screen, Bobo's respondents' active editing as viewers seeking images that meet their urgent cultural needs. But these are grown women, with their attention focused on the majority of the film in which Celie is already an adult and performed by Goldberg. Children are noted as a responsibility and a burden to adult women who in the film may not even be their biological mothers, and the respondents use this as a space to discuss schooling, segregation, and parenting more widely. But nothing specific is said about the film's initial focus on girls: the child actors are figures in a bucolic landscape on which adult struggles are later built. Something of this carries over into *Schindler's List*, enabled partly by Spielberg's experience of directing *The Color Purple* and featuring children as contexts and augmentation for a primarily adult story. In the next chapter I consider *Schindler's List* alongside *Empire of the Sun*, which places the child foursquare at the center of the narrative against a backdrop of war.

7

War Child

Empire of the Sun, *Schindler's List*, and *War Horse*

There are many war children in Spielberg's work, placed at the center of a theater of war that usually excludes them as active combatants. This chapter explores children in war, and children changed by war—children subject to adult violence, or forced to behave like adults or pass as adults. If we use the words "infantile" or "childish" to designate the adult behaving younger than their years (as we have seen, a frequent charge against Spielberg), the war child is "adultish": war makes phrases such as "growing up too fast" and "old beyond her years" particularly pertinent to the child caught in adult-determined circumstances. Of course, much of a child's reality is adult-determined, but war (and the war film genre) fashions unique conditions. Outside of specific child soldier–themed films, the cinematic war child—certainly those represented by Hollywood as caught up in war—is not usually a combatant but a civilian, commonly articulated as victim. Indeed, "civilian" is one of those words, like "child," that is often harnessed to that contested word "innocent." War subjects the child to violations—of their family, of their own body. The war survivor may be injured or orphaned, war confronts the child with harrowing experiences and visions, and it may remove them from safety and familiarity (as a refugee). Previous discussions in this book have focused on imperiled children separated from home, a child-framed alien finding a home in the suburbs, and a future home that nurtures the organic child and expels the robotic one. The children of this chapter are violently displaced from home. Unlike the American child most commonly referenced in U.S. war cinema (home-front children protected by geography from the spaces of combat), the children of this chapter are war's active targets, war's collateral refugees, war's too-young participants. While the majority of Spielberg's children are American, here they are mostly European.

War culture (literature, film, propaganda) commonly excludes the child. Wars may be waged because of territorial and political threat, but war stories often narrativize and humanize their subjects by identifying women and children as the prime raison d'être of conflict ("fighting for those back home") while simultaneously distancing them from the action. As David Slocum puts it, "The presence of women in films about war . . . symbolizes . . . the feminine or domestic sphere for which battles among men are fought" (2006, 9). The febrile contradictions of war cinema have focused more on gender (Tasker 2011; Bronfen 2012, 43–73; Basinger 2016; Williams 2004) than on childhood and minority, where the prime example of a field-establishing discussion is Karen Lury's brilliant chapter focusing on children in European war films in *The Child in Film: Tears, Fears and Fairy Tales* (2010). Women and children are, then, an excluded justification, the reason war is waged even as and when they are also deemed incapable of understanding its traumatic realities. This is particularly true of American war culture focused on twentieth-century conflicts featuring adult male soldiers who are often themselves only just post-childhood, deployed away from their compatriot women and children. It is not so true of cultures under occupation, and cultures within which women and children kill, are killed, and witness violence close-up. That Spielberg's supreme contribution to the war film is often cited as the combat- and squadron-focused *Saving Private Ryan* suggests confirmation of this model.[1] However, though women remain rare in Spielberg's war stories, children are highly visible. This is not just because of the obsession with family that runs through all generic forms in which the director works; children become equally intrinsic to war scenarios as any other human. And once again they turn the screw of affect: the presence of an imperiled child in a situation where acts of killing are central exacerbates emotion and tension.

However, Spielberg also uses this canvas to present more diverse views of children and child's-eye views, more contradictory representations: a prisoner child in an occupied war zone (*Empire of the Sun*), a child rendered a racial enemy/alien within her own nation (*Schindler's List*), a family fleeing invaders on home territory (*War of the Worlds*—a science fiction pretext sets off a war cinema invasion/refugee narrative), and an animal-as-child story in which a horse combatant is passed between young owners on different sides of conflict (*War Horse*, where the eponymous horse/child moves from home front to combat zone like his young soldier owner, a foil for child and adolescent characters across territories). With the exception of *War of the Worlds*, all of these are historical dramas focused on the two world wars of the twentieth century. Spielberg also visits this history in the farcical comedy *1941*, which I will not be discussing here even though it shares a common Pearl Harbor context with the far darker *Empire of the Sun* (though set entirely around a military community in California). Despite its enjoyment of childish adults, *1941* features no children. Because of its enjoyment of childish adults, it merits mention later when I consider childness and childishness displaced beyond children's bodies and identities.

Critical writing on war films usually follows the cue of the films themselves in positing children caught up in conflict as victim or symbol, representing the wholesomeness of peacetime, and—because they are also entirely irrelevant to the man's primary work on the battlefield—endangered as potential collateral wastage. Lury notes, "In films involving war, children are often ciphers for adult anxieties, fantasies and fears. It remains necessary for children to be different from adults since this makes them blameless" (2010, 106). However, the bold move of Spielberg's *Empire of the Sun* is its refusal of this victimized and marginalized position. Instead, it stages a relationship to war that is richly multifaceted. The young hero Jamie/Jim is set free by war; its machines are (sometimes) his toys; war provides a context within which to try out adult personae while also continuing to play at being a child. Before exploring this in detail, I want to pause on two models of mainstream war culture: the familiar idea that war functions to "man up" boys, and a secondary notion that it does just the opposite, provoking adult men into a state of dangerous childishness.

Coming of Age and Lethal Adolescence: *Saving Private Ryan*, *War of the Worlds*, and *War Horse*

Lynda Boose reads the "boy-eternal" as a figure for war cinema. For her, the cult of youth cannot be distinguished from both violence and contempt for the feminine, being ultimately a resonant image of America itself: "Judging from such signs as America's heroized mythology of baby-faced gunfighters like Billy the Kid or from its traditional representation of its national historical self as the 'young,' 'new,' and 'innocent' nation, one could say that this country has always valorized male adolescence" (2006, 280).

World War II films are often built around a romantic subplot or context, justifying the presence of women as facilitators of heterosexual love stories. However, Boose notes that U.S. films about the Vietnam War almost entirely exclude women, first substituting romance with father-son-focused Oedipal tropes, before foreshadowing the end of the nuclear family when violent sons displace disciplinarian fathers, resulting in an anarchic vacuum of authority ("war is a chaotic moral landscape with no fathers on hand, a war fought by boys led by boys, a space abandoned to the rule of frightened and lethally armed adolescents" [281]). For Boose, the war film depicts in miniature "the culture of American masculinity that the latter half of the twentieth century has shaped: an image of wanton boys, killing for their sport" (284). This book has shown Spielberg marketed as the boy eternal par excellence, but his war stories are usually identified as the work of a more mature director tackling historical violence in order to honor his parents' generation—war stories told by a baby boomer not called on to fight in Vietnam. Yet youth is central to Spielberg's war films; the lost boys of combat build dark Peter Pan stories in which the young are politically and militarily prevented from growing up. Marilyn Young notes that World War II was part of Spielberg's childhood play landscape: "This was war as men of Steven Spielberg's generation played it on the street when they were boys: storming beaches, house-to-house fighting, sharpshooters in doorways, vulnerable human beings against tanks, always outnumbered" (2006, 316). It was also a setting for his juvenile films. But it is the family that has grown within these scenarios as he has gotten older, and it is his adherence to the family that rescues his filmic war scenarios from Boose's dark Vietnam War–era vision.

Saving Private Ryan is not just about World War II, though it conforms to the structure of such a film in its justifying family wraparound, its benign view of paternalistic authority, and its surrogate-father/son narrative that does not dissipate into the anarchy of the American Vietnam film. In resurrecting the heart and heroism of a justified war ("the only refuge for the righteous fighting man has been World War II"; Young 2006, 316), *Ryan* manages to both outdo most Vietnam war films in its horror spectacle and undo the nihilism of the Vietnam film subgenre through recourse to the traditional nuclear family. The image of the family it presents thus both predates the Vietnam War (in its World War II setting) and postdates—survives—it. The Rockwellesque opening view of the bereaved mother is then brought full circle in the concluding view of the present-day elderly Ryan, surrounded by his biological family, grieving for his substitute soldier-father. This is indeed a family-justified war film.[2] However, the family is not only present in these narrative bookends; kinship structures develop within the unrelated troupe whose mission is precisely to save young Private Ryan after his brothers have all been killed. The film's dominant familial relation here is brotherly, because of Ryan's importance in relation to his dead brothers, and because of the platoon bonding of the troupe. When he is eventually found, Ryan refuses to go with Miller, vowing that he will stay "with the only brothers that I have left." This sibling surrogacy coexists with a parent-child relation that, as in many Spielberg productions, inserts itself into a nonfamilial narrative, with the commanding officer Captain John Miller (Tom Hanks), a former schoolteacher, as the mission's father figure. Two of the original mission "brothers" die before Ryan is even discovered, reinforcing the idea that endangered children (even adult children) are also risky to others as well as at risk themselves. Real children pose even more danger: when one of the troupe helps a little girl and her refugee family in a desecrated French village, and is shot in the process by enemy fire, Miller declares "*That's* why we can't take children." This may seem like a remarkably un-Spielbergian message, but the film has already demonstrated that the team itself functions as children to Miller's father figure regardless of age.

Spielberg's next foray into war scenarios, *War of the Worlds*, more clearly suggests the man-making power of the military for boy children, though this is subsumed in a wider narrative of paternal crisis. Earlier I discussed this film as a showcase for Dakota Fanning's burgeoning talent, but narratively it is another divorce story in which a failing father, Ray (Tom Cruise), redeems himself in extreme circumstances. However, this does not take place on the regular battlefield. Even though the film's title features the word "war," it is a science fiction action adventure shot through with a strong strain of horror, focused on the family. Its dominant masculinity story is told not through the heroism of defeating aliens but through Ray forging a better relationship with his kids. He proves himself in the battleground of the family—instead of "manning up," he learns to "father up." This is introduced through the protracted rebellion of his teenage son, Robbie (Justin Chatwin), who, it turns out, is a better father to his little sister, Rachel (Fanning), than is Ray. Indeed, Robbie refuses to call Ray "Dad." He is a near adult—stealing Ray's car, acting up—and the fleeting war scenario is an opportunity for coming of age through heroic violence. Indeed, in the balance of genres, it is once again the child who inflects a multigenred story in one direction or another.

All three family members travel as refugees through scenes of devastation akin to those of *Schindler's List* or *Empire of the Sun*, except here the scene is mainland United States. I argued in the previous chapter that these three protagonists seem to be acting in three different genre films: Ray's story is male melodrama (made so because of the pull of children), Rachel's is horror, but Robbie—driven to tip the adolescent balance of his development toward adulthood—emphasizes the film's war focus. When the soldiers finally appear, he pleads with them to let him join up so he can "get back at them." Whether this refers to the aliens per se, or is an act of distinction from his father, is questionable: the father-son argument that ensues suggests that Robbie is motivated by disdain toward Ray, who is trying to deliver the children back to their mother so he can be alone again.

The military thus offers Robbie escape from a failing family, and solidarity through an accepted gesture of manhood. The scene in which he finally joins the army ("I need to be here," he pleads to his father. "You've got to let me go") takes place in the film's one true battle sequence, with the alien tripods adopting a scorched-earth tactic as burning (human) military vehicles fly through the air. But we do not see Robbie earning manhood on-screen. Such is the violence of the scene into which he runs that he is then presumed dead, only to reappear for the final tableau, simply embracing Ray and finally calling him Dad. Uneasily, he is still a child identified relationally through his father rather than through heroic or wanton violence.

Spielberg's next war film was *War Horse* (2011), an adaptation of Michael Morpurgo's 1982 novel. Most attention has been focused on the second word of the title (the horse as forced combatant), but I want briefly to think about the film's meditation on children and war. For all the focus on Joey, the eponymous horse taken from his rural English life and conscripted to "serve" in the World War I trenches, this is another coming-of-age story about children caught in historical violence. The film's first image is of the birth of a baby—Joey the foal (I will consider Joey as the film's primary child in the next chapter). He is the "war horse" that coheres the episodic stories of a series of young people who develop individual (parent-like) relationships with him as charge. First there is Albert (Jeremy Irvine), who socializes him into becoming a member of a human farming team away from the equine mother-son dyad into which he was born. War breaks out, and as well as a call for young men to enlist, there is a call for horses to be sent to the front. But while Joey is fit for service, Albert is not. The horse is sold to Captain Nicholls (Tom Hiddleston), and Albert tries to join up too. Nicholls realizes Albert is too young to serve (the enlistment age in World War I was eighteen, though initially boys were protected from active service at the front until nineteen). Nicholls then makes a promise "man to man" to Albert that he will care for Joey equally well. Age and boyhood are, then, at the center of the struggle over (nonhuman child) Joey.

This brief stint with Captain Nicholls notwithstanding, for much of his story Joey is cared for by teenage children. Nineteen-year-old Irvine plays Albert at the start as significantly younger than the actor's actual age; since it is only by the end of the war that Albert is old enough to join up and search for Joey at the front, we must assume that when he accepts this "man-to-man" promise he is only fifteen (Morpurgo describes Albert as "barely past thirteen" at the story's opening [2007, 7]). Nineteen-year-old David Kross, playing the young German soldier Gunther, who takes over the care of Joey when he transfers to German hands after a disastrous cavalry charge, is joined by the even younger Leonard Carrow playing Gunther's fourteen-year-old brother, Michael, one of the many underage boys on both sides who joined up by lying about their age.[3] One of the film's most brutal sequences begins as Gunther rescues Michael from deployment to the front by riding Joey at full gallop, picking Michael bodily from the marching line and escaping to a hiding place in a remote windmill. They are soon caught, and summarily shot for desertion. Not since *Schindler's List* have we seen grown men shooting boys in a Spielberg film. The care of Joey then passes to Emily, a farm girl played by fourteen-year-old Céline Buckens. Despite the sentimentalized representation of her delicate nature (Emily is the film's Little Nell or Little Eva,[4] spirited but sickly), her attitude toward Joey briefly strips him of gender—with only her grandfather as company, she has no peers and so makes Joey her best friend. Ultimately, her death is the means by which Joey is returned to Albert in the film's denouement. *War Horse*'s promotional campaign focused on the translation from book to play to film, and on Spielberg's cinematic trickery in representing the brutal experience of animals at war (because of course "no animals were harmed"; Sultan, one of the fourteen horses that played Joey, walked down the red carpet at the London premiere).[5] But also significant was

Spielberg's now-familiar use of a mix of known and unknown actors, particularly those too young to yet be famous. In the United Kingdom, *The Observer*'s review section featured a large-scale celebration of "Spielberg's Youth Team" (Ojumu and Solomons 2012, 4–5)—eight young men, including rookie actors (except Hiddleston and Benedict Cumberbatch; Kross was also an experienced child actor, having starred in *The Reader*), all (just) adult but some playing children; actual child actors Buckens and Carrow are not mentioned.

Crucially, while Spielberg may offer his young actors a passport to adult success, none of *War Horse*'s "youth team" are heroically transformed into mature adults through their experience of war within the story. Emily, Michael, and Gunther die unheroic deaths; Albert is blinded and scarred, redemption only coming for him by reuniting with Joey. The film's final tableau, in which the two (adult/equine) boys return to the parents' farm, might see them four years older but does not romanticize the changes they have undergone, though violence also seems an absurd interruption in a landscape of bucolic continuity. The most convincing sequence of "manning up" comes early in the film when Albert and Joey work together to conquer an unplowable stony field, making a show of hard labor in order to keep Joey on the farm (and in Albert's care). Commenting on the sweat and effort, the villainous Lyons (David Thewlis) remarks to Albert's drunkard father, "He's more of a man than you." *War Horse*'s World War I story chooses not to follow the combat film tradition of showing war making men of boys or sending them away to protect those back home; it either kills them or send them home simply as older boys. Boose argues that the Vietnam combat film infantilizes men, giving them the lethal toys that ensure they never grow up. *War Horse* does show young men's bodies being wasted for the political struggles of aged politicians (and young Joey is also an emblem of that), but it does not heroize the violent adolescence of Boose's model.

A more widespread image of the child caught in war—as combatant or civilian—is that war robs children of childhood. Private Ryan remains in his own mind a child to Captain Miller (Hanks), even though he is an old man in the graveside wraparound. Robbie in *War of the Worlds* wants to be militarily "adultized," is presumed to have been wasted as teenage cannon fodder, then returns to his father's arms as a boy again. *War Horse*'s Albert only wants to go to war to be with Joey, with which he has forged a surrogate parent relation—he is a (human) child with an (animal) child. He does not come of age because of war, but through his love for Joey, going to war not to save his homeland but to bring back his "child." We will see several examples of child-adult crossovers in *Schindler's List* at the end of this chapter. *Empire of the Sun*, to which I now turn, shows further the complexity of Spielberg's war children, oscillating between childhood, childishness, adolescent tenacity, and adultlike mimicry, as well as other non-aged identities. This seriously challenges the linear view of childhood as a golden phase from which the child is untimely ripped by military conflict, never to return.

Jamie/Jim/Christian: *Empire of the Sun*

The child is the center of *Empire of the Sun*, but he is also a surprisingly shifting figure—and only sometimes a child. Spielberg promoted the film as the story of a loss of innocence (Forsberg 2000), but it shows that a child subject to adult experiences is not necessarily a child robbed of innocence. *Empire* was adapted by Tom Stoppard from J. G. Ballard's semi-autobiographical novel of the same name; though not science fiction (Ballard's favored genre), it is nevertheless a story articulated in Ballard's customary affectless neutral style, and therefore an odd source for such an affecting filmmaker to adapt. Yet *Empire* has epic scale, is set in Spielberg's favorite war, and once again articulates a boy child wrestling with identity and impotence, following Jamie Graham (played by a thirteen-year-old Christian Bale) from family life to loss of family, through domestic privilege to imprisoned privation.[6] World War II is raging elsewhere but only impinges on his wealthy expatriate life when the Japanese invade Shanghai in the wake of the attack on Pearl Harbor. The invasion violently separates him from parents and home; Jamie roams the streets of Shanghai, nearly succumbing to starvation, and is eventually imprisoned with other Europeans and Americans at Soochow internment camp, on the edge of an airfield. With tenuous adult protection (the Fagin-like opportunist Basie [John Malkovich], the noble Dr. Rawlins [Nigel Havers], the unmotherly surrogate Mrs. Victor [Miranda Richardson]), Jim (as Basie renames him—"a new name for a new life") embraces the parentless freedom of the camp and learns to survive and thrive through manic opportunism. After four brutal years, U.S. planes end the Japanese control of China, and Jim is reunited with his parents.

Center stage throughout *Empire* is James/Jamie/Jim—and therefore the then-unknown young Christian Bale. There are few scenes that do not foreground him, as he negotiates a complex oscillation between performances of child, adolescent, and adult. Indeed, most positive critical responses to the film focus on Bale as standout star, tipped for an Oscar nomination (which did not come) (I. Davies 1988; Andrew 1987). The *Village Voice*'s Andrew Sarris was particularly eulogistic, calling Bale's "the most electrifying child performance I have ever seen on the screen. . . . He not only holds *Empire of the Sun* together, he drives it relentlessly, hysterically, heroically forward by his own irresistible momentum" (1987, 109). That this is a highly "adult" film (sometimes violent, grimly unrelenting) with a child as focalizer made it particularly tricky to market to adult audiences on its initial release—the stellar adult cast essentially function as support. As is the case with *A.I.*, one of Spielberg's most important essays on childhood is not a film that children will watch. How, then, do children function in films for adults? Did using a child in marketing *Empire of the Sun* (or *A.I.*) contribute to these films' relatively disappointing reception with adult audiences initially? The questions of genre that I have addressed throughout this book emerge here in a specific way: How does the child refract the war film, a genre sometimes marketed to (boy) children (through comics and games), but in a filmic form that may not be targeted at children?

Another common positive reading of the film was that *Empire* is a coming-of-age exercise for its director (says Richard Corliss in *Time*, "So Spielberg decided to take the manly course of growing up onscreen" [1987, 48]). One British critic even noted that a child protagonist was precisely what enabled Spielberg to tackle adult issues, since he is ill at ease with adult emotions tackled head-on.[7] Though it investigates childhood in an adult frame, *Empire* has usually been read as a coming-of-age story for Jim. However, this is an interpretation I will contest—Jim tries out many ages, eluding a linear, irreversible move from younger to older, from innocence to experience. The film also uses the child to think about war (and the war film genre) as a civilian event. Marilyn Young cites Michael Sherry as pointing out that "we rarely witness bombing raids from below" (2006, 316), but in a sense this is exactly what *Empire* delivers. It also does not conform to that familiar trope of looking at adult events through a child's eyes by way of critiquing those events—Jim is too enemy-identified, too in love with Japanese heroism and military firepower for all that. This intricate negotiation of the to-and-fro trajectory of the child/adult is a crucial contribution to the cinema of childhood.

As the film opens, Jamie—a colonial middle-class schoolboy who has only ever lived in Shanghai—attends a private British-style cathedral school and lives in a genteel European-colonial house in the International Settlement, attended by a staff of Chinese servants.[8] On the cusp of adolescence, he is curious and playful, with the confidence denoted by privilege enabling him to address adults without fear. He boldly declares himself an atheist and has consequently "resigned" from the Boy Scouts. So he is older than *E.T.*'s Elliott and *A.I.*'s David (both unambiguous child figures), reaching for adult discourse, yet still surrounded by boys' toys. Though the first shot of him is as a school chorister surrounded by a line of uniformed boys, he does not engage with other children until he becomes a prisoner, and he has no siblings. This is in marked contrast to Spielberg's girls, who are mostly knitted into sibling networks. In this first pre-invasion sequence Jamie only interacts with adults—as child to parent, as employer to servant, and as would-be equal to British upper-class men.

Nor is his toy fixation entirely childish. War planes strongly resonate across this child/adolescent/adult divide. Like Spielberg, Jamie is (and Ballard was) an aviophile. He is rarely seen without a toy plane or a copy of *Wings* magazine in this homebound first act, marking him out as both a child and a Spielberg surrogate. Toy planes are narrative activators but are also symbolically resonant: at the Lockwoods' party, pursuit of his flying balsa-wood model plane across the garden and into the surrounding fields takes him to a burned-out crashed Japanese fighter plane, in which he playacts a dogfight (his first overt identification with the invading enemy) and encounters a troupe of Japanese soldiers camped on the edge of Shanghai waiting for the "attack" directive. Spielberg's fascination with flight and its technologies has been present since his early juvenile films—it has even been argued that his Peter Pan obsessions were derived from his interest in flight, not his belief in eternal childhood. The child's presence, then, enables *Empire* to oscillate between (child's) play and (war) history: it is arguably more of a love letter to flight than even *Hook, Catch Me If You Can, E.T.*, or *Always*.

But the plane is not the only object on which Jamie, and thus *Empire*, fixates. Perhaps because it focuses increasingly on material privation, the film is careful in its use of and focus on materially valuable objects, primarily food (jealously possessed before it is consumed, the object of elaborate transactions). The play possessions and home reminders that Jamie carries with him through his refugee and prisoner journey are also profoundly significant of the childhood he both leaves and continues to sporadically inhabit, and they are placed and used in the film with great care. We get to know Elliott in *E.T.* in the environment of his bedroom—a child world that adults enter so rarely that an alien can be securely hidden there. David's strangeness in *A.I.* is first established in the home, but his futuristic bedroom is kitted out with adult-chosen objects, and play is performance more than pleasure for him.

One of *Empire*'s key threads is initiated in an early sequence in Jamie's bedroom, replete with model planes and aviation paraphernalia. Here Spielberg explicitly restages Norman Rockwell's painting *Freedom from Fear* (1943), in which mother and father hover over sleeping children; in Spielberg's rendition of this the parents dote on and worry for just their singleton child Jamie (figure 14). Two images—Rockwell's original and a frame from *Empire*—are published side by side in Virginia M. Mecklenburg's tour de force volume, *Telling Stories: Norman Rockwell from the Collections of George Lucas and Steven Spielberg* (2010), which accompanied the Smithsonian American Art Museum exhibition of 2010–2011. The

FIGURE 14 Spielberg explicitly restages Norman Rockwell's *Freedom from Fear* in *Empire of the Sun*.

bedtime tucking-in ritual (revisited in many Spielberg films) is here orchestrated in an overtly Oedipal fashion: Jamie's father, John (Rupert Frazer), drifts in, but neither mother, Mary (Emily Richard), nor Jamie seems to acknowledge him. Despite a pervasive stiff-upper-lip British distance, mother and son are locked in a communication that excludes the father. As Lester Friedman notes (2006, 204), this is not the case with the Rockwell original, in which the father seems almost as close to the children as the mother. Spielberg's visual quotation is then not a gesture of nostalgia but an ironic comment: Rockwell's painted parents are successfully protective, Jamie's filmic parents turn out to be the opposite. Mecklenburg quotes Spielberg remembering the painting from his father's pile of *Saturday Evening Post* magazines, but crucially he remembers it as an image with just a boy child, not two children (at least one of Rockwell's children appears to be a girl—and there is a doll on the floor). Spielberg reminisces about the painting as if it already is a still from *Empire*:

> I remember having a sense that when the mother and father both come in to the children's bedroom to tuck in the boy, they must really love him. It must be a solidly happy family, a family unit, that hasn't been shattered by divorce or illness. That has always been the American Dream, the great concept of the American unit, the American family. The fact that they are both there in the room, and the father's holding a newspaper with bad news about the war overseas—they're looking at the boy, thinking, if the war keeps going, in a few more years he could be drafted or enlist, and also thinking that we are here, living in freedom and at this moment our child is safe because our country is protecting all of us. But they're not smiling; they're not flaunting that freedom. (Mecklenburg 2010, 111–112).

This resonant fantasy of what the painted parents are thinking is drenched in such acute anxiety about boys becoming "lethal adolescents" that the sleeping girl might as well not be there. Of course, *Empire* features a British family already in a war zone, while Rockwell's image features an American family safely tucked up in the unoccupied United States.[9] John's newspaper headline reads "Japanese occupy Shanghai," so the war really has come home.[10] The sequence gets darker: John leaves the room, and Jamie conjectures to his mother about whether we might be simply God's dream, or whether he is our dream. Mary attempts to replace this philosophizing with the suggestion to "dream of flying" as she kisses him good night; to a Freudian, flying is sexual, but this consciously refers to the toy culture of Jamie's room (of course it may be both). Rockwell's painting contains only one toy (that doll); Spielberg's scene contains many, because toys (however apparently trivial) help Spielberg tell important stories about children. There is also a historical overlay here: though Jamie's toys are of the 1930s and 1940s (his room resembles a nostalgic museum of childhood), the toy-stuffed bedroom in itself is a more postwar consumer-culture child space. Jamie has the kind of bedroom a baby boomer might occupy ten or twenty years later (Spielberg's own, perhaps), yet here it is filled with toys from an earlier moment.

His mother departs, and he stares at the planes dangling from his ceiling: a mobile shot begins with Jamie's perspective on the ceiling-pinned models, then rises above him, turns, and catches his face illuminated by magical uncanny light that evokes a more science fiction–inflected cinematographic style. Then, in a reverse shot, we see—as if through Jamie's eyes—the hovering planes, moving a little. If Jamie is indeed acting on his mother's instructions, this dream of flying is a dark one: the illumination of Jamie's face, the movement with no obvious cause, suggests *Poltergeist* or *Close Encounters of the Third Kind*. Elliott's toy cupboard speaks of the fantasy conflicts of the *Star Wars* universe; Jamie's toys intimate a dark historical reality, and there is a direct continuum between his toy planes and their full-scale adult counterparts. When toward the end of the film the U.S. Air Force closes in on the airfield next to Soochow camp, Jim exults as if this early playacted air raid has finally come to life. War and its technology are exciting as well as frightening—war is where boy toys grow into reality.

Homelessness, Orphancy, Freedom

Home and family life are, then, initially identified with order and abundance. One of the last acts of the Grahams as a family unit is their attendance at a fancy dress party, carefully designed to both contrast and foreshadow the deprivation to come—Westerners play (like children) while the serious business of war encroaches. Leisure is a register of infantilization. The family's costumes are elaborate and inconsonant, the parents' referencing a fairy tale of European culture—Mary is a Pierrot (she will indeed soon shed tears), and John is a pirate (Spielberg had yet to make *Hook*, but Peter Pan was already a strong touchstone). But Jamie is Sinbad: his costume is a gaudy Orientalist parody, yet the absurd outfit may hint that he is about to become a traveler, an adventurer. The symbolism does not end there: as he tucks in to the party feast (only the first of his desperate encounters with food, though here it is greed, not need), his father and a Chinese businessman talk politics while an unidentified guest dressed as a skeleton looks on, like a memento mori in a Renaissance painting.

The costume play also marks out the Grahams, and their style of family life, from their Chinese counterparts. The drive to the party is one of the film's most surreal scenes. Locked into their chauffeur-driven Packard, Jamie gazes through the mobile frame of the car window onto a highly cinematic vision of otherness—a chaotic market, bloodied animals, panicked crowds escaping the advancing Japanese. If imperial history has too often characterized colonizer as adult to colonized as child, here in the twilight of British involvement with mainland China the protected Westerners are identified with play while the real world outside of the car is marked by adult concerns: violence, sex, war. An ethereal string and choral score focuses the boy as privileged viewer, wondering at the rolling spectacle, as if he is animating a traveling shot in a movie played out just for him (sure enough, farther along the Wang Poo Road they pass the Capital Cinema—one of many references to the source novel's movie saturation). All Jamie/Bale can do is passively spectate. A Chinese boy shouts urgently through the window at him, "No mama! No papa!," the brief eye contact of boy with boy underlining similarity as well as difference. They do meet again later on more perilous terms, when it is Jamie who now has "no mama, no papa," and the other boy steals his shoes. By then Jamie is just beginning his own apprenticeship as thief, trader, opportunist, and vagrant. But in the film's opening act, "home" is Jamie's parents, their suburban mansion as well as the mobile safety of their luxury (American) car—home, then, is not-China within China. Later "home" becomes more precarious, a temporary function of particular locations and dysfunctional human connections (internment camps, unreliable adults). Once Jamie is violently dislocated from family, his "unfixity" from childhood begins. The film (like the book before it) suggests that the notion of home (just like that of childhood) for this Japanese-admiring English boy who has only ever lived in China has always been complex and uncertain. That he does not exclaim, "There's no place like home" when finally reunited with his family suggests that those critics who argue that he is irrevocably changed are correct. But this is not entirely true: Jamie's inexhaustible resourcefulness is bound up with his ability to make home everywhere. This is required of the refugee as well as the colonizer.

Nevertheless, Spielberg chooses to stage the split of son from mother as supreme melodrama. As we have seen, some of the director's most tearfully agonized moments display the violent severance of child from its love object: David cast into the woods by his human mother in *A.I.*, Elliott's parting from E.T., Celie torn from her sister in *The Color Purple*. Jamie's loss of his mother is more epic but equally personalized. The family tries to flee the Japanese invasion in the Packard, but this home-surrogate bubble is rammed by a tank (privilege cannot save the Grahams), so they must get out and merge with the dense crowds. In the crush of panic, Mary loses John's hand, and the surge separates them; John shouts, "Stay together—hang on to Jamie!" as he recedes. Clearly, they are rather worse at protecting their offspring than the fleeing Chinese families who successfully hold fast to their children, for Mary promptly loses Jamie. Dropping his little toy plane, he lets go of her hand to retrieve it, and she is gone. Bale then performs Jamie as a much smaller child through infantilizing gestures: he holds his head, then reaches out toward her disappearing figure in wild desperation. Screaming, "Mum! Mummy!" he linguistically regresses from the older child's familiar term for a mother to the nomenclature of one much younger. If this image of the lost boy were not heartbreaking enough, Spielberg then deploys a classic melodrama shot taken from Mary's point of view: the crowd presses her away from her son, who becomes smaller and smaller in the distance, and she reaches to him with one ardently outstretched arm, fingers spread (figure 15). The focus on two Western figures in a heaving sea of fleeing bodies posits the

FIGURE 15 In a nuanced performance, Christian Bale becomes a younger Jamie in *Empire of the Sun*, within an action sequence that is also a moment of supreme melodrama.

(othered) crowd as primary threat, rather than the invading tanks. Though neither parent is able to help Jamie, the mother's final insistence is that he (like E.T.) should "Go home!"

However, home is no longer home—when Jamie finally returns, he finds it has been possessed by the Japanese. Mary has indeed been there: her bare footprint is visible in a dusting of talcum powder on her bedroom floor, framed by marks that suggest a violent struggle. If home is the primary context for the child's identity formation, here it begins to turn him into something else because it is itself now something else. Of course, "home" becoming "unhomely" is foundational to Freud's *unheimlich* and is reflected in the looking-glass world Jamie's home has become: the dusty footprint with its connotations of sexual violence suggests the repressed returning—the beating heart of the uncanny. But here there is also a political inversion of ownership and propriety that systematically exposes the impotence of the child. Jamie must break into his own home like a thief; his former amah is there looting the furniture (she slaps rather than nurtures him); he now squats the building not as its owner but as an occupying vagabond. This makes plain that as a child (and an expatriate one at that), Jamie never had power over his own house anyway. Children's homes are "theirs" only by virtue of their parents' rights: Jamie's new orphancy means that he cannot belong in his house because it cannot belong to him. Furthermore, the colonial Westerners (and indeed the Chinese themselves) also have few rights in a China under occupation. The child is therefore an apposite figure for the refugee.[11] Of course, Jamie's uncanny relationship with home is historically loaded: he occupies his house in a way which suggests that as a child it was never his (it was only his parents' through colonial occupation). Women may struggle to find "a room of one's own"; children may (if they are lucky) become themselves in the rooms in which they grow up, and which they are destined to leave. Spielberg has yet to direct the empty nest emptying out that the director Lee Unkrich articulates so poignantly in the leave-taking of Andy in *Toy Story 3*; Jamie leaves loose ends, unexhausted toys, unfinished childhood.

Leaving, however, is also liberation. If war can make the child's impotence and minority ever more acute, it can also equalize the child (for good or ill), who as a prisoner of war or refugee is given no special privileges simply because he is a child. There is a positive side to this equalization: children's fiction has long deployed orphan protagonists (from *The Secret Garden* to the *Series of Unfortunate Events* books), who are free to embark on ever-more-exciting adventures because they lack parental control. Though the novel *Empire of the Sun* is based on J. G. Ballard's own childhood experiences in Lunghua camp, Ballard was in fact interred with his parents, and he reports that initially this brought them closer than ever.[12] I will say more in the last section of this chapter about the principle of adults reminiscing themselves back into the child they were, narrating their childhood memories as if from a child's point of view. But James Graham is not James Ballard, especially when he also becomes Christian Bale as directed by Steven Spielberg. The fictional Jamie is set adrift for dramatic reasons—Ballard writes, "In my novel the most important break with real events is the absence from Lunghua of my parents. I thought hard about this, but I felt that it was closer to the psychological and emotional truth of events to make 'Jim' effectively a war orphan" (2008, 82). This also enables Ballard—and Spielberg—to engage with the fact that "the camp was, in effect, a huge slum, and in any slum it is the teenage boys who run wild" (83).

Jamie's liberation through estrangement (from parents, from school) thus begins in the home but defamiliarizes home. We have seen that Spielberg uses dinner table scenes to anchor child to home (*A.I.*'s David is accepted by his adoptive family courtesy of that spaghetti dinner), but only *Empire* makes the content of the scene (food) more important than the ritual, though not at first. In his early days as a war orphan, Jamie adheres to the apparatus of meals as a way of preserving the familiar: he forages on the house's dwindling resources but eats at the table with knife and fork, donned in his school uniform, complete with necktie. Though brilliantly backlit—bright sun floods in through gauzy curtains—he still lights a candle on the table. It is a touching image in which various life phases collide—ostensibly here a child is behaving "properly" according to traditional codes of table manners, but the child also mimics an adult dinner scenario. Then he plays a game that no doubt would have been taboo under his parents' jurisdiction—catapulting a spoon into a glass. These are elements of play invented in the shoot and not present in the shooting script. One image particularly seems to prefigure the dinner table scene from *A.I.*, which I discussed earlier, framed to show the Oedipal triptych as fully present: Spielberg frames Jamie through two ornate wooden Carver chairs, entirely empty of mother and father.

Food remains the focus and the means that signals time passing, as Jamie begins to starve, foraging like a feral animal.[13] Spielberg's shot, a little later, of the desperate child positioned behind a table cluttered with a curiously opulent wasteland of opened, empty tins is bookended by a similar shot much later, when the deprivation of imprisonment is terminated by a U.S. supply airdrop. Jim then is caught behind a burst-open capsule of abundance—life-sustaining but also absurdly luxurious items (chocolate, coffee, Spam, a copy of *Life* magazine). As he drinks a can of evaporated milk, Bale performs a curiously ageless scream—infantile but exultant in its conscious grasp of survival. But this is much later; in the kitchen of his home, he is just starting a journey of slow starvation. When the water fails to come out of the tap, Jamie devours the liquid contents of a case of liqueur chocolates before drunkenly riding his bike around the kitchen, echoing the intoxicated E.T., who was also left alone with the contents of the food cupboard. Jamie, it seems, is now also an alien in his own home.

As the struggle for food intensifies beyond home, the rituals around consuming it are subsumed into the bartering and exchange economies of mess tins and queuing. Once Jamie leaves the building he has called home, he is not freed into a world of anarchy—he is after all a child who boasts that he is writing a book on contract bridge and thrives in rule-bound systems. Looking to the amoral Basie for protection (who first assesses the value of Jim's teeth—gold teeth can be extracted and sold—before trying to sell him to an old Chinese man), Jim soon realizes he must become a trader, or himself be traded, or die. There is an intimation in Ballard's book that the boy's body might be worth something sexually even if it is worthless as food or labor, but, as Freidman points out, Spielberg glosses over this taint of pedophilia (Basie's accomplice Frank simply answers Jim's question "Why can't you sell me?" with "You're worth nothing—you're just skin and bone"). The pervasive accusation against Spielberg—that (at least up until *Munich*) he has trouble representing sexuality—seems to be borne out by this elision.[14]

Jim's only resources are, then, class and education, so he uses his class-endowed cultural capital of complicated words as currency to buy Basie's attention—words become elite exchange objects, perhaps suggesting to Basie a finer life than that of the cabin steward he once was. In *A.I.* artificial children are luxury commodities for adults to purchase. In *Empire* children are accessories enabling adults to gain advantage. En route to camp, Basie favors two other children over Jim, whose more acute newly orphaned vulnerability suggests a better advantage, even though they are first encountered as Basie loots the shoes from their mother's corpse. Unlike Bale's virtuoso performance, Paul (Nicholas Dastor) and his sister (Edith Platten) are required to do little more than just *be* self-evident images of numb child misery, brimming with tears and grief. Just as Basie exploits the children as accomplices or covers, enabling passage into a more advantageous world, so Spielberg once again deploys their tearful images to turn the screw of affect. Indeed, most of the film's children are supporting players, performing

FIGURE 16 "You're an American now": Jim replaces a pinup with his cherished print of Rockwell's *Freedom from Fear*.

necessarily one-dimensionally as background victims, or as childhood emblems gesturing playfulness despite the deprivations of the camp. By contrast, Bale performs as someone trying to piece himself together, trying to build himself, trying out different possibilities for himself. Alongside these bereaved children he is as yet an intermediary, empathy with their victim status evident in how vociferously he protests Basie's amorality in stealing from a corpse that is still a mother. Soon, of course, Jim will be doing this for himself: once in the camp, he distinguishes himself from the less active interned children by learning a survivor's opportunism. Food is the prime currency of negotiation, but he also tirelessly trades exchanged objects and, increasingly, the possessions of the dead (Dr. Rawlins calls him a pragmatist, an adult word that Jim smartly passes on to Basie, but that also sticks to him as long as he cannot be a child).

However, there are some objects that Jim keeps close in the camp—his Japanese flying jacket, his wooden suitcase full of significant objects (a reproduction of the Rockwell painting, torn from a magazine, which Spielberg imitated earlier; the toy plane that caused Jim to lose his mother). These are unpacked and displayed wherever he sleeps, to signify and then re-signify home—in a bunk under the care of Mr. and Mrs. Victor, or when he briefly takes up residence in the U.S. men's quarters. Here he pins the Rockwell over the previous occupant's girlie pinup (figure 16)—ascension to the savvier men-only U.S. barracks is something of a coming-of-age moment that distances the British boy from his homeland (Basie says, "Don't let me down kid. You're an American now"), though occlusion of the saucy picture confirms that Jim wants to hold on to prepubescence. His sexuality/asexuality remains a moot point given that he surreptitiously watches Mr. and Mrs. Victor's sexual encounter later. However, in the barracks picture switch he chooses one fantasy (home, parents) over another (sexualized women).

Almost as soon as Jim arrives in the U.S. quarters, he is asked to leave: Basie is hospitalized and charges Jim with looking after his possessions, failing to recognize the boy's physical impotence, and on a later hospital visit Jim is accused of dereliction of duty in allowing Basie's possessions to be looted. Bale performs Jim's response as a suddenly crestfallen child, looking overwhelmed, stricken: "They were bigger than me." Jim's/Bale's oscillation between child, adult, and all points in between infects the men-only billet with childishness, making it a playground in which bullies push around weaker boys. As in peacetime, Jim is mostly seen with adults—Basie and the Americans, the heroic Dr. Rawlins, who keeps his education on track, and the emotionally distant Mr. and Mrs. Victor. The Japanese commander calls him "difficult child"; he is also a child only and always with difficulty. Too vulnerable to be an American adult and too wily to be one of the British-colonial minors, across the film Bale performs a developmentally unstable identity that oscillates between older child, small child, teenager, "adultish," and something else that is feral, un-aged, and entirely the creation of the unique camp experience. So he leaves the U.S. quarters and walks out into the open camp: he has been tolerated as an honorary American only because of his trading value, he admires the military Japanese, and his only friend is a Japanese boy on the other side of the boundary fence, with whom he cannot talk. He is and is not British; he is and is not a child. His physical lack of belonging (as an intern) is an outward sign of his developmental shiftiness (as not-child, not-adult).

But it is temporary: Basie admits that he also both has and has not a home in a telling exchange with Jim:

> "Basie where do you live?"
> "Here"
> "I mean after the war"
> "Somewhere else"

Jim is unsettled, expecting to return to his home (and childhood?) at the war's end.[15] As yet, he is perhaps more suspended and homeless than Basie, who is at least "here." Though he returns to the British dormitory (where Mrs. Victor begins to mother him), the fit is imperfect. However, this placelessness makes him briefly a unifying figure, for no one is at home in the camp (not least the Japanese). Jim sings an exalted Welsh lullaby in homage to the young kamikaze pilots setting off for death ("Suo Gân," with lyrics articulated from a mother to a child)—his song becoming part of their ritualistic preparation. It is a supremely emotional moment, but is predicated on profound unease. Everyone across the hushed camp listens, and (in an improbable Spielbergian gesture) even the Japanese commander brims over with tears. It seems that the child's song has unified all sides around young men's sacrifice rather than lethal adolescence. Of the novel (which does not contain such a moment) Belinda Kong writes: "Ballard can quite easily be accused of ethnography and even orientalism in his seemingly essentializing and certainly broad-stroked portraits of 'the Chinese' and 'the Japanese,' 'the British' and 'the Americans.' Yet he exhibits all too well how effortlessly, beneath this veneer of human beings' self-brandings, such alibis as empire, nation, and race can come undone in the space of the fallen polis, how any life can revert back to the bare state of species identity" (2009, 294).

What, then, is an unutterably bleak articulation of baseline equality in Ballard (in stateless abjection we are all the same) becomes in Spielberg a poignant gesture of reconciliation that will hopefully unify all audiences—after all, he does not want to alienate Japanese filmgoers, China has allowed him to shoot the film in Shanghai, and (venal as the key American in this film is) it must sympathetically speak to the experience of the former allies. A child may be the most appropriate figure to provide this access.

We have seen Spielberg's children caught up in a number of manifestations of consumer culture—*Jurassic Park*'s theme park visitors, Elliott's toy collection, and David as himself a commodity, a toy/gift for adults. Yet Spielberg's children are also consuming participants (even David has his own AI toy). Understandably, Spielberg would place the suburban child within his culture through the material objects that define contemporary childhood, yet while this is relatively benign in *E.T.*, it becomes part of *A.I.*'s critically dystopian discourse, reflecting negatively backward onto present attitudes toward the parental ownership of children. *Empire* also uses the child to think about consumerism and uses the child's beloved objects to think about childhood, but it separates items of need from items of greed, maintaining a strong focus on material circulation in an economy of deprivation. Objects of desire wash up most surreally as the war closes and the interns leave the camp in search of food. The progress of the exhausted prisoners of war's journey is marked by the bodies of those who could go no further, and the possessions they have discarded. There is another significant "light moment" here, when a dazzlingly backlit Jim throws his suitcase of treasures into an expanse of glittering water—it floats, like the coffins bobbing on the Huangpu River at the film's opening (we will see it again at the film's close, floating through Shanghai, jostling with those coffins—Jim's childhood is discarded, but also kept safe, in the suitcase).

Those still surviving arrive at the Nantao Stadium, which is stuffed full of items ransacked from the homes of European colonizers. As one of the film's most surreally brilliant sequences, this is also where its discourse on the exchange of objects comes to rest: the stadium looks like a warehouse for film props or a toy cupboard for colonial adults. Of course, it is the mausoleum of the West's occupation of the East, and since these objects could not help the war -effort, they have been dumped in a setting of spectacle. Focus on children's bedrooms has shown Spielberg to be acutely interested in resonant clutter; the Ballardian influence here suggests further questions about what happens when "rich pickings" (Basie's favorite phrase, which he "caught" from Jim) become rubbish. Nothing here will feed them—unless it is music for the soul (a woman sits down and plays a sonata on a white piano that perhaps was once hers). When Jim finds the family's Packard limousine, it marks a stark difference between the privileged child he was and the deprived in-betweener he now is. Spielberg's camera focuses on absurd objects of opulence—chandeliers and ornate furniture, paintings, a full-size concert harp, classical statues—and illuminates them to look strangely dead as night falls. The prisoners appear zombielike as they move on from the stadium in the white moonlight, as if they too are already dead.

"I Can Bring Everyone Back"

We have seen many moments when the child's affinity to light functions to both idealize and terrify. The child is magnetized as well as illuminated by light; going toward the light signifies curiosity as well as death. In *Empire of the Sun* that curiosity is a function of control, narcissistically rendered: the desire to find the origin of the light and what it is develops into a child's fantasy that he switched the light on in the first place, or was the only one to see it. *Empire* seems to be aware of the psychological model, derived from Freud, in which the baby believes himself to be the king of the world—an infantile omnipotence that can develop into narcissism or megalomania. Of course, as child, refugee, prisoner of war, and war orphan, Jim is more impotent than omnipotent. Any sense of right his character exudes early in the story is a legacy of colonial privilege; his controlling outbursts later in the film are symptoms of his attempt to grasp or perhaps perform control because it is exactly what he lacks.

But at three particularly sublime moments, Spielberg and his director of photography Allen Daviau deploy light as a language for articulating Jim's uncertain relationship to childhood, a spectacular tool for illuminating his childish megalomania.[16] While children often function as signifiers of impotence, childish narcissistic fantasy also makes them potent with self-belief. Spielberg has described *Empire* as a film about the end of childhood rather than childhood extended into adulthood—about the child having to grow up too fast. Certainly Jim becomes increasingly "adultish" in order to survive, and if childhood is partly defined as a certain *lack* of adult powers, the acquisition of power ought also to denote adulthood. But the light-led sequences to which I now briefly turn show Jim in the grip of a sense of self-potency that is more child-delusional than adult-potent. When younger Jamie contemplated the planes dangling from his bedroom ceiling, they began to move around, and the lighting became more sinister—inflected as science fiction rather than the domestic war film—foregrounding the child as (or soon to be) imperiled. Yet later key moments of supreme narcissism suggest he ultimately believes he has countered peril with power.

The first takes place in the Cathay Hotel—his father thinks that the family will be safe there whereas in fact he has moved them to the epicenter of war. Jamie lies in bed playing with his toy plane and a flashlight, creating huge shadows on the ceiling as if trying to find his own bedroom in this alien space. Moving to the window, he intervenes as the Japanese naval boats signal to instigate the final push on Shanghai—Jamie joins in with his own flashlight Morse code (as an act of play, or in a self-important desire to involve himself in adult matters). He seems to radiate the light, which he in turn radiates upon the Japanese ships with his flashlight. Having already stated that he is an atheist, he now seems to be putting himself in God's place. A huge explosion then hurls him across the room, and the camera quickly swings around to focus on both the boy thrown to the floor and simultaneously his triple reflection in the mirrors of the dressing table, which spectacularly fragments him while also seeming to catch him in a spotlight of guilt. Clearly the aghast child believes he has caused the war finally to conflagrate, as when his father bursts in he cries, "I didn't mean it! It was a joke!" The sequence is replete with cinematic reflexivity, yet it also manages to drill down into the nuances of a child's confusion in adult scenarios—shame follows narcissism, self-aggrandizement is mixed with mortification. Here, too, a child is used to catalyze one of the film's most dynamic action sequences.

There are a number of moments in the film when a scene change is signaled not by a cut or fade to black but by an image of Jim's face fading to white. The Nagasaki/Nantao Stadium sequence concludes in this way. The interns arrive at the Nantao Stadium and soon are hurried on by guards. Jim becomes adult/carer to his dying surrogate mother Mrs. Victor, who in turn becomes childish as she allows him to feed her water from his closed palms, kissing his hands as she sits in an opulent chair in the middle of the sea of looted Western objects, like a child in a too-large toy cupboard. Refusing to leave her (as Basie has left him), he instructs her to pretend she's dead. By this point in the film, the adult actors are performing as if they have got to the bottom of themselves, with enervated desperation and strangely calm weariness. Miranda Richardson here gesturally suggests quiet derangement, but she allows herself to be guided by Jim, half smiling and enjoying the possibility of a game. Jim flops theatrically onto the floor; Mrs. Victor uses the last of her energy to playact death. By dawn she *is* dead: Jim's instruction to "pretend you're dead" seems to have become a reality. However, in the spirit of *Catch Me If You Can*, performing an illusory omnipotence can actualize real power: the action and signs of power denote potency. Believing he is in control and grown up might be at least as effective as Jim actually *being* grown up. An intensely bright (atomic) light then washes across the wide landscape, and Jim whispers "Mrs. Victor" (he later says that he thought the flash was effected by her soul going to heaven). Then comes the fade to white on Jim's face. He also later articulates this bleached moment as "like God taking a photograph," which suggests that God is at some remove from the nuclear actions of humans, that God was not there to take Mrs. Victor's life away, and perhaps therefore that it was Jim who did it with his pretending (his words coming real)—God just stood by, watched, recorded. While this might resonate with the larger question of why God allowed the war in the first place, here it pinpoints a smaller drama of singular childhood, with the atheist boy oscillating between belief/unbelief in God and believing that he *is* God.

Jim's tragedy is, then, the child's: feeling that he is omnipotent when he is anything but, believing he is king of the world perhaps because he is privileged, or loved, or indeed British (he continues to declare his nationality as if this will make a difference). As all directors know, projecting the illusion of omnipotence can have its uses. Like children of the empire (British, not Japanese) in hero stories before him, this spirit of omnipotence has helped Jim survive. That it is a delusional, and narcissistic, sense of omnipotence also means it can crumble when he is given the chance to be a boy again—when he is mothered (by Mrs. Victor), when his mother finds him again (the final fade to white on Jim's face, which I will turn to in a moment), and when Dr. Rawlins picks him up like a baby. This is an earlier encounter with light in the form of explosions, when, as the U.S. Air Force bombs the airfield next to the camp, Jim exults in the attack, like an animated spectator watching a war film.

Poignantly, here Bale's performance greets the bombing with the very same gesture he made when he lost his mother—his arms flail and he grasps disbelievingly at his head. He regresses to excited child, screaming at the planes, "B51—Cadillac of the sky!" Yet even here he makes a claim on the event, babbling to Dr. Rawlins, "I touched them! I could feel their heat! I could taste them in my mouth!" and then babbling, "Do you remember how we helped to build the runway? If we'd died like the others our bones would be in the runway—in a way it's *our* runway!" This is partly because throughout Jim has been unable to choose sides: he is the bomber and the bombed, the plane-fixated child, the plane-fixated director, and the U.S. pilot who here waves to him reassuringly from his cockpit. Dr. Rawlins must establish a boundary ("No it's *their* runway, Jim"—an homage to David Lean's *Bridge on the River Kwai*) and then holds the child fast in the most parental touch he experiences since the Shanghai separation. Then, Jim's/Bale's face struggles with a range of emotions as he calms down from psychotic, childish, adolescent raving, finally welling up at the realization that the megalomania has been masking: "I can't remember what my parents look like. I used to play Bridge with my mother in her bedroom. I used to comb her hair and watch her. She had dark hair" (figure 17). Rawlins/Havers catches Jim's/Bale's contagious tears (tears seem once again to be an appropriate articulation of an experience beyond the edge of the known world), and he carries him to safety as a little boy, while Jim endorses the restoration of order, and parent-child relations, by reciting his Latin homework.

Both the outbreak of war and the U.S. bombing sequences are, then, exemplary Spielbergian moments because, while dynamically action-driven and epic, they also use a fine child performer to oscillate between potent and impotent, adult-child and child-adult, offspring and minor. If Jim believes he can instigate wars, he also believes he can restore life. Early in the film Dr. Rawlins asks him to do CPR in an attempt to revive a woman on the edge of death. As he pumps away, her eyes briefly move, apparently focused on Jim, who cries, "She just looked

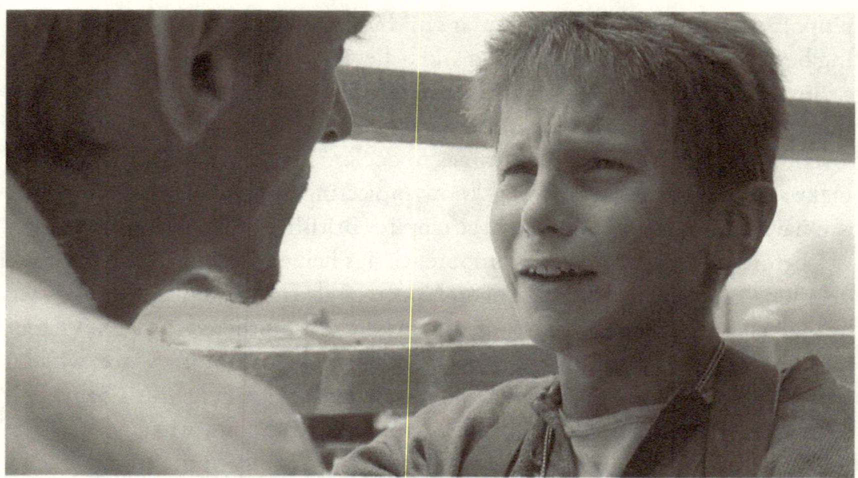

FIGURE 17 "I can't remember what my parents look like": Jim (Christian Bale) catches up with his grief in *Empire of the Sun*.

at me! I've done it! I can bring her back to life!" While Rawlins explains that it was the simple effect of moving blood into the dead woman's brain, Jim is left with the impression that "I can do it again!" Later in the film, when his young Japanese friend has been shot, Jim revisits the technique. A sublime backlit moment signals the boy's death, and then Jim looks at his own hands, as if they are capable of all sorts of mysteries. We then watch from the dead boy's point of view as Jim looms down, his head blotting out the sun and choral music suggesting that this will be a Spielbergian sentimental redemption moment. The attempt at artificial respiration is held for an uncomfortably long time (over a minute), with the haloing blue/silver of the sun behind Jim's head flaring across his image. Jim pumps and pumps, repeating the mantra "I can bring everyone back. Everyone. I can bring everyone back. Everyone." Then there is a surprising, almost subliminal, countershot: from Jim's point of view, he is doing CPR on a schoolboy dressed in Jamie's cathedral school uniform. It is of course his childhood self he would bring back, as if childhood could be reinstigated and inhabited as an act of will. However a shot-countershot subsequently reveals that this will not be a redemption: Jim has simply succeeded in pumping blood out of the dead boy's mouth. But he may have succeeded in his other mission: reviving his childhood self. Has his own boyhood died like his Japanese friend, or can Jim succeed in at least resurrecting himself?

Child Laborer, Child Soldier

These readings have suggested something more complex than a loss-of-innocence story. While clearly Jamie/Jim develops from unthinking overprivilege to canny manipulator of the internment experience, he does not leave behind childish things when he becomes adult before his time—he does not simply move from innocence to experience. As with a number of films encountered in this study, here too Spielberg challenges the linear idea of childhood as a phase that one moves through and outgrows—despite his own promotion of the film as just that. Remember earlier the director imagining the parents of Rockwell's *Freedom from Fear* "looking at the boy, thinking, if the war keeps going, in a few more years he could be drafted"? Jim has a closer relationship to combat than a child should. An act of foolish valor (his infiltration of the land mine–infested margin beyond the perimeter fence) has enabled him to join the barracks-like U.S. men's quarters, operating rather like the billet of a boot camp film.[17] While there he is not just an honorary American but a foot soldier at the forefront of a civilian war waged across the black market economy. Is Jim then child or adult, civilian or participant? *Empire* shows the close proximity of these roles to be mutually subversive. Spielberg's beloved military planes resonate across the border between child's toy and adult weapon.[18] When he first arrives at the camp and labors alongside the adults, Jim risks himself by wantonly embracing a Japanese plane parked on the airfield. Welder's sparks fly all around him (another light effect that blazes when one of Spielberg's children hovers on a threshold or crosses sides), and he is momentarily imperiled as a guard threatens to shoot him for the transgression. But he is saved by three young Japanese pilots, who recognize his ageless passion for the flying machine. That these airmen, and later his teenage Japanese friend, salute him suggests that he is recognized as an active combatant. Indeed, once transformed into the boy wonder of the camp black market, he is never seen without his Japanese flying jacket. When the Americans finally liberate the camp, the commander accepts Jim's surrender (proffered with a tin of evaporated milk—his final food exchange) and also salutes him. That he is constantly being told to slow down, to rest, suggests he is always at work. In fact, as they part for the last time, Basie reassures Jim that finally the boy "can retire." Jim is then either a child soldier or a child worker; either way, these are not the child roles he was born to, or those that Spielberg is thought to idealize.

The (temporary) loss of a toy thus propels Jamie/Jim into precarious post-childhood, but he does not become an adolescent in the postwar sense of the term. Nor does he become an adult. Nor is this necessarily a place from which he cannot return. Rather than growing up when he gets to the camp, in fact he enters a liminal zone from which he perhaps returns at the story's conclusion, and at moments throughout. The reunion scene is something of a coda: in a Red Cross center (a broken glass house), children run around playing, ministered to by immaculate old-school nurses. The children grow still as a group of parents arrive; the two sides inspect each other, across a space. The children look vagrant, but the parents—well-dressed, well-fed—do not seem to have changed. Some children eagerly present themselves at the front, but Jim holds himself farther back in the crowd, looking like he does not expect much, and also that he does not belong in a crowd of children. He seems to recognize his father (though this is not reciprocated), but as soon as his mother sees him, she knows him. They stare at each other, but he only believes it is her when he uses his primate fingers to scrutinize her piano-playing fingers and feel the texture of her hair. Her fingernails are long, well manicured—the fingers of a leisured woman; Jim's are short and dirty—the fingers of a working man. His face softens; mother and son embrace, and though the father is left out, he chokes back tears. But an extreme close-up of Jim's eyes over her shoulder, staring into the distance as if confronting his experience, initially intimates that he cannot go back. However—finally—the eyes close. If he has been holding on while an orphan, he can now "retire." Indeed, they close as if he is performing the act of dying.[19] But it is also a moment that evokes another sense of the word "surrender"—submitting to a surrender of self, from the Old French *surrendre*, meaning "give up, deliver over." The final image is of Jim's suitcase bobbing in the river as downtown Shanghai is liberated. Perhaps (coffin-like) this contains his dead childhood self, or perhaps it is his refugee self, if still exiled. This is an uncharacteristically open ending for Spielberg, leaving self-determined childhood experience floating in a strange limbo, even as the child surrenders to his mother's embrace.

However, it may be that Spielberg's closure and Jim's redemption have already come earlier in the film. As the most mainstream of directors, Spielberg's films favor moral resolutions; as an edgily amoral science fiction writer, J. G. Ballard does not. The camp scenario stages a negotiation of these positions via the unsettled child, with Jim figuring out what friendship is while also learning how to survive (and Basie posits these as mutually exclusive). His only friendship is with the Japanese boy across the wire—a friendship struck up through the non-value-based exchange of passing the boy's model aircraft back and forth. Ultimately this relationship is the sign that Jim is redeemed: at one point he has appealed to Basie to let him live in the American quarters "because I'm your friend," but Basie only values trading relationships (Jim's final words to him attest to the one thing Basie taught him, "that people would do anything for a potato"). Once the war has ended, the boy offers Jim a mango but is shot by Basie's gang. Jim protests that the boy was his friend, and the sign of this was that "he gave me a mango!," to which Basie responds—referring to the food parcels being dropped by the American liberators—"I'll give you a whole goddam fruit salad. There are Frigidaires falling from the skies!" Basie can only understand the material value of objects; Jim sees friendship in the gesture of giving up an object—surrendering it. It is this that enables him finally to reject Basie, which—more than reuniting with his mother—is the film's moment of closure. Rejecting the bad parent here is a more powerful gesture of active childhood than accepting the good. Indeed, the arms into which he sinks at the end are also those that so clumsily lost him in the first place.

The Memory of Childhood: *Schindler's List*

One thread running through this book focuses the child's experience as framed and imagined by the adult, but this has been supplemented by visions of the child reinterpreted, and owned, by the child performer. There are other—remembered—children buried in these texts. *E.T.*'s much-celebrated sense of authenticity derives not just from Henry Thomas's performance but from the narrative's widely promoted proximity to Spielberg's biographical childhood. The historical child (Spielberg) is, then, used in marketing to suggest that as a film *E.T.* speaks directly from the heart of childhood. This may mitigate the sense that it is the articulation of adults ventriloquizing the child. The films under discussion here suggest both: adults can and do speak from their child selves, and they use children to represent this. But children in performance also re-author the templates written for them by adult screenwriters.

Empire of the Sun is another such child-reflective, autobiography-as-fiction source in which the adult J. G. Ballard "remembers" his prisoner-of-war child self as a war orphan (even though he was well parented). A flurry of refutation news stories around the release of Spielberg's film saw fellow Lunghua camp survivors protesting the inaccuracy of the film's—and Ballard's—overemphasis on trauma and deprivation. The reality, they argued, was more civilized. At the same time, some film reviewers criticized Spielberg for sanitizing Ballard. On the one hand, then, Ballard's grittier account of internment is deemed authentic (because of that familiar critical privileging of dark pessimism over happier schmaltz), while its cinematic revision is accused of Spielbergian sugarcoating. Ballard was not a war orphan, and—if his co-survivors are to be believed—the camp experience was tolerable. Still, Spielberg (whose film is nearer to this "reality" than Ballard) is beaten with the stick of sentimentality. Indeed, Ballard himself distinguishes memoir from novel in *Miracles of Life*, which stresses the fictionality of *Empire* and the relative comforts of his own experience. That said, *Empire* was marketed as autobiographical fiction predicated on childhood memories of deprivation, and therefore occupies an uneasy middle ground between fiction and remembrance. Of course, narrative cinema is not history, nor is it made by historians. There is the real and there is the actual. Spielberg is often caught between the two, to the detriment of perceptions of his "seriousness."

The other form of child-anchored war remembrance with which Spielberg is concerned is Holocaust testimony: adult-remembered (usually) childhood suffering that functions to bear witness to the veracity of historical events. Ballard uses historical experience to refract memory into fiction. The testimony of trauma as part of remembrance is distinct from remembered trauma distilled as fiction, yet both of these inform Spielberg's filmmaking. I have not engaged in an intensive adaptation-focused comparison of Ballard's book and Spielberg's film here, nor do I want to think about *Schindler's List*—to which I now turn—in terms of the fictive representation of memory, or film as testimony or remembrance. But psychologically- or psychoanalytically informed questions about truth and memory posed by literary theorists around autobiographical fiction are particularly interesting given that there are buried children here, themselves accessed only through knotted skeins of remembering.

Spielberg set up the Shoah Foundation in 1994 in the wake of his profound experiences making *Schindler's List*, in order to document survivor testimonies, initially by Jews remembering the Holocaust.[20] Many of the Shoah Foundation's original testimonies are by adults remembering childhood experiences in the context of war—as a testimony to lived events, rather than as the fictional revision of lived events, which was Ballard's approach to revisiting his childhood internment. *Schindler's List*'s producer Branko Lustig was a child prisoner at both Auschwitz-Birkenau and Bergen-Belsen, from where he was liberated at age twelve in 1945. Reports of the anniversary commemoration of the liberation of Auschwitz in January 2014 (which Spielberg attended) focused on the fact that many of the increasingly elderly returning survivors were only children when they were liberated. The Shoah Foundation contains multiple views of childhood delivered by adult voices, the adult and the child being of course the same person, separated and refracted by time and experience. Reading these testimonies requires a dark, internalized version of the perspectivism I have drawn on throughout this book—the adult view of what it is to be a child. Time and again, however, interviewees appear to narrate their way right back to the moment of childhood they recount so as to be once more in the midst of it. This time travel or time ellipsis is a fecund area for psychoanalysts and trauma theorists, and is widely discussed in the plethora of academic materials on Holocaust testimony and theories of memory.

Children's testimony in other cultural contexts is of course routinely discredited—the disbelieving of sexual abuse victims as part of a long history of identifying children with lying, even when children grow up and reflect on childhood abuse that may not be believed. Yet against this, the reminiscences of Holocaust survivors are among the most historically significant witness statements of the twentieth and twenty-first centuries, within a cultural context that has made Holocaust denial illegal within (to date) seventeen European nations, plus Canada and Israel. The remembered child persists. Indeed, *Schindler's List* is not just a (controversial, fictionalized) text of remembrance; it instigated the Shoah Foundation's formalized collection of memory, which is also child-anchored. Spielberg has said that he was first inspired to establish the foundation by the Holocaust survivors who approached him on set, who wanted to pass on the stories of their young lives and bear witness to those who were lost. The foundation's guidelines for those conducting survivor interviews to deposit in the archive are mindful that many of these oral history narrators were very young at the time of the Holocaust. In the section titled "Establishing the Profile of the Interviewee," interviewers are advised to "familiarize themselves with the interviewee's personal, religious, educational, and socio-economic background. The interviewee's age at the time of the historical event also helps the interviewer understand the interviewee's perspective about his/her experience. A survivor who was eight years old at the outbreak of World War II saw and understood his/her world differently than someone who was 15 or 20 years old."[21]

To compare this historical testimony and documentation with the memory embedded in a fictional novel may seem like a disrespectful maneuver. Important work has also been done on the refraction of traumatic memory across time (e.g., Felman and Laub 1992; Caruth 1995; Erll 2011), but it is not the work of this chapter to develop that. While the foundation's testimonies strive to present personal truths as clearly as possible and take great pains to try to avoid documentarian pitfalls about distortion of material and interviewer agendas, a text such as Ballard's *Empire of the Sun* deliberately refracts autobiography into fictional form. Both, however, rely upon adults drawing on the child—late twentieth-century adult fermentations of mid-twentieth-century child experiences from the same war. *Empire of the Sun* is Spielberg's adaptation of Ballard's adaptation of his own childhood, with Bale performing a character only tenuously anchored to Ballard as an actual child. *Schindler's List* is also an adaptation of a literary text—Thomas Keneally's 1982 Booker Prize–winning historical novel *Schindler's Ark*, which drew on survivor testimonies and is fictional biography to Ballard's fictional autobiography. Both of these key Spielberg texts are fiction films interpreting fictional writings that use adult memories of real children-turned-adults caught in historical events, from a perspective of forty or fifty years on. It is, then, not enough to read the image of the child in these films as instances primarily of 1980s or 1990s American cinema. The child is a function of adult remembering framed by history, not just the historical events that these text foreground (the war, the Holocaust) but the psychobiographical histories of author and reminiscer, pulled by desire and misremembering.

In the midst of this pull of adult voices and world events, we have then found the intricate form of Christian Bale's Jim. *Schindler's List* contains no singular images of complex children, but extensive views of child figures. I do not want to revisit the heated debate among Holocaust documenters, filmmakers, Jewish scholars, and film critics about the merits and problems with this film. While it was lauded (as well as castigated) on release, garnered Spielberg his first Best Director Oscar, and took the Holocaust out of the realm of art house cinema and into mainstream theaters (as the NBC TV series *Holocaust* had done on small screens in 1978), critical debate since has circulated around its Americanization of Jewish history;[22] its representation of the Holocaust from the point of view of the Nazis (it "depicts the Nazi slaughter of Polish Jewry almost entirely through German eyes"; Gourevitch 1994, 51); its happy ending ("Sentimentality also marred the conclusion of the film with its triumphal march of the survivors"; Strauss 1994); its audacity in daring to make "the unimaginable imaginable, the unrepresentable representable" (Loshitzky 1997, 2; this was explicitly against Claude Lanzmann's view expounded in his 1985 film *Shoah*).[23] I want instead to look at *Schindler's List* as a development of Spielberg's thinking about childhood—though this indeed involves discussion about point of view and memory, which touches on the film's controversies. It is a fictionalized version of the true story of the German entrepreneur Oskar Schindler, who moves to Poland to profit from servicing the war effort but, having witnessed the liquidation of the Kraków ghetto, saves surviving Jews by enlisting them to work in his factory. The film's children are primarily positioned to augment moments of acute affect (as if this story were not affecting enough already).

The most famous of these is the image of the "girl in red," performed by the three-year-old Polish child Oliwia Dabrowska. This nonspeaking character is perhaps the most iconic presence in the film—the most repeated poster/DVD packaging image features a small child's hand, with a visibly red coat cuff, being protectively held by an adult hand. No star images here: color and smallness are the star. Within the film the girl in red has a symbolic (as well as marketing) importance that far outstrips her fleeting appearance in the harrowing ghetto liquidation sequence. Lury notes that the presence of the child as an "emotive figure, can be used to 'stand in' for many deaths. . . . the child's narrative function is effectively to act as a metonym for wider suffering" (2010, 107). This is nowhere more evident than with the figure credited as Red Genia, though her symbolic function is reinforced by the fact that her name is never given in the film.[24] She is therefore associated entirely with and as childness and the color of her coat—an emblematic innocent, and a walking sign of shed blood.[25] She also primarily functions in the impact her image makes on Schindler (Liam Neeson), who spies her amid the appalling violence from his hilltop vantage-point—the one pop of color in a largely monochrome film. As she toddles through the streets alone, sometimes against the tide of the fleeing crowds (the script refers to her as "a bright moving target"), the musical score underlines the message that children should learn from these images (a children's choir swells up with the popular Yiddish song "Oyfn Pripetshik," about a rabbi teaching children).[26]

One of the many criticisms of *Schindler's List* is that it narrates the story of the Shoah from the point of view of the perpetrators,[27] an argument partly countered by Miriam Hansen's analysis of Itzhak Stern (Ben Kingsley)'s privileged point-of-view moments (2001, 135). If Genia is an image function primarily serving Schindler's narrative arc, she also exists independently of any diegetic adult view, Jewish or Nazi. In the context of this book it is not surprising that Spielberg would choose a child to articulate these privileged moments of extreme peril. Cutting away from Schindler's viewpoint, we follow little Genia into a building as she finds a hiding place under a bed. Night falls, and an SS death squad makes its way through the ostensibly deserted buildings, picking children out from their small hiding places. Genia is not explicitly murdered here; she is only later recognized by the red coat (witnessed again by Schindler) on one of the corpses exhumed and carted away for incineration. Indeed, Spielberg generally refrains from showing the deaths of tiny children—those picked out by SS rifles usually look like teenagers—as if size were a permit for violent imagery.

Popular readings of this archetypal figure of innocence suggest that she is there both as a moral counterpoint to atrocity and as a function of Schindler's conscience: these are the two turning points in his resolve to help the Jews. A common critical position is to say, "we will never know what changed Schindler's heart," but the child image is the answer given by Spielberg's film. Soon after the vision of her corpse, he is seen packing all his money into suitcases in preparation for bribing (or buying) his 1,200 people from the Plaszów forced labor camp commandant Amon Goeth (Ralph Fiennes). As he does so, Billie Holiday's voice is heard quietly in the distance singing "God Bless the Child," a song that laments child poverty and impotence and explicitly connects racial minority (Holiday as celebrated African American singer) to age minority. It initially seems to come from the radio or a gramophone, but since it runs across a temporally elliptical sequence as Schindler gets ready to change his life (and those of others), this is clearly not just a song lending contemporary atmosphere (it was recorded in 1941) but a song providing a heavy-handed extradiegetic commentary.[28] Schindler then proceeds to draw up his list, insisting that "the children—all the children" be included.

Of course, it is hard to justify the use of small children as workers in a munitions factory, but it is part of the twisted moral landscape that Schindler occupies that not only must he ingratiate himself with Nazis (and remain apparently a good Nazi himself) if he is to protect his workers but also must appear to profit from slave labor and must be seen to keep children in his labor force. When the women and girls are sent to Auschwitz-Birkenau by mistake (rather than to his new factory in Czechoslovakia), the guards initially allow him to reclaim the women but not the girls. He protests that he owns the children and needs them for specialist war work. Thinking on his feet, he holds up Danka Dresner's/Anna Mucha's small hand to a guard saying, "These are mine—their fingers polish the insides of shell metal cases." This use of the child's small body would be monstrous in another context (though of course small children have also been used in the production of this film), but here the illusion of child labor is salvation.

Although Dabrowska is around the same age as Cary Guffey from *Close Encounters*, her role is not sustained enough to require significant performance skills. Nevertheless, Spielberg was aware that the child might be curious about the work she was doing and made her promise that she would not watch the film of which she became the symbol until she was eighteen. When he received the Order of the Smile from the Polish children at Łęg, which I discussed in chapter 1, he had told his child interviewers, "In *Schindler's List*, which is not a film for children, there are only Polish children and they are excellent actors" (Palowski 1999, 146). But this message ("not a film for children") and his explicit instruction to Dabrowska contradict the moral of the song "Oyfn Pripetshik." The fact that the Holocaust has, since the 1990s, become such an important subject in Western children's education suggests that this ought *primarily* to be "a film for children," lest we forget (though perhaps not for three-year-olds—even though it depicts the murder of three-year-olds). Spielberg's anxiety about the age limits on who should and should not see this film (rated 15 in the United Kingdom and R in the United States) became even more acute when Dabrowska reported in 2013 that she defied the director's advice that she "grow up into the film." Instead of age eighteen, she watched it at age eleven. She later recalled: "It was too horrible. I could not understand much, but I was sure that I didn't want to watch it ever again in my life" (Pulver 2013). This became widely misreported as evidence that "maybe it's all Spielberg's fault" when his child actors go "off the rails."[29] Though she is now proud of her involvement and regrets not listening to Spielberg, the question of who should experience historical horror remains, as well as how extreme it should be—and whether images involving children are worse. Even Spielberg admits censoring himself: "The SS had a lot of marksmen, and just for fun, placing bets, they threw babies out of the windows alive and shot them like skeet. I wouldn't show that in the movie. I couldn't, even with dolls" (quoted in Malcolm 1994).[30]

Children are, however, seen here in extreme peril, though—aside from Genia—the key child characters mostly survive: the bespectacled Danka (the script gives her age as fifteen, but Anna Mucha was twelve when she played the role), inseparable from her mother; the vulnerable Olek Rosner (played by four-year-old Kamil Krawiec), who escapes the line of children being sent to their deaths and lends his face to one of the most resonant images of the film. But children are also identified with the perpetrators: there is a brief glimpse of a complete Jewish family welcoming the Sabbath in the film's opening scene, but the first active children we see are Polish, marching with invading German troops. Polish children also throw dung at families forced into the ghetto, and a monstrous child mimes a smiling throat-cutting gesture at a train destined for Auschwitz. The sound of crying children functions as a shorthand for fear or despair throughout the film, infecting viewers with those same emotions; many children are seen and heard screaming as they are torn from their parents (primarily boys taken from mothers' arms in the gender segregation process).

We have seen Spielberg using children to turn the screw of affect in multiple scenarios. As if the Holocaust were not emotionally charged enough, the child must still serve as emotive intensifier. Yet as Goeth is shown around the under-construction Plaszów, we see a children's playground slide being put into place and are told there will be a kindergarten, so initially it seems that perhaps this will not be a particularly dark place for children. However, Goeth, known for randomly shooting anyone at any time for no apparent reason, soon kills his teenage houseboy, Lisiek (Wojciech Klata), following a trembling confession about his failure to remove stains from the bathtub. Goeth as the prime representative of Nazi evil is here focused through individual psychopathy, with random child murder as its apotheosis. The ebbs and flows of affect are carefully, sequentially manipulated: it is arguably the moment when a child is summarily shot dead earlier in the ghetto liquidation sequence that forces the audience to recognize where *Schindler's List* is heading. In a film of terrible moments, one of the worst is when Plaszów's smallest children march out of the kindergarten singing a rousing song and are loaded into carts presumably headed for the gas chambers at nearby Auschwitz-Birkenau (the older children are spared because they can work). This comes just after their parents are granted a brief elation at their own reprieve; they then explode with desperate panic as the children are driven off. Once again the perceived suffering of children affected those on set before infecting the audience: "While many scenes were painful to film, several of the filmmakers pointed out two particularly difficult sequences," and this is one of them; the unit publicist Anne Marie Stein had to walk away as it was filmed (USC Shoah Foundation 2014, 114; 116). As the scene plays out on-screen some children try to escape and are roughly handled into submission by pursuing guards. Then we follow small Olek Rosner as he slips away unnoticed, escaping into a building as Genia had done earlier. He makes his way around potential hiding places, only to find them already stuffed with children. Eventually he reaches the latrine and drops down through the toilet hole into the cesspool below, where he stands, chest deep in excrement and isolated in a pool of light, confronted by Danka and others already crouched in this unimaginable refuge. Two circles of light are cast onto the liquid filth, ostensibly created by daylight pouring through the toilet holes. Though the children ought to be evading capture by clinging to darkness, instead they cluster in the pools as if caught by searchlights. Alongside red-coated Genia, Olek standing in excrement but gazing up to the light is one of the film's dominant images, the child's mute expression combining fear, pleading, and yearning (figure 18).

Beyond this there are few moments of active child performance. In one chilling camp lineup, Goeth shoots an adult suspect over a stolen chicken, and a

FIGURE 18 Olek Rosner (Kamil Krawiec) evades capture in *Schindler's List*.

crying boy (Adam Siemion) steps forward and speaks up in a way that protects all the men. He is rewarded with a work permit for Schindler's factory, and his rapid chattering to his new boss, promising that he will be a model worker, provides a rare moment of humor. We have seen this boy previously in the ghetto liquidation sequence. Here Danka calls him Adam; the two perform as if they have a backstory as child sweethearts. Though he is Jewish, he is working to help the SS soldiers, but he has the authority to put Mrs. Dresner and Danka "in the good line." Mrs. Dresner reads this power of life and death, delivered from child to adult, as a coming-of-age moment, responding, "You are not a boy any more. I am saying a blessing for you." Another key scene features the Nazis throwing a birthday party for Schindler at which two of the laboring girls—one very young (Magdalena Dandourian performing the real-life Nuisa Horowitz), one an older teenager—present a humble cake. The party stops as Schindler kisses the young girl in a paternalistic fashion, then kisses the teenager more sexually. This is risky, violating the Nazi antimiscegenation laws, and he is imprisoned for it.

These vignettes of horror and tragedy require brief agonized displays from often quite young children, but few performances are sustained. Most child actors in *Schindler's List* simply stand mutely next to adults; few speak lines. Of course, using children as resonators is a risky strategy for Spielberg in developing a "serious" art project (though mass-entertainment child-friendly films can also be art). They have been his most dependable emotional faucets, so the familiar act of centering on the child seems to conform simply to the tried-and-tested strategy of "Spielbergization." He said, vehemently, that he did not want *Schindler's List* to be an entertainment film, so these are ostensibly rather different kinds of "message children." But the child here is still used for emotive intensification, not an unfamiliar strategy in wider popular representations of the Holocaust (*Sophie's Choice*; *Life Is Beautiful*; *The Boy in the Striped Pajamas*), partly because many testimonies remember childhood but also because the horror becomes ever more horrific the younger the victims are seen to be. The scene in which hordes of possessions looted from those herded onto cattle trains are being sorted for Nazi profit by Jewish forced laborers becomes most affecting when we see a pile of child's toys—dolls in particular as a metonym for the piles of bodies to come.

While *E.T.* seals his Peter Pan–esque child identification, we have seen that later with *Empire of the Sun* using a child as focalizer does not necessarily risk Spielberg's (then) newly acquired "adult" status: with that film he was seen to have grown up precisely because of the mature performance of Bale. But *Schindler*'s children are less developed and precisely more sentimentalized. Indeed, even his young actors had trouble believing in this as a serious enterprise, and the director falls on the old technique of "being" rather than acting:

> Behind a reconstructed Birkenau barrack two girls are building a snowman. It is freezing. Several of the actors playing German SS guards are wearing large overcoats. They put them around the children to keep them warm. Spielberg

> rounds up several young girls and wants to rehearse a scene in which they are frightened and are calling for their mothers. Nothing doing—all the faces are smiling when they are yelling, "Mama! Save me! Help!" Dagmara, who is an interpreter for the extras, tells the children to think of something scary, like meeting a wolf in the forest. The children cannot believe that in Spielberg's film things could be scary. (Palowski 1999, 66)

These are children who, as we saw from discussion of the Order of the Smile ceremony, grew up on *E.T.* and have integrated it into Polish children's culture. Spielberg is thus read by his background actors not as Jewish memorializer but as children's entertainer with a distinct worldview.

Those 1,200 people Schindler saved were and are known as *Schindlerjuden*,[31] and Keneally's novel was inspired by the campaigning of one of them (Poldek Pfefferberg) for world recognition of Schindler's achievement. The story of Pfefferberg, a Holocaust survivor whose testimony feeds into a novel, is not that of an adult remembering the child self: he was a young man when the war broke out, a teacher, and fought in the Polish army.[32] But many of Spielberg's characters are very young. Some surviving *Schindlerjuden* who were characterized in the story are seen as themselves in the film's concluding tableau, when they place stones on Schindler's grave in Jerusalem, accompanied by the actors who performed them on film. Magdalena Dandourian, Kamil Krawiec, and Anna Mucha all perform characters who were actual children in the Holocaust and survived (Nuisa Horowitz, Olek Rosner, and Danka Dresner, respectively), so these child actors are able to accompany the real-life (and now elderly) people they play to pay homage at Schindler's actual grave in the film's documentary end sequence.

This in itself is visually emblematic of the recent focus on children as the objects of remembrance. The Shoah Foundation's mission is now explicitly educational: the foundation's collection of survivor testimonies, the largest in the world, has been digitally archived so as to be searchable by anyone, but particularly children. "Imagine if young people could experience eyewitness accounts of such crimes against humanity. Would it change them? Could it change the world? The Survivors of the Shoah Visual History Foundation know it can," intones Morgan Freeman, voicing the fundraising documentary *The Shoah Foundation Story with Steven Spielberg*.[33] Holocaust Remembrance Day now often takes the form of handing stories over to the youngest generation, the best guarantee of carrying remembrance far into the future.[34] Spielberg is explicit about this when he articulates the mission of the foundation through the image of a contemporary child connecting with an older person by watching them recount their own childhood experience: "It almost becomes an adoption, and a child adopts a grown-up." *Schindler's List*'s concluding image of Magdalena Dandourian hand in hand with Nuisa Horowitz, Kamil Krawiec hand in hand with Olek Rosner, and Anna Mucha hand in hand with Danka Dresner is, then, more powerfully emblematic of the ongoing work of remembrance (past child with present child) than the more famous Liam Neeson accompanying (Oskar's widow) Emilie Schindler, as he does in the same tableau. This reverse-generational connection is all the more emotive because it seems to bypass the intervention of adulthood, as child viewer links with remembered child. Among many others, Alfred Garwood (2020) has reflected on the need to pass his Holocaust childhood on to contemporary children, but this recent desire to speak was preceded by a long silence for many. Franciszek Palowski asks Ryszard Horowitz (brother of Niusia, who presented Schindler with his birthday cake in the film) why he had not discussed his childhood experiences with his sons, and Ryszard replies, "They are too young." Yet, as Palowski reflects, "As a prisoner in Auschwitz . . . he was younger than his older son Daniel is now" (1999, 64). Hovering over this, then, is a question about the appropriate age for certain narratives and images, and here *Schindler's List* itself as a film also has a bearing. Genocide education is now common in many schools, making use of survivor testimony. Sometimes contravening its classification, *Schindler's List* is also frequently screened to high school–age children as a teaching aid. Yet Spielberg insists that it is "not a film for children." Nevertheless, children inherit—adopt—the previous generation's trauma as if, in the image of Art Spiegelman's *Maus*, history has bled onto them. The hand-in-hand concluding tableau of *Schindler's List*—old child linked to young performer—is a far more audience-friendly moment of closure.

8

Family Finds a Way

Adult Children, the Nonhuman Child, and Chosen Families

In *Catch Me If You Can*, a twenty-seven-year-old Leonardo DiCaprio "passes" as a teenager and grows to young adulthood through the story. It is common practice to cast over-eighteens in child roles to bypass child employment restrictions; one popular survey, *Child Stars, Then and Now*, even contains a section titled "I'm Not a Kid but I Played One on TV!" (Durkee 2008, 142–143). However, DiCaprio's character is constantly being referred to as "a kid," even as he ages; he is also positioned as child/offspring by his painful ongoing relationships with his failing biological parents (a mother who has all but left him; a father who cannot function effectively in society), and through his more successful surrogate father-son relationship with Tom Hanks's Carl Hanratty. Though *Catch Me If You Can* is based on the real-life Frank Abagnale's autobiography and was originally developed for production by Spielberg and direction by other helmers (most notably Gore Verbinski), this cluster of concerns make it vintage Spielberg subject matter. Keith Uhlich (2003) reads it as Spielberg's masterpiece, on the grounds that "autobiography is inherent to the best art"—but he means Spielberg's, not Abagnale's.

This book has been primarily concerned with child performers and "childness" as borne out by the bodies and skills of young actors. However, this chapter will look at a range of films that infantilize adults and show them relationally to be child figures, whatever their age. This underpins the idea that family will out, however far a story seems to stray from the actual nuclear family. As Jeff Goldblum's Ian Malcolm says in *Jurassic Park*, "Life finds a way." Family does, too, even when its usual structures are denied or dismantled, and even when there are no children evident. Indeed, if there is anything in Spielberg's films as ubiquitous as childhood, it is family. This is not just a question of shoring up a traditional institution, since in addition to genetic families there are surrogate and symbolic families, often welded together through nonbiological links. The parenting of children, as well as the "childness" of parents, is part of this story.

So, turning our attention to how the child as offspring functions in all-adult scenarios closes the circle of children in Spielberg: from adults positioned as sons or daughters to adults who stand in as parents. Sometimes, within these familial dynamics, the adult will behave like a child; sometimes the denoted child figure will resist. We have seen how critical and reception responses to Spielberg frame his corpus as one extended self-analysis, working through the traumas and pleasures of childhood, divorce, and—later—fatherhood across decades of filmmaking. The familiar extratextual story around the director brand reinforces this: at key career junctions Spielberg has reflected on his own position as father or son as a framework for presenting and promoting the content of a film (*E.T.*, *Empire of the Sun*, *A.I.*), and we saw in chapter 4 how an imagined filial relation was superimposed onto the relationship between the son (Spielberg) and (older) father (Kubrick) around the inheritance of *A.I.* As Chuck Stephens (1997) quips, Spielberg has "been taking his Oedipal angst to the bank" ever since *The Sugarland Express*.

A feedback loop of promotional factoids, interview tidbits, and a "preferred" line on how a film is to be received thus feeds the autobiographical into the public realm, and journalists and critics duly use this to form the interpretations of critical writings, which then in turn become ways of reading the films. Language is telling here: Richard Corliss even supplants a father-child relationship onto filmmakers and viewers, presenting the first three *Indiana Jones* films as three episodes of familial storytelling, since viewers of these films "have two surrogate storytelling dads, George Lucas and Steven Spielberg": "Tell me a story, Dad"; "'Next night: Tell me another story, the same but different'"; "Third night: 'Tell me another story, Dad, the same, but different . . . and better'" (1989, 52). Nancy Griffin also reads these friends and collaborators as a kind of cinematically gestating couple. "The blockbuster hits of the '80s," she writes, are the "children or stepchildren of Spielberg and Lucas" (1989, 94). Family even describes franchise formation, with Spielberg articulating the Indiana Jones series as a "family" of related titles. Having designed the conclusion of *Indiana Jones and the Last Crusade* as closure for the franchise, he found himself reanimating the family line with the fourth film: "My goal was to make this movie a blood relative of the first three" (Hiscock 2008, 25). Even in his seventies, the former Peter Pan continues to be framed as a sometime grown-up child passing as an adult, or as an adult who still would play the child, as a son of television, or of Hollywood, or—now—as some kind of cinematic father.

Alongside adult children in screen families, another premise of this discussion is that even when the family is absent, it is present. The practice of analyzing nonfamily groups in familial terms is well established in film analysis, including psychoanalytically inflected readings of Oedipal struggles between generationally separated men, or the feminist focus on mother-daughter bonds among women. What, then, are the limits of childhood in the stories I turn to here—the Spielberg-helmed *Indiana Jones* quartet (the recent fifth installment, *Dial of Destiny*, was directed by James Mangold, so will not be discussed here), *Close Encounters of the Third Kind*, *The Sugarland Express*, and others? Who are the children when a family is adults only? Is the child still present even in films featuring only all-grown-up adults? Or no humans at all? These questions are interrelated: even when there are no children, the child endures—adults become children relative to other (parent figure) adults. But Spielberg also specializes in a particular formation of adult Peter Pans (often, though not always, men), who regress, or who do not/cannot grow up, or who eschew a normal developmental trajectory through "inappropriate" behavior. The slapstick of *1941* might be a prime case here, but foolish playfulness can also be the purview of adults. If some of his children are "adultish," many of his adults are childish. From *Sugarland Express* to *Hook* to *The Fabelmans*, there are multiple examples of adults who fail to be adults or are more childish than their children. Reversing some of the issues of chapter 7, here we find adults *as* children, and child figures who are not minors.

Adult Childishness: *The Sugarland Express* and *Close Encounters of the Third Kind*

Adult infantilization is frequently the preserve of men in Spielberg's films. It is not necessarily an unequivocally celebrated trait of authenticity or refusal; Roy Neary's infantilism may have been central to his spiritual journey in *Close Encounters of the Third Kind* (1977), but Spielberg has since said that he would not write the character that way if he had his time again. Childish women also feature and are more ambivalent figures, particularly since adult childishness only ever destabilizes the family, anxiously displacing those who surround the grown-up baby who must take responsibility or step back so that the Peter Pans can find family in other locations and connections. Spielberg's first theatrical feature was already exploring this. *The Sugarland Express*'s story of a young couple whose baby has been taken by the welfare department is a road movie featuring dazzling Spielbergian car-chase set pieces, but with the question of how family is made and broken and remade at its heart. Lou Jean Poplin (Goldie Hawn) and jailbird father of their child, Clovis (William Atherton), steal a car in pursuit of their baby (Baby Langston), who has been given by the welfare services to an older, richer couple. En route they kidnap a patrolman Maxwell Slide (Michael Sacks), who becomes complicit in their quest and something of a protector. As a road movie melodrama, the narrative is fully determined by Lou Jean's need to get her baby back, and this separation has two effects: family is invented where it has been dismantled, and adults play children.

In place of "natural" family, the triptych of Lou Jean, Clovis, and Maxwell mutates into a differently identified ramshackle surrogate family, despite their captive-captor relationship. They share their family snapshots, Lou Jean mothers Maxwell, and Clovis becomes brotherly. One heartbreaking moment positions Lou Jean as a daughter to her own absent biological father, and sister to the captive Maxwell. Pursuing the on-the-run trio, the police stage a broadcast by the father over the police radio, presumably hoping he will make a paternally persuasive plea for her return. Instead, he pours out a lifetime of spleen, stating that she is no good, and her mother would have been ashamed of her. Maxwell is alone in the car when this is aired; when Lou Jean returns, he turns off the radio as a kindness, sparing her the sound of her own father publicly disowning her. In the midst of a story in which a woman attempts to bring her nuclear family back together, she is severed from her birth family, but Maxwell's kindness confirms a different kind of (chosen) family emerging in the close confines of the car as he tells her she is a good woman. In the absence of family, other families are constructed.

This warmth is contrasted to the plight of the unfortunate Baby Langston, as the action cuts from one nongenetic family to another—the runaway adults in the stolen car, and Baby Langston in his foster home. The child himself as a fleshly being ever eludes Lou Jean and functions as a miserable reminder of unhappy families for the viewer. Indeed, he hardly features at all; Spielberg has said, "The baby *is* irrelevant" (Tuchman 1978, 53). But this is not entirely true: the baby is the prime plot motivation and—seen from the woman's point of view—is central. His misery also underpins the film's (unusual for Spielberg) nihilism. When not crying or being carried from place to place, he is seen playing alone, surrounded by a desert of immaculate lawn in the front yard of the affluent but cheerless middle-class house. The age, control, wealth, and formality (of the stable foster carers) are contrasted unfavorably with the youth, spontaneity, poverty, and warmth (of the on-the-run genetic parents). *Sugarland* thus posits an ideal—though divided—family of three children (mother, father, baby) that is never there (Lou Jean only gets Baby Langston back in the "what happened next" script that concludes the film, by which time Clovis is dead) and an alternative family formation of nonrelated adults (mother, father, and kidnapped friend). These are set against a socially sanctioned but unsatisfactory family of too-old adults who look more like grandparents than parents and fail the baby in other ways—at one point they grotesquely allow the crying toddler to be interviewed by the press. Of course, given that the actor performing the youngster is so tiny—one year old when the shoot started and therefore unable to "perform crying" in Henry Thomas fashion—the screams can only be real (figure 19). That this baby actor is Harrison Zanuck, son of *Sugarland*'s producer Richard D. Zanuck (and therefore grandson of the legendary studio head Darryl F. Zanuck),[1] is another indication of what filmmakers will allow (their) children to experience to get the footage in the can.

FIGURE 19 Distressed Baby Langston (Harrison Zanuck) is paraded in front of the press in *The Sugarland Express*.

Early as this film is in his oeuvre, and despite the fact that it is based on a true story, *The Sugarland Express* has been read (familiarly) as a personal Spielbergian tale: Joseph McBride conjectures that "Lou Jean's compulsive need to reunite her family at all costs expressed the childlike pain Spielberg continued to feel over his own family breakup, for which, at the time it occurred, he primarily blamed his mother" (2010, 219). Since *The Fabelmans*, guilt and blame in this cinematic auto-melodrama have been supplanted by a more nuanced view of adult relationships. "There are no villains in this at all," Spielberg said in 2022 of his latest film. "There are simply choices, and we're not villains for making those choices" (Zacharek 2022). Though the Peter Pan syndrome has long been associated with the director's infantile men, the infantile mother is also part of Spielberg's biographical filmmaking. McBride quotes the director's mother, Leah, as saying, "We're all for immaturity in my family. . . . The rule at home was, 'Just don't be an adult.' Who needs to be anything but ten?" Spielberg is further quoted as glossing this with "We never grew up at home, because *she* never grew up" (McBride 2010, 42). This was amply fleshed out by Michelle Williams's Oscar-nominated performance as a version of Leah in *The Fabelmans*, of which Spielberg has said, "She was more of a peer than a parent, because she wanted us all to call her Lee, not mom" (Apatow 2023). Lou Jean is, however, not Leah and is more unsettling than Spielberg's other mothers. Uneducated, incompetent, and socially ineffective, she is nonetheless guileless and motivating, and she gathers a form of stardom as the media follow the chase and well-wishers cheer her on through the journey. While worrying over her ability to be a fit mother, the film also celebrates her natural maternalism as an effect of her own childlikeness, as when at a gas station the police watch her, charmed, when she plays with a little boy.

There is, then, an ambivalence about childish adulthood in this film—it can be heroic or neglectful, enabling or dangerous. Goldie Hawn's performance manifests a kind of infantile restlessness, as if she is channeling a distracted child.

Veronica Geng reads this as showcasing Spielberg's mastery of nondirective narrative and performance:

> His characters have been obsessed, but in a distracted way, like children who don't hear what you're saying because something catches their eye off to one side. . . . In *The Sugarland Express*, Lou Jean, determined to get to her baby, isn't so much hellbent as dreamily stubborn. Words of caution she tunes out, like a kid fixating on the promise of a Carvel down the road, yet her angle of vision keeps veering off. For all her purpose, her eyes drift away from the point or the point drifts away from her. . . . She's like her baby Langston, who giggles with irrelevant pleasure at police tramping through his foster-parents' house, or Barry, in *Close Encounters*, skittering away from his mother and evading her eye to scan the sky for the "toys." (1981, 57)

The "infantile" is, then, a mode of being and is performed as such—it is not necessarily a regression or a failure to progress. It may be more common in those young in years but is also a behavioral possibility and (here) a stylistic tic: distraction, evasiveness, and (inappropriate?) pleasure. I place "inappropriate" in parentheses because it is a mobile but resonant term that may or may not be—as it were—appropriate here. Adults (or those policing the socially acceptable) commonly name "inappropriate behavior" as age-shifted actions or interactions—the too-sexualized child, the infantile adult who cannot adhere to agreed boundaries in a responsible manner. Adults may be "inappropriate" because obsession distracts their focus from the "proper" responsibilities of adulthood (the most regular charge against *Close Encounters of the Third Kind*'s Roy Neary).

But it is not just Lou Jean who is the adult child (in a film that has cordoned off actual children to the margins of the story). *Sugarland* infantilizes both of its couple-on-the-run protagonists: if they cannot *have* their baby they will *be* babies (as chief cop Tanner realizes, "They're nothin' but a couple of kids"). When a well-wisher holds up a sign that reads "God Bless the Child" (the name of the song that, as we saw in the previous chapter, accompanies Schindler's resolution to save his mostly adult workers), this could be referring to Lou Jean as well as Baby Langston. Perhaps *Sugarland*'s most magical scene is when the journey, briefly, stops. The couple hole up overnight in a used car lot overlooking a drive-in cinema, snuggling down to watch the movie next door over the fence. "If Baby Langston were here we'd be a real family," Lou Jean says as Road Runner and Wile E. Coyote play out on the screen.[2] In the absence of audio, Clovis improvises a soundtrack to the animated movie, which (fittingly for such a chase-activated film) always revolves around restless pursuit and erratic movement. Spielberg is not generally admired for his handling of intimate scenes, but here he conveys the couple's romantic connection through child's play and via screen entertainment for children.

So who else in Spielberg's work "never grows up"? The infantilization of adult players is something to which Spielberg has continued to return - his oeuvre is almost as interested in adult children as it is in actual children. This is not the relational infantilization that positions the Jews of *Schindler's List* as subordinate to Schindler-as-protecting-adult, which is a power relation rather than a performed identity; those actors perform primarily adults trapped in captivity and torment. More comic figures include Tom Hanks as Viktor Navorski in *The Terminal*, whose unalloyed qualities of trust and guilelessness ultimately save him. The character is unfortunately rendered an infantilized buffoon by virtue of his foreign otherness: he arrives at JFK Airport with an invalid passport and visa (of which he is stripped) as his country (the fictional Soviet bloc nation Krakozhia) has undergone a revolution while he was in the air. He is invalid, with no way in and no way out, and is less than a minor (even a child has its own passport, or is an adjunct of its parents'). He is simply told, "You are a citizen of nowhere." This "nowhere" is the no-man's-land of the airport terminal, in which he must carve out a precarious life. The infantilization of the marginalized man-child is expressed in some inventive ways: while awaiting his interview with Homeland Security, he is put in a small taped-off pen in a larger open space (like a child's playpen), where he shaves as if to demonstrate his manhood; the game of "homemaking" involves him in turning the objects of travel into the domestic detritus of a life in a room made his own in the margins of legitimate life.

It is not just because this film is very loosely "based on a true story" that it is hard to imagine the Victor character as a woman.[3] With the notable exception of the adolescent "precog" Agatha (Samantha Morton) in *Minority Report* (a female savant role, performed more commonly by males), childish men (both celebrated and criticized) are more evident than infantile women in Spielberg. *Hook* is, among other things, a story that addresses adults who carry unresolved childhood within them, and who show their failure fully to grow up by being too adult (Peter's workaholism and paternal incompetence at the start of his story). Reconnecting with playful childishness saves Peter and makes him a better father. This is popularly thought to be a typical Spielberg conclusion: men who are not children but function as such through displays of childishness or uncanny innocence. The former is manifested as the child out of place, out of body, the child rendered grotesque because it inhabits an all-grown-up body. The latter is an idealized quality that characterizes some Spielberg heroes and also his habit of attaching himself to those figures in the promotion of the films. All examples of adult childishness in Spielberg's films are therefore not the same: to continue a quote from earlier, the positive mode is what Peter Biskind has called Spielberg's "better self as the inner child, the innocent youth we used to be" (1998, 363).

There are, then, two forms of child's play acted out by adults: a disruptive childishness often marked as "inappropriate," and a more "wondrous" childlikeness signaled as a form of gift. The obverse of "better self as inner child," the manifestation of "bad childishness" in those who should know better, is one trope explored in *Kick the Can*, Spielberg's contribution to the portmanteau film *Twilight Zone: The Movie*. Residents of a care home for the elderly are given the gift of youth, but playfulness turns out to be not such a blessing. This sounds like a Spielbergian experiment in the limits of childishness, but as a very short film, *Kick the Can* is slighter than that. The elders learn that there is a merit in lifelong experience, and playfulness is what should be recaptured—and indeed what rejuvenates the geriatrics—not actual youth itself. In the short night in which the older people are replaced by younger versions of themselves, the child actors' roles are perfunctory. Only one resident chooses to stay a child, playing out his memories of wanting to be Douglas Fairbanks Jr., and then exiting the window in a manner reminiscent of Peter Pan.

The most sustained child-adult is Roy Neary (Richard Dreyfuss) in *Close Encounters of the Third Kind*, a film the director also wrote. Spielberg went out of his way to cast a man-child as centerpiece to a film populated and created by adult children. Though he has said that "there's an easy gateway to children for me. I find it's very natural directing children, even more natural than directing grownups," he qualifies this by pinpointing the "big kids" with whom he has a regular directing relationship:

> I have a good time directing people who have never grown up, like Richard Dreyfuss. It's very easy to direct Richard because, like me, he's wearing Peter Pan clothes. It was even great directing Harrison Ford, because he's a big kid. He's a little more serious and he's a little more sobering but he is a big floppy kid. I kind of have an easier time directing people like that, who still have a little bit of the kid stuff left over from childhood, than I do directing someone who takes acting and performance so seriously that there's no room for mistakes, no room for humour. (Warhol and Jagger 1982, 47–48)

This became the signal line taken in promotion, even across the decades. In casting, he said in 2007, "what I was really looking for were actors who were still closer to their own memories of their own childhood. Richard Dreyfuss was a bigger kid than the children he was raising in his suburban house."[4]

Dreyfuss's Neary does not start as this within the diegesis, however: he is initially a responsible working-class man with a family to feed. Infantilization creeps up on him as his reality and experience (the aliens he encounters one night on a lonely country road) drift away from his family's (who did not see the aliens and do not believe him), and he is eventually left alone to follow his obsession. This takes the form of a shape that has been imprinted on his mind by the aliens, which he tries to represent (through deranged sculpture-building) but does not understand; it turns out to be the shape of a mountain that will be the location of the culminating "close encounter." Neary must overcome the skepticism of his family and the might of military and government personnel, whose job it is to keep him away from the mountain even as he has been called to it by the aliens. The film's final spectacular showpiece has the extraterrestrials revealing themselves to earth (in child form, as we saw in chapter 3), with the now unencumbered but vindicated Neary being taken into the mothership, leaving the world (and his family) behind.

This may be the film's climax, but what happens to Neary in suburbia is equally telling. While he remains in the clutches of his human family, he appears to go mad and is increasingly disturbing to his wife and children. Because we were there with Roy, we have privileged access to the truth of his experience of the aliens, but his family members were not, so they do not, and the two truths conflict. He is regressively irresponsible (variously read as monstrous or as a charmed, Spielbergian alter ego) because he (like toddler Barry Guiler) has a supposed insight beyond bourgeois/rational reality. Yet Spielberg does not take this unilateral position; when family is concerned, he cannot help but complicate things. Though it would be much simpler for Roy to cast off the encumbrance of family as he embarks on his journey (as Dennis Weaver does in *Duel*, which was perhaps the last time Spielberg treated family as an undesirable, avoidable entity), the domestic scenes when Neary loses his grip on "appropriate" adult behavior are a far more painful film within a film. Once his family relationship has entirely broken down, he heads off without so much as a backward glance, a latter-day incarnation of an earlier-1970s New Wave hero who might have been played by a Jack Nicholson or a Dennis Hopper. As he enters the mothership, no commonplace fatherly thoughts such as "Will I ever see my kids again?" seem to trouble him. But I am more interested in what comes before—Neary's infantile modes of expression, and his family's (particularly his children's) consequent struggle.[5]

Early in the film, a sequence in which he plays with a train set does double service to set him up as both a poor father (refusing to be disturbed by his children's needs) and a comical child (fixated on toys). As we saw in chapter 3, the train set also features in the story of Spielberg as "playing with toys" in his job: an interview with *American Cinematographer* in January 1978 captions a photo of the director setting up the prop with his technical crew, noting his youth and filmmaking as child's play: "Looking about twelve years old in this photograph, Spielberg gleefully contemplates the model train layout which his protagonist man-child . . . plays with in the picture. Spielberg himself favors bigger toys—such as the largest interior set ever constructed and a Mother spaceship supposedly a mile in diameter" (Lightman 1978, 41). Within the story, the train set is more interesting than the child: when his eldest son, Brad (played by twelve-year-old Shawn Bishop),[6] requests help with mathematics ("Dad, do my problems for me"), Neary resists interruption from play, replying, "I don't have to do your problems for you. You do your problems for you. That's why I graduated so I don't have to do problems." Ascendance to adulthood is, then, expressed as transcendence of "problems." When he does concede, it is to offer a misjudged explanation about fractions, involving a ghoulish narrative around a train wreck he orchestrates on the train set—the child is threatened that life (or death) depends on his ability to judge the correct answer. Bishop performs a response that is fearfully hesitant. As this bizarre parenting strategy unfolds, Brad's younger brother Toby (played by Dreyfuss's nephew, eight-year-old Justin Dreyfuss) is seen climbing into the family's playpen, where he smashes a baby doll to pieces. The message is plain: bad fathering, borne out by the adult's wish to keep playing despite the presence of children he should be parenting, is framed by a child figuratively destroying an image of childhood. We never find out if bad fathers create child monsters in this universe, since mercifully these unhappy children are taken away by their mother (Teri Garr as Ronnie) in due course.

But before she does, the family disintegrates further. Roy is hemmed in by unfulfilled promises: Ronnie reminds him he promised everyone a cinematic outing to a family film; Brad reminds him he promised goofy golf. But Roy is only excited by any of these options when he realizes that the film is *Pinocchio* ("I grew up with Pinocchio!" he says, though the parenting here suggests little growing up has taken place). This is of course just one of the references to Disney's film-as-leitmotif across Spielberg's work, endorsing "wishing on a star" and pretend boys becoming real boys. But while the father here is child-identified, the child considers himself too old for Disney ("Who wants to go and see a dumb cartoon rated G for kids?"). Roy's response is threatening: "How old are you?" he asks. "Eight" comes the reply. "You wanna be nine?" says Roy, to which the child of course replies "Yes." "Then you're gonna see *Pinocchio* tomorrow night." Ronnie sardonically responds by parenting the parent: "That is a wonderful way to win over your children." It may be, of course, that Ronnie is too adult while Roy is insufficiently adult: she is strict, but sometimes his childishness makes him an equal playmate for the children. When five small boys sneak in on Roy, batting him on his rear, he responds as a mock monster. In a heartbreaking tableau of child reassuring adult, when Roy's obsession begins to take hold, his boys try to make it all right, impressing him, or living up to him, by declaring a belief in the aliens they have never seen, and helping with his baffling sculptures. Dreyfuss's disordered performance would read rather differently without these poignant supporting performances by his young costars, children augmenting the man-child and signaling the devastating impact of Roy's strangeness on his family.[7]

There is a switch point in *Close Encounters* when Neary turns a corner, and the film shifts genre. Ronnie is orchestrating the family meal, with the camera following a bowl of mashed potatoes from person to person around the table until it shares Toby's perspective on Roy as he begins to play with his food (as children are told not to do). Roy's distress is seen from the position of the arrayed children. He begins to sculpt his potato rather than eat it, and everyone else falls silent—the substance is not most important as food (indeed, the spectacle seems to put the others off their food) but as material for comprehending his derangement (pointing to the potato, he says, "This *means* something"). In another context it might be viewed as playful, but the wrongness of an adult male making mountains out of food is distressing. The youngest child, Silvia (played by three-year-old Adrienne Campbell), has been naturalistically chattering but soon joins the others in disturbed silence. Brad begins to cry, and Roy joins him. "Well, I guess you've noticed there's something a little strange with Dad," he says, licking potato off his finger (Silvia copies him). "It's OK though—I'm still Dad."

But is he? That this is the moment when the film shifts from family melodrama to science fiction makes it also the moment that wife and children are left behind. Though melodrama continues to inflect Roy's increasing obsession/breakdown, this singular scene is the film's supreme articulation of family agony. There is of course bombastic melodrama at the heart of the showstopping sci-fi climax (returning veterans, surging music, a lost child running into the arms of its mother), so it would not be entirely true to say that when Roy escapes his family he escapes from one genre (womanly melodrama) into another (manly science fiction)—melodrama runs across these two half films. But this scene provides a familial complexity that is too easily forgotten once Roy hits the road for Devil's Tower. Despite the fact that the audience knows he is right, Dreyfuss performs the scene as if he is King Lear descending into madness but retaining some of the self-perspective of sanity, while wife and children look on with fear and (at this stage) compassion. His performance speaks to their understanding of the situation rather than his, while of course their surrounding performances give credit to an alternative possibility (which is not the truth of the film's story) that Dad has gone mad, and the family is in peril as a result. This seems to me to be part of an entirely different film than the fireworks of its spectacular alien-soaked opening and conclusion. When at home (roughly the first hour of the film), Roy is challenging, threatening, angry; he fails to respond to his wife, and he frightens his children. He is sometimes funny (to an adult's ear); he is mostly unsettling, even monstrous. When on the road (roughly the second hour of the film), having left his family behind to—as it were—follow his star, he becomes the film's heroic adult male, infused by a different (positive) form of childishness. The mashed potato scene pivots between the two.

Roy then enters full play (or frustrated artist) mode, aggressively throwing modeling clay around before having a temper tantrum. The score veers between horror and melodrama, as he cries up to the stars, "Tell me!" (as wondrous child) while sitting on the children's garden swing (as regressive adult). When Roy breaks down in the shower, Brad—himself in tears—calls his father a "crybaby";[8] the scene cuts repeatedly to the pained eyes of the children looking on from behind their bedroom doors. A traumatized adult child will in turn traumatize his children. Roy then seems to resolve to give it up and turn back to the family, but he is halted by the intervention of another toy in his den, a small rotating musical model of the Disney Pinocchio, which randomly plays a few notes of "When You Wish upon a Star." This reactivates the quest, with Roy throwing garden matter into the house to construct an even bigger formation of the mountain (the boys still want to be like their dad, with Toby—who poignantly tries to help—asking, "Dad, after this can we throw dirt through my window?"). Ronnie then bundles herself and the children into the car and leaves, knocking a tricycle across the road as she departs—and the melodrama of the film largely departs with them. From here on in, *Close Encounters* takes the form of science fiction adventure, and Roy's childness also shifts tone: he becomes the story's wondrous questing hero rather than its damaged father, culminating in being chosen by the childlike aliens to enter the mothership, as if he were their child kin.

So, somewhere around about the mashed potato scene, *Close Encounters of the Third Kind* shifts genre from melodrama-interrupted-by-sci-fi to science-fiction-inflected-by-melodrama. There is, in this middle phase, a collision of two incompatible realities, and while the film plumps for one (the existence of aliens, the credibility of Roy's experience—psychic reality proven to be empirical reality), for the duration of that awkward dinner table scene the viewer can apprehend both and experience contradictory truths. This is done through an interplay between the children's views of their father, and their father's (mostly) childish view of everything—until at the conclusion he "mans up" and shows he can see as they are seeing. The showstopping sequences in the first hour of the film are the loss of little Barry from his mother's grasp, and the unbalancing of Roy. Though there are some spectacular "close encounter" moments, these seem only to have importance for their impact on the witnessing humans. The finale sequence is of course the final "third kind" encounter section, an overwhelming conclusion that tends to deflect attention from the family-focused concerns of earlier. And let us not forget that it is in these family-focused sequences that Spielberg chooses to locate his "signature image," that of the small boy framed by the awful white light in the doorway.

Close Encounters is, then, two films uneasily welded together. It moves from home-based to road- and space-based. In the shift from one focus to another, Roy becomes less infantilized and more "adultized" as his experience gains credence, though still with a Spielbergian "wondrousness" about him. Curiously, as the film progresses the presence of actual children diminishes. The genre shift from melodrama to science fiction cannot be attributed to the presence (or lack) of women, since women remain fairly constantly represented throughout the film (Teri Garr's frustrated wife may disappear, but Melinda Dillon's searching mother remains). It is children who disappear—Roy's children leave, Barry remains abducted, and even the child that is Roy changes the tone of his childishness through his quest—and with them goes melodrama in this more recognizable form. Close encounters around the dinner table give way to those around the mothership.

Hook takes these motifs in a different direction. Spielberg has acknowledged that though interested in the Peter Pan story throughout his life (he even directed a play version of it as a child [Bahiana 1992, 14]), he came to this adaptation somewhat too late. The film suffers from an inflated budget put to work on too limited a script, and it was critically reviled (the subject matter left the director vulnerable to vicious critiques) as well as initially underperforming at the box office. The story conjectures that Peter Pan grew up, becoming Peter Banning (Robin Williams), a nominal family man who is a workaholic corporate lawyer, letting down his children, Jack (Charlie Korsmo) and Maggie (Amber Scott), in numerous ways. Banning takes his family on a winter visit to see Wendy (Maggie Smith), the grandmother of his wife, Moira. Peter has a mysterious connection with Wendy, who lives in London, although he only remembers that in early life, as a foundling, Wendy helped secure him an adoptive family in the United States—nothing before that. One night Jack and Maggie are abducted by Captain Hook (Dustin Hoffman), and Tinkerbell (Julia Roberts) takes Peter to Neverland to get them back—in the process lifting his amnesia about his origins. Peter must behave like a child in order to find his past self and activate its power: happy thoughts enable flight; imagination makes invisible food real; the lost boys kill adults but spare him, and render him an honorary child when they realize he is really eternal child Peter.

Hook may seem a highly significant text for this study: the collective group of lost boys created employment for a range of young actors (who earned the Outstanding Young Ensemble Cast in a Motion Picture award at the Fourteenth Youth in Film Awards);[9] the story's motivating quest is the return of Banning's children; and Banning himself is really that famous eternal child of J. M. Barrie's imagination, a leitmotif of Spielberg's career. In this story Peter has chosen to grow up because of the love of a woman (he has met Moira while visiting Wendy) and then must reverse the "adulting" in order to refind the magical child. In fact, the film presents as a huge, unwieldy symptom of child obsession, largely driven by the plot itself. Dark threads running through the film include the death of a child (Rufio, played by Dante Basco), which we know to be a great rarity in Spielberg stories. Unlike Neary in *Close Encounters*, the child-man as performed by Williams is mostly repressed; adopting childishness is a plot device that denotes power, and the more significant result of Peter's awakening is not infantilization but a renewed awareness of the magic of fatherhood. *Hook* is also, as Tim Morris points out, one of a spate of films between 1986 and 1996 to feature fantasies of returning to childhood—"an adult transformed into a child or a child who inhabits an adult body" (2000, 121). Of the six cited by Morris, half feature Robin Williams (the others are *Jumanji* [1995] and *Jack* [1996]), significant both as an indicator of Williams's skills and star persona, and also of the defining nature of his role as Banning.

Other families prevail in *Hook*. This is probably most interesting for the child-hating Hook character (and the film is of course named for him, not Pan). Playing the title character, Dustin Hoffman embraced an alternative domestic coupling, set apart from the nuclear family Peter must recuperate. Hook and sidekick Smee, as performed by Hoffman and Bob Hoskins, camp it up "like two married people": "It became like *The Dresser*," Hoffman has said. "We're two old queens" (Docherty 1992, 31). Recalling *The Sugarland Express*, Smee and Hook's domestic setup of nonrelated "married people" is perhaps the film's most dynamic alternative family unit, even more than the lost boys as street gang. Of the multiple chosen families that Spielberg dramatizes, *Hook*'s is a queer alternative.

Nonhuman Children: *War Horse*

War Horse starts with the birth of a baby—a horse baby, anxiously watched over by a boy (Albert, played by Jeremy Irvine). The foal—soon to be named Joey—is enveloped into his (equine) mother's care, but when they are separated the human boy becomes its mother, brother, and protector. *War Horse* is full of actual, symbolic, and surrogate family structures the likes of which we have seen across Spielberg's work, but the most remarkable family here is cross-species, between Joey and his various human parent/carers/abusers, as well as his brotherly relationship with fellow warhorse Topthorn, which (as with some human siblings) begins in rivalry, moves through love, and ends in self-sacrifice and grief. There are many overlapping symbolic and actual families in *War Horse*, but perhaps it is Joey who is the most consistent child, not the film's various grooms and boy soldiers. Like the Tyrannosaurus Rex nuclear family in *The Lost World*, sometimes animal families require the parent-like protection of humans to ensure their survival. Such animals do function narratively like children, being cared for or abused by humans, and subject to endangerment strategies like victim children. The first part of this chapter has asked when and why adults perform childishness, and how this might contribute to the story of Spielberg's children. But how are nonhumans able to flesh out symbolic and functional child roles, and what does this do to and for the actual children in the narrative? This book has already discussed at length at least one Spielbergian child who is *not* human, so how appropriate would it be to read David in *A.I.* as an animal like Joey the horse? Or to read Joey most literally as pet-as-child, satisfying parental desire just as David does? How do animals help us to understand what a "real" child might be, or not be?

We use the word "anthropomorphism" to mean human attributes inappropriately projected onto a nonhuman, usually an animal, a pet. However, since etymologically the word is formed of the Greek *anthropos*, meaning human, and *morphe*, meaning form, the most literal anthropomorphized character in Spielberg's work is David, who takes the form of a human but is not one. Though Joey does not look like a human in the way that David does, he is physically situated as the next best thing to an anthropoid being, since his duty is to support people on his body and to carry out their work in agriculture, transport, and war. As a companion animal, Snowy in *Tintin* is his detective-master's best friend, but like many a silent fictional dog, he knows more than he can say and behaves with the wisdom of a sleuth coworker. Further down the evolutionary chain—and however vehemently the scientists of *The Lost World* argue for the family bond of the T-Rex nuclear unit (mom, dad, and abducted baby)—the fact that those beasts also attack and eat (human) children in their bid to reunite their own (dinosaur) family makes them harder to anthropomorphize. (Indeed, this is exactly what makes the *Jurassic Park* joke reference in *Toy Story*, featuring sweet, dumb, talkative Rex, so funny.) As for the shark in *Jaws*, it is a lone predator. Though family stories proliferate in the wider narratives of that film, the great white's only humanization came extradiegetically, in the production problems around the model shark that came to be known as Bruce.

In chapter 7, I proposed that *War Horse* is not a film about Joey but about his teenage carers—children or very young adults caught in war scenarios that damage them more than "manning them up"—and in this way Spielberg mounts a spectacular critique of war through its young combatant victims. *War Horse* began its cultural life with Joey at its center, yet with each creative development from Michael Morpurgo's 1982 novel the horse's centrality has been displaced. The novel is narrated in Joey's voice, but the development of the London National Theatre's stage production silenced this first-person narrative and the focus turned to the phenomenal puppeteer skills that made the wood-and-cloth horse seem so real. Still, Joey was the star. Spielberg's film did not reinstate Joey's voice (though he could easily have done so in voice-over), introducing instead a stronger focus on the sequence of young people who surround him. The love and admiration of Devon farm boy Albert, patrician army captain Nicholls (Tom Hiddleston), German teen soldier Gunther (David Kross), and Belgian peasant Emily (Céline Buckens) function to position Joey/animal as child to these humans as adults, even though—apart from Nicholls/Hiddleston—the characters are mostly children (though Buckens is the only child actor performing a key role in the film, aged fourteen when it was shot; Irvine and Kross were both nineteen but played younger).

It might then be said that Joey passes through a variety of surrogate families, serving as child to the needs of other lonely children. The first relationship encounter Spielberg presents is when the (human) boy Albert tries to coax the (equine) boy away from his mother with an apple, but the foal is called back. When his father buys the young horse and Albert starts breaking him in, gaining trust by recognizing how much he must be missing his mother, childhood seems to transfer from the young human to the young horse. Joey is then passed on to others, who denote different roles: upper-class Nicholls sees him as a sporting partner; Gunther tries to protect him as he protects his younger brother; Emily plays out the familiar story of a girl with a horse passion. So while Joey has lost his voice, he remains the narrative focus, cohering the episodic story across enemy lines as he is passed from British to German to Belgian owners, with the quadruped child as transnational peace emblem. This borderless figure thus promotes Morpurgo/Spielberg's anti-war story: war equalizes not only because war spreads suffering equally across all sides, but because enemies are also capable of caring for and abusing Joey in equal measures.

The horse also occupies an uneasy zone between chattel and subject, just like the child. As a soldiering animal, Joey is told several times that he is "in the army now," but he is also a machinelike asset whose function (like that of other child soldiers) is to facilitate war: as a mount he participates in a cavalry charge; as a slave he pulls heavy artillery. He is a worker, not a pet, but his labor is most like the child labor examined in chapter 7: exploitative, hard, pushed to the borders of death. Like the young soldiers, he is a sentient coworker—part of a "band of brothers"—so he seems yet another boy warrior in this extended investigation of that figure. Like a child, he rarely controls his own experience, requiring care and protection while attracting cruelty and indifference. There are many human children in *War Horse*, but it is the horse that functions as the film's central contradictory cypher-child. All of which brings us back to *A.I.* and Donna Haraway.

If children are everywhere in Spielberg, is everyone also a child? If horses and robots and aliens are children born outside of human gestation, what are the limits of childhood, and can it be entirely uncoupled from biological genesis? Haraway famously pronounced that we are all cyborgs, and though David's science fiction identity is that of android, not cyborg, his story positions him as empathic kin, and his robot descendants both become and replace us. The utopian project of Haraway's "A Cyborg Manifesto" envisions "a cyborg world [that] might be about lived social and bodily reality in which people are not afraid of their joint kinship with animals and machines, not afraid of permanently partial identities and contradictory standpoints" (2004, 13). Building on this, Haraway has written about her kinship with dogs, going beyond the customary anthropomorphism of pets to trouble at the leaky distinction between species. Entering into a relationship with a companion animal, the human becomes more doglike and the dog more human, and neither is therefore the "pure" species they originally were in an "implosion of nature and culture" (16). Something similar takes place in the interrelationship between child and animal in *War Horse*, but this goes beyond a trans-species closeness or transmission of characteristics. Children must adult-up as carers, and the horse exposes the vulnerability of the done-to child as used and passive. Each is primarily and relationally meaningful in the context of each other, exposing the inequalities and brutality to which each is subject.

Children, Otherwise: The *Indiana Jones* Franchise

Spielberg has said that his sets are like families, and—though collaborative up to a point—he is of course very much in charge. As families go, the ones constructed in the filmmaking process are mostly cooperative, but with an overseeing patriarch. "I am open to input from everybody," he said in 1981. "I make my movies in as much of a family situation as I can tolerate" (Reiss 1981, 39). We have seen that in multiple ways family is both inside and outside of (serving the promotion of) his creative practice. There are few films that have nothing to say about family. Even *Amistad*, which has few children and then only fleetingly glimpsed as traumatized witnesses to horror, contains moments such as when a desperate slave woman, seeing her companions whipped on the deck of the ship, clasps her baby in a blanket and slips quietly over the side. Death in the sea, at a time of her choosing, is better than what she and her baby face on the ship or when they reach the Americas. This also serves to underline slavery's double abomination in relation to family, both destroying it and using reproductive power as a means of generating more "chattels" (babies born on plantations were legally owned slaves at the time of *Amistad*'s story).

Other films may feature few children but still configure relational children out of adult bodies. In *Munich*, Eric Bana's Avner, a Mossad agent enlisted to enact the Israeli state's revenge against militant terrorist group Black September for the killings at the Munich Olympics in 1972, is acutely tormented by his forced estrangement from wife and baby. His past unspools and threatens the future: his own father (also a Mossad agent) was absent; his mother was distant, and gave him to a kibbutz to be brought up; his wife considers that "Israel is your mother." As an action drama about terrorism and its aftermath, the film focuses on absent family from Avner's point of view, looking backward at his own neglect, and forward at the impact of his mission on the next generation. He has trouble separating work and personal relationships, cries about his distant baby, and is repeatedly seen looking into a kitchen showroom at the spectacle of domestic bliss for sale. "You could have a kitchen like that one day," he is told. "It costs . . . but home always does." Though his wife and child are endangered by his work, the cost is presented as primarily to the father/son—Avner himself—whose trauma is of the grown-up abandoned child who must do his duty for the state parent, in the process passing on the legacy of absent parents.

The *Indiana Jones* franchise is a much more family-friendly rendition of an abandonment dynamic among fathers and sons. This starts as the story of a single man with no strings attached, but as it develops it increasingly focuses on family. It was modeled on 1930s and 1940s Saturday movie matinee fare for children that Spielberg and George Lucas (as co-originator and coproducer) watched on TV in the 1950s—Pauline Kael called this being "hooked on the crap" of childhood (1981, 134). These are not films for small children, however; as the franchise develops, they become more "adult" in some ways, which has the contrary effect of rendering the eponymous hero more of a child. In the series' first outing, *Raiders of the Lost Ark* (1981), Indy is an independent, free man, unencumbered by family; by *Indiana Jones and the Last Crusade* (1989), he is very much a son; and by *Indiana Jones and the Kingdom of the Crystal Skull* (2008), he is a feckless/failing but ultimately redeemed father (the film even ends with a wedding).

The first title was received as popcorn entertainment, with little room for characterization or more serious personal or political questions. "The actors are mostly just bodies carrying pieces of plot around," observed Kael again (1981, 133), while David Denby was cuttingly clear: "There are no real people in the work of Lucas and Spielberg" (1981, 70). The subsequent three Spielberg-directed films went some way toward complicating this. Narratively, the stories move their eponymous college professor–adventurer hero away from youth, since they are loosely chronological, and because Harrison Ford has stayed in the role, aging before our eyes (although James Mangold's *Dial of Destiny* uses *de*-aging technology to make him youthful again in flashback scenes). At the same time, they become progressively focused on Indiana's positioning in and for the family.[10]

Horror-inflected content also moved *Indiana Jones and the Temple of Doom* into a higher classification bracket, edging the franchise upwards (in terms of audience age) as it incarnates the "family adventure film"—a loose New Hollywood genre aimed at adults as well as older children (see Krämer 2006). In the United States, *Temple of Doom* was part of the argument that resulted in the Motion Picture Association of America creating the PG-13 category (an argument persists that the film would have garnered an R rating had family-friendly Spielberg's name not been attached to it). In the United Kingdom, it received a PG, but only after numerous changes were made to its sometimes ghoulish imagery. The British Board of Film Classification (BBFC) faced difficulties in the 1980s with family films that were also part of a franchise (Bond, the *Star Wars* films, and the *Indiana Jones* films), due to an established audience that already included children expecting to be able to consume the next iteration in these popular series as a matter of course, whatever the content (see Barber 2012, 121–122). When that content becomes more adult, this is a problem both for young audiences and for the franchise. James Ferman, then BBFC chief examiner, said that the version of *Indiana Jones and the Temple of Doom* that was originally sent to the board for classification would even struggle to get a 15 rating, and would more likely receive an 18. For a family adventure film, this would have been disastrous and suggested a mismatch between content and projected (child-inclusive) market. The case study on the BBFC website states that UK distributor "UIP worked closely with the BBFC to implement the changes noted in the cuts list to achieve a PG, with James Ferman even travelling to Los Angeles to work with the producers of the film as part of the process. With the amendments made the BBFC classified the film PG in June 1984."[11] This was around the time the BBFC changed its name from British Board of Film Censors to the British Board of Film Classification, and what *Temple of Doom* experienced was clearly a form of censorship in order to protect a young audience and target the most profitable classification band. However, Spielberg has since said that he regrets *Temple of Doom*'s horror effects. In the United Kingdom at least, classification of family fare must take into account the likelihood that images would upset children, and Spielberg accepted, in a TV interview, that he would not allow children of ten and under to see the film (Harmetz 1984, C12). Part of the problem was clearly that, as Spielberg and Lucas said in a joint statement, "A story with children in jeopardy is going to get more emotional reaction than a story with Indiana Jones battling Nazis" (quoted by Harmetz 1984, C12). Children in jeopardy is less likely to be (what adults consider to be) appropriate subject matter for children in the audience. David Denby noted in his review, "At the preview I attended, a boy sitting behind me, perhaps eight years old, whimpered through the whole movie" (1984, 72). These are clearly not the tears of children grieving the departure of *E.T.*

Raiders is a swashbuckling romp about the American archaeologist's swag grab of other nations' treasures, which now shows definite signs of age and worrying racial bias. Indiana's path around the globe is marked by the franchise's trademark "red line" animation, with journeys represented by moving lines crossing antiquated colonial-era maps. The world of these maps is that of imperial rule or demarcated difference, across which Indiana is free to traverse. Multiple crowd scenes that designate "natives" of Nepal, Egypt, and a nonspecified South American location as biddable subordinates or dangerous "others" suggest infantilization of the subaltern. The only actual children to feature are a gaggle of Egyptian street kids surrounding Indiana when he himself is surrounded by armed enemies, who then must lower their weapons and release him so as not to harm the children ("Next time it'll take more than children to save you," threatens Indiana's dastardly adversary). In this fleeting scene, North African children effectively function as a human shield to get the white adventurer out of trouble, with no narrative justification given for why they treat him as such a hero. It is as if the writers (even such experienced hands as Lawrence Kasdan, penning the screenplay, and George Lucas and Philip Kaufman, originating the story) simply ran out of ideas and brought in the cute kids as a last resort to move the plot on. A small baby-like monkey also latches on to Indiana and his entourage and is able to perform a Nazi salute like some tiny monstrous infant. And, like the street urchins, the child-monkey saves Indiana, though at the same time sacrificing himself (he eats poisoned dates meant for his new master).

The next film, the prequel *Indiana Jones and the Temple of Doom* (1984), which is set in 1935 (*Raiders* was set in 1936), was received as significantly more racist, and Spielberg has since spoken against it. It is, however, also more interested in children and family than its predecessor—not that this redeems it any. Indiana, his child sidekick Short Round (2023 Oscar winner Ke Huy Quan, also known as Jonathan Ke Quan), and showgirl Willie Scott (Kate Capshaw, later to be Spielberg's wife) escape the peril of the customary prologue sequence and find themselves in rural India, where they are surrounded by the pleading, praying hands of a multitude of villagers. Here at least Indiana shows some cultural sensitivity, speaking to them in Sinhala and chastising Westernized Willie for her lack of respect. The village boys have all been stolen and enslaved in a temple, overseen by a child maharaja; the hero is able to free the boys (there is a telling sequence in which he beneficently releases their chains) and return them to their parents. The most reprehensible scenes of the film feature a Kali-focused death

FIGURE 20 Ke Huy Quan delivers *Indiana Jones and the Temple of Doom*'s standout performance as surrogate son Short Round.

cult, including crazed worshippers who carry out human sacrifice. India refused to host the shoot because of the problematic content of the script, so the village and temple sequences were shot in Sri Lanka.

The one redeeming aspect of *Temple of Doom* remains Ke Huy Quan's remarkably naturalistic performance as Indiana's feisty young friend Short Round (figure 20), whose family was killed, we are told, when the Japanese bombed Shanghai, and Indiana "caught him" (and semi-adopted him) when the boy attempted pickpocketing. Of course, we know that the relationship will not last, since, though made three years earlier, *Raiders of the Lost Ark* is set a year after *Temple of Doom*, by which time the child has gone. Still, the film's primary relationship is Indiana with Short Round. Willie is an interloper, a far less street-smart third member; the trio never quite become the film's surrogate mom, dad, and baby, as the man-and-boy buddy partnership precedes the arrival of the woman. It is Short Round who rescues Indiana after the Kali cult has drugged him and forced him to function as one of their followers; Short Round tells his father figure that he loves him (and this, after the delirious Indiana has hit the child). The declaration brings Indy back to himself, though he does not reciprocate. Of Short Round, Kael felt that "a good case could be made for his being the true (and invulnerable) hero of the adventure" (1984, 104).

Short Round was Quan's first role; he did not know who Spielberg and Lucas were when he was cast at the age of twelve and had never seen any of their films.[12] He was not allowed to watch himself on-screen for the whole of the shoot, all the better to facilitate a naturalistic performance. "Steven and George purposely did it that way, so I could just be myself and not worry about being on camera," he has said in interview as an adult. "In fact, I was never allowed to watch playback. I shot the entire movie without ever looking at myself on screen, and the very first time I saw the movie was the LA premiere at Mann's Chinese Theater" (Goh 2022). This enforced unselfconsciousness certainly worked for the performance, but it put the child actor in a rather different workplace category than his adult peers and was a strange introduction to screen acting. Quan subsequently became an established child actor, later appearing in the ensemble of children in the Spielberg-produced *The Goonies* and in some TV roles. As an adult he graduated from the University of Southern California's filmmaking program and worked in action choreography and as assistant director to Wong Kar-Wai. But he only returned to acting much later, with an acclaimed performance in *Everything Everywhere All at Once* (2022). It was during the awards season promotion for this film that he gave Spielberg credit for a visionary approach to diverse casting, despite the racist reputation of *Temple of Doom*. "We're talking about something that was done almost 40 years ago," he said in late 2022. "It was a different time. It's so hard to judge something so many years later. . . . I really don't have anything negative to say about it" (Lee 2022). Cultural relativity and historical context may be moot points in relation to this film, but clearly the work he got as an Asian child actor was initiated by Spielberg favoring him. The director "was the first person to put an Asian face in a Hollywood blockbuster," Quan argues. "Short Round is funny, he's courageous, he saves Indy's ass. That was a rarity then. For many years after that, we were back to square one" (Lee 2022). We have seen how many child actors have, as he puts it, "an expiration date," but the young actor was also negotiating being Asian American (he was born in Vietnam of Chinese parents, and emigrated to the United States via a Hong Kong refugee camp). After the success of *Temple of Doom*, he "thought the road moving forward would be easy. Boy, was I wrong. Then, being an Asian actor in the late 1980s and early 1990s was even more difficult." These perspectives are not given to redeem *Temple of Doom*, but the story of racism, stereotyping, and also opportunity that Ke Huy Quan encountered as a child actor, both on and off the screen, is more complicated and contradictory than can be pinned to this single film, which for the actor was a positive production experience.[13]

Indiana Jones and the Last Crusade consolidates and crystallizes child-adult relationships by making Indiana the child—not as a minor, but identified as such in relation to his father. At first the father figure is elusive. Über-archaeologist Professor Henry Jones (Sean Connery) has disappeared while leading a quest to find the Holy Grail, the subject of his life's work. Indiana is set the job of tracking Henry down, though it is clear that the father has been "missing" from the son's life for far longer: they have not talked for twenty years, and in a brief flashback vignette of the boy Indy (played by River Phoenix) trying to engage with his father, his emotionally unavailability is evident. Henry is soon found in an Austrian castle, a prisoner of the Nazis, but how the pair escape, meet Hitler, find the Grail, and survive the dramatic finale is not as significant for the film—or the way in which it was received and identified with Spielberg's own biography—as the relationship between Indy and Henry. On first meeting, Henry calls Indy "Junior," and though Indy initially responds, "Yes, sir!," his usual response is "Don't call me Junior!"

We learn that the son's name is in fact Henry Jones Jr., and Indiana is just a nickname taken from a pet dog (more animal and child conflation). Though he retains "Jones," Indiana has cast off the paternal nomenclature and refuses the diminutive of Junior. Some of this is explained in a central exchange in which Indiana (hardly the man of action who swaggers through *Raiders*) lays out his decades-old festering childhood grievances: not only was his father never "there for him," but he "taught me was that I was less important than people who'd been dead for 500 years in another country." Henry gives a different perspective on this, claiming that his son only became "interesting" when he was older, and that neglect was a gift. "Actually I was a wonderful father," retorts Henry. "Did I ever tell you to eat up, go to bed, wash your ears, do your homework? No, I respected your privacy, and I taught you self-reliance." This tough—indeed, near-absent—love does not come from the handbook of good fathering as authored by Spielberg. To be fully redeemed Henry must show emotion, which he only does when he thinks his son has perished over a cliff. The film was received as a more "grown-up" narrative than the first two in the franchise: the headline of Nancy Griffin's profile of the director around this release is "Manchild in the Promised Land," with a strapline reading "Like Indiana Jones, Steven Spielberg has improved with age. But can he incorporate this newfound adulthood into his movies?" (1989, 86), a perspective that dominated Spielberg reception through the 1980s and into the 1990s—indeed, even beyond his "serious" work and Oscar wins. But why should it be that being son to father is a more "grown-up" storyline than being surrogate father to unrelated son (*Temple of Doom*) or having no observable family at all (*Raiders*)? And what happens to the "adulting" narrative when Indy becomes a full parent?

The period between *Last Crusade* and *Indiana Jones and the Kingdom of the Crystal Skull* (2008) saw a shift in Spielberg's work, a new critical acclaim following *Schindler's List* in 1993, and a number of films that presented a take on failing, absent, or surrogate fathering. The child in the family became more mobile, was frequently biologically unconnected, or else was estranged. Indiana's relationship with Short Round in *Temple of Doom* was both buddy and familial, but the later surrogate/biological parenting of *Crystal Skull*, which finds the older Indiana in a quarrelsome but paternal relationship with Mutt (played by twenty-one-year-old Shia LaBeouf) is soon properly validated when Indy discovers that he is actually Mutt's genetic father after all. A scene early in the film seems to suggest a return to the single, free hero status of Indiana that began the series. The 1950s-set *Crystal Skull* commences in a secret military location reminiscent of White Sands, with Indiana landing in an atomic test location—a fabricated small town that looks like a parody of suburbanized tract house 1950s Americana. Model moms, dads, and kids are arrayed like shop-front dummies in kitchens, living rooms, and yards in preparation for a test atomic blast, an exercise to find out what happens to small-town America under nuclear attack. As the test bomb is detonated, this synthetic domestic idyll is vaporized. Indiana manages to escape not just the bomb but also the trappings of domestication in a lead-lined fridge. He then commences the customary quest, free of family encumbrance (a photo on Indy's desk reveals that father, Henry, has passed away).

But this solo life does not last long: he is soon inveigled into a relationship with biker boy Mutt, which leads him back to Mutt's mother, Marion Ravenwood (Karen Allen), who was the love interest of *Raiders of the Lost Ark*. Mutt's real name—Henry Jones—is Indy's, and also his grandfather's; Marion has preserved the patronymic despite Indiana's abandonment of her before their marriage. Mutt, it emerges, was conceived soon after the timeline of *Raiders*, with Indiana subsequently cast as an absconding father before he even knew he was a father at all. Late fatherhood is focused through thoughts about aging and abandonment: Jim Broadbent's Stanforth opines to Indy, "We seem to have reached the age where life stops giving us things and starts taking them away." Like father, like son: Indy steps up to the role adopted by Henry in *Last Crusade* with history-repeating recriminations. "Why don't you stick around, Junior?" asks Indy of his son, to which Mutt replies, "I don't know—why didn't you, Dad?" As soon as fatherhood is affirmed, it is failing but it also becomes a form of recognition to be passed between men in a dynasty. "Somewhere your grandpa is laughing," quips Indiana ruefully. It is Mutt who gives his father the most ageist grief, inviting him onto his motorbike with "Get on, Gramps," and remarking backhandedly, "For an old man you ain't bad in a fight. What are you, like, eighty?" And then the film ends with the marriage that was scheduled and abandoned decades ago. The older couple beam like their younger selves, and paternity is formalized. This shift from son position to father position between *Last Crusade* and *Crystal Skull* is, then, a formation, within one franchise, of male familialism that is also expressed across Spielberg's work through a variety of genres. Of course, Indiana is biologically connected to Henry and Mutt, but they are strangers first. Estrangement, or literal strangeness (he did not even know he had a son), is itself a kind of fragile male bond, a commonality between nongenetic men, even as the men themselves seem to run away from the very notion of family as fast as they can. So, as children must go their own way, parent and child functions are decoupled from biology. Here paternity (usually surrogate) fares better than genetically connected fathering.

Spielberg's Chosen Families

Emphasizing the dark side of Spielberg, James Kendrick traces a drama of family fragmentation across this body of films (2014, 190), but I find the opposite: where there is no family, it comes into being—imaginatively assembled, often from nongenetic parts. Viktor's new kinship in *The Terminal* is a positive rendition of alternative bonds. Motivated to travel to New York in a final quest for his late father, he must find an alternative family in the limbo of the airport terminal itself because "Uncle Sam" is so hostile to him as an alien other. With Viktor miles from home and in a nation (Spielberg's) that will not welcome him, his airport friends—blue-collar workers, people of color, transitory workers—overtly declare, "We're your family now." Viktor's surrogate community does not arise from family failure—it is not the result of breakdown, failure, or absence of biological parents, but this is unusual in Spielberg. More commonly, far from endorsing a suburban dream through the nostalgic glow of its young inhabitants' lives, family is a receptacle of failure and loss, and a troubled environment. But children are resilient, finding their way into other relationships that function alternatively—or better—as "family." These are queerer, nongenetic alliances, suggesting the persistence of care rather than the ubiquity of a dominant patriarchal nuclear structure. Just as his troubled children lend themselves to interpretations of idealization, so Spielberg's families disintegrate and re-form themselves in a different array.

Men are usually the instigators of breakdown—Spielberg's dysfunctional mothers are rarer (Williams 2017). If the message of *Hook* is that finding one's child self gives a route through to authentic and loving paternity, it is not borne out by other Spielberg stories of fathering. Lacking or problematic relationships between fathers and offspring are, then, stories of adults who are centrally defined by their problematic relationship with their children. Why else would Spielberg bother to show, albeit fleetingly, the family David Mann leaves behind when most of *Duel* is spent on the road? Frank Abagnale Sr.'s failure in *Catch Me If You Can* functions solely as the narrative spur for his son's compensatory exploits. In a similar gesture, Spielberg takes the grand political events covered by *Lincoln* (like *Munich*) and subjects them to interior familial motivations. *Lincoln* consistently counters antislavery political struggle and triumph with the president's wife's maternal despair and their sons' disquiet. Lincoln may be a successful father of the nation, but this is at the expense of his role as father to one dead son and two living, one of whom wants to risk his life fighting in the war while the other suffers for his father's absences.

Despite the historically significant public events that protagonists such as Lincoln or *Munich*'s Avner influence, family remains a key reference point, and public impact is qualified by private paternity. *Catch Me If You Can*, *Lincoln*, and *Munich* are all based on real events: the specter of the child let down by the father inflects historical drama with melodrama. Children also learn resourcefulness from this, and (lest that sound like a Pollyanna compensation) it is an "adulting" process that is usually painfully hard-won. Lincoln's tricksy conclusion situates the president's young child Tad (played by thirteen-year-old Gulliver McGrath) squarely in the midst of its culminating trauma, while simultaneously separating and isolating him. The final scene is of a theatral production, which we imagine to be the one at the famous Ford's Theatre, where Lincoln is about to be assassinated. But then an announcement interrupts the performance, indicating that at *another* theater—Ford's Theatre—the president has been shot. Having spent much of the film alongside Lincoln as he grapples with politics and history while failing to be the father his children and his wife think he should be, the film's point of view now switches to the perspective of the *son*, who is watching another performance away from his father. *Lincoln* thus ends with the image of the child hearing the public announcement of his father's death in a public setting while having the most private of connections to the news. Instead of being in Ford's Theatre to witness the most famous plot points of Lincoln's story, Spielberg has chosen to position this section of the film with the distraught child, layering the most radical fatherly absence onto the sequence of paternal loss demonstrated throughout. While much of this book is preoccupied with child's-point-of-view films, some of the works discussed here might be called "father's-point-of-view films." In *Lincoln*, the son functions to underline this for much of the film—until this final scene, when it shifts back to a more familiar Spielbergian perspective with the child.

In his discussion of *Empire of the Sun*, Lester Friedman points out the key changes that transform Jamie's father from Ballard's book into Spielberg's film via Stoppard's script. The literary John Graham is heroic and courageous, while the filmic Graham is cowardly and self-serving—not a predictable translation given Ballard's penchant for dystopian darkness, and Spielberg's sunnier reputation. While Ballard's Graham provides a strong example to his son, Spielberg's Graham fails his son, causing Friedman to conclude that viewers "who compare the book to the film can readily see how the director altered this figure according to his own persistent pattern of weak or absent biological fathers" (2006, 201).[14] In Spielberg's film, Graham's failure is so fundamental that it ultimately causes the breakdown of his family: though it is Jamie's mother who lets go of the boy's hand, losing him in the crowd, the father has already led his family into peril. In turn, Jamie becomes a lost boy who must find community where he can, oscillating between variable father figures—the Fagin-like Basie (John Malkovich), the positive mentor Dr. Rawlins (Nigel Havers), and the benign but soon absent Mr. Victor (Peter Gale). None of these is "enough," but cumulatively they function as midwives in the birth of a different Jamie. Across Spielberg's work, numerous young adults and adolescents are positioned relationally through father figures—the junior soldiers mentored by senior officer figures in *War Horse*, for example. And though *Saving Private Ryan* is a film about an imperiled biological family (three out of four sons dead) whose remaining son is rescued by the military, substitute father-son and fraternal relationships more securely replace genetic ones, standing in for blood relations. Spielberg repeatedly returns to the military "Band of Brothers," even referencing this in *The Fabelmans* when young Sammy directs the teenage cast of his war film, itself an exact re-creation of his real teen film *Escape to Nowhere*: "Your platoon, they've been wiped out. These guys, they're your family!" It is as if, in a male-dominated genre such as the war film, the inflection of melodrama that Spielberg brings insists on family as a prime metaphor for connecting men. Given that he cannot help showing how poor men can be at actual fathering, he rescues them through other bonds. This is an unusual twist of genre, and story, for male protagonists and audiences. Of course, adult males come to parent unrelated children in other genres too—Dr. Alan Grant's/Sam Neill's turn to fatherhood in *Jurassic Park* is more secure than John Hammond's/Richard Attenborough's grandfathering. Biological fathers also behave with complex compassion, especially in Spielberg's later films: in *The Fabelmans,* the father is at his best when he lets his wife go and allows the family to split. Family, like children, is then often not what it seems in Spielberg.

Afterword

The Fabelmans

A *Time* magazine cover story from 1985 laid out many of the familiar autobiographical riffs this book has explored in the story of Spielberg's relationship to, and representation of, children and childhood: that his films are his children, that each new film "is like another chapter in the autobiography of a modern Peter Pan," even that his name translates into German as "play mountain," which is exactly what his supposed alter ego in *Close Encounters* does. "Each picture," writes the author of the profile, Richard Corliss, "has allowed him to remake his own childhood, then to generalize it so it touches millions of once-again kids" (1985). On December 5, 2022, another *Time* cover feature made Spielberg once again the story, through an interview sparked by his remarkable remaking of family in the form of *The Fabelmans*, which plays some different notes. Though generically distinct, the film has a particular relationship with *E.T.* read as a divorce story, but, as Stephanie Zacharek points out in this profile, "The children who connected with *E.T.* at the time of its release 40 years ago are now the grown-ups to whom *The Fabelmans* is speaking" (2022). Indeed, in *The Fabelmans* the director inhabits a new tone but exposes threads that have been there all along if we would only trouble to look.

Young Sammy Fabelman is taken to see Cecil B. De Mille's film *The Greatest Show on Earth* (1952) as was Spielberg on his first cinema outing, and this sets rolling an obsession with filmmaking as both escape and therapy, nurtured by a family that is by turns dysfunctional, loving, and tempestuous. Sammy's mother, Mitzi (Michelle Williams, the image of Spielberg's mother, Leah Adler, even wearing Leah's own jewelry for the shoot), was, like Leah, a concert pianist who gave up her artistic career to bring up her children. "But she raised four kids,"

Spielberg said in an extended discussion with Judd Apatow for the Writers Guild of America East. "We stopped her from allowing her dream to come true" (Apatow 2023). Unlike previous images of mothers and fathers who fail their children in Spielberg's films, *The Fabelmans* is remarkable for its late-life understanding of the restrictions that motherhood enforces. It also boasts a renewed observation of paternal compassion, borne out here by Paul Dano as Burt, a pioneering electronics whizz and computer innovator, rational and scientific in contrast with the artistic and pleasure-focused Mitzi. The family is frequently joined by Bennie, Burt's best friend and (as we eventually discover) Mitzi's lover. Here, then, Spielberg revisits his parents' unconventional dynamic: in the film as in life, his mother is "let go" by his father so she can be free to marry the man she loves.

This is a malleable family structure: Spielberg described his home, which is rendered pretty much verbatim in the film, as "a unique sort of strange story," with the third adult seemingly always there: "We thought it was natural to have kind of like two dads" (Apatow 2023).[1] *The Fabelmans* is described as semi-autobiographical, but it is closer to the actual details of Spielberg's life than this phrase suggests. Biographical sources show that the characters look like, act like, and in at least one instance have the same name as their real-life models. The films that teenage Sammy makes are replications of the actual films the teenage Spielberg made with his scout troupe and school friends. If public discourse around Spielberg, family, and children has had him remaking his own story over and again, never quite letting go of unresolved childhood scenes, this self-mythologizing film was reviewed, and indeed playfully promoted by Spielberg, as "exposure therapy" (Breznican 2022), or a $40 million exercise in creative autopsychotherapy.[2]

Sammy as a child is played first by young Mateo Zoryan and then, as a teenager, by nineteen-year-old Gabriel LaBelle, himself a veteran of the child acting profession. Familiar riffs from a long career directing children are more refashioned than revisited, and it is the child's working relationship with filmmaking and his choices around creative sacrifice that come to the fore. Sammy must learn to be ruthless; his uncle counsels him to choose art over family in a way that Mitzi as a mother could not. Growing up in this lively petri dish, the young Sammy must witness adult truths, but crucially he only recognizes these when he sees them through the lens. When assembling footage of a family camping trip that has Bennie in tow, he recognizes, after the fact and through his editing viewfinder, evidence of the illicit love affair he had missed with his own unalloyed eyes. He confronts his mother with what he sees, an act that is both guilty confession (I saw you, I was looking) and angry attack (Look what I saw! Look what you've done to me!). As Michael Schulman (2022) pointedly observes, this is mostly an act of power and vengeance against the mother: "All this time, we thought we were dealing with Peter Pan. It turns out that Spielberg was Prince

Hamlet." Mitzi is childish, admitting to selfishness when finally choosing lover over husband, and inflicting the astonishing burden of requiring her child to withhold the secret of her infidelity from his sisters and father, which Spielberg says he had also done. What transpires is a strange complicity between the mother and the son who now knows too much: on accepting one of the two Golden Globes the film won, Spielberg said, "I've been hiding from this story since I was 17 years old" (Mondello 2023); as Judd Apatow aptly observes, "And that's enough to screw up your whole childhood." The question remains: *Has he* been hiding? Or has this all been hiding in plain sight? What of *E.T.*? What of *Catch Me If You Can*? What of the numerous variations on family, and of lovingly rendered parental failure, that this book has explored?

In *The Fabelmans*, Spielberg also hands the Peter Pan mantle back to the woman—and remember that it is mostly women who have historically played the role of Pan onstage. "My mom always referred to herself as Peter Pan, the little girl who never wanted to grow up," he said in another *Fabelmans* promotional interview. "She loved being in our lives as our friend more than our mom. She befriended us more than parented us" (Zacharek 2022). Sammy throws himself into filmmaking as a life obsession, and so close is the child filmmaker to the director of the film (and so crystalline is the line from biographical detail to filmic action) that the director answers all questions on the publicity campaign not through addressing filmic character and narrative but with further self-revelation. He attributes his subsequent faith in the ability of film to supplant the truth of real life to the child's realization of adult sexuality, revealed only through the editor's lens: "What's weird for me is that I didn't believe the truth that my eyes were telling me. I only believed what the film was telling me. And so that became my truth for many things. If the film told me the truth, I would believe it to be a fact" (Zacharek 2022). Whether or not this actually happened (Spielberg's public self-analysis sometimes runs to myth), was there ever a more resonant cinematic primal scene? Learning sex from cinema not through content but through optics (figure 21)?

Something of this has been prefigured in the representation of childhood throughout Spielberg's cinema. The films have told us that this is what a (usually boy) child is, and this has become a truth of childhood. That which is seen on-screen is glued by the emotion of superb child performances to a collective Western sensibility of what it is to be a child, even if we dig down and find these very representations to be wildly troubling and contradictory. The episodes narrated by *The Fabelmans* are familiar to anyone with even a cursory knowledge of Spielberg's origins story: a life-altering first encounter with cinema, a developing obsession with filmmaking technology, parlaying storytelling prowess to fit in as a Jew in Waspish Midwestern suburbia and high school hostility, the buzz of adulation from live audiences, the fallout of divorce. It is also a love letter to his parents, shifting the balance of sympathy in favor of the father, who in *E.T.*

FIGURE 21 Cinema mediates adult truths to Sammy Fabelman (Gabriel LaBelle) in *The Fabelmans.*

had simply absconded ("he's in Mexico with Sally") but is now understood as self-sacrificial and inspirational, providing the child with technological power even as the mother denotes her restless artistry.

These are the familiar building blocks of the director's publicly avowed biography, and it is not surprising that *The Fabelmans* would stick to these narrative beats. The surprising elements that this swan song–toned story delivers gather together many of the odd strands evident through Spielberg's work, which cuts against all those historical charges that he reinforces conservative notions of the family and delivers mawkish views of the child: a nonconventional family structure including a more benign view of family making, breaking, and remaking itself; children who are driven and ruthless as well as questing and creative, but are seldom sentimental, least of all about themselves; mother and father figures who are neither idealized nor vilified, and through which a politics of social change is woven.

When I began work on this book, I approached Spielberg's office requesting an interview, as my own film analytic method on other projects has turned to oral history, particularly as a way to illuminate untold stories. It may seem that, after more than half a century as the world's most famous filmmaker with copious interview materials in the public realm, there is nothing untold about Steven Spielberg, and yet another work-focused conversation would be superfluous. I was not interested in probing personal issues; I hoped instead to garner more information than was available in the public sphere about how he directs children. After sending the request via several different avenues, I received a polite rebuff from his people, stating that Spielberg was working on his own project about his childhood and would not be contributing to my discussion of the child in his films. It is now clear that this project was *The Fabelmans*, or else an early exploration that formed the origins of *The Fabelmans*, or perhaps a larger canvas of self-analytic work of which *The Fabelmans* became one creative avenue of exploration. There may be more Fabelman families in the drawer marked "drafts" that will appear before he is done, fleshing out other facets of the fragmentary memory archive that forms his writerly and directorial source pool. It may be that Spielberg emerges as the perfect case for the next iteration of psychoanalytic screen interpretation not as subject-to-be-analyzed through those surrogate self-portraits but as a coinvestigator in a memory field that is originally only his, but which has itself been inflected by highly public yet still partial plays on childhood. Who else has been able to revisit these personal scenarios across five decades (and counting), aided by such generous budgets, technological prowess, and thespian talent?

The opportunity to fantasize and dramatize oft-repeated (if already selected) biographical vignettes and re-render them for mass public entertainment is unprecedented, but it is also weirder than it seems. Spielberg's childhood, pitched across the highly personal and the highly publicized, is no longer only his own. The private made so public, and so profitable, may seem in this case to be a subjective realm, entirely emptied out through sheer overillumination, and therefore unworthy of further conversation. Yet this in itself is both interesting and unique: while it is common for an artist to revisit their own stories across a life, it is rare for someone to do this quite so visibly, using real children to playact the episodes, in the process building a formation of childhood that seems to have become something of a cultural given, a set of "truths" about what the child is, with an avowed desire to connect to "all of our" incarnations of childhood. Separating out what is the mere marketable story for a film release, and what is singular, complex, and perhaps bizarre in this public psychodrama formed of child players pinned to some enormous historical, fantastical, and family canvases has been the subject of this book—but there is further work to be done.

Of course, childhood has never been "one thing" here—by virtue of the performers playing it out, and the differently gendered and genred, historical and narrative inflections of each film. Each child role is a particular iteration of something differently understood and half repeated across time, across films, with each child actor's interpretations taking the story in a direction only partly shaped by their director. The copious public material signaling the autobiographical seam running through even the most unlikely of popular cultural offerings, telling a story of an auteur profile built in the public realm, is a shared narrative partly trotted out by the director in publicity interviews, partly told by the critics in career analysis, but also in no small way performed and nuanced by Spielberg's young actors. Their own creative input and career agendas have of course shaped the result, and I have tried to credit children with originality and skill and independent impulse, even when enveloped by the apparatus of monolithic productions they are charged to "carry." This is compounded when their fellow adult actors have failed to credit their professionalism, creativity, or expertise or else have attributed it to the director's preternatural skill with children, or to the freaky overreaching of too-early adultization on the part of children themselves. Even in *The Fabelmans*, when the young Zoryan performs that small viewer of *The Greatest Show on Earth* and then re-creates the train wreck scene on camera as a novice child filmmaker, Spielberg directs the scene but cannot entirely control the child within it, neither himself as memory nor the small boy who bears him out. The father gets the film's first line—"Mommy and Daddy will be right next to you"—tutoring the small boy on his first cinema experience. But the father cannot "have" the boy's experience for him, just as no parent can "have" their children's pain for them. Nor can Spielberg "be" all the children in his frame. Children are active actors—in the most driven sense of the word. They are not puppets. This book has tried to give Steven Spielberg's childhood visions back to the children who have incarnated them. Within Spielberg's cinematic childhoods, children themselves have enabled the emergence of something far stranger, more complex, and powerfully child-originated.

Acknowledgments

This book has been through a long gestation, during which I presented versions of chapters at numerous university colloquiums and conferences, eliciting lively discussion, for which I am very grateful. Academic friends have helped me in so many ways and made this a better book. Many thanks to Murray Pomerance for his unfailing interest and impeccable critical judgment. Michael Hammond, James Jordan, Lester Friedman, and Peter Kramer gave sound perspectives and encouragement. I have benefited greatly from the input of researchers and Spielberg specialists in a wider context, and those who commissioned me to write shorter publications on Spielberg's work or led forums in which I participated: Nigel Morris, Michael Lawrence, and Matt Melia. I would also like to thank two of my graduate students for their engagement across the common ground between this and their own projects on children and film (Amanda Stevenson) and 1980s U.S. science fiction and practical effects (Jared Robinson). The editorial team at Rutgers University Press, particularly Lesley Mitchner and Nicole Solano, have been wise and encouraging support. Thanks also to Helen Wheeler, Daryl Brower, and Susan Ecklund for meticulous work on the manuscript, and to Tim Clifford for hard work on the index, and Georgia Williams, who gave valuable help at earlier stages.

Finally, Mark Kermode: you have been the most incredible support, an incisive reader of drafts, and an inspirational and ever-patient companion to this work and to me. Thank you. This book is also for you.

An early version of the discussion of Henry Thomas's audition tape, which now appears in chapter 2, was first published as "The Tears of Henry Thomas," *Screen* 53, no. 4 (Winter 2012): 459–464. An early version of the analysis of the dinner table scene in *A.I.* appeared as "The Laughter of Robots," in *The Last Laugh: Dark Humors of Cinema*, ed. Murray Pomerance (Detroit: Wayne State University Press, 2013), 209–222.

Notes

Introduction

1 Thomas Becon, "The Demands of Holy Scripture," written in 1550, in Becon (1844), 607.

2 James Gallagher reports that the first baby born using the DNA of three people was in Jordan in 2016 ("Baby Born from Three People's DNA in UK First," BBC, May 9, 2023, https://www.bbc.co.uk/news/science-environment-65538866).

3 Despite spawning a TV series with the word as a title (http://www.imdb.com/title/tt4033780/), "adultish" has not entered common currency but is useful for this discussion.

4 The "new sociology of childhood," arguably instigated by Ariès's *Centuries of Childhood* but intensifying through the 1990s and into the present century, is addressed by A. James, Jenks, and Prout (1998).

5 "Child Actors/Child Stars: Juvenile Performance on Screen, 8th–9th September 2011," David Puttnam Media Centre, University of Sunderland, UK.

6 In *Witness: The Making of Schindler's List*, Franciszek Palowski reports that Spielberg told him "that the only films he considered his personal creations were those like the one he made of his little daughter in front of a TV set—like all those taken by a proud and loving father. His other films are all the result of teamwork—by the director, scriptwriter, production designer, camera crews, and even the people in advertising and promotion" (1999, 24).

Chapter 1 "You Are the Child"

1 The sled was bought along with a call sheet and storyboard from *Citizen Kane* and is now housed at the Academy Museum in Los Angeles. As Spielberg explained in an interview with Ali Plumb, "It was at home for a while, then it was in my office, but I think it really belongs in a museum so everybody can see it" ("Steven Spielberg: Movies That Made Me," BBC iPLAYER, March 28, 2018, https://www.bbc.co.uk/iplayer/episode/p061mx4v/movies-with-ali-plumb-steven-spielberg-movies-that-made-me). See also Michael Juliano, "Here's How These 5 Pieces Ended Up on Display at the Academy Museum," *Time Out*, October 28, 2021, https://www

.timeout.com/los-angeles/news/heres-how-these-5-pieces-ended-up-on-display-at-the-academy-museum-102821.

2 Pomerance wrote in 2008: "Spielberg (still, at 61!) is critically conceptualized as a prodigious 'wunderkind' and, as Lester Friedman has observed . . . , the true Citizen Kane of Hollywood—therefore a freak." Pomerance also wrote, "Spielberg's former wife Amy Irving and a gaggle of his friends including Dan Aykroyd and the late John Candy collaborated on his fortieth birthday to make a film of some thirty minutes length called Citizen Steve. Tightly following the syntax and shot structures of Orson Welles's Citizen Kane (1941), the film lovingly spoofed an enigmatic czar of Hollywood" (2008).

3 The final sequence of *Raiders of the Lost Ark* and the first sequence of *Kingdom of the Crystal Skull* even reference Kane's cavernous concluding warehouse.

4 Orson Welles rather petulantly claimed that Spielberg's sled was a fake, however: see Brady 1990, 577–578.

5 Spielberg continued, "When you look at Rosebud you don't think of fast dollars, fast sequels and remakes. This to me says that movies of my generation had better be good."

6 In return, Spielberg has said that Truffaut "in real life was a child of heart. . . . He had a real aspect of himself that was like a child." Childishness was, Spielberg has attested, one of the qualities he looked for in casting his adult actors in *Close Encounters*. From *Steven Spielberg: 30 Years of Close Encounters*, written, directed and produced by Laurent Bouzereau. This promotional special feature was included in the 2007 DVD rerelease but is also available on YouTube at https://www.youtube.com/watch?v=_1JoYLdZ_II.

7 Spielberg's purchased sled was, of course, the one that got away. Three were made, and two perished in the flames: the first in a take that was not used in the film, the second in the take that concludes the final film. Because that second take was successful, the third sled was spared to survive into movie posterity.

8 Though McBride reports that "there were at least a dozen other young filmmakers besides Steven who were busy making their own amateur movies in town on a regular basis" (2010, 76).

9 Spielberg was also interviewed about his filmmaking by another local TV show, McBride quotes Spielberg's father as saying, "He was sixteen or seventeen, but he handled it just like he'd been doing it for years" (2010, 76).

10 McBride (2010, 70–108) provides a comprehensive account of Spielberg's early filmmaking up to the age of eighteen; see also Steve Poster's extensive interview with Spielberg in *American Cinematographer* in February 1978, where he discusses this early work (Poster 2000). I will turn to *The Fabelmans*' rendition of this phase in the afterword of this book.

11 The connection between the young filmmakers is even more circular, with the adult Spielberg directly drawing a teenage would-be auteur Abrams to Spielberg's own early work. Abrams "was profiled in a newspaper article about his participation in a young film-makers' festival in Los Angeles. In a coincidence straight out of a movie, Spielberg read the article and hired Abrams and a friend to repair some 8mm reels that he had knocking around from his own teenage movie-making days" (Puckrik 2011).

12 One of his high school friends made an observation about Spielberg's focus as a teenage filmmaker that resonates with some of the points this book makes about the slipperiness of age: though technically a child filmmaker, he was already (as will be said of his child actors later) older than his years: "He is still childlike in the sense that he is still fascinated with magic and a sense of wonder, but he was one of the

least childish fourteen-year-olds I have ever seen. He was very focused, and that's not a fourteen-year-old's characteristic. If anyone I knew was going to make it, I thought he was going to, because he was so driven and committed" (Rick Cook quoted by McBride, 2010, 97).

13 Spielberg's *Raiders of the Lost Ark* (1981) also inspired two other young filmmakers, Chris Strompolos and Eric Zala, to make a shot-for-shot remake of the film during their school vacations between 1982 and 1989. When this came to wider attention in 2003, Spielberg congratulated them. See Windolf 2004, 4–7 for the story up to 2003; in 2015, the story of the boy's filmmaking exploits was itself the subject of the documentary *Raiders!: The Story of the Greatest Fan Film Ever Made* (dir. Jeremy Coon and Tim Skousen).

14 Once he became a father, Spielberg discussed his children's responses to his films on a number of occasions. The child (Max) who closed his eyes at the scary parts of *E.T.* "wants to see *Jaws*," he reported in 1989, "but I won't show it to him. I won't show him anything real violent or scary" (Griffin 1989, 94).

15 This is distinct from legendary 1950s and 1960s exploitation production company AIP's formula for identifying its target youth audience, which it also termed "The Peter Pan Syndrome," and which deems that "a) a younger child will watch anything an older child will watch; b) an older child will not watch anything a younger child will watch; c) a girl will watch anything a boy will watch; d) a boy will not watch anything a girl will watch; therefore: to catch your greatest audience you zero in on the 19-year-old male" Cited by Robin Bean and David Austen in "U.S.A. Confidential," *Films and Filming*, November 1968, and quoted by Thomas Doherty, *Teenagers and Teenpics* (Boston: Unwin-Hyman, 1988), 157. This audience identification was central to the rise of the blockbuster in the 1970s, where Spielberg was a key player; it also impacts on his preference for boy protagonists over girls.

16 McBride (2010, 109–114) covers this initial period at Universal in detail, deploying confused press materials and interviews he conducted with those still alive.

17 "I called her Miss Crawford, and she insisted on calling me Mr Spielberg. I asked her to call me Steven, but she wouldn't; she knew I was just a scared kid, and she was setting an example . . . for the rest of the cast and crew to follow" (Anthony 1982).

18 A lone *L.A. Times* article tried to bring clarity to the situation but only confused the age conundrum further: "It's axiomatic that actors hedge about their ages. What's lesser known is that directors can be equally coy. In 1975 a babyfaced Steven Spielberg got great mileage in the press for landing his first professional directing assignment before he was 21." But this cite records "which would have made him 23. Spielberg, by now 35 by the same records, would not comment" (Goldstone 1981).

19 Famously, Shirley Temple was deprived of a whole year of childhood experiences as those around her falsely aged her down by a year from the age of five onward. She was told only on her twelfth birthday that it was really her thirteenth.

20 In 1976, Robin Wood also reflected on the child in American cinema, in an essay reprinted in his collection *Explorations in Film: Personal Views* (2006, 189–212). Here he links American literature's ubiquitous "figure of the naturally wise child from whom corrupt or sophisticated adults can (and should) learn, and whose moral judgements the reader is encouraged largely to accept" to the child across the history of U.S. cinema.

21 This is from an article from a publication titled *Success: The Magazine for Achievers*, in which Spielberg is named "1982 Achiever of the Year" and says, "I'm more concerned with audience response than with how much money a film makes" ("Extraterrestrial Success," January 1982, 17).

22 In his excoriating critique of Spielberg, Andrew Britton refuses this idea that he straddles the filmmaker-audience divide by virtue of his universalizing youth, on the grounds of money: "He *isn't* out there in the audience being thrilled as he was as a boy, but he wants to be, and he has contrived to become unconscious of why he can't. . . . Steven Spielberg is actually a grown-up man making large amounts of money . . . but he sincerely believes that he is on the edge of his seat with the rest of us, and his simple-mindedness is the sincere expression of a genuine bent: he really wishes that adult life didn't make a difference—though no doubt the money helps" (1986, 33).

23 J. Hoberman's "Good Steven" and "Bad Steven" segregate according to audience effect through a scale of sentiment and sadism, on the one hand "out-Disney[ing] Disney," on the other terrorizing audiences "in the name of fun" (Hoberman 2007, 122; also quoted by Kendrick 2014, 9). This recalls the child filmmaker who, as discussed previously, would terrify his friends in order to film their terror.

24 A comparison might be made with Ed Wood, also a visionary director with recognizable style and thematic consistency, but vilified rather than canonized. Unlike Wood's, Spielberg's films are of course accomplished, lucrative, and Oscar-winning—but the proposition of auteur status is apparently ridiculous enough for a 2002 BFI dossier on auteurism aimed at high school students to begin its section on the director, "Spielberg? Auteur? In the same sentence or breath? Surely not. In box office terms, Steven Spielberg is the most important and influential filmmaker of his generation. But an auteur? Surely such success should preclude inclusion? Where is the evidence?," *Auteur Theory/Auteurs: 16+ Source Guide* (London: BFI National Library, 2002), archived at https://www.scribd.com/doc/25372836/Auteur-theory-auteurs-16-guide.

25 Higonnet notes that nineteenth-century and early twentieth-century women painters were consigned to painting children (1998, 9), and the taint of childhood as a nonserious subject has affected her own work: "My own academic field dismisses the subject of the child as being trivial and sentimental, good only for second-rate minds and perhaps women" (1998, 13).

26 He adds, "Yet it's the women who shove their men into the movie theaters each weekend," suggesting that the woman's picture ambition may be more commercial than feminist.

27 Nigel Morris also discusses the politics of critical responses to Spielberg in the introduction to his impressive 2007 monograph, *The Cinema of Steven Spielberg: Empire of Light*.

28 Kaplan's comments on Dickens, in many ways equivalent to Spielberg in mainstream reach, echo responses to Spielberg: "Dickens' sentimentality is a joy to those who respond to it but an embarrassment to those whose sense of taste and reality it offends" (1987, 7). Though it is not the role of *Steven Spielberg's Children*, exploring the conjunctions and influences between Dickens and Spielberg would be a significant next research step.

29 "The tear-filled worship of sacred sentimentality in Victorian culture came through the philosophy and literature of the moral sentiments that the early Victorians read, studied, and breathed as their childhood air" (Kaplan 1987, 9). Spielberg's relationship to the work of Norman Rockwell (whom he collects) is surely important here, as a foundational set of images linking his 1940s and 1950s childhood back to the morality of a just war inscribed in patriotic images of family and community.

30 In the periodization narrative of Thomas Schatz (1992), the advent of films like *The Exorcist* and *Jaws* effected a transition from auteur-identified "American renaissance" filmmaking to the era of the blockbuster and family adventure film.

31 However, in her illuminating overview, Winfried Herget notes that the word "sentimental" was first used pejoratively in 1780, in a curiously modern sense, to mean a hypocritical person, "faking feelings that are not really there" (1991, 2).

32 Defender of cinematic sentiment Clive Marsh—who identifies it as a quasi-religious experience—notes that the word is used in relation to literature and film to mean that "short cuts are taken, tough and complex situations are oversimplified" (2004, 8).

33 Fred Kaplan cites one contemporary critic of Dickens, who also connects tears to money: "Henry Hallam in 1847 responded to the death of Dickens' Paul Dombey by remarking, 'I am so hardened as to be able to look on it in any light by pure business,' suggesting that Dickens had manipulated the dramatic situation, eliciting from his readers feelings that he himself did not have in order to appeal to a debased popular taste for the purpose of selling more books" (1987, 47).

34 *Oxford English Dictionary*, s.v. "sentiment," https://www.oed.com/dictionary/sentiment_n?tab=meaning_and_use#23615218.

Chapter 2 The Lemonade Stand of Cinema

1 Jasper Rees accuses Spielberg of "deposit[ing] his unmistakable pawprints" on the story, though "there are splendid flourishes that could only come from him: . . . Bradlee's kid making a mint selling lemonade as the paper's top brass set up camp in the editor's home" (2018); Scott Marks writes that "not since *1941* has Spielberg slathered on the comic relief with such a leaden hand. . . . there's an insufferable running gag involving Bradlee's adorable little daughter and a lemonade stand" (2018).

2 All quotes from Weeks, who wrote one of a spate of press items about children being fined for running stands: "If lemonade stands are symbols of the American dream, and if lemonade stands are under attack in the United States, then the American dream is under attack." Weeks cites an enraged mother of a fined child: "The message to kids is, there's no American dream" (2011).

3 The same comparison features in one of many mixed reviews: Marks argues that "the awfulness" of Marina's presence "stands out almost as much as a colorized red dress in a black-and-white movie" (2018). See also Geoffrey Macnab, for whom Marina symbolizes "innocence amid evil," "another little girl here who looks in on the antics of the adults" (2018).

4 Protective legislation differs in the United States on a state-by-state basis but covers areas such as the limitation of children's working hours and the provision of on-set education, and also includes and updates to the Coogan Law: there are differences in its implementation from state to state, which means that productions can target locations that offer more favorable working environments for children. For further information, see "Coogan Law," SAG-AFTRA: Membership & Benefits, https://www.sagaftra.org/membership-benefits/young-performers/coogan-law, accessed February 2025. The 2015 Child Performers Protection Act (https://www.congress.gov/bill/114th-congress/house-bill/3383/text) attempted to close loopholes in protection legislation from state to state. For further information, the "Entertainment Legislation" section of the BizParentz website is useful: http://www.bizparentz.org/entertainmentlaws/krekorianact.html.

British legislation protecting child actors (which had a bearing on Spielberg's employment of British actors in films that are partly shot in the United Kingdom) includes the 1933 Children and Young Persons Act, which determines that only children over age fourteen can work, and then for limited hours, but with the marked exception of children working in the entertainment industries, who can be any age but must be licensed; "Child Employment," GOV.UK, https://www.gov.uk/child-employment/performance-licences-for-children, accessed February 2025. Support organizations have also sprung up in this century, including the Looking Ahead program, set up in 2003 by the Actors Fund and SAG-AFTRA to support performers between the ages of nine and eighteen and their families (https://www.lookingaheadprogram.org/) and the BizParentz Foundation (http://www.bizparentz.org/home.html).

5 See also Lury discussion of risk in her chapter on performing children (2010, 145–189).

6 Andrea Darvi reports on one stage mother who fed her child poor food in the hope of stunting its growth, thus keeping it small (i.e., childish) enough for a longer career (1983, 50).

7 See Diana Serra Cary's revealing 1996 memoir of her life as the 1920s child actor "Baby Peggy" Mongomery. She also penned a wider history of the child star era in which she argues, "With rare exceptions, all of the children described in this book, including the writer, suffered such severe psychological traumas as a consequence of our early careers that most of us were obliged to seek professional help in some form before we could begin to function as emotionally stable adults" (1979, vi). The journalistic account by the former child actor Andrea Darvi also draws on numerous stories, particularly concerning the actions of stage mothers, that "border on child abuse" (1983, 50): sending sick children to work, dodging the rules to extend their hours, and using drugs as an aid to performance.

8 She reports in her autobiography *Child Star* that she felt a year had been taken from her; see also Valerie J. Nelson, "Shirley Temple Black, Iconic Child Star, Dies at 85," February 11, 2014, https://www.latimes.com/local/obituaries/la-me-shirley-temple-black-20140211-story.html. The deceit was, of course, an example of the common practice of extending a child's "playing age" and thus career.

9 See "'Potter' Class Graduates with No Child-Actor Woes," *San Diego Union-Tribune*, July 5, 2011, http://www.signonsandiego.com/news/2011/jul/05/potter-class-graduates-with-no-child-actor-woes/ and "Child Star . . . Doomed from the Start,?" posted by BCTC Deja on "BCTC Deja Blogspot—Lindsay Lohan Research Blog," May 3, 2011, http://bctcdeja.blogspot.com/2011/05/child-stardoomed-from-start.html.

10 The recent shift in perceptions of the fortunes of child stars has refocused the object of blame culture: "Many parents, television executives and others who work with young performers see cases like [Lindsay Lohan's] (Ms. Lohan, 21, has been to rehab three times this year) as the exception, and more attributable to family dynamics than the entertainment industry" (Navarro 2007).

11 The young Christian Bale preferred Amblin to Disneyland: "Disneyland was fun," Christian said afterwards, "but I liked Steven's offices more. He has lots of arcade games, and you don't have to pay for them" (G. Brown 1988, 22).

12 This is a consistent message, echoed by Elle Fanning, whose older sister Dakota was directed by Spielberg in *The War of the Worlds*: "The 13-year-old Somewhere star, whose latest film *Super 8* is produced by Spielberg, tells the Press Association, 'Steven said it's really important to have movies and have your regular life. He really is an advocate for still staying in school—I go to regular school—and he thinks you should have that as well.'" Fanning quoted in "Spielberg's Career Advice for Elle Fanning," Teen Hollywood, August 3, 2011, http://www.teenhollywood.com/2011/08/03/spielbergs-career-advice-for-fanning.

13 "A Tiffany & Co. crystal vase—a wedding gift from Spielberg and his wife, Kate Capshaw—and the size 2–3T top he wore as Barry Guiler are among the few

mementos of *Close Encounters* that he keeps in the suburban Birmingham home he shares with Michelle and their two dogs" (C. White 2001). See also "Former 'Close Encounters' Child Star Cary Guffey: 'I Still Get Fan Mail,'" *Inside Edition*, September 2, 2017, https://www.youtube.com/watch?v=c3zZXZEnHxo.

14 Despite as a child starring in significant films for adult audiences, Osment has felt the need for darker roles once he became an adult: "I'm most well known for being a good kid and the moral center of the movie. So, in college, the most fun I had was to play as bad guys. It's telling that most of my current roles are dark and nasty" (Parkin 2014).

15 Bale's biographers cite hours in the publicity machine that—if true—surely flout child labor laws, including "ten hours of interviews a day with few breaks" and "over 160 interviews with newspapers, television, magazines, and radio" (Cheung and Pittam 2012, 13).

16 *Evening Standard* website, "Drew Barrymore: People Should Shut Up about My Wild Past, I'm Proud of It," August 24, 2010, https://www.standard.co.uk/showbiz/starinterviews/drew-barrymore-people-should-shut-up-about-my-wild-past-i-m-proud-of-it-6506274.html.

17 The casting director Melissa Skoff discusses emancipation as a fast track to a nonrestrictive employment environment for a child, and though there are children "who are emancipated who don't have spectacular careers and they miss out on a normal high school life," it is also "hard when we have a child as the lead" who is not emancipated, because of the restricted hours they can work. See Kondazian 2000, 371.

18 "Although, due to her emancipation," write Barrymore's biographers, "the law considered Drew two years older than she actually was, the film's producers ran into difficulties when it came to getting the censors to approve her steamier moments" (Ellis and Sutherland 2003,128)

19 Reported in "Barrymore Hails 'Mentor' Spielberg," editorial, *Daily Express*, January 12, 2009, https://www.express.co.uk/celebrity-news/79606/Barrymore-hails-mentor-Spielberg.

20 The celebrated UK documentary strand that began as *Seven Up!* (and is now known as *The Up Series*) has traced the growing up and growing old of a group of British children at seven-year intervals, from the age of seven in 1964 to (so far) the age of sixty-three in 2019 (dir. Paul Almond [1964] and Michael Apted [1970–2019], Granada Television, https://www.imdb.com/title/tt0058578/). It was frequently referenced in reviews of Richard Linklater's *Boyhood* (2014), a feature filmed across twelve years that charted the growing up of two children and their families, for real and as their characters. Spielberg's version of *Seven Up* is the regular promotional events around an *E.T.* rerelease, at which the core team is reassembled for interviews, and the differences between then and now are rehearsed—the middle-aged Henry Thomas may be accompanied by a prop bicycle. Reporting on a press conference for the 2012 reissue featuring Barrymore, Thomas, and Spielberg, Anthony Breznican notes, "The child stars of E.T. have long since grown up, and now have children of their own. Steven Spielberg is the father of seven and the grandfather of three. Thirty years after their movie about a little lost alien made an indelible mark on kids of the '80s, the three principal players find themselves introducing the movie to their own next generation" (2012).

21 MacNaughton in interview with Mike Avila, in "E.T. The Extra-Terrestrial's Robert MacNaughton on Deleted Scenes, Teasing Drew Barrymore, and So Much More," SYFY, September 4, 2017, https://www.syfy.com/syfywire/et-the-extra-terrestrial-star-on-deleted-scenes-teasing-drew-barrymore-wild-et-fans.

22 Illustrated souvenir program *Close Encounters of the Third Kind* (New York: Encounter Enterprises, 1977), 9.

23 In *Little Girl Lost*, Barrymore cites the director's advice to her as the best she has ever received: "Drew, you can't act your character, you've got to *be* your character" (Barrymore 1990, 59).

24 This wider sense of play is central to the sociology of childhood and of course has many functions. As Henry Jenkins writes, "Children's play is not ideologically innocent; it is the primary means by which they absorb the values of their society and master both their own bodies and other culturally significant materials" (2007, 165). He also stresses that play "contains a counter-social potential: it may be used to express the child's feelings of outrage over the expectations imposed upon him or her by the social formation, over the pressure to conform to rules that constrain instinctual life and frustrate personal desire" (166).

25 Karen Lury addresses something akin to this in her discussion of Michael Kirby's 1972 essay "On Acting and Not-Acting": "What Kirby suggests is that while child performers may not apparently be 'doing' anything, they are, by their very presence in the film, 'done to'" (2010, 162).

26 Summarizing a history of childhood theories, Warner argues that children have been culturally characterized via two dominant themes, the first of the child as tabula rasa ("the idea of candor, innocence, whiteness, littleness, belongs to a moral ideal that is typified by the child"), the second of the child as providing a morally superior focus of point of view: "the child's superior wisdom, the assumed vantage point of innocence and the greater access to fantasy, leaves the adults in the audience to see their own absurdity and hardness through the eyes of the child" (1993, 43–44). Warner pinpoints Spielberg's films for children as "built on a kind of duplicitous flattery of the child" who is presented as "knowledgeable and wise in a way that adults are not. . . . parents need to be led by their children. In a way this is a sort of compensatory fairy tale . . . [b] ecause basically children have probably never been so powerless" (50–51). Interesting as Warner's analysis is, I think she gets this wrong about Spielberg, whose performed children—as I hope this book demonstrates—are rather more complex than this.

27 "Can another Academy Award nomination be far behind?" asked Catherin Ryan Hyde in 2001 of *A.I.* (http://www.kidactors.com/haley/default.asp).

28 "A Tribute to Director Steven Spielberg," Directors Guild of America event on June 11, 2011, moderated by Michael Apted—the director of most of the aforementioned episodes of the Granada television *Up!* series, tracing children's changing lives in Britain since the 1960s. Apted later became president of the DGA. See Director's Guild of America, "A Tribute to Director Steven Spielberg," June 11, 2011, archived at https://www.dga.org/Events/2011/08-august-2011/75th-Spielberg-Event.aspx#anchor.

29 Ke Huy Quan's experience shooting *Indiana Jones and the Temple of Doom* is very particular: he did not know who Spielberg was until after the completion of principal photography. This is more credible perhaps—considering that he spent the first part of his life in Vietnam and Hong Kong in the 1970s and early 1980s—than that the British actor Ruby Barnhill "admitted she 'had no idea' of the Oscar-winning director's reputation when she won the role" of Sophie in *The BFG*. "The BFG: Ruby Barnhill on Her Film Role as Sophie," BBC News, July 21, 2016, https://www.bbc.co.uk/news/av/uk-england-manchester-36861418.

30 Osment's father, Eugene—himself an actor in Los Angeles—"put his own career on hold and became his son's acting coach, training the boy in the drama tradition he'd studied in college, accompanying him to shoots, teaching him how behave during press junkets, and later, how to conduct interviews" (Copel 2001).

31 Osment elaborates on his parents' "normalization" strategies: "They emphasized school as the most important thing and really kept my feet on the ground. . . . When I was younger, making those movies took about two or three months and for the rest of the year I would be in a regular school, so that enabled me to have friends who weren't in the industry and a life that was separate from Hollywood" (Hiscock 2015).

32 This approach is underpinned by new work in the sociology of childhood, which credits childhood agency, a new paradigm developed in the 1980s and 1990s that calls "for children to be understood as social actors shaping as well as shaped by their circumstances" (A. James, Jenks, and Prout 1998, 6).

33 See the clip, including Spielberg's reflective comments from a retrospective interview, at http://www.youtube.com/watch?v=HzUZheS7cXY and in the DVD extra, bundled together with various reissues of the film this century on DVD and Blu-ray, "E.T. The Extra-Terrestrial: The 20th Anniversary Celebration," written, directed, and produced by Laurent Bouzereau (this is cited on the DVD menu as "The Evolution and Creation of E.T.," though this title does not appear on the film itself). Several other versions are regularly posted on YouTube, and augmented by pages of viewers' comments praising the performance.

34 For a comprehensive account of children on the stage in Victorian Britain, see Steedman 1995, 130–148.

35 The theater reviewer Doctor Judd wrote years later of Cordelia Howard: "Such a shower of tears as swept over that theatre! Actors and auditors were alike affected. . . . her parents' fortunes were made from that very night." "How Uncle Tom's Cabin Came to Be Dramatized," *The Billboard*, March 17, 1906, collected at the Uncle Tom's Cabin & American Culture multimedia archive held at the University of Virginia, http://utc.iath.virginia.edu/saxon/servlet/SaxonServlet?source=utc/xml/media/onstage-notices/osar48c.xml&style=utc/xsl/utcprint.xsl&print=yes&clear-stylesheet-cache=yes.

36 Lury also discusses child actors who, by reducing the crew on set to tears, are guaranteed to make future audiences cry, including the celebrated weeping work of Margaret O'Brien and Mandy Miller in the 1940s and 1950s (2010, 151–153).

37 Men's tears may also be more prized than women's: Steve McQueen was offered the role of Roy Neary in *Close Encounters of the Third Kind* but had to admit he could not cry on camera (Morton 2007, 130). Richard Dreyfuss could, and had certain "childlike" qualities, and so he got the part.

38 Yule attributes this story to Phillips, but the only cited source is her not entirely reliable tell-all tale of Hollywood Babylon in the 1970s and 1980s, *You'll Never Eat Lunch in the Town Again*. However, this is close to the tactic used on *E.T.*, in which Spielberg takes the young cast chronologically to the point where they will never see their alien friend again in order to elicit maximum tears.

39 From *The Evolution and Creation of E.T.*, produced and directed by Laurent Bouzereau and included as a special feature on the *E.T.* Special Edition DVD released by Universal to mark the 2002 release of the director's cut.

40 Spielberg interviewed in *The Evolution and Creation of E.T.*

41 Thomas has said of the goodbye scene, "I had worked so much with the E.T. character, and it had become very tangible to me. I could just draw on what was going on in the scene" (Sunshine 2012, 146).

42 Copjec writes: "My initial premise is this: crying was an invention of the late eighteenth century. I offer as proof of this thesis the fact that at this precise historical moment there emerged a brand new literary form—melodrama—which was specifically designed to give people something to cry about. Now I realize that some of you are saying to yourselves, 'I think she's got her dates wrong. I seem to remember

something about people crying before then. Weren't there even professional mourners in some former societies?' I will grant you this: tears were shed from time to time before the eighteenth century, and even as a public duty, but never before was there such a universal weeping, such a general social incitement to cry" (1999, 249).

43 As reported by Robert MacNaughton (Michael) in *The Evolution and Creation of E.T.* (2002).

44 Loudon Wainwright was "quite unprepared for, even embarrassed by the damp mix of snuffles" despite the fact that he had been forewarned that "*E.T.* was a 10-hankie picture" (1982, 7).

45 *E.T.* was for Sutcliffe "a jerry-built machine for extracting human emotions," and he quotes Universal's Sid Sheinberg (who was of course in the business of promoting the film) as saying, "It was like a religious experience. . . . It must be a bit like the way people feel if they've seen God" (2002, 1).

46 Mooallem also reports that "a psychologist named Richard Sloves looked into it and discovered that these children had fathers that, like Elliott's, had recently left home after a divorce." This is then once again referred back to Spielberg's biography: "And this, of course, was precisely the trauma that Spielberg was channeling too: the loneliness and disorientation that followed his own parents' separation—the foundational experience of Spielberg's childhood" (2016).

47 David Robb quotes special effects driver Carl Pittman, who claimed he encountered Spielberg in the chaos after the crash (1982c, 1, 30), but both Farber and Green (1988, 233–234) and LaBrecque (1988, 75–76) dispute this. There is a suggestion that Pittman was confusing Spielberg with his longtime collaborator Frank Marshall.

48 This is transcribed by LaBrecque (1988, 9) from the casting director Marci Liroff's day sheet. Michael Fenton's casting agency, for which Liroff worked, soon refused the job as they do not secure extras. Fenton is, of course, a celebrated Hollywood casting director, and his is the adult voice heard on the Henry Thomas audition tape.

Chapter 3 Boyhood and the Child's Alien Body

1 Even though this was a smokescreen to put the media off the scent that it was in fact an alien-themed film, the title is resonant, and Spielberg insists that the story he started with, and the issue that then made *E.T.* his "most personal" film, is not alien contact but that of the boy caught in a divorcing family.

2 *Close Encounters of the Third Kind* "Production Information," 1977, p. 3, archived in the microfiche collection of the British Film Institute Reuben Library, London.

3 *Steven Spielberg: 30 Years of Close Encounters*, written, directed, and produced by Laurent Bouzereau. This promotional special feature was included in the 2007 DVD rerelease but is also available on YouTube at https://www.youtube.com/watch?v=_1JoYLdZ_II. This quote occurs at around 6.15 minutes.

4 Wilson's fascinating 2003 analysis focuses on the death or loss of children in independent and art cinema, primarily from the perspective of the adults who experience that loss.

5 From Bouzereau's short film *Steven Spielberg: 30 Years of Close Encounters*, collected as a DVD extra but also available online. The quote is from the final section, archived as part 2 on YouTube https://www.youtube.com/watch?v=xfVeo1reSeg.

6 Neary of course has his own playful creative triggers—drawing, model trains, modeling mashed potatoes—that mark him out as a particular form of "kidult."

7 This conflation of formations of play inside and outside the film is also noted by Vivian Sobchack, but as a strategy of disavowal: "By emphasizing its own vision as child-like and revelling in its own technology (as do the playful aliens), *Close Encounters* disavows alliance with traditional patriarchal institutions and traditional paternal behaviour" (1991, 15–16).

8 McBride disagrees, finding Cary's a nuanced performance: "As that pajama-clad Barry stands in the shadowy doorway, his expression changes in a single close-up from initial trepidation to quizzical amusement and, finally, to an almost rapturous joy" (2010, 285).

9 The production head Stanley Jaffe objected to the child abduction story ("What the hell is this? . . . This is not the movie I bought"), canceling the film for a brief time until the producer Julia Phillips persuaded him and Spielberg to trial two possible storylines, one in which Barry is abducted, one in which he is remains safe with his mother (Morton 2007, 160).

10 They "tuckered out so quickly that the crew ended up not using them for most of the shots that they had been hired for" (Morton 2007, 190).

11 Balaban reports that this Rambaldi creation was entirely operated by levers and bellows, including an individual lever to make the Adam's apple move (2002, 151–152).

12 See McBride (2010, 279) for an account of the alien's genesis and for Rambaldi's work on Puck. Shakespeare named Puck for the magical hobgoblin of English folklore—a sprite or demon identified as male.

13 Though he does write that Truffaut was "filled with innocent, childlike, Peter Pan–ish sexual innuendoes" (Spielberg 1985, 41).

14 See Morton's account of the filming of the alien encounter (2007, 187–190).

15 "No-one thought to put a trap door in their costumes, and it takes them each a full ten minutes to get into and out of their skin tight leotards" (Balaban 2002, 63).

16 Balaban notes that by the time of filming the scene, which took many more days than anticipated, the "unruly kids of three weeks ago are now acting calmer and more professionally than the rest of us" (2002, 62).

17 In "Children as Bait" (Williams 2020), I analyze the ways in which the blockbuster exploitation flick *Jaws* considers human bodies as meat, and—rather than protecting children from on-screen violence—exposes and subjects them to it.

18 *E.T. the Extra-Terrestrial* press notes, United International Pictures (UK) and Universal, no author credit or pagination, accessed at British Film Institute Reuben Library.

19 This image appears in Sunshine 2012, 78.

20 This is sometimes extended to include the outer teenage circle of Michael's friends—C. Thomas Howell (Tyler), Sean Frye (Steve), and K. C. Martel (Greg).

21 The interview also notes that performing in *E.T.* inspired De Meritt to take up a camera himself: "Matthew has begun an 8mm movie project of his own. Following the example of Steven Spielberg, who began film-making as a teenager, Matt and two friends are filming a ghost story" (S. L. Jones 1983, 73).

22 Bellamy writes, "He is rarely seen as a whole—bits and pieces of him pop up unexpectedly, his head peeks out from among the dolls, his long knobby fingers crawl up from under a table" (2009, 97).

23 At which point, according to Marina Heung, E.T. behaves "like the man of the house enjoying a leisurely day at home": "Donning a man's plaid dressing-gown, he goes downstairs, checks the refrigerator for food, drinks a couple of beers, reads the paper, and turns on the television" (1983, 84).

24 "He's a cross between DNA and photosynthesis and made out of love," Spielberg said in a promotional interview (Gray 1982, 38). The first draft script was predicated on eight "Rules of E.T.'s Universe":

* All adults in the movie are shot from the waist down, except for mom.
* Adults are the villains.
* E.T. is a plant, neither male nor female.
* Aliens aren't here to destroy, they come to observe and make contact.
* Elliott has a psychic connection with E.T.
* E.T. has healing powers but they are limited (i.e. he can't cure cancer).
* Science is the threat.
* Everytime E.T. says a word, he has to say it twice.

(Sunshine 2012, 16)

25 However, Spielberg has said, "I made the creature a botanist vegetarian who never eats meat, only junk food, vegetables, and Coors" (Sunshine 2002, 86). According to this he is, then, a plant that eats plants.

26 See, for example, the preface in Stephens 2002, ix–xiv, and the introduction in Pomerance and Gateward 2005, 1–18. Stephens notes the propensity in preadult films and books "to engage in attempted social intervention by privileging variants of a 'sensitive male' schema (or postfeminist masculinity) and perforating the hegemonic masculinity associated with patriarchy and against which preferred masculinities are depicted" (xi). The presexual or asexual prepubescent boy is also, as Pomerance and Gateward point out, freed by certain narrative trajectories being closed off (2005, 5).

27 See the online fan site starwarsforum for a list of *Star Wars* toys by year of introduction, https://www.starwarsforum.co.uk/threads/a-complete-list-of-palitoy-star-wars-products-1978-1983.33956/.

28 The girl—credited only as "Pretty Girl"—is performed by Erika Eleniak, who has continued with an acting career in television and film as an adult.

29 See Brode 1995, 114, though he does not cite any references.

30 The last part of the title was added because preview audiences did not know what "E.T." stood for.

31 "E.T. Starring in Sales of Toys," *New York Times*, December 13 1982, https://www.nytimes.com/1982/12/13/business/et-starring-in-sales-of-toys.html.

32 See Noel Brown 2012, 44–45 for a discussion of this.

33 From *Letters to E.T.* (1983). This book contains no pagination at all, so page references cannot be given, and authorship/editorship is unclear.

Chapter 4 Real Boys and Synthetic Children

1 Available for consultation in the clippings files both at the Margaret Herrick Library in The Academy of Motion Picture Arts and Sciences, Los Angeles, and at the British Film Institute Reuben Library film title clippings.

2 For a young performer who grew up on Spielberg's 1980s films, the impact of then starring in one that itself throws back to the 1980s is huge. Tye Sheridan has said, "I told him that his movies had been such a huge part of my childhood from *ET* to *AI* and it just goes on and on—*Jurassic Park* and *Jaws*"—indeed, we might say to *Ready Player One* itself. *Ready Player One* DVD extra documentary *Game Changer: Cracking the Code.*

3 De Line, interviewed in *Ready Player One* DVD extra documentary *Game Changer: Cracking the Code.*

4 As Truffaut said to Spielberg in 1977; Sragow 2000, 113.

5 This is a profoundly moving and heroic declaration, but no less affecting is the moment when the eponymous android in *Robot & Frank* (2012, dir. Jake Schreier) "reassures" Frank that he is not a real person anyway, while urging him to "reformat" his android brain so that all digital evidence of the crime they have committed together (as well as any personality Frank is attached to) will be erased. The android as family adjunct has become a rich source of filmic inspiration since *D.A.R.Y.L.* and *A.I.*, including the *Android Kunjappan Ver. 5.25* (2019, dir. Ratheesh Balakrishnan Poduval; like *Robot & Frank*, this is another robot-as-elder-carer story); *After Yang* (2022, dir. Kogonada, in which the humanoid robot is purchased as sibling to a family's adoptive only child); and *Robot Bror* (2022, dir. Frederik Meldal Nørgaard, a Danish children's film).

6 The poster accompanied, and also helped to launch, the extraordinarily elaborate online game *The Beast*, devised to promote the film, and to this day recognized as a unique example of early online interactive storytelling. One textual element from the poster has attracted particular curiosity: the fictional credit Sentient Machine Therapist Jeanine Salla (neither the role nor the person exists), who is the starting point for the multiple online murder-mystery clues that spread out across the multiple sites and platforms of *The Beast*; see Trueman 2001, 58 for an overview. Since *The Beast* has little connection with the narrative of the film, or its discourse on childhood, and it is not a game aimed at children, I will not be discussing it in any detail.

7 V. Alan White's essay on *A.I.* (2008) is entirely focused on whether David passes the Turing test.

8 Though as Donna Haraway famously points out in her 1985 "Manifesto for Cyborgs" (Haraway 2004), the sense in which we are all cyborgs now means we will never more be truly orga. David is android rather than cyborg, but he eventually comes to embody the only vestiges of humanity.

9 The uncanny perfection of Osment-as-David was achieved through a makeup process developed by the Stan Winston Studio that involved shaving any peach fuzz off the actor's skin to make it unnaturally smooth, and coating it with a sealant that lent it an unblemished sheen, applied each day in just twenty minutes, "a crucial factor while observing the nine-hour work days and three-hour schooling sessions dictated by the Screen Actors Guild and child labor laws" (Fordham 2001, 70).

10 Rice (2017) likens Johnson-Johnson's racist rhetoric about "the big lie" to Hitler's use of the phrase in *Mein Kampf* (see pp. 2001–2004; see also Kendrick 2014).

11 In this, David's journey is like a reverse version of the young hero of the 1985 film *D.A.R.Y.L.*, the title acronym standing for Data-Analyzing Robot Youth Lifeform. The boy Daryl (Barret Oliver) escapes the U.S. military–funded AI experiment that created him and passes as a "real boy" in small-town America. He may be technically closer to cyborg than robot—he has the brain of an android but a body made of "normal" boy-like growing flesh, so convincing that we are told that even doctors could not tell the difference. Daryl quickly learns to love, and—very different than David's situation—is adopted by parents who truly love him back, even when they find out what he is and how he was made. The film concludes, in the words of one of the scientists leading the D.A.R.Y.L. project, with the statement that "a machine becomes human when you can't tell the difference anymore." This is entirely in the spirit of the famous Turing test, which Daryl clearly passes. It may be enough for Gigolo Joe to be able to enunciate "I am—I was," but the affirming, reflective

moment of being told by his adoptive father "You are a real person—you are real" enables Daryl's journey to full emotional selfhood.

12 As Kendrick discusses, love is *forced* on David by human selfishness—he has no choice in what is a purely commercial decision: "His condition has been deliberately manufactured, programmed into him to make him a better product" (2004 189, citing Kreider 2003, 36).

13 The mother-son pain also transferred behind the camera: shooting the scenes between Monica and David was "so wrenching that Haley's real mother has difficulty watching them" (Copel 2001). However, the British director Ken Russell's son Alex Verney-Elliott reports a lachrymose father-son moment when "we both wept in unison at the closing scene" of *A.I.* in the cinema (2011). Naremore begins and ends his analysis of *A.I.* with a meditation on his copious tears—for his own childhood—across five separate viewings (2005).

14 Spielberg also made his actors mime with food ten years earlier in *Hook*'s imaginary food fight; see Murray Pomerance's fascinating 2008 discussion of this scene in the context of a wider analysis of food as a metonym for sex in Spielberg.

15 "The passion of laughter is nothing else but a sudden glory arising from sudden conception of some eminency in ourselves, by comparison with the infirmities of others" (Hobbes 1928, 32).

16 Children have long been used to think about monstrosity, whether viewed as premoral/amoral creatures of unfettered nature, or as the embodiment of original sin. Hell itself gets its name from a mythological child, the half-girl and half-corpse child of Loki in Norse mythology; Hel guarded the realm of the dead. Closer to Spielberg's cultural context, the cycle of demon child horror films in the 1960s and 1970s (*Rosemary's Baby*, *The Exorcist*, *The Omen*) is an obvious cultural touchstone for more recent monstrous children. However, in *A.I.* it is arguably Martin—manipulative, spiteful, violent, yet still understandably threatened by his cuckoo child rival—who is the film's most monstrous child.

17 Wilson cites David alongside Boris Karloff's melancholic mummy and his Frankenstein's monster, and Rutger Hauer's too-mortal fallen angel replicant in the first *Blade Runner* film: "Each of these humanoids doubles the condition of human beings sundered between untroubled mechanism and organic turbulence. These divided figures are our siblings, our familiars, revealing the burdens that cleave to our souls" (2006, 125). See *The Mummy* (1932, dir. Karl Freund); *Frankenstein* (1931, dir. James Whale) (both Karloff); and *Blade Runner* (1982, Ridley Scott) (Hauer).

18 However, the most common cinematic robot is a mechanical being with an unchangeable alloy face. We usually read into its fixed visage a range of dark emotions—gravity, sadness, threat. More positive emotions such as delight or mirth are difficult to discern in the blank manufactured expression. Unless it was cast that way by its maker, the metal robot cannot smile, and may lack lungs or diaphragm and so cannot project laughter's force. However, it may be capable of sardonic humor—indeed, as with Marvin the Paranoid Android from *The Hitchhiker's Guide to the Galaxy* or C-3PO from *Star Wars*, depression and anxiety are a source of humor. A creature of high science, historically the cinematic robot has been imbued with deep seriousness. For David, roboticness takes him close to the grave child of horror.

19 Though just why Hobby's highly advanced corporation, capable of producing a robot child who can love and a robot gigolo who presumably can sustain an erection, cannot produce convincing blinking or sleep, or laughter, is one of the glitches in the film's science fiction realism.

20 The press notes to *A.I.* endorse this, citing the producer Kathleen Kennedy giving Osment plaudits across the adult-child border: "I think Haley is the most extraordinary child actor to come along in a long, long time. . . . And I hesitate to use the word 'child,' as Haley is every bit the consummate professional trained actor that any adult would be."

21 He said in the *Ready Player One* DVD extra documentary *Game Changer: Cracking the Code*, "My whole cast had tons of ideas. . . . They had ideas about who they were, in both the real world and the OASIS. And if they were good ideas——right into the movie."

22 There have been some inroads into creating convincing robotic performers since the production of *A.I.*; see "Robot Actor Makes Stage Debut in Japan," BBC News, November 11, 2010, https://www.bbc.co.uk/news/av/technology-11732995; Rebecca Keegan, "A.I. Robot Cast in Lead Role of $70M Sci-Fi Film," *Hollywood Reporter*, June 24, 2020, https://www.hollywoodreporter.com/news/general-news/ai-robot-cast-lead-role-70m-sci-fi-film-1300068/.

23 Abramowitz also reports that "Spielberg does not consider himself an artist. 'I feel like I continue to aspire to be one, but Stanley always was one'" (2001).

24 There are multiple Davids in Barrie's subsequent writing, including in the first text about Peter Pan and one in Barrie's last play, *The Boy David*, about the biblical King David.

25 Of course, this was just one of the many false starts to Spielberg's *Pan* projects, which only came to fruition seven years later with *Hook*.

26 This is a development of an existing problem with AI-human interactions: Stan Winston, who created the robotic toy Teddy for the production, discusses how, working on a project with MIT to create real animated AI beings, they have discovered that the "biggest chance to get a human being to actually interact with a robot is if it looks real—if it looks organic, acts organic" (Cornea 2007, 272).

Chapter 5 Girl/Daughter

1 These are also adaptations of best-selling novels, so the actors additionally carry the expectations of wide popular readerships.

2 See https://www.youtube.com/watch?v=35eLZTepTwo. The widespread irritation at Fanning's screaming is evidenced in responses to this compilation as well as some review criticism. Of course, screaming is often what girls and women are required to do all too frequently in genre films—as Ariana Richards's audition tape, discussed in chapter 6, evidences.

3 *Variety* picked up on the political contexts of each adaptation of Wells's novel: "Wells' original reflected attitudes about the British Empire as well as the rapid rise of science and technology; Orson Welles' panic-inducing 1938 radio broadcast (which had a New Jersey setting, as does Spielberg's film) arrived less than a year before World War II broke out; and the George Pal/Byron Haskin 1953 feature was very much a product of the anti-communist Cold War mentality" (McCarthy 2005).

4 "*War of the Worlds* Production Information," Paramount Pictures/Dreamworks, 2005, 6–7, archived in the British Film Institute Reuben Library clippings files.

5 "*War of the Worlds* Production Information," 15.

6 The "EDGE—Teen Stars" series is pitched to its readership as being focused on young celebrities: "Welcome to Teen Stars! Whether you're already a fan, or just want to find out more, this series has something for everyone who's into the teen celebrity scene." See https://www.hachettechildrens.co.uk/books/detail.page?isbn

=9781445106625; see also http://abdopublishing.com/series/6-big-buddy-biographies for the Big Buddy series on child-focused celebrities (many of them children themselves) and http://www.mitchelllane.com/CRRB/CRRBPT.php for the Robbie Reader Contemporary Biography series.
7 Mooallem (2016) reports that Barnhill told him, "I don't want to be an actress anymore. I'd like to be a director. I don't think I'll ever be as brilliant as Steven is, though," while Spielberg contributes to this exchange of self-deprecation: "She made three movies in the span of time it took me to make one!"

Chapter 6 Clever Girls

1 The film refers to the male Alan Grant by his surname and to the female Ellie Staddler by her given name, a patriarchal convention that I will only continue for clarity's sake, because of the film's consistent use of these forms.
2 Even the author Michael Crichton recounts the origins of the novel in gendered terms: "My wife was pregnant with my first child, and I found that I couldn't walk past a toy store without buying a stuffed toy. And what I was buying, more often than not, were stuffed dinosaurs. My wife couldn't understand it. We knew we were having a girl. Why was I buying all these dinosaurs? And I would say, 'Well, girls like dinosaurs, too.' But it was clear that I was sort of obsessed with dinosaurs; and the whole idea of children and dinosaurs, and the meaning of what that was" (Shay and Duncan 1993, 3).
3 This is underpinned by the film's soft feminism, usually articulated by Ellie. When Malcolm stares into the T-Rex enclosure and opines, "God creates dinosaurs. God destroys dinosaurs. God creates man. Man destroys God. Man creates dinosaurs," she completes the formulation: "Dinosaurs eat man. Woman inherits the earth." Given that the film concludes with the humans fleeing and the (female) dinosaurs controlling Ilsa Nublar, this turns out to be wiser than any of the pithy one-liners voiced by Malcolm.
4 The final girl was famously identified by Carol J. Clover in her brilliant book *Men, Women and Chain Saws: Gender in the Modern Horror Film*, (1992), a model of the tenacious young woman who survives to dispatch the monster, which has been hugely influential on film theory, gender studies, and indeed the evolution of the horror film itself. However, Clover's final girl is invariably a young woman in her late teens or twenties, or older. Girl heroes, of course, frequently prevail in children's fiction and films for young audiences, but the two are seldom positioned in a common narrative frame.
5 *Jurassic Cast Podcast*, "Ariana Richards interview," https://www.youtube.com/watch?v=Lar6vq7LrmU.
6 *Jurassic Cast Podcast*, "Ariana Richards interview."
7 Richards also reports that when a hurricane hit the island as filming was concluding, the cast and crew had to take cover in the hotel, resulting in an off-duty appearance of Nasty Steven who we encountered earlier: "Steven Spielberg came over to talk to me and Joey and say 'Hey, how are you guys doing? Are you doing OK?' And he started telling us ghost stories . . . to try to distract us. And—seriously—Steven's ghost stories actually scared me more than the hurricane" (*Jurassic Cast Podcast*).
8 Seb Patrick (2011), "*Jurassic Park*: Ariana Richards interview," *Den of Geek*, Oct 24, 2011, archived at https://www.denofgeek.com/movies/18232/jurassic-park-ariana-richards-interview.
9 "Reel Women in Technology (Reel WiT) Award," NCWIT, accessed February 2025, https://www.ncwit.org/project/reel-wit-award.

10 Motion Picture Association—Film Ratings, accessed February 2025, https://www.mpaa.org/film-ratings/.

11 British Board of Film Classification, "BBFC: PG Parental Guidance," accessed February 2025, www.bbfc.co.uk/rating/pg.

12 The statement about the film on the BBFC website continues:

> While the Compliance Officers were assured of their PG recommendation, given the potential for the film to unduly frighten children with the intensity of the film's threat and horror-like scenes, the BBFC arranged a test screening for an audience of 200 children, aged 8 to 11, in June 1993. The children were invited from five schools both in and outside London, with the intention of surveying their views of the film and whether it would be appropriately rated at PG or should be classified 12 instead.
>
> A report of the event describes the reaction of most of the audience as one of "cheerful terror" rather than "genuine anguish." A questionnaire given out after the screening revealed that there was some degree of anxiety for several members of the young audience—37% did not feel certain that the children in the film would be alright—but overall 96% said that they enjoyed the film "a lot," including all of the 8 year olds. Just one child ticked "not at all."
>
> Given a choice of phrases to describe their experience of the film—"too frightening for me" or "good and scary"—only 13% of the children said "too frightening" and 82% chose "good and scary." The BBFC therefore had to choose a rating that would not deny the 82% the opportunity to enjoy the dino-thrills. A 12 or 15 could not accommodate that, as those certificates would prohibit the admittance of anybody under those ages (in 1993, the 12A rating did not exist). The BBFC opted to award a PG certificate, but with a warning attached: "contains sequences which may be particularly disturbing to younger children or those of a sensitive disposition."

See "Education/Case Studies: *Jurassic Park*" (no author or date cited), https://www.bbfc.co.uk/case-studies/jurassic-park. Traumatic and pleasurable fear responses are, then, weighed against each other, and a decision of harm, protection, or the freedom of children to watch was made on the basis of statistical majorities.

13 British Board of Film Classification, "BBFC: 12/12A - Suitable for 12 Years and Over As," accessed February 2025, www.bbfc.co.uk/rating/12.

14 A deleted scene included in the DVD release features a board meeting of InGen, Hammond's company, using photos of the injured Cathy that form part of her parents' lawsuit being passed around as evidence of the need to depose Hammond from his CEO role in favor of his more despicable nephew.

15 For example, *Jaws*, *Empire of the Sun*, *Jurassic Park*, *Schindler's List*, *War of the Worlds*, *War Horse*, *Ready Player One*, and *The BFG*; others had looser literary bases (e.g., *Minority Report*, *Catch Me If You Can*).

16 It was nominated in eleven categories for the Academy Awards, including Best Picture, and won none, holding the record of being the title that at that time had the most Oscar nominations with no wins. It did win other awards, including Golden Globes and at the Directors Guild of America Awards.

17 Bobo cites the "mandate, given dominant media coverage, that Black people should not have positive responses to the film"; a panel of four Black male journalists debating the film deemed it "the most racist depiction of black men since *The Birth of a Nation* and the most antiblack family film of the modern film era" (1995, 92).

18 Bobo transcribes key moments of the qualitative interviews to reflect the varied positions on some controversial issues, including on Spielberg as director choice:

ANNE: I got angry that Spielberg, white man . . .
PHYLLIS: . . . had to do it . . .
ANNE: . . . did it. I got really upset with that. I felt violated in that sense.
PHYLLIS: I was just glad somebody did it.
GRACE: I didn't feel angry. I'm glad somebody did it. If he had not done it, I don't know too many other people who would have even tried—
WHITNEY:—or who would have had the money or the financial backing.

(1995, 122)

19 The section of Walker's memoir also includes a letter from the public relations director of the National Association for the Advancement of Colored People that "applauds your efforts," situating Walker as an important "behind the camera" force in this instance, and arguing for increased representation in the film industry: "'The Color Purple' is a perfect demonstration of the significant contribution that Blacks have been ready and willing to make to the movie industry," calling for the inclusion of "more Black people both in front of and behind the camera in upcoming films" (1996, 237).

Chapter 7 War Child

1 This also extends to TV, with the series he co-devised and executive-produced that form a tryptic in this genre: HBO's *Band of Brothers* (2001), HOB/Playtone/DreamWorks' *The Pacific* (2010), and Apple TV+'s *Masters of the Air* (2024).

2 Michael Hammond, in his incisive account of the 1990s war film, reads it as a "celluloid memorial" (2002, 69). Indeed, both films that won Spielberg the Best Director Oscar (*Saving Private Ryan* and *Schindler's List*) conclude in a similar fashion with families gathered around a grave.

3 My own grandfather, born in 1901, tried to join up in a similar fashion, but his age was discovered.

4 Doomed girl characters from Charles Dickens's *Old Curiosity Shop* and Harriet Beecher Stowe's *Uncle Tom's Cabin*, respectively.

5 "*War Horse* Film Preview: Watch Joey on the Red Carpet," *Horse and Hound*, January 9, 2012, http://www.horseandhound.co.uk/news/war-horse-film-preview-watch-joey-on-the-red-carpet-311033; see also Claire Suddath, "Training the Horses in Steven Spielberg's *War Horse*," *Time*, January 5, 2012, http://entertainment.time.com/2012/01/05/training-the-horses-in-steven-spielbergs-war-horse/.

6 Ballard is quoted as being particularly pleased that Spielberg tackled his novel because "he has an unequalled gift for handling children" (Peachment 1987).

7 "The boy-wonder director, who had manifest trouble coping with adult themes in *The Color Purple*, here has the gift of a boy hero (played by Christian Bale) and of a subject that allows his visionary surrealism to take wing" (Andrew 1987, 13).

8 Which looks rather like another Spielbergian suburb—the Amhurst Avenue sequences were actually filmed in the affluent London suburb of Sunningdale.

9 Elsewhere Spielberg remembers the artist as synonymous with a more optimistic "Technicolor" America; he says in the press notes for *Indiana Jones and the Kingdom of the Crystal Skull*, which is set in the 1950s, that the decade "means the bright young faces that Norman Rockwell loved to paint" (press notes, *Indiana Jones and the Kingdom of the Crystal Skull* cuttings file, British Film Institute Reuben Library).

10 The original Rockwell headline is unclear on the folded newspaper of the painting, but unequivocally signals conflict abroad: "BOMBINGS KI . . . HORROR HIT." "KI" here is presumably the start of the word "kill."

11 Other (peacetime) children in Spielberg have very different relationships to home as physical space: Elliott in *E.T.* is so closely identified with his bedroom that he has superior powers of ownership over it even than his mother; Barry in *Close Encounters* is given the power to move around his house, and leave it at will, when under the spell of the aliens. However *A.I.*'s David only passes through his adoptive parents' house, is ejected from it, and goes—as it were—to meet his maker, in the place he was born/made but was not a home. Celie in *The Color Purple* is passed around within houses which are men's property, but comes to own her own space.

12 "The most important consequence of internment was that for the first time in my life I was extremely close to my parents. I slept, ate, read, dressed and undressed within a few feet of them in the same small room, in many ways like the poorer Chinese families for whom I had felt so sorry in Shanghai. But I revelled in this closeness, which I assume has been a central part of human behaviour throughout most of its evolution" (Ballard 2008, 79).

13 Murray Pomerance (2008) discusses how Spielberg captures ravenousness in *Empire*: "The rice scene is something of a watershed in Spielberg's development, in the sense that it could only have been realized in the form we see in the film by a filmmaker whose instinct told him to imagine instinct: a hunger that transcended appetite and manners, that was inseparable from the ravenous body that satisfied it."

14 When asked by Martin Amis why he shies away from representing "adult relationships," the director testily replied—astonishingly—"I think I have an incredibly erotic imagination. It's one of my ambitions to make everyone in an 800-seat theatre come at the same time" (1987, 154).

15 When the war finally does end, Jim is left alone in the camp, cycling around and around it as he had cycled around his house. There is some ownership in his confidence underpinned by the jaunty contemporary choral music. But the bleached-out white/gray/neutral palette makes it look more like a nowhere—an afterlife perhaps—than a somewhere.

16 For his work on *Empire*, Daviau won a BAFTA for Best Cinematography and the American Society of Cinematographers Award for Outstanding Achievement in Cinematography, and he was nominated for an Oscar.

17 The scene in which Jim shimmies into the no-man's-land beyond the fence on an errand for Basie is performed as action-adventure, with dark comedy coming from the appalling spectacle of the American adults betting over the child's survival chances.

18 Objects of warfare cannot so easily be separated from objects of peace in this film. Even the canisters of food that are dropped by the U.S. Air Force to save the civilians are shaped like bombs, as was sometimes necessary when bomber planes were used in humanitarian airdrops. The agent of salvation mimics the agent of death.

19 Lester Friedman writes movingly of his own emotional response to this sequence at the start of his discussion of *Empire* in *Citizen Spielberg*.

20 More recently, the Shoah Foundation's brief has extended to include other persecuted groups and victims of genocide worldwide.

21 USC Shoah Foundation "Interviewer Guidelines," updated 2012, https://sfi.usc.edu/explore/collecting_testimonies.

22 Writes Monica Strauss, "*Schindler's List* remains a Hollywood production. . . . By relying on the traditional entertainment-industry formula of sex, violence, and

sentiment, Spielberg undermines the film's serious message.... the movie indulges in what I call 'Holocaust porn'" (1994).

23 Alan Mintz debates the positions for and against *Schindler's List* in measured detail in his chapter "The Holocaust at the Movies: Three Studies in Reception" (2001, 125–158).

24 Roma Ligocka has claimed in her novelistic memoir of being a Jewish child in wartime Kraków (2003) that she is the girl in the red coat, a fact she realized when watching Spielberg's film, which was itself a catalyst for confronting her past. However, Ligocka survives and Genia does not; Genia's role is primarily symbolic rather than character-driven.

25 Spielberg had already tried this color strategy in *Empire of the Sun*, when Jamie in his red school uniform, about to lose his mother, is overwhelmed by a crowd, undifferentiated as a group and color graded down into duller tones.

26 Here it is sung by the Li-Ron Children's Choir. The version accompanying Genia's sojourn simply repeats the opening verse and refrain, translated as: "On the hearth, a fire burns / And in the house it is warm / And the rabbi is teaching little children / The alphabet. / Refrain: See, children, remember, dear ones / What you learn here / Repeat and repeat yet again, 'Komets-alef: O!'"

27 Extreme political objections to *Schindler's List* exploded in tandem with popular praise for the film, so the reception response oscillated widely. *Shoah* director Claude Lanzmann was among the most vociferous critics, as was the philosopher Marie-José Mondzain: "Films of fiction, for example the 'Holocaust' series or *Schindler's List* (1993), can have no bearing upon history or politics. The roles of executioners and victims are not distributed in the same manner." (Desplechin et al. 2010, 137).

28 The lyrics we hear run: "Yes, the strong gets more / While the weak ones fade / Empty pockets don't ever make the grade / Mama may have, Papa may have / But God bless the child that's got his own / That's got his own."

29 Dabrowska's statements were widely recirculated and exaggerated at every turn, sparking articles such as Steve Rose's "Should Children Be Allowed to Act in Harrowing Films?," which teetered on the edge of former-child-star-goes-off-the-rails stories in its presentation: "Oliwia Dabrowska has spoken of her 'years of trauma and shame' after her role in Steven Spielberg's *Schindler's List*. How have other child actors reacted to their roles in disturbing movies—and how do directors protect them?" Exaggerating the distress of Dabrowska, it then misreports the fate of Linda Blair from *The Exorcist* before concluding, "But Drew Barrymore went off the rails after doing *ET*. So maybe it's all Spielberg's fault?" (Rose 2013).

30 The phrase "even with dolls" is interesting here: How else *could* he do it?

31 Some sources simply cite the number saved as in excess of 1,000, but Schindler's gravestone in Jerusalem cites the number as 1,200.

32 Pfefferberg (who renamed himself Leopold Page when he moved to the United States) worked as a consultant for Spielberg and is a character in the film.

33 Included as a bonus feature on the 2013 DVD edition of *Schindler's List*.

34 See also Janina Bauman's 2004 analysis of the use of Holocaust testimony in child education and Shoshana Felman's more wide-ranging 1992 analysis of the use of trauma testimonies in a graduate class that itself fell into crisis.

Chapter 8 Family Finds a Way

1 This is Harrison Zanuck's only on-screen role—he has since become a producer himself. This baby actor easily tops Drew Barrymore as the most Hollywood-connected young performer discussed in this book.

2 Clovis has less of a stake in the baby's return, saying, "You're my wife, and I love you, even if we don't get the baby."

3 The real Mehran Karimi Nasseri passed away at terminal 1 of Charles de Gaulle Airport in Paris in 2022, a place he called home from 1988 to 2006. On his request, he was allowed to return and live there for his final months.

4 *Steven Spielberg: 30 Years of Close Encounters*, written, directed, and produced by Laurent Bouzereau. This promotional special feature was included in the 2007 DVD rerelease but is also available on YouTube at https://www.youtube.com/watch?v=_1JoYLdZ_II. This quote occurs at around 5.20 minutes.

5 I have written elsewhere (Williams 2017) about the demonization of Teri Garr's Ronnie, mother/wife in *Close Encounters*, presented as a nagging figure of convention who is nevertheless focused on protecting family.

6 The casting of the children is discussed briefly in Morton 2007, 136.

7 Murray Pomerance perceptively explores a number of adult male children in "The Man-Boys of Steven Spielberg" (2005).

8 Spielberg returns to this when discussing *The Fabelmans*, as this is what the young Spielberg did when he saw his father crying in his mother's arms around the time of their marriage breakup: "It was easier to wedge pieces of his story into . . . the masculine anguish of *Close Encounters*" (Zacharek 2022).

9 These awards, for performers between age five and twenty-one, are known as the "kid Oscars," and multiple child cast members of *Hook* were included in the citation for this award.

10 Like the fifth and final cinematic outing in the franchise, which was not directed by Spielberg, I will also not be writing about either TV series *The Young Indiana Jones Chronicles* (1992–1993) or *The Adventures of Young Indiana Jones* (2002–2008) here.

11 The correspondence and examiner's documents are appended to the case study on the BBFC site for this film. See https://www.bbfc.co.uk/education/case-studies/temple-of-doom.

12 "It was not until I finished filming [*Temple of Doom*] that George and Steven screened their movies for me. I saw *Star Wars* and *Raiders of the Lost Ark* for the very first time, and I realized, 'Oh my God. These filmmakers are really successful, and they're very, very famous'" (Goh 2022).

13 He continues, "In Hollywood, very, very few child actors make smooth and successful transitions into adult acting. It's very difficult for many, but I think it's a hundred times—a thousand times—more difficult when you are an Asian actor" (Goh 2022).

14 Friedman's discussion of father figures in *Empire of the Sun* usefully ranges across a number of men who mentor Jamie/Jim (2006: 199–215).

Afterword

1 Joseph McBride reports, '"Some of [the Spielbergs'] Phoenix neighbors found Leah's romantic history a bit outré. 'I was always confused as to who [Steven's] father was,' says Steven's friend Chris Pischke. Katherine Galwey recalls that Leah 'told me she loved both men. She said she couldn't marry 'em both, so she married Mr. Spielberg'" (2010, 75).

2 Though Spielberg—revelatory as he sometimes is—will usually give and take away in the turn of a sentence: "'It's like making a movie, you know, and realizing with this movie, what have I just done? Has this been $40 million of therapy? 'And the answer is?' 'Whoever spends $40 million in therapy?' he laughed" (Lim and Orvedahl 2022).

References

Author's note: Some materials were gathered at the Margaret Herrick Library at the Academy of Motion Picture Arts and Sciences in Los Angeles (production and biographical files) and the British Film Institute Reuben Library in London (film title files). Many of these clippings, saved onto microfiche, omit page references, or add page numbers running from 1 onward. These are marked here with an asterisk (*) in lieu of direct page references but can be located and consulted in these locations via publication information.

Abramowitz, Rachel. 2001. "Regarding Stanley." *Los Angeles Times*, May 6. https://www.latimes.com/archives/la-xpm-2001-may-06-ca-59783-story.html.

Alcott, Louisa May. 1869. *Little Women*. Boston: Roberts Brothers.

Aldiss, Brian. 1969. *Supertoys Last All Summer Long, and Other Stories of Future Time*. London: Orbit.

———. 2001. "The Mind behind A.I." BBC News, September 20. http://news.bbc.co.uk/2/hi/in_depth/sci_tech/2001/artificial_intelligence/1542794.stm.

American Cinematographer. 1978. "Spielberg Speaks about 'Close Encounters.'" 59, no. 1 (January): 39–42, 88.

Amis, Martin. 1987. "Steven Spielberg: Boyish Wonder." In *The Moronic Inferno, and Other Visits to America*, 147–154. London: Penguin.

Anderson, Mark Cronlund. 2007. *Cowboy Imperialism and Hollywood Film*. Lausanne: Peter Lang.

Andrew, Nigel. 1987. "Oscar Favourites Paraded in Hollywood." *Financial Times*, December 18, 13.

Anthony, George. 1982. "Kings of Inner Space." *Marquee*, July–August 1982.*

Apatow, Judd. 2023. "Episode 105: Steven Spielberg & Tony Kushner, 'The Fabelmans' (in conversation with Judd Apatow)." Writers Guild of America East. February 23. https://www.wgaeast.org/onwriting/episode-105-steven-spielberg-tony-kushner-the-fabelmans-in-conversation-with-judd-apatow/.

Argent, Daniel. 2001. "Steven Spielberg as Writer from *Close Encounters of the Third Kind* to *A.I.*" *Creative Screenwriting* 8, no. 3 (May/June): 49–53.

Ariès, Philippe. 1962. *Centuries of Childhood: A Social History of Family Life*. Translated by Robert Baldick. New York: Vintage.

Arms, Gary, and Thomas Riley. 2008. "The 'Big-Little' Film and Philosophy." In *Steven Spielberg and Philosophy: We're Gonna Need a Bigger Book*, edited by Dean A. Kowalski, 7–37. Lexington: University Press of Kentucky.

Aronson, Virginia. 2000. *Drew Barrymore*. Philadelphia: Chelsea House.

Audissino, Emilio. 2010. *L'infanzia nel cinema di Steven Spielberg*. Imperia, Italy: Ennepilibri.

Austin, Chuck. 1977. "Director Steve Spielberg [*sic*]." *Filmmakers' Newsletter* 11, no. 2 (December): 28–30.

Avila, Mike. 2017. "*E.T. The Extra-Terrestrial*'s Robert MacNaughton on Deleted Scenes, Teasing Drew Barrymore, and So Much More." SYFY, September 14. https://www.syfy.com/syfywire/et-the-extra-terrestrial-star-on-deleted-scenes-teasing-drew-barrymore-wild-et-fans. Accessed December 4, 2018.

Bahiana, Ana Maria. 1992. "*Hook*." *Cinema Papers*, no. 87 (March/April): 12–16.

Balaban, Bob. 2002. *Spielberg, Truffaut and Me*. London: Titan Books.

Balázs, Béla. 1970. *Theory of the Film: Character and Growth of a New Art*. Translated by Edith Bone. New York: Dover.

Ballard, J. G. 1984. *Empire of the Sun*. London: Gollancz.

———. 2008. *Miracles of Life: Shanghai to Shepperton, An Autobiography*. London: Fourth Estate.

Barber, Sian. 2012. "More Than Just a 'Nasty' Decade: Classifying the Popular in the 1980s." In *Behind the Scenes at the BBFC: Film Classification from the Silver Screen to the Digital Age*, edited by Edward Lamberti, 110–126. London: British Film Institute/Palgrave Macmillan.

Barker, Felix. 1978. "Felix Barker on the Royal Film." *Evening Standard*, March 14.*

Barker, Olivia. 2013. "'Former Child Star' Now Looks Good on a Résumé." *USA Today*, October 6. https://eu.usatoday.com/story/life/people/2013/10/06/child-star-success-generation/2924991/.

Barrie, J. M. 1911. *Peter Pan and Wendy*. London: Hodder and Stoughton.

Barrymore, Drew. 2015. *Wildflower*. London: Virgin Books.

Barrymore, Drew, with Todd Gold. 1990. *Little Girl Lost*. New York: Pocket Books/Simon and Schuster.

Basinger, Jeanine. 2016. "The Wartime American Woman on Film: Home-Front Soldier." In *A Companion to the War Film*, edited by Douglas A. Cunningham and John C. Nelson, 89–105. Chichester: Wiley Blackwell.

Bauman, Janina. 2004. "Entering the World of a Holocaust Victim: Schoolchildren Discuss a Ghetto Memoir—a Case Study." In *Representing the Shoah for the 21st Century*, edited by Ronit Lentin, 77–85. New York; Berghahn Books.

Bayer, Ann. 1986. "Spielberg: Husband, Father and Hitmaker." *Life*, May, 148–156.

Bazalgette, Cary, and David Buckingham, eds. 1995. *In Front of the Children: Screen Entertainment and Young Audiences*. London: British Film Institute.

Bazalgette, Cary, and Terry Staples. 1995. "Unshrinking the Kids: Children's Cinema and the Family Film." In *In Front of the Children: Screen Entertainment and Young Audiences*, edited by Cary Bazalgette and David Buckingham, 92–108. London: British Film Institute.

Becon, Thomas. 1844. *Prayers and Other Pieces of Thomas Becon*, edited by John Ayre, S.T.P. Vol 4, The Parker Society, Cambridge, UK: The University Press.

Bellamy, Dodie. 2009. "Phone Home." In *Life as We Show It: Writing on Film*, edited by Brian Pera and Masha Tupitsyn, 83–105. San Francisco: City Lights.

Bentley, Rick. 2016. "'BFG' Director Steven Spielberg Influenced by Walt Disney." *Fresno Bee*, June 26. https://www.fresnobee.com/entertainment/movies-news-reviews/article85593317.html.

Bergson, Henri. 2008. *Laughter: An Essay on the Meaning of the Comic*. Rockville, MD: Arc Manor.

Bernstein, Robin. 2011. *Racial Innocence: Performing American Childhood from Slavery to Civil Rights*. New York: New York University Press.

Bick, Ilsa J. 1992. "The Look Back in 'E.T.'" *Cinema Journal* 31, no. 4 (Summer): 25–41.

Biskind, Peter. 1998. *Easy Riders, Raging Bulls: How the Sex-Drugs-and-Rock 'N Roll Generation Saved Hollywood*. London: Bloomsbury.

Black, Shirley Temple. 1989. *Child Star: An Autobiography*. New York: Warner Books.

Blum, Carol. 1995. "Sentiment." In *The Blackwell Companion to the Enlightenment*, edited by John W. Yolton, Roy Porter, Pat Rogers, Barbara Stafford, 487–488. Oxford: Blackwell.

Bobo, Jacqueline. 1995. *Black Women as Cultural Readers*. New York: Columbia University Press.

Bobrow, Andrew C. 1974 "Filming The Sugarland Express: An Interview with Steven Spielberg." *Filmmakers' Newsletter* 7, no. 9–10 (Summer): 30–34.

Boose, Lynda. 2006. "Techno-Muscularity and the 'Boy Eternal': From the Quagmire to the Gulf." In *Hollywood and War: The Film Reader*, edited by J. David Slocum, 275–286. New York: Routledge.

Bradshaw, Peter. 2001. "A.I.: Artificial Intelligence." *The Guardian*, September 21. https://www.theguardian.com/film/2001/sep/21/1.

Brady, Frank. 1990. *Citizen Welles: A Biography of Orson Welles*. London: Hodder and Stoughton.

Bratton, Jacky, Jim Cook, and Christine Gledhill. 1994. "Introduction." In *Melodrama: Stage, Picture, Screen*, edited by Jacky Bratton, Jim Cook, and Christine Gledhill, 1–8. London: British Film Institute.

Breskin, David. 1985. "Steven Spielberg: The Rolling Stone Interview." *Rolling Stone*, October 24. http://davidbreskin.com/magazines/1-interviews/steven-spielberg/.

Breznican, Anthony. 2012. "'E.T.' Reunion: How Steven Spielberg Coached His Kid Stars." *Entertainment Weekly*, October 5. https://web.archive.org/web/20210403000925/https://ew.com/article/2012/10/05/et-reunion-spielberg-drew-barrymore/?amp=true.

———. 2022. "What Scared Steven Spielberg about *The Fabelmans*—And How Tony Kushner Pushed Him Past It." *Vanity Fair*, November 21. https://www.vanityfair.com/hollywood/2022/11/awards-insider-what-scared-steven-spielberg-about-the-fabelmans.

Britton, Andrew. 1986. "Blissing Out: The Politics of Reaganite Entertainment." *Movie*, nos. 31/32 (Winter): 1–42.

Brode, Douglas. 1995. *The Films of Steven Spielberg*. New York: Citadel Press.

Bronfen, Elisabeth. 2012. *Specters of War: Hollywood's Engagement with Military Conflict*. New Brunswick, NJ: Rutgers University Press.

Brooks, Peter. 1994. "Melodrama, Body, Revolution." In *Melodrama: Stage, Picture, Screen*, edited by Jacky Bratton, Jim Cook, and Christine Gledhill, 11–24. London: British Film Institute.

———. 1995. *The Melodramatic Imagination: Balzac, Henry James, Melodrama, and the Mode of Excess*. New Haven, CT: Yale University Press.

Brown, Geoff. 1988. "Surprise for Shanghai." *The Times*, March 19, 22.

Brown, Noel. 2012. *The Hollywood Family Film: A History, from Shirley Temple to Harry Potter*. London: I. B. Tauris.

———. 2017. *The Children's Film: Genre, Nation and Narrative*. London: Wallflower.

Buckland, Warren. 2006. *Directed by Steven Spielberg: Poetics of the Contemporary Hollywood Blockbuster*. New York: Continuum.

Business Wire. 2014. "Newcomer Ruby Barnhill Has Been Cast as 'Sophie' in Spielberg's Adaptation of Roald Dahl's 'The BFG.'" December 16. https://www.businesswire.com/news/home/20141216005085/en/Newcomer-Ruby-Barnhill-Cast-%E2%80%9CSophie%E2%80%9D-Spielberg%E2%80%99s-Adaptation.

Callahan, Dan. 2003. "Arrested Development." *Senses of Cinema*, "The Question Spielberg: A Symposium," no. 27 (July). http://archive.sensesofcinema.com/images/27/spielberg/sugarland_express.jpg&imgrefurl=http://archive.sensesofcinema.com/contents/03/27/spielberg_symposium_position_papers.html/.

Campisi, Jessica, and Saeed Ahmed. 2018. "For Kids Getting Busted for Running Lemonade Stands without Permits, These Guys Are Here to Help." CNN, June 11. https://edition.cnn.com/2018/06/11/us/lemonade-stands-country-time-trnd/index.html.

Canby, Vincent. 1984. "Screen: 'Indiana Jones,' Directed by Spielberg." *New York Times*, April 23, C21.

Carson, Tom. 1986. "Boy Wonder." *L.A. Weekly*, January 10.*

Caruth, Cathy. 1995, *Trauma: Explorations in Memory*. Baltimore: Johns Hopkins University Press.

Cary, Diana Serra. 1979. *Hollywood's Children: An Inside Account of the Child Star Era*. Boston: Houghton Mifflin.

———. 1996. *What Ever Happened to Baby Peggy: The Autobiography of Hollywood's Pioneer Child Star*. London: St. Martin's Press.

Castle, Alison. 2005. *The Stanley Kubrick Archives*. Cologne: Taschen.

Cheung, Harrison, and Nicola Pittam. 2012. *Christian Bale: The Inside Story of the Darkest Batman*. Dallas: Benbella Books.

Chi, Paul. 2013. "*Jurassic Park* Kids: Where Are They Now?" *People*, April 5. https://people.com/movies/jurassic-parks-joseph-mazzello-and-ariana-richards-today/.

Chia, Daniel. n.d. "Exclusive Interview with Haley Joel Osment." Pts. 1–3. https://web.archive.org/web/20071122064014/http://www.homeofthegiants.com/haleyjoelosmentINTERVIEW.htm.

Child Survivors' Association of Great Britain. 2005. *Zachor: Child Survivors Speak*. London: Elliott and Thompson.

Clark, Alex. 2016. "Mark Rylance: 'I Was Amused Steven Spielberg Offered Me the Part." *The Guardian*, July 31. https://www.theguardian.com/culture/2016/jul/31/mark-rylance-interview-steven-spielberg-the-bfg.

Clover, Carol J. 1992. *Men, Women and Chain Saws: Gender in the Modern Horror Film*. London: British Film Institute.

Coleman, John. 1978. "Close Encounters of the Third Kind." *New Statesman*, March 17.*

Collodi, Carlo. 1881. *The Story of a Puppet*. Later published as *The Adventures of Pinocchio*, Tipografia dei Fratelli Bencini, 1883.

Cook, Bruce. 1977. "Close Encounters with Steven Spielberg." *American Film* 3, no. 2 (November): 24–29.

Cook, Tommy. 2012. "Henry Thomas and Kathleen Kennedy Talk *E.T. the Extra-Terrestrial*, *Jurassic Park 4*, *Lincoln*, Steven Spielberg, and More." Collider, September 30. http://collider.com/et-henry-thomas-kathleen-kennedy-interview/.

Copel, Lib. 2001. "Acting Older Than His Age." *Washington Post*, July 2. https://www.washingtonpost.com/archive/lifestyle/2001/07/02/acting-older-than-his-age/61b60037-6cde-4651-a7fa-309e87b86d3c/?noredirect=on&utm_term=.d916634182cc.

Copjec, Joan. 1999. "More! From Melodrama to Magnitude." In *Endless Night: Cinema and Psychoanalysis, Parallel Histories*, edited by Janet Bergstrom, 249–272. Berkeley: University of California Press.

Corliss, Richard. 1981. "The New Hollywood: Dead or Alive?" *Time*, March 30, 66–71.

———.1982. "Cinema: Steve's Summer Magic." *Time*, May 31. https://time.com/3833695/e-t-poltergeist-steven-spielberg-movie-review/w.

———.1985. "Show Business: I Dream for a Living." *Time*, July 15. time.com/archive/6704465/show-business-i-dream-for-a-living/

———. 1987. "The Man-Child Who Fell to Earth." *Time*, December 7, 48.

———. 1989. "What's Old Is Gold: A Triumph for Indy 3." *Time*, May 29, 52–54.

Cornea, Christine. 2007. *Science Fiction Cinema: Between Fantasy and Reality*. Edinburgh: Edinburgh University Press.

Cunningham, Hugh. 2006. *The Invention of Childhood*. London: BBC Books.

Czach, Liz. 2012. "Acting and Performance in Home Movies and Amateur Films." In *Theorizing Film Acting*, edited by Aaron Taylor, 152–165. New York: Routledge.

Darvi, Andrea. 1983. *Pretty Babies: An Insider's Look at the World of the Hollywood Child Star*. New York: McGraw-Hill.

Davies, Ivor. 1988. "Here's Looking at You, Kid!" *Sunday Express*, February 7, 10–12, 14, 41.

Davies, James. 1975. "Jaws." *Daily Express*, December 27.*

Davis, Ivor. 1982. "ET, the Lovable Little Monster Who's Earning Steven Spielberg One Million Dollars a Day." *Daily Express* August 18, 16–17.

Dawn, Randee. 2022. "With a Comeback Like No Other, Ke Huy Quan Can Again Embrace His Dream of Acting." *Los Angeles Times*, November 7. https://www.latimes.com/entertainment-arts/awards/story/2022-11-07/ke-huy-quan-can-again-embrace-his-dream-of-acting.

Delano, Anthony. 1978. "Watch This Space!" *Daily Mirror*, February 18.*

Denby, David. 1981. "Movie of Champions." *New York*, June 15, 68, 70.

———. 1984. "Lost in the Thrill Machine." *New York*, June 4, 72–74.

Desplechin, Arnaud et al. 2010. "Conversations at the Mill." In *Cinema and the Shoah: An Art Confronts the Tragedy of the Twentieth Century*, edited by Jean-Michel Frodon, 107–145. Albany: State University of New York Press.

Dick, Leslie. 1997. "Sight and Sound A-Z of Cinema. R Road." *Sight and Sound* 7, no. 11 (November): 22–24, 26.

Diorio, Carl. 2001. "'A.I.' Stirs Ad Men's Angst." *Variety* September 15, 8, 41.

Docherty, Cameron. 1992. "Fairytales of Hoffman." *The Scotsman*, Weekend section, 28 March, 31.

Driscoll, Catherine. 2002. *Girls: Feminine Adolescence in Popular Culture and Cultural Theory*. New York: Columbia University Press.

Durkee, Cutler. 2008. *Child Stars, Then and Now*. New York: Time Inc. Home Entertainment.

Eberl, Jason T. 2007. "'Please Make Me a Real Boy': The Prayer of the Artificially Intelligent." In *The Philosophy of Stanley Kubrick*, edited by Jerold J. Abrams, 235–246. Lexington: University Press of Kentucky.

Ebert, Roger. 2001. "A.I. Artificial Intelligence." Roger Ebert.com, June 29. https://www.rogerebert.com/reviews/ai-artificial-intelligence-2001.

———. 2011. "He Just Wanted to Become a Real Boy." Roger Ebert.com, July . https://www.rogerebert.com/reviews/great-movie-ai-artificial-intelligence-2001.

Ebert, Roger, and Gene Siskel. 1991. *The Future of the Movies: Interviews with Martin Scorsese, Steven Spielberg, and George Lucas*. Kansas City: Buena Vista Media.

Ellis, Lucy, and Bryony Sutherland. 2003. *Drew Barrymore: The Biography*. London: Aurum Press.

Elsaesser, Thomas. 1986. "Tales of Sound and Fury: Observations on the Family Melodrama." In *Film Genre Reader*, edited by Barry Keith Grant, 278–308. Austin: University of Texas Press.

Erll, Astrid. 2011. *Memory in Culture*. London: Palgrave Macmillan.

Esquire. 1975. "Directors of the 9th Era." February.*

Farber, Stephen, and Marc Green. 1988. *Outrageous Conduct: Art, Ego, and the* Twilight Zone *Case*. New York: Arbor House.

Feeley, Gregory. 1999. "Film; The Masterpiece a Master Couldn't Get Right." *New York Times*, sec. 2, July 18 . https://www.nytimes.com/1999/07/18/arts/film-the-masterpiece-a-master-couldnt-get-right.html.

Felman, Shoshana. 1992. "Education and Crisis, or the Vicissitudes of Teaching." In *Testimony: Crises of Witnessing in Literature, Psychoanalysis, and History*, edited by Shoshana Felman and Dori Laub, 1–56. New York: Routledge.

Felman, Shoshana, and Dori Laub, eds. 1992. *Testimony: Crises of Witnessing in Literature, Psychoanalysis, and History*. New York: Routledge.

Felperin, Leslie. 1998. "The James Gang." *Sight and Sound* 8, no. 6 (June): 47.

Fisher, Bob. 1999. "A Transcendent Career Foretold." *American Cinematographer* 80 no. 2 (February): 30–40.

Fordham, Joe. 2001. "Mecha Odyssey." *Cinefex*, no. 28 (October): 64–93.

Forsberg, Myra. 2000. "Spielberg at 40: The Man and the Child." In *Steven Spielberg Interviews*, edited by Lester D. Friedman and Brent Notbohm, 126–132. Jackson: University Press of Mississippi.

Freer, Ian. 2001. *The Complete Spielberg*. London: Virgin Books.

Friedman, Lester D. 2006. *Citizen Spielberg*. Urbana: University of Illinois Press.

Friedman, Lester D., and Brent Notbohm, eds. 2000. *Steven Spielberg: Interviews*. Jackson: University Press of Mississippi.

Frosh, Stephen, Anne Phoenix, and Rob Pattman. 2002. *Young Masculinities: Understanding Boys in Contemporary Society*. Basingstoke: Palgrave.

Garber, Marjorie. 1993. *Vested Interests: Cross-Dressing and Cultural Anxiety*. New York: HarperCollins.

Garry, John P. 2009. "Strange Days and the Post-revisionist Era: The Possibility of Redemption." *Film International* 5, no. 39 (June): 36–49.

Garwood, Alfred. 2020. *Holocaust Trauma and Psychic Deformation: Psychoanalytic Reflections of a Holocaust Survivor*. London: Routledge.

Gateward, Frances, and Murray Pomerance, eds. 2002. *Sugar, Spice and Everything Nice: Cinemas of Girlhood*. Detroit: Wayne State University Press.

Gay, Michael, and George Lynn. 1975. "They Were the First—and They Loved It!" *The Sun*, December 27.*

Geng, Veronica. 1981. "Spielberg's Express." *Film Comment* 17, no. 4 (July–August): 57–59.

Gilchrist, Roderick. 1975. "Children Can Watch Jaws." *Daily Mail*, November 7.*

Gittins, Diana. 2005. "The Historical Construction of Childhood." In *An Introduction to Childhood Studies*, edited by Mary Jane Kehily, 25–38. Maidenhead: Open University Press.

Gledhill, Christine, ed. 1987. *Home Is Where the Heart Is: Studies in Melodrama and the Woman's Film*. London: British Film Institute.

Goh, Yang-Yi. 2022. "The Many Lives of Ke Huy Quan." *GQ*, April 8. https://www.gq.com/story/ke-huy-quan-everything-everywhere-all-at-once.

Goldrup, Tom, and Jim Goldrup. 2002. *Growing Up on the Set: Interviews with 39 Former Child Actors of Classic Film and Television*. Jefferson NC: McFarland.

Goldstone, Patricia. 1981. "Movie Directors Can Stay Forever Young." *L.A. Times*, March 8.*

Gordon, Andrew M. 2008. *Empire of Dreams: The Science Fiction and Fantasy Films of Steven Spielberg*. Lanham, MD: Rowman and Littlefield.

Gordon, George. 1975. "How One U.S. Family Reacted." *Daily Mail*, November 7.

Gottlieb, Carl. 2005. *The Jaws Log*. Expanded edition. New York: HarperCollins.

Gourevitch, Philip. 1994. "A Dissent on Schindler's List." *Commentary* 97, no. 2 (February): 49–52.

Grant, Katie. 2016. "BFG Star Ruby Barnhill: My Parents Sent Me to My Audition Thinking I'd Be Rejected." *inews*, July 19. https://inews.co.uk/news/entertainment/bfg-star-ruby-barnhill-parents-thought-i-fail-audition-14848.

Gray, Marianne. 1982. "Why I Really Wanted to Film *E.T.*" *Photoplay* 33, no. 12 (December): 34–39.

Grenier, Richard. 1991. *Capturing the Culture: Film, Art and Politics*. Washington, DC: Ethics and Public Policy Centre Publications.

Griffin, Nancy. 1989. "Manchild in the Promised Land." *Premiere* 2, no. 12 (June): 86–94.

Grodal, Torben. 1997. *Moving Pictures: A New Theory of Film Genres, Feelings, and Cognition*. Oxford: Clarendon Press

Gross, Larry. 1995. "Big and Loud." *Sight and Sound*, August, 6–10.

Hammond, Michael. 2002. "Some Smothering Dreams: The Combat Film in Contemporary Hollywood." In *Genre and Contemporary Hollywood*, edited by Steve Neale, 62–76. London: British Film Institute.

Handyside, Fiona, and Kate Taylor-Jones, eds. 2016. *International Cinema and the Girl: Local Issues, Transnational Cultures*. Basingstoke: Palgrave Macmillan.

Hansen, Miriam Bratu. 2001. "*Schindler's List* Is Not *Shoah*: Second Commandment, Popular Modernism, and Public Memory." In *Visual Culture and the Holocaust*, edited by Barbie Zelizer, 127–151. New Brunswick, NJ: Rutgers University Press.

Haraway, Donna. 2003. *The Companion Species Manifesto: Dogs, People and Significant Otherness*. Chicago: University of Chicago Press.

———. 2004. "A Manifesto for Cyborgs: Science, Technology, and Socialist Feminism in the 1980s." In *The Haraway Reader*, 7–45. New York: Routledge.

Harlan, Jan, and Jane M. Struthers, eds. 2009. *A.I. Artificial Intelligence: From Stanley Kubrick to Steven Spielberg: The Vision behind the Film*. London: Thames and Hudson.

Harmetz, Aljean. 1984. "'Indiana Jones' Stirs Ratings Debate." *New York Times*, May 21, .C12.

Harris, Anita. 2004. *Future Girl: Young Women in the Twenty-First Century*. New York and London: Routledge.

Hazlitt, William. 2004. "On Wit and Humour." In *Selected Essays of William Hazlitt 1778 to 1830*, edited by Geoffrey Keynes. Whitefish, MT: Kessinger Publishing.

Heathwood, Gail. 1978. "Steven Spielberg." *Cinema Papers*, no. 16 (April/June): 318–321, 379.

Heffernan, Teresa. 2018. "A.I. Artificial Intelligence: Science, Fiction and Fairy Tales." *English Studies in Africa* 61 (1): 10–15.

Herget, Winfried. 1991. "Towards a Rhetoric of Sentimentality." In *Sentimentality in Modern Literature and Popular Culture*, edited by Winfried Herget, 1–14. Tübingen: Gunter Narr.

Heung, Marina. 1983. "Why E.T. Must Go Home: The New Family in American Cinema." *Journal of Popular Film and Television* 11 (2): 79–85.

Heywood, Colin. 2001. *A History of Childhood: Children and Childhood in the West from Medieval to Modern Times*. Cambridge, UK: Polity Press.

Hibbert, Claire. 2012. *EDGE: Teen Stars: Dakota Fanning*. London: Hatchette Children's Group.

Higonnet, Anne. 1998. *Pictures of Innocence: The History and Crisis of Ideal Childhood*. London: Thames and Hudson.

Hinton, Leslie. 1977. "The UFOs Are Coming." *The Sun*, November 24.*

Hirschberg, Lynn. 1984. "Will Hollywood's Mr. Perfect Ever Grow Up?" *Rolling Stone*, July 19–August 2, 34–35, 38.

Hiscock, John. 2008. "How We Brought Indy Back to Life." *Daily Telegraph*, May 14, 25.

———. 2015. "Haley Joel Osment: 'I'm Not the Kid from The Sixth Sense Any More.'" *Daily Telegraph*, June 20. https://www.telegraph.co.uk/film/entourage/haley-joel-osment-interview/.

Hobbes, Thomas. 1928. *The Elements of Law, Natural and Politic*. Cambridge: Cambridge University Press.

Hoberman, J. 2003. "*A.I.*: The Dreamlife of Androids." In *The Magic Hour: Films at the Fin De Siècle*, 76–81. Philadelphia: Temple University Press.

———. 2007. "Laugh, Cry, Believe: Spielbergization and Its Discontents." *Virginia Quarterly Review* 83 (1): 119–135.

Hollywood Reporter. 1968. "Universal Pacts Pamela McMyler, Steve Spielberg." December 12.*

Holmes, Martha Stoddard. 2009. "Peter Pan and the Possibilities of Child Literature." In *Second Star to the Right: Peter Pan in the Popular Imagination*, edited by Allison B. Kavey and Lester D. Friedman, 132–150. New Brunswick, NJ: Rutgers University Press.

Horse and Hound. 2012. "*War Horse* Film Preview: Watch Joey on the Red Carpet." January 9. http://www.horseandhound.co.uk/news/war-horse-film-preview-watch-joey-on-the-red-carpet-311033.

Horton, Andrew. 1978. "Hot Car Films and Cool Individualism: Or, What We Have Here Is a Lack of Respect for the Law." *Cineaste* 8, no. 4 (Summer): 12–15.

Hull, Bob. 1969. "22-Year-Old Tyro Directs Joan Crawford: 'A Pleasure'." *Hollywood Reporter*, February 17, 8.

Jackson, Kathi. 2007. *Steven Spielberg A Biography*. London: Greenwood.

Jackson, Kathy Merlock. 1986. *Images of Children in American Film: A Sociocultural Analysis*. Metuchen, NJ: Scarecrow Press.

Jacobs, Lea. 2008. *The Decline of Sentiment: American Film in the 1920s*. Oakland: University of California Press.

James, Allison, Chris Jenks, and Alan Prout. 1998. *Theorizing Childhood*. Cambridge, UK: Polity Press.

James, Henry. 2010. *What Maisie Knew*. London: Penguin.

Janos, Leo. 1980. "Steven Spielberg: L'Enfant Directeur." *Cosmopolitan*, June, 236–239, 345.

Jenkins, Henry, ed. 1998. *The Children's Culture Reader*. New York: New York University Press.

———. 2007. *The Wow Climax: Tracing the Emotional Impact of Popular Culture*. New York: New York University Press.

Jenks, Chris. 1996. *Childhood*. 2nd ed. London: Routledge.

Jones, Samuel L. 1983. "Matthew de Meritt: The Scout in the E.T. Costume." *Boy's Life* 73, no. 10 (October): 72–73.

Jones, Theresa. 2009. "Peter and Me (or How I Learned to Fly): Network Television Broadcasts of Peter Pan." In *Second Star to the Right: Peter Pan in the Popular Imagination*, edited by Allison B. Kavey and Lester D. Friedman, 243–263. New Brunswick, NJ: Rutgers University Press.

Jurassic Cast Podcast. n.d. "The Guys at Jurassic Cast Interview Ariana Richards about Her Time Playing Lex in Jurassic Park and The Lost World." https://www.dailymotion.com/video/x69xlry.

Kael, Pauline. 1977. "The Greening of the Solar System." *New Yorker*, November 28, 174–178, 181.

———. 1981. "Whipped." *New Yorker*, June 15, 132–135.

———. 1984. "A Breeze, a Bawd, a Bounty." *New Yorker*, June 11, 100, 103–106.

———. 1987. "The Pure and the Impure." In *Taking It All In: Film Writings 1980–1983*, 347–355. London: Arrow Books.

Kaplan, Fred. 1987. *Sacred Tears: Sentimentality in Victorian Literature*. Princeton, NJ: Princeton University Press.

Kaplan Peter W. 1982. "The Rosebud Legacy." *Washington Post*, June 9. https://www.washingtonpost.com/archive/lifestyle/1982/06/10/the-rosebud-legacy/51a53f08-1a5e-4e44-81e5-0099f1af7c3d/.

Kavey, Allison B., and Lester D. Friedman, eds. 2009. *Second Star to the Right: Peter Pan in the Popular Imagination*. New Brunswick, NJ: Rutgers University Press.

Kendrick, James. 2014. *Darkness in the Bliss-Out: A Reconsideration of the Films of Steven Spielberg*. London: Bloomsbury.

Keneally, Thomas. 1982. *Schindler's Ark*. London: Hodder & Stoughton.

Kilday, Gregg. 1982. "Spielberg's Tract: Surprise in the Suburbs." *Los Angeles Herald-Examiner*, June 11.*

Kiley, Dan. 1983. *The Peter Pan Syndrome: Men Who Have Never Grown Up*. New York: Avon Books.

Kim, Ellen A. 2001. "A.I.: Haley Joel Osment Interview." Hollywood.com, June 27. http://www.hollywood.com/feature/AI_Haley_Joel_Osment_Interview/470090.

King, Susan. 1999. "Actor Has a Sense for Spooky Role." *Los Angeles Times*, August 13. https://www.latimes.com/archives/la-xpm-1999-aug-13-ca-65205-story.html.

Kondazian, Karen, with Eddie Shapiro. 2000. *The Actor's Encyclopedia of Casting Directors: Conversations with over 100 Casting Directors on How to Get the Job*. Los Angeles: Lone Eagle.

Kong, Belinda. 2009. "Shanghai Biopolitans: Wartime Colonial Cosmopolis in Eileen Chang's Love in a Fallen City and J. G. Ballard's Empire of the Sun." *JNT: Journal of Narrative Theory* 39, no. 3 (Fall): 280–304.

Kowalski, Dean A., ed. 2008. *Steven Spielberg and Philosophy: We're Gonna Need a Bigger Book*. Lexington: University Press of Kentucky.

Krämer, Peter. 1998. "Would You Take Your Child to See This Film? The Cultural and Social Work of the Family Adventure Movie." In *Contemporary Hollywood Cinema*, edited by Steve Neale and Murray Smith, 294–311. London: Routledge.

———. 2006. "Disney and the Family Adventure Movie since the 1970s." In *Contemporary American Cinema*, edited by Linda Ruth Williams and Michael Hammond, 265–279. Milton Keynes: Open University Press and McGraw-Hill.

———. 2017. "Spielberg and Kubrick." In *A Companion to Steven Spielberg*, edited by Nigel Morris, 212–226. Chichester: Wiley Blackwell.

Kreider, Tim. 2003. "*A.I.: Artificial Intelligence*." *Film Quarterly* 56, no. 2 (December): 32–39.

Kroll, Justin. 2015. "Steven Spielberg to Direct Sci-Fi Film 'Ready Player One'." *Variety*, March 25. https://variety.com/2015/film/news/steven-spielberg-to-direct-sci-fi-film-ready-player-one-1201460039/.

LaBrecque, Ron. 1988. *Special Effects: Disaster at "Twilight Zone": The Tragedy and the Trial*. New York: Charles Scribner's Sons.

Laderman, David. 1996. "What a Trip: The Road Film and American Culture." *Journal of Film and Video* 48, no. 1/2 (Spring–Summer): 41–57.

Lambie, Ryan. 2018. "Olivia Cooke Interview: *Ready Player One*, Spielberg, Working Class Accents." *Den of Geek*, March 26. https://www.denofgeek.com/movies/olivia-cooke-interview-ready-player-one-spielberg-working-class-accents/.

LaSalle, Mick. 2001. "Artificial Foolishness." *San Francisco Chronicle*, June 29. https://www.sfgate.com/movies/article/Artificial-foolishness-A-I-starts-out-2905798.php.

Lawrence, Michael, and Susan Smith, eds. 2012. "Child Performance Dossier." *Screen* 53, no. 4 (Winter): 436–439.

Lebeau, Vicky. 2008. *Childhood and Cinema*. London: Reaktion.

Lee, Ann. 2022. "'I Didn't Have a Single Audition for a Year': Goonies and Indiana Jones Child Star Ke Huy Quan on Finding Fame Again." *The Guardian*, November 14. https://www.theguardian.com/film/2022/nov/14/ke-huy-quan-goonies-indiana-jones-asian-actors-everything-everywhere-all-at-once.

Leggatt, Matthew. 2021. "'Why Can't We Go Backwards, for Once?': Nostalgia, Utopia, and Science Fiction in Steven Spielberg's *Ready Player One*." In *Was It Yesterday: Nostalgia in Contemporary Film and Television*, edited by Matthew Leggatt, 179–195. Albany: State University of New York Press.

Leishman, Rachel. 2018. "Ariana Richards on *Jurassic Park*, Her Art, and the Jeff Goldblum Craze." The Mary Sue, September 12. https://www.themarysue.com/ariana-richards-interview/.

Letters to E.T. 1983. New York: G. P. Putnam's Sons.

Lightman, Herb. 1978. "Spielberg Speaks about 'Close Encounters'." *American Cinematographer*, January, 39–42, 58, 59, 95.

Ligocka, Roma. 2003. *The Girl in the Red Coat*. New York: Random House.

Lim, Kay, and Reid Orvedahl. 2022. "Steven Spielberg on Making 'The Fabelmans': 'It Was Cathartic for Me'." CBS News, November 6. https://www.cbsnews.com/news/steven-spielberg-on-making-the-fabelmans/.

Lipworth, Elaine. 2014. "Drew Barrymore: 'I NEVER want to repeat my upbringing'." *Mail on Sunday*, May 11. https://www.dailymail.co.uk/home/you/article-2623423/Drew-Barrymore-I-NEVER-want-repeat-upbringing.html.

Lopate, Phillip. 1997. "When the 'I' in a Film Is a Child's." *New York Times*, March 16. https://www.nytimes.com/1997/03/16/movies/when-the-i-in-a-film-is-a-child-s.html.

Loren, Scott. 2008. "Mechanical Humanity, or How I Learned to Stop Worrying and Love the Android: The Posthuman Subject in *2001: A Space Odyssey* and *Artificial Intelligence: A.I.* " In *Stanley Kubrick: Essays on His Films and Legacy*, edited by Gary D. Rhodes, 211–231. Jefferson, NC: McFarland.

Loshitzky, Yosefa, ed. 1997. *Spielberg's Holocaust: Critical Perspectives on Schindler's List*. Bloomington: Indiana University Press.

Loynd, Ray. 1977. "Surprising Turns for Two Hit Filmmakers." *L.A. Herald-Examiner*, December 9.*

Lury, Karen. 2010. *The Child in Film: Tears, Fears and Fairy Tales*. London: I. B. Tauris.

Lyus, Jon. 2011. "Exclusive Interview: Ariana Richards on *Jurassic Park*." Heyuguys, October 24. https://www.heyuguys.com/exclusive-interview-ariana-richards-on-jurassic-park/.

MacCabe, Colin. 2005. "Midnight in America." *The Independent*, arts section, July 1, 8–9.

Macnab, Geoffrey. 2018. "The Post Review: Spielberg's Newspaper Drama Matches Up to Spotlight." *The Independent*, January 17. https://www.independent.co.uk/arts-entertainment/films/reviews/the-post-review-tickets-watch-steven-spielberg-trailer-meryl-streep-tom-hanks-a8163456.html.

Malcolm, Derek. 1994. "This Week's Reviews: Schindler's List." *The Guardian*, February 17. https://www.theguardian.com/film/News_Story/Critic_Review/Guardian_review/0,,530821,00.html

Mann, Karen B. 2005. "Lost Boys and Girls in Spielberg's Minority Report." *Journal of Narrative Theory* 35, no. 2 (Summer): 196–217.

Marks, Scott. 2018. "The Post—Spielberg's Stagiest Work to Date." *San Diego Reader*, January 10. https://www.sandiegoreader.com/news/2018/jan/10/movie-review-post-spielbergs-stagiest-work-date/.

Marsh, Clive. 2004. *Cinema and Sentiment: Film's Challenges to Theology*. Eugene, OR: Wipf and Stock.

Marshall, William. 1988. "Empire of the Kid." *Daily Mirror*, March 22, 16–17.

Maslin, Janet. 1987. "Film: Spielberg's 'Empire of Sun' [*sic*]." *New York Times*, December 9, C25.

Mattern, Joanne. 2006. *Dakota Fanning*. Hallandale, FL: Mitchell Lane.

McBride, Joseph. 2007. "Review of Citizen Spielberg." *Cineaste* 32, no. 2 (Spring): 80–82, 92.

———. 2010. *Steven Spielberg: A Biography*. 2nd ed. Jackson: University Press of Mississippi.

McCarthy, Todd. 2005. "War of the Worlds." *Variety*, June 28. https://variety.com/2005/film/awards/war-of-the-worlds-2-1200524860/.

McCartney, Jenny. 2005. "War of the Worlds." *Sunday Telegraph*, review section, July 3, 6.

McDonald, Frances. 2012. "Wrong Laughter: Laughing Away the Human in Richard Powers' Galatea 2.2." In *Unveiling the Post-human*, edited by Artur Matos Alves, 115–122. Leiden, NL: Brill.

McGavran, James Holt, ed. 1999. *Literature and the Child: Romantic Continuations, Postmodern Contestations*. Iowa City: University of Iowa Press.

Mecklenburg, Virginia M. 2010. *Telling Stories: Norman Rockwell from the Collections of George Lucas and Steven Spielberg*. New York: Abrams, in association with the Smithsonian American Art Museum.

Miller, Henry. 1977. "SF Spectacular by 'Jaws' Prodigy Rivals 'Star Wars'." *Daily Telegraph*, November 21.*

Mintz, Allan. 2001. *Popular Culture and the Shaping of Holocaust Memory in America*. Seattle: University of Washington Press.

Mondello, Bob. 2023. "Spielberg Shared His Own Story in 'Parts and Parcels'—If You Were Paying Attention." NPR, March. https://www.npr.org/2023/03/06/1160818590/steven-spielberg-the-fabelmans.

Mooallem, Jon. 2016. "Inside the Mind of Steven Spielberg, Hollywood's Big, Friendly Giant." *Wired*, July 2016. https://www.wired.com/2016/06/steven-spielberg-the-bfg/.

Morpurgo, Michael. 1982. *War Horse*. London: Kaye and Ward.

Morris, Nigel. 2007. *The Cinema of Steven Spielberg: Empire of Light*. London: Wallflower Press.

Morris, Tim. 2000. *You're Only Young Twice: Children's Literature and Film*. Urbana: University of Illinois Press.

Morton, Ray. 2007. *Close Encounters of the Third Kind: The Making of Steven Spielberg's Classic Film*. New York: Applause Theatre and Cinema Books.

Moss, Robert F. 1981. "Director Steven Spielberg: New Epic, Big Stakes." *Saturday Review*, June, 12–15. https://www.unz.com/print/SaturdayRev-1981jun-00012/.

Mulvey, Laura. 1994. "'It Will Be a Magnificent Obsession': The Melodrama's Role in the Development of Contemporary Film Theory." In *Melodrama: Stage, Picture, Screen*, edited by Jacky Bratton, Jim Cook, and Christine Gledhill, 121–133. London: British Film Institute.

Munns, David P. D. 2009. "'Gay, Innocent, and Heartless': Peter Pan and the Queering of Popular Culture." In *Second Star to the Right: Peter Pan in the Popular Imagination*, edited by Allison B. Kavey and Lester D. Friedman, 219–242. New Brunswick, NJ: Rutgers University Press.

Myles, Eileen. 2001. "Our Love Is Real, but We Are Not." *Village Voice*, July 31, 43.

Naremore, James. 2005. "Love and Death in *A.I. Artificial Intelligence*." *Michigan Quarterly Review* 44, no. 2 (Spring): 257–284. https://quod.lib.umich.edu/cgi/t/text/text-idx?cc=mqr;c=mqr;c=mqrarchive;idno=act2080.0044.210;g=mqrg;rgn=main;view=text;xc=1.

Navarro, Mireya. 2007. "When Childhood Is a Tough Role." *New York Times*, September 23. http://www.nytimes.com/2007/09/23/fashion/23hollywood.html.

Neale, Stephen. 1989. "Issues of Difference: *Alien* and *Blade Runner*." In *Fantasy and the Cinema*, edited by James Donald, 213–223. London: British Film Institute.

Nelson, Thomas Allen. 2000. *Kubrick: Inside a Film Artist's Maze*. Bloomington: Indiana University Press.

Newsweek. 1977. "Close Encounter with Spielberg." November 21, 98–99.

Nichols, Peter M. 2003. *The New York Times Essential Library: Children's Movies*. New York: Times Books.

Nodelman, Perry. 2002. "Making Boys Appear: The Masculinity of Children's Fiction." In *Ways of Being Male: Representing Masculinities in Children's Literature and Film*, edited by John Stephens, 1–14. London: Routledge.

O'Connor, Jane. 2008. *The Cultural Significance of the Child Star*. London: Routledge.

Ojumu, Akin, and Jason Solomons. 2012. "Spielberg's Youth Team." *The Observer*, review section, January 8, 4–5.

Olson, Debbie. 2017. *Black Children in Hollywood Cinema: Cast in Shadow*. London: Palgrave Macmillan.

Olson, Debbie, and Andrew Scahill, eds. 2012. *Lost and Othered Children in Contemporary Cinema*. Lanham, MD: Lexington Books.

Olya, Gabrielle. 2019. "30 Former Child Stars Striking Hollywood Gold." Yahoo!Finance, April 24. https://finance.yahoo.com/news/bella-thorne-30-other-former-090000031.html.

Orgeron, Marsha. 2007. "'I Came Back as Nobody': An Interview with the Former Baby Peggy." *Framework* 48, no. 1 (Spring): 4–22.

Pace, Patricia. 1996. "Robert Bly Does Peter Pan: The Inner Child as Father to the Man in Spielberg's Hook." *The Lion and the Unicorn* 20, no. 1 (June): 113–120.

Palowski, Franciszek. 1999. *Witness: The Making of Schindler's List*. Translated by Anna and Robert G. Ware. London: Orion.

Parisi, Paula. 2019. "Ready Player One' Juxtaposes Real, Virtual via VFX from Three Shops." *Variety*, February 21. https://variety.com/2019/artisans/production/spielberg-ready-player-one-vfx-1203144265/.

Parkin, Simon. 2014. "Haley Joel Osment Returns." *New Yorker*, October 29. https://www.newyorker.com/culture/culture-desk/haley-joel-osment.

Parry, Becky. 2013. *Children, Film and Literacy*. Basingstoke: Palgrave-Macmillan.

Patrick, Seb. 2011. "Jurassic Park: Ariana Richards Interview." *Den of Geek*, October 24. https://www.denofgeek.com/movies/18232/jurassic-park-ariana-richards-interview.

Peachment, Chris. 1987. "The Film of the Booker: Chris Peachment Talks to JG Ballard about Spielberg's Film Adaption of the Author's Prize-Winning Novel." *The Times*, November 28. www.jgballard.ca/media/1987_nov28_times_newspaper.html.

Perkowitz, Sidney. 2010. *Hollywood Science: Movies, Science and the End of the World*. New York: Columbia University Press.

Perry, George. 1998. *Steven Spielberg: The Making of His Movies*. London: Orien.

Petley, Julian. 1988. "The Sun Landing." *The Guardian*, March 17. https://www.jgballard.ca/media/1988_march17_guardian.html.

Phillips, Julia. 1991. *You'll Never Eat Lunch in the Town Again*. New York: Random House.

Plantinga, Carl. 2009. *Moving Viewers: American Film and the Spectator's Experience*. Berkeley: University of California Press.

Playboy. 1975. "On the Scene—Steven Spielberg Into the Jaws of Fame." June, 168.

Plotz, Judith. 2001. *Romanticism and the Vocation of Childhood*. New York: Palgrave.

Pollock, Dale. 1981. "The Graying of a Crapshooter." *L.A. Times*, June 10, 1, 4.

———. 1983a. "Spielberg Philosophical over 'E.T.' Oscar Defeat." *L.A. Times*, April 13, 1, 4.

———. 1983b. "The Movie Godfather." *Marquee*, June/July, 1–2.*

Pomerance, Murray. 2005. "The Man-Boys of Steven Spielberg." In *Where the Boys Are: Cinemas of Masculinity and Youth*, edited by Murray Pomerance and Frances Gateward, 132–154. Detroit: Wayne State University Press.

———. 2008. "Digesting Steven Spielberg." *Film International* 6, no. 2 (April): 24–37. https://intellectdiscover.com/content/journals/10.1386/fiin.6.2.24.

———. 2017. "Close Encounters of the Paternal Kind: Spielberg's Fatherhoods." In *A Companion to Steven Spielberg*, edited by Nigel Morris, 258–275. Oxford: Wiley Blackwell.

Pomerance, Murray, and Frances Gateward. 2005. "Introduction." In *Where the Boys Are: Cinemas of Masculinity and Youth*, edited by Murray Pomerance and Frances Gateward, 1–18. Detroit: Wayne State University Press.

———, eds. 2005. *Where the Boys Are: Cinemas of Masculinity and Youth*. Detroit: Wayne State University Press.

Poster, Steve. 2000. "The Mind Behind *Close Encounters of the Third Kind*." In *Steven Spielberg: Interviews*, edited by Lester D. Friedman and Brent Notbohm, 55–69. Jackson: University of Mississippi Press.

Powers, James. 1978. "Dialogue on Film: Steven Spielberg." *American Film*, September, 43–53.

Prince, Stephen. 2000. *A New Pot of Gold: Hollywood under the Electronic Rainbow, 1980–1989*. Oakland: University of California Press.

Projansky, Sarah. 2014. *Spectacular Girls: Media Fascination and Celebrity Culture*. New York: New York University Press.

Puckrik, Katie. 2011. "JJ Abrams: 'I Called Spielberg and He Said Yes." *The Guardian*, August 1. https://www.theguardian.com/film/2011/aug/01/jj-abrams-spielberg-super-8.

Pulver, Andrew. 2013. "'Red Coat Girl' Traumatised by Experience of Watching Schindler's List." *The Guardian*, March 4. http://www.theguardian.com/film/2013/mar/04/schindlers-list-actor-traumatised-by-film.
Pye, Michael, and Lynda Myles. 1979. *The Movie Brats: How the Film Generation Took Over Hollywood*. New York: Holt, Rinehart and Winston.
Rees, Jasper. 2018. "*The Post* Review—Spielberg's Glorious Paean to Print." *The Arts Desk*, January 18.https://theartsdesk.com/film/post-review-spielbergs-glorious-paean-print.
Reilly, Sue. 1981. "By Raiding Hollywood Lore and His Childhood Fantasies, Steven Spielberg Rediscovers an Ark That's Pure Gold." *People*, July 20, 74–78.
Reiss, David. 1981. "Raiders of the Lost Ark: An Interview with Steven Spielberg." *Filmmaker's Monthly* 14, no. 9/10 (July/August): 30–39.
Rich, Frank. 1977. "The Aliens Are Coming!" *Time*, November 7, 34–36.
Rice, Julian. 2017. *Kubrick's Story, Spielberg's Film: A.I. Artificial Intelligence*. Lanham, MD: Rowman and Littlefield.
Richardson, Alan. 1999. "Romanticism and the End of Childhood." In *Literature and the Child: Romantic Continuations, Postmodern Contestations*, edited by James Holt McGavran, 23–43. Iowa City: University of Iowa Press.
Robb, David. 1982a. "Spielberg Denies He Was at 'Twilight' Chopper Crash Scene." *Variety* (weekly), December 15.
———. 1982b."Spielberg Denies Presence at Fatal 'Twilight' Crash." *Variety*, (daily), December 10.
———. 1982c. "'Zone' Probe Asking Whither Spielberg." *Variety* (weekly), December 1, 1, 30.
Rose, Jacqueline. 1993. *The Case of Peter Pan, or The Impossibility of Children's Fiction*. 3rd ed. Philadelphia: University of Pennsylvania Press.
Rose, Steve. 2013. "Should Children Be Allowed to Act in Harrowing Films?" *The Guardian*, March 14. http://www.theguardian.com/film/shortcuts/2013/mar/04/children allowed-act-harrowing-films.
Rosenfield, Paul. 1985. "TASTE MAKERS: People Who Shape and Define Matters of Taste: PAULINE KAEL: AND YOU CAN QUOTE THAT. . . ." *Los Angeles Times*, December 22. http://articles.latimes.com/1985-12-22/entertainment/ca-20081_1_pauline-kael.
Royal, Susan. 1982. "Steven Spielberg in His Adventures on Earth." *American Premiere*, July, 17–25.
Rudd, David. 2009. "Animal and Object Stories." In *The Cambridge Companion to Children's Literature*, edited by M. O. Grenby and Andrea Immel, 242–257. Cambridge: Cambridge University Press.
Samuels, Shirley, ed. 1992. *The Culture of Sentiment: Race, Gender, and Sentimentality in Nineteenth-Century America*. New York: Oxford University Press.
Sánchez-Eppler, Karen. 1992. "Bodily Bonds: The Intersecting Rhetorics of Feminism and Abolition." In *The Culture of Sentiment: Race, Gender, and Sentimentality in Nineteenth-Century America*, edited by Shirley Samuels, 92–114. New York: Oxford University Press.
Sandhu, Sukhdev. 2005. "Close Encounter of the Wrong Kind." *Daily Telegraph*, July 1, 17.
Sarris, Andrew. 1982a. "E.T." *Village Voice*, June 15, 59.
———. 1982b. "Is There Life after E.T.?" *Village Voice*, September 21, 47–48.
———. 1987. "A Boy's Own Story." *Village Voice*, December15, 109.
———. 1996. *The American Cinema: Directors and Directions 1929–1968*. Boston: Da Capo Press.

Schatz, Thomas. 1992. "The New Hollywood." In *Film Theory Goes to the Movies: Cultural Analysis of Contemporary Film*, edited by Ava Preacher Collins and Hilary Radner, 8–36. New York: Routledge.

Schickel, Richard. 1981. "Slam! Bang! A Movie Movie." *Time*, June 15, 54–55.

———. 2012. *Spielberg: A Retrospective*. London: Thames and Hudson.

Schober, Adrian, and Debbie Olson, eds. 2016. *Children in the Films of Steven Spielberg*. Washington, DC: Rowman and Littlefield.

Schrodt, Paul. 2012. "Henry Thomas, the Kid from *E.T.*, on the Anniversary and His Perfect Improvised Audition." *Esquire*, October 9. https://www.esquire.com/entertainment/movies/interviews/a16176/henry-thomas-et-interview-13541489/.

Schruers, Fred. 2001. "They Sing the Body Electric." *Premiere* 14, no. 10 (June): 51–53, 107.

Schulman, Michael. 2022. "With 'The Fabelmans,' Steven Spielberg Finally Phones Home." *New Yorker*, September 20. https://www.newyorker.com/culture/notes-on-hollywood/with-the-fabelmans-steven-spielberg-finally-phones-home.

Seabrook, John. 2003. "It Came from Hollywood." *New Yorker*, December 1, 54–63.

Sears, Rufus. 1993. "It's Big!" *Empire*, no. 50 (August): 72–84.

Semlyen, Phil de. 2016. "Steven Spielberg Says The BFG Is the Most Ambitious Mo-Cap Character Ever." *Empire*, April 26. https://www.empireonline.com/movies/news/steven-spielberg-says-bfg-ambitious-mo-cap-character-ever/.

Shay, Don, and Jody Duncan. 1993. *The Making of Jurassic Park*. London: Boxtree.

Short, Sue. 2011. *Cyborg Cinema*. London: Palgrave Macmillan.

Silet, Charles L. P., ed. 2002. *The Films of Steven Spielberg: Critical Essays*. Lanham, MD: Scarecrow Press.

Sinyard, Neil. 1992. *Children in the Movies*. London: Batsford.

Slocum, J. David. 2006. "Introduction: Seeing Through American War Cinema." In *Hollywood and War: The Film Reader*, edited by J. David Slocum, 1–22. New York: Routledge.

Sobchack, Vivian. 1990. "On the Virginity of Astronauts." In *Alien Zone: Cultural Theory and Contemporary Science Fiction Cinema*, edited by Annette Kuhn, 103–115. London: Verso.

———. 1991. "Child/Alien/Father: Patriarchal Crisis and Generic Exchange." In *Close Encounters: Film, Feminism, and Science Fiction*, edited by Constance Penley, Elisabeth Lyon, Lynn Spigel, and Janet Bergstrom, 2–30. Minneapolis: University of Minnesota Press.

———. 2008. "Love Machines: Boy Toys, Toy Boys and the Oxymorons of *A.I.: Artificial Intelligence*." In *Science Fiction Film and Television* 1, no. 1 (Spring): 1–14.

Spielberg, Steven. 1985. "He Was the Movies." *Film Comment* 21, no. 1 (January–February): 40–41.

———. 1988. "Dialogue on Film." *American Film* 13, no. 8 (June): 12–16.

———. 2014. "Introduction: Face to Face with Testimony." In *Testimony: The Legacy of* Schindler's List *and the USC Shoah Foundation*, edited by the USC Shoah Foundation, ix–xiii. New York: HarperCollins.

Sragow, Michael. 2000. "A Conversation with Steven Spielberg." In *Steven Spielberg Interviews*, edited by Lester D. Friedman and Brent Notbohm, 107–119. Jackson: University Press of Mississippi.

———. 2011. "Outtakes from My 1982 Rolling Stone Talk with Spielberg, as the Charles Shows 'E.T.'." *Baltimore Sun*, August 19.*

———. 2012. "'E.T.' Turns Thirty." *New Yorker*, October 3. https://www.newyorker.com/culture/culture-desk/e-t-turns-thirty.

Stam, Robert. 2000. *Film Theory: An Introduction*. Oxford: Blackwell.
Staples, Terry. 1997. *All Pals Together: The Story of Children's Cinema*. Edinburgh: Edinburgh University Press.
Steedman, Carolyn. 1995. *Strange Dislocations: Childhood and the Idea of Human Interiority 1780–1930*. Cambridge, MA: Harvard University Press.
Stephens, Chuck. 1997. "Spielberg's *Lost World*: Franchise, Fatherhood, a World without Dung." *Film Comment* 33, no. 4 (July–August): 12–14. https://www.filmcomment.com/issue/july-august-1997/.
Stephens, John, ed. 2002. *Ways of Being Male: Representing Masculinities in Children's Literature and Film*. London: Routledge.
Stettin, Monte. 1975. "From Television to Features . . . Steven Spielberg." *Millimeter* 3, no. 3 (March): 20–25.
Stevens, Stephanie. 2017. "25 Celebs You Didn't Know Were British." Kiwi Report, February 26. http://www.kiwireport.com/25-celebs-didnt-know-british/.
Strauss, Monica. 1994. "Dissent on Schindler's List." *The New York Review*, June 9. https://www.nybooks.com/articles/1994/06/09/dissent-on-schindlers-list-3/.
Studlar, Gaylyn. 1996. *This Mad Masquerade: Stardom and Masculinity in the Jazz Age*. New York: Columbia University Press.
———. 2001. "Cruise-ing into the Millennium: Performative Masculinity, Stardom, and the All-American Boy's Body." In *Ladies and Gentlemen, Boys and Girls: Gender in Film at the End of the Millennium*, edited by Murray Pomerance, 171–183. Albany: State University of New York Press.
Suddath, Claire. 2012. "Training the Horses in Steven Spielberg's *War Horse*." *Time*, January 5. http://entertainment.time.com/2012/01/05/training-the-horses-in-steven-spielbergs-war-horse/.
Sunshine, Linda, ed. 2012. *E.T. the Extra-Terrestrial: From Concept to Classic: The Illustrated Story of the Film and the Filmmakers*, with an introduction by Steven Spielberg, screenplay by Melissa Mathison, interviews by Laurent Bouzereau. New York: HarperCollins.
Sutcliffe, Thomas. 2002. "ET . . . Loving the Alien (Or: The Incredible True Story of How, 20 Years Ago, a Geeky Little Extra-Terrestrial Became Stranded in an American Suburb and Changed Our World For Ever)." *The Independent*, March, review section, 1.
Swertlow, Frank. 1984. "Success as in $pielberg." *L.A. Herald-Examiner*, September 4.*
Tan, Ed S., and Nico H. Frijda. 1999. "Sentiment in Film Viewing." In *Passionate Views: Film, Cognition, and Emotion*, edited by Carl Plantinga and Greg M. Smith, 48–64. Baltimore: Johns Hopkins University Press.
Tasker, Yvonne. 2011. *Soldiers' Stories: Military Women in Cinema and Television since World War II*. Durham, NC: Duke University Press.
Taylor, Philip M. 1992. *Steven Spielberg*. London: Batsford.
Taylor, Ruth. 1975. "Plumb Petrified by Bambi, Turns to Serene Squaliformes." *Canyon Crier*, September 22.*
Thirkell, Arthur. 1982. "Exciting and a Tearjerker." *Daily Mirror*, December 11, 18.
Thomas, Bob. 1978. *Joan Crawford*. London: Weidenfeld and Nicolson.
Thomson, David. 1982. "Goldie Gets Serious." *Film Comment* 18, no. 6 (November–December): 49–55.
———. 2002. "Alien Resurrection." *The Guardian*, sec. 2, March 15, 2–4.
Tieck, Sarah. 2010. *Dakota Fanning*. North Mankato, MN: Abdo.
Time. 1975. "Summer of the Shark." June 23, 32–35.

Toulson, Leslie. 1975. "It Could Shock Women Frigid." *The Sun*, December 27.
Travers, Peter. 2001. "A.I./Artificial Intelligence." *Rolling Stone*, June 29. https://www.rollingstone.com/tv-movies/tv-movie-reviews/a-i-artificial-intelligence-127906/.
Trueman, Paul. 2001. "Kubrick's Strange Afterlife." *The Guardian*, sec. 2, April 30, 58.
Tuchman, Mitch. 1978. "Close Encounter with Steven Spielberg." *Film Comment* 14, no. 1 (January–February): 49–55.
Tuite, Patrick B. 2009. "'Shadow of [a] Girl': An Examination of *Peter Pan* in Performance." In *Second Star to the Right: Peter Pan in the Popular Imagination*, edited by Allison B. Kavey and Lester D. Friedman, 105–131. New Brunswick, NJ: Rutgers University Press.
Turan, Kenneth. 2005. "They're Here!" *Los Angeles Times*, June 29. https://www.latimes.com/archives/la-xpm-2005-jun-29-et-world29-story.html.
Twain, Mark. 1884. *Adventures of Huckleberry Finn*. London: Chatto and Windus.
Uhlich, Keith. 2003. "The Major and the Minor." *Senses of Cinema*, no. 27 (July). https://www.sensesofcinema.com/2003/steven-spielberg/spielberg_symposium_position_papers/#uhlich.
USC Shoah Foundation, ed. 2014. *Testimony: The Legacy of* Schindler's List *and the USC Shoah Foundation*. New York: HarperCollins.
Ventura, Michael. 1982. "Spielberg on Spielberg." *L.A. Weekly*, June 11–17, 10–14.
Verney-Elliott, Alex. 2011. "Eyewitness: Ken Russell, by His Son." *Slipped Disc*, December 7. https://slippedisc.com/2011/12/eyewitness-ken-russell-by-his-son/.
Wainwright, Loudon. 1982. "*E.T.*, Don't Phone, Go Home." *Life*, July, 7.
Walker, Alice. 1982. *The Color Purple*. New York: Harcourt Brace Jovanovich.
———. 1996. *The Same River Twice: Honoring the Difficult*. London: Women's Press.
Warhol, Andy, and Bianca Jagger. 1982. "Steven Spielberg." *Interview*, July, 43–48.
Warner, Marina. 1993. "Through a Child's Eyes." In *Cinema and the Realms of Enchantment*, edited by Duncan Petrie, 36–62. London: British Film Institute.
Watson, Keith. 2018. "Sixty Seconds with Henry Thomas." *Metro*, October 9. https://www.metro.news/sixty-seconds-with-henry-thomas/1262304/.
Weeks, Linton. 2011. "America's Attack on Lemonade Stands." NPR, July 19. https://www.npr.org/2011/07/19/138461324/americas-attack-on-lemonade-stands.
White, Constance. 2001. "Down to Earth: Cary Guffey, *Close Encounters of the Third Kind*'s Boy Wonder, Grew Up in the Real World and Went into Finance." *People*, June 18. https://web.archive.org/web/20080917160944/http://www.people.com/people/archive/article/0,,20134692,00.html.
White, V. Alan. 2008. "A.I. Artificial Intelligence: Artistic Indulgence or Advanced Inquiry?" In *Steven Spielberg and Philosophy: We're Gonna Need a Bigger Book*, edited by Dean A. Kowalski, 210–226. Lexington: University Press of Kentucky.
Wigmore, Barry. 1982. "The Little Green Hero." *Daily Mirror*, July 5, 22–23.
Williams, Linda Ruth. 2004. "Ready for Action: *G.I. Jane*, Demi Moore's Body, and the Female Combat Movie." In *Action and Adventure Cinema*, edited by Yvonne Tasker, 169–185. Abingdon: Routledge.
———. 2012. "The Tears of Henry Thomas." *Screen* 53, no. 4 (Winter): 459–464.
———. 2013. "The Laughter of Robots." In *The Last Laugh: Dark Humors of Cinema*, edited by Murray Pomerance, 209–222. Detroit: Wayne State University Press.
———. 2017. "'Who Am I, David?' Motherhood in Spielberg's Dramas of Family Dysfunction." In *A Companion to Steven Spielberg*, edited by Nigel Morris, 243–257. Oxford: Wiley Blackwell.

———. 2020. "Children as Bait." In *The Jaws Book: New Perspectives on the Classic Summer Blockbuster*, edited by I. Q. Hunter and Matthew Melia, 133–144. London: Bloomsbury Academic.
Wilson, Emma. 2003. *Cinema's Missing Children*. London: Wallflower Press.
Wilson, Eric G. 2006. *The Melancholy Android: On the Psychology of Sacred Machines*. New York: State University of New York Press.
Windolf, Jim. 2004. "Indiana Jones Rides Again." *The Guardian*, May 14, 4–7.
———. 2008. "Steven Spielberg." *Vanity Fair*, January 2. https://www.vanityfair.com/news/2008/02/spielberg_qanda200802.
Wojcik, Pamela Robertson. 2016. *Fantasies of Neglect: Imagining the Urban Child in American Film and Fiction*. New Brunswick, NJ: Rutgers University Press.
Wojcik-Andrews, Ian. 2000. *Children's Films: History, Ideology, Pedagogy, Theory*. New York: Routledge.
Wollen, Peter. 1993. "Theme Park and Variations." *Sight and Sound*, July, 6–9.
Wood, Gaby. 2002. *Living Dolls: A Magical History of the Quest for Mechanical Life*. London: Faber.
Wood, Robin. 1986. *Hollywood from Vietnam to Reagan*. New York: Columbia University Press.
———. 2006. "Images of Children." In *Explorations in Film: Personal Views* 189–212. Rev. ed. Detroit: Wayne State University Press.
Woods, Judith. 2016. "How Steven Spielberg Gave the Father of The BFG Film's Young Star a Big Friendly Giant Break." *The Telegraph*, July 16. https://www.telegraph.co.uk/films/2016/07/16/how-stephen-spielberg-gave-the-father-of-the-bfg-films-young-sta/.
Young, Marilyn. 2006. "In the Combat Zone." In *Hollywood and War: The Film Reader*, edited by J. David Slocum, 315–324. New York: Routledge.
Yule, Andrew. 1996. *Steven Spielberg: Father of the Man: His Incredibly Life, Tumultuous Times and Record-Breaking Movies*. London: Little, Brown.
Zacharek, Stephanie. 2022. "Steven Spielberg Waited 60 Years to Tell This Story." *Time*, November 16. https://time.com/6234045/steven-spielberg-interview-the-fabelmans/.
Zelizer, Viviana A. 1994. *Pricing the Priceless Child: The Changing Social Value of Children*. Princeton, NJ: Princeton University Press.

Filmography

The Adventures of Tintin (dir. Steven Spielberg, 2011)
The Adventures of Young Indiana Jones (created by George Lucas, produced by George Lucas and Rick McCallum, various directors, 2002–2008)
After Yang (dir. Kogonada, 2021)
A.I. Artificial Intelligence (dir. Steven Spielberg, 2001)
Altered States (dir. Ken Russell, 1980)
Always (dir. Steven Spielberg, 1989)
Amazing Stories (TV series produced by Steven Spielberg et al., multiple directors, 1985–1987)
Amblin' (dir. Steven Spielberg, 1968)
Amistad (dir. Steven Spielberg, 1997)
Android Kunjappan Ver. 5.25 (dir. Ratheesh Balakrishnan Poduval, 2019)
Band of Brothers (TV miniseries produced by Steven Spielberg et al., multiple directors, 2001)
The BFG (dir. Steven Spielberg, 2016)
The Birth of a Nation (dir. D. W. Griffith, 1915)
Blade Runner (dir. Ridley Scott, 1982)
Bohemian Rhapsody (dir. Bryan Singer, 2018)
Bonfire of the Vanities (dir. Brian De Palma, 1990)
Boyhood (dir. Richard Linklater, 2014)
The Boy in the Striped Pajamas (dir. Mark Herman, 2007)
Bridge of Spies (dir. Steven Spielberg, 2015)
Bridge on the River Kwai (dir. David Lean, 1957)
Catch Me If You Can (dir. Steven Spielberg, 2002)
The Cat in the Hat (dir. Bo Welch, 2003)
Charlie's Angels (dir. McG, 2000)
Charlotte's Web (dir. Gary Winick, 2006)
Child's Play (dir. Mike Norris, 1988)
Citizen Kane (dir. Orson Welles, 1941)
Close Encounters of the Third Kind (dir. Steven Spielberg, 1977)
The Color Purple (dir. Steven Spielberg, 1985)
Coraline (dir. Henry Selick, 2009)

Dark Passage (dir. Delmer Daves, 1947)
D.A.R.Y.L. (dir. Simon Wincer, 1985)
The Day the Earth Stood Still (dir. Robert Wise, 1951)
Duel (dir. Steven Spielberg, 1971)
Empire of the Sun (dir. Steven Spielberg, 1987)
E.T. the Extra-Terrestrial (dir. Steven Spielberg, 1982)
Everything Everywhere All at Once (dir. Daniel Kwan and Daniel Scheinert, 2022)
The Exorcist (dir. William Friedkin, 1973)
Eyes (section of portmanteau made-for-TV film *Night Gallery*, dir. Steven Spielberg, 1969)
The Fabelmans (dir. Steven Spielberg, 2022)
The First Movie (dir. Mark Cousins, 2009)
Frankenstein (dir. James Whale, 1931)
The Goonies (dir. Richard Donner, 1985)
The Greatest Show on Earth (dir. Cecil B. De Mille, 1952)
Heaven's Gate (dir. Michael Cimino, 1980)
Hitchhiker's Guide to the Galaxy (dir. Garth Jennings, 2005)
Holocaust (TV miniseries produced by Herbert Brodkin and Robert Berger, dir. Marvin J. Chomsky, 1978)
Hook (dir. Steven Spielberg, 1991)
Indiana Jones and the Dial of Destiny (dir. James Mangold, 2023)
Indiana Jones and the Kingdom of the Crystal Skull (dir. Steven Spielberg, 2008)
Indiana Jones and the Last Crusade (dir. Steven Spielberg, 1989)
Indiana Jones and the Temple of Doom (dir. Steven Spielberg, 1984)
Jack (dir. Francis Ford Coppola, 1996)
Jaws (dir. Steven Spielberg, 1975)
Jumanji (dir. Joe Johnston, 1995)
Jurassic Park (dir. Steven Spielberg, 1993)
The Lady in the Lake (dir. Robert Montgomery, 1947)
Life Is Beautiful (dir. Roberto Benigni, 1997)
Lincoln (dir. Steven Spielberg, 2012)
The Lost World: Jurassic Park (dir. Steven Spielberg, 1997)
The Maltese Falcon (dir. John Huston, 1941)
Men of Boys Town (dir. Norman Taurog, 1941)
Minority Report (dir. Steven Spielberg, 2002)
The Mummy (dir. Karl Freund, 1932)
Munich (dir. Steven Spielberg, 2005)
1941 (dir. Steven Spielberg, 1979)
The Omen (dir. Richard Donner, 1979)
Pan (dir. Joe Wright, 2015)
Peter Pan (dir. P. J. Hogan, 2003)
Pinocchio (dir. Ben Sharpsteen et al., 1940)
Pinocchio (dir. Guillermo del Toro, 2022)
Poison Ivy (dir. Katt Shea Ruben, 1992)
Poltergeist (dir. Tobe Hooper, 1982)
The Post (dir. Steven Spielberg, 2017)
Prancer (dir. John Hancock, 1989)
The Quiet Man (dir. John Ford, 1952)
Raiders of the Lost Ark (dir. Steven Spielberg, 1981)
Raiders!: The Story of the Greatest Fan Film Ever Made (dir. Jeremy Coon and Tim Skousen, 2015)

The Reader (dir. Stephen Daldry, 2008)
Ready Player One (dir. Steven Spielberg, 2018)
Robot & Frank (dir. Jake Schreier, 2012)
Robotbror (*My Robot Brother*) (dir. Frederik Meldal Nørgaard, 2022)
Rosemary's Baby (dir. Roman Polanski, 1968)
Saving Private Ryan (dir. Steven Spielberg, 1998)
Schindler's List (dir. Steven Spielberg, 1993)
Seven Up! (TV documentary series, dir. Paul Almond and Michael Apted, 1964–2019)
Shoah (dir. Claude Lanzmann, 1985)
The Sixth Sense (dir. M. Night Shyamalan, 1999)
Sophie's Choice (dir. Alan J. Pakula, 1982)
Star Wars (dir. George Lucas, 1977)
Steven Spielberg: 30 Years of Close Encounters (dir. Laurent Bouzereau, 2007)
The Sugarland Express (dir. Steven Spielberg, 1974)
Super 8 (dir. J. J. Abrams, 2011)
Switched at Birth (dir. Waris Hussein, 1991)
Taken (TV miniseries produced by Steven Spielberg et al., multiple directors, 2002)
The Terminal (dir. Steven Spielberg, 2004)
Terror (dir. Norman J Warren, 1978)
Toy Story (dir. John Lasseter, 1995)
Toy Story 2 (dir. John Lasseter, 1999)
Toy Story 3 (dir. Lee Unkrich, 2010)
Twilight Zone: The Movie (dir. Joe Dante, John Landis, George Miller, Steven Spielberg, 1983)
Uptown Girls (dir. Boaz Yakin, 2003)
The Wallace and Ladmo Show (TV series produced by Russell Cunningham and Sharon Kelley, dir. Sharon Kelley, 1954–1989)
War Horse (dir. Steven Spielberg, 2011)
War of the Worlds (dir. Steven Spielberg, 2005)
West Side Story (dir. Steven Spielberg, 2021).
The Young Indiana Jones Chronicles (produced by George Lucas, multiple directors, 1992–1993)

Index

About the Author

LINDA RUTH WILLIAMS is professor of film at the University of Exeter, United Kingdom. She is the author of five books, including *The Erotic Thriller in Contemporary Cinema*, and coeditor of *Contemporary American Cinema*. Her research focuses on anglophone cinema since the 1970s, and the work and visibility of women in film history and the contemporary screen industries.